Tools of Progress

Tools of Progress

A German Merchant Family in Mexico City, 1865–Present

Jürgen Buchenau

University of New Mexico Press
Albuquerque

08 07 06 05 04   1 2 3 4 5

Library of Congress Cataloging-in-Publication Data

Buchenau, Jürgen, 1964–
Tools of progress : a German merchant family in Mexico City,
1865–present / Jürgen Buchenau.— 1st ed.
      p. cm.
Includes bibliographical references and index.
  ISBN 0-8263-3087-8 (cloth : alk. paper)
  ISBN 0-8263-3088-6 (pbk. : alk. paper)
  1. Casa Boker (Firm)—History.
  2. Hardware industry—Mexico—Mexico City—History.
  I. Title.
HD9745.M64C373 2004
381'.45683'09233107253—dc22
                                        2003026993

Design and composition: Maya Allen-Gallegos
Typeset in Berkeley 10.5/12.5
Display type set in Humanist 521, 770, and 970

Contents

Illustrations

Tables

Maps

Figures

Abbreviations

AHSRE	Archivo Histórico de la Secretaría de Relaciones Exteriores
BDM	Bund Deutscher Mädels
CAAH	Colegio Alemán Alexander von Humboldt
CFM	Compañía Ferretera Mexicana
CTM	Confederación de Trabajadores Mexicanos
IMF	International Monetary Fund
Junta	Junta de la Administración de la Propiedad Extranjera
NAFTA	North American Free Trade Agreement
NSDAP	Nationalsozialistische Deutsche Arbeiterpartei
PRI	Partido Revolucionario Institucional
UET	Unión de Empleados y Trabajadores de la Compañia Ferretera Mexicana
VDR	Verband Deutscher Reichsangehöriger in Mexiko

Preface

On a February evening in 1984, I boarded a plane bound for Paris from Mexico. For the past seven months, I had held an unpaid internship at the Casa Boker, a hardware store in downtown Mexico City, in preparation for a career in economics. My Spanish improved every day that I was in Mexico, yet I still felt alien to that country. I lived with an elderly German woman born in Mexico City who only rented rooms to German men. I worked with my great-uncle, Gunther Boker, his sons Klaus and Pedro, his brother Helmuth, and two other ethnic Germans, all of whom spent much of the day speaking German to each other even though they were natives of Mexico. A farmer's son from rural northern Germany, I was not well adapted to life in the world's largest city and I lost 15 pounds to encounters with the *cantina* food that I had grown to love. As my plane took off, I was determined to leave Mexico in general and the Casa Boker in particular far behind me.

Today, that windy February evening seems like ages ago. My time in Mexico shaped me in more and different ways than I had imagined possible then. The major in economics gave way to a fascination with Latin American history—a fascination lived out, paradoxically, in graduate school in the United States rather than Germany or Mexico. In the course of my studies of the rich ethnic diversity of Mexico at the University of North Carolina at Chapel Hill, my mind kept returning to its "perennial," unassimilated Germans. While I worked on a very different project for my dissertation on the history of Mexico in world affairs, I slowly assembled data from government documents and interviews, hoping to make the Bokers the subject of a journal article. Years later, after the death of the older Bokers, I was finally able to consult the company and family archive housed in the Casa Boker. This archive conveyed to me a unique, in-depth understanding of the identity, business, and politics of one immigrant family. Seven years ago, during a conference at Yale University at which I presented preliminary findings, Professor Friedrich Katz, a fellow historian and transnational traveler in the triangle Mexico-United States-Germany/Austria, encouraged me to "think bigger" than an article. Thus the idea for a book was born.

Writing this study has been an intensely personal experience in another way as well. My wife, Anabel Aliaga-Buchenau, herself a product of German and Spanish cultures and a fellow academic whose insights contributed greatly to this book, and my children, Nicolas and Julia, tolerated a husband and father who spent too much time holed up in his study or away from them on research trips. Meanwhile, their own efforts to negotiate identity as immigrants and first-generation "United Statesians," respectively, have also helped me to continually rethink the experiences of immigrants.

This study would not have been written without the help of a large number of people. I particularly want to thank Alan Knight for his careful reading of the manuscript, and Max Friedman, Carol Hartley, Gil Joseph, Karen Racine, Emily Rosenberg, Friedrich Schuler, and Steve Topik for providing suggestions on earlier versions and/or chapters. Silke Nagel and Brígida von Mentz provided advice on German and Mexican repositories, and Víctor Macías displayed the rare generosity of sharing several important sources from his own research. Patrick Jones from the UNC Charlotte Cartography Lab designed the maps used in this book. At the University of New Mexico Press, Associate Director David Holtby offered excellent advice and encouragement. My colleagues in the History Department at UNC Charlotte, and particularly Lyman Johnson, have inspired and supported me in many ways. Friends and family provided hospitality during my research trips, especially Carlos Agüeros, Dennis Brehme, and Pablo Pellat in Mexico City, Marike van der Veen Estepp in Washington, D.C., and Alfredo and Ingrid Aliaga in Germany. Finally, forty-eight interview subjects gave generously of their time and allowed me to learn their views of the story related in these pages. Without diminishing the significance of the other interviewees, I must single out Pedro and Klaus Boker, the current directors of the Casa Boker, for their patience in answering my questions and for granting me access to the archive of Boker, S.A. de C.V. I also wish to acknowledge the valuable financial assistance of the Dupont Foundation, the Southern Regional Education Board, the University of North Carolina at Charlotte, the University of Southern Mississippi, Wingate University, and particularly the National Endowment for the Humanities, which awarded me a year-long research fellowship.

This book is dedicated to the memory of three members of my *gran familia*. My grandmother Gabriele Buchenau masked the profound shaping of her personality by the country of her birth through a frank dislike of all things Mexican and therefore inadvertently helped her grandson become a historian of Mexico. Her own hidden transcript served as the point of departure of this investigation of a merchant family between German origins and a Mexican present. My uncle Half Zantop and my aunt Susanne Zantop, professors at Dartmouth College whose lives ended far too soon in a savage act of violence, were role models for Anabel and me, both as human beings and as academics. Having traveled down the same road before us, they spent their lives working for social justice, peace, and—perhaps most importantly—understanding and accepting the "other." We will never forget their example.

—Charlotte, February 2003

> You cannot understand the Mexicans unless you are one yourself.
>
> —Franz Böker

Introduction

On a Saturday evening in the summer of 1915, Franz Böker left his spacious office in his family's department store in the historic downtown district of Mexico City.[1] It had been another difficult day for this German merchant in a year remembered by Mexicans as the bloody climax of the Mexican Revolution, and by Germans as the first full year of World War I. As the director of the Casa Boker, a company due to celebrate its fiftieth anniversary, Franz had just determined that the day's retail sales amounted to 1 measly gold peso. He had spent much of the past year fighting off the demands of a series of warlords for acceptance of their paper currencies, each one rendered worthless when the next faction seized Mexico City. To survive in this climate, Franz had coordinated his actions with those of fellow foreign investors, among them English and French entrepreneurs whose relatives faced his own family members in the trenches of eastern France. Like most of his colleagues on the Comité Internacional, the committee that represented foreign interests in Mexico City, he longed for the old regime of dictator Porfirio Díaz (1876–1911), when the Casa Boker had become one of the premier commercial establishments in Mexico.

When Franz arrived at his home in the suburb of Colonia Roma, he realized that his business problems had not remained behind in his office. Instead, he faced private worries that paralleled the uncertainties in his company. One of his family's servants greeted him at the door to inform him that his wife, Luise, had just given birth to her fourth child. As he looked at his infant boy, Helmuth, who lay in a crib in a corner of the house where he would be safe from stray bullets, Franz wondered how to pay 150 employees and feed a family of 6 on 1 peso. He also pondered how he could raise Helmuth and his other three children in German cultural traditions. In a country riddled with revolution, this foreign merchant facing financial hardship found it ever more difficult to maintain the boundary he had constructed between his Mexican business world and his German private world—a boundary predicated in part on the elite status of his family.[2] This eventful day represents just a tiny fragment of a merchant family's

1

five-generation-long journey from the status of German immigrants to blue-eyed Mexicans.

The Boker clan, which still owns the Casa Boker, one of the oldest businesses in the capital, provides important insights into both Mexican and immigration history. The history of the family and its company reflects that of modern Mexico: a country that has muddled through various economic development strategies; violent and unpredictable political change; the rise of U.S. influence and consumer culture; and the conflicted relationship between Mexicans and foreigners. The story demonstrates the importance of European merchants in the process of economic modernization in the late nineteenth century and also reveals how revolution, globalization, and the rise of U.S. influence marginalized merchant families in a metropolis that has become the world's largest city. Finally, it shows that modern Mexico, unlike Argentina and the United States, is not a nation of immigrants. Like the works of Oscar Lewis, Larissa Lomnitz and Marisol Pérez-Lizaur, and David Walker, this study places individual and family behavior in the context of larger historical processes.[3] It is neither business nor immigration history in the traditional sense. Rather, it combines both in a study of one family and its business in order to provide a unique look at the long-term relationship between business practices and constructions of identity and, thus, between political economy and cultural history.[4]

This approach transcends such worn dichotomies as "local" versus "foreign" and "insiders" versus "outsiders" by demonstrating that one family could be at once commercial insiders and cultural outsiders. Unlike the U.S. entrepreneurs studied by John M. Hart, among others, the Bokers were not shrewd opportunists who gouged Latin American countries for profits to be reinvested in the home country. They had no imperial ambition, and little interest in helping German geopolitical objectives.[5] Their decisions followed the needs of a family business—until today the dominant form of enterprise in Latin America—and thus were not always designed to maximize profit.[6] The pioneers of the business sought a steady stream of capital to Germany, but ended up constructing an expensive department store that economically anchored the family in Mexico for generations to come. Yet the Bokers did not blend easily into their host society: the first Mexican-born members of the family spoke Spanish with a German accent and supported the return to greatness that Adolf Hitler had promised the German people. More recently, the family has been "neither coffee nor milk": torn between their status as descendants of an old German family and a country that has finally claimed that clan as its own.[7]

From the Vanguard of Modernization to the Rearguard of Globalization

The Casa Boker began its existence on November 1, 1865, when Franz's father, Robert Böker, a young merchant from the town of Remscheid in western Germany, invested in a small hardware store in Mexico City. This investment was part of a transnational strategy that also sent family members to Buenos Aires, Melbourne, New York City, and St. Petersburg to sell iron and steel items produced in the Böker firms. From its modest beginnings, Robert's company soared to national prominence over the next three decades. "The first hardware business of real importance," the Casa Boker was not just an outpost of German commerce in Mexico.[8] Instead, it sold as many U.S. and British products as German, and it eventually distributed almost 40,000 different products. The Casa Boker also became one of the first foreign-owned businesses to reinvest a large part of its profits in Mexico. In 1900, it moved into a glamorous department store built at the cost of 1.5 million gold pesos, then the most expensive commercial building in Mexico City. Admiring observers soon dubbed the enterprise the "Sears of Mexico."[9]

The rapid rise of the Casa Boker highlights the prominent position of foreign merchants in nineteenth-century Mexico. These merchants took advantage of the weakness of the Mexico City elite following the Wars of Independence (1810–21). Not only did the wars contribute to a severe economic crisis that lasted forty years, but an anti-Spanish backlash in the 1820s also led to the departure of most of Mexico's *peninsulares,* or native-born Spaniards, who formed the country's backbone of international and wholesale trade. The sons of European exporters and producers filled the void and soon came to dominate overseas trading. Aided by their familial ties, these young merchants prospered despite the fact that the poverty of most Mexicans limited their market geographically and socially.[10] As the Mexican economy recovered in the second half of the nineteenth century, the traditional *almacén,* or warehouse store, gave way to specialty and department stores that took advantage of the elite's appetite for foreign-made goods. The French set up Mexico City's most important garment and jewelry establishments; the Germans controlled the sale of hardware, drugs, and musical instruments; and new peninsulares dominated the retail trade. All of these import businesses thrived as economic growth during the Díaz dictatorship created a middle class that discovered the new culture of consumption.

Nonetheless, the Casa Boker could not in fact become the "Sears of Mexico." As the modernization of the Díaz era benefited a relatively small percentage of the population, the Mexican market for hand tools, cutlery, and housewares remained limited. Unlike the real Sears, Roebuck in the United States, the Casa Boker could not fully develop as a department store, as the French monopoly on garments kept it out of the lucrative textile sector. Even at a time when industrialization began to transform Mexico, the Bokers did not invest heavily in domestic manufacturing. Most importantly, the Casa Boker predominantly catered to a customer base of male professionals rather than casual shoppers waiting to be seduced into buying. In the twentieth century, they came to oppose the very consumer culture that their beautiful building had helped pioneer—a fact that displayed the importance of attitudes in their business strategies. As Franz Böker saw it, the ethos of a *königlicher Kaufmann,* or kingly merchant, distinguished Germans from other foreign entrepreneurs in Mexico. The Bokers believed that kingly merchants succeeded due to their excellent reputation rather than because of slick advertising, and that trust rather than persuasion defined the relationship with their customers. Meanwhile, in the United States, Sears, Roebuck, and other department stores created dream worlds, or "lands of desire," through aggressive advertising that catered to the emotional needs of both male and female customers.[11] The Bokers' reluctance to take advantage of the emerging consumer culture demonstrates their resistance to integration into the Mexican bourgeoisie. While the Bokers sold the tools of progress, progress would ultimately pass them by.

Because of these limitations and the enormous cost of its fancy building, the Casa Boker entered a period of stagnation between 1900 and 1942, a tumultuous period marked by the Mexican Revolution and the Great Depression. The revolution not only attacked the foundations of the Porfirian political system and the landowning rural elite. Revolutionary violence also destroyed the Bokers' network of distribution, and the victorious leaders questioned the privileges of foreign investors in Mexico. Nevertheless, the Casa Boker turned a hefty profit at a time when World War I had made imported goods scarce; Mexican neutrality blunted most of the effects of Allied blacklisting of German firms, and the Bokers isolated their business from revolutionary nationalism by giving it the appearance of a purely Mexican enterprise. In the succeeding decades, the successful co-optation of its workers in a company union allowed the Casa Boker to avoid the strikes of the Lázaro Cárdenas era (1934–40).

The Casa Boker also weathered the growth of U.S. influence at the expense of that of Germany and other European powers. Since the founding of the company, the Bokers had recognized the significance of the United States in devising a transnational business strategy. Robert Böker came to Mexico on a U.S. passport, established close ties with U.S. producers, and associated with both the German and "American" communities in Mexico City. The Casa Boker became the principal Mexican customer for producers such as Remington and Studebaker, and it resisted German pressures to reduce its stock of U.S. and British items. Its status as an outlet for U.S. goods persisted through World War I despite the efforts of the Woodrow Wilson administration to eliminate German commerce in the Western Hemisphere. Even after the Nazi seizure of power in Germany, the Bokers' decision to continue their association with Allied producers and Jewish employees kept the company out of trouble until May 1942, when Mexico entered the war on the side of the Allies.

This event marked the beginning of the decline of the Casa Boker. The U.S. government treated the Mexican Bokers as "enemy aliens" and subjected them to a campaign to drive out Axis influence in the Americas. In June 1942, a government agency seized control over the business and depleted its inventory and cash reserves. When the Bokers once again took possession of their firm in 1948, Mexico City had changed forever. The year before, a new competitor, Sears, Roebuck, had opened its first store in Mexico City. While Sears expanded into the suburbs and to other Mexican cities, the Casa Boker gave up the sale of toys, kitchenware and many other product lines available today in the catalogs of its rivals. Even worse, an accelerated process of industrialization created a Mexican hardware industry; and to help this industry, the Mexican government adopted protectionist measures that kept out imports. In addition, a new "consumer nationalism" drove many Mexicans away from the imported products that had once awarded their buyers a cachet of modernity.[12] Although the Bokers adjusted by selling Mexican items, they never regained their old market share. Most recently, competition from U.S. corporations such as Wal-Mart and Home Depot has contributed to the downsizing of the Casa Boker, and the enterprise is no longer a major outlet for U.S. products.

From Trade Conquistadors to Blue-Eyed Mexicans

Not coincidentally, the growth, stagnation, and decline of the Casa Boker corresponded to the family's parallel journey from adaptation to acculturation and assimilation. This journey has driven the family toward the entrepreneurial bourgeoisie of the capital—only one tiny part of the socially and culturally diverse patchwork that we call Mexico, but the largest denominator in which a discussion of national identity in such a diverse society makes analytical sense. In turn, this journey reflects three phases in the life cycle of the German community. A proto-diaspora dominated by single male merchants gave way to a family-based ethnic enclave that sought to replicate German culture thousands of miles from home. Since 1945, this enclave has disintegrated into a poly-diaspora characterized by national identities that span the range from recently immigrated Germans to blue-eyed Mexicans.

Robert Böker commenced this journey by practicing adaptation, which José Moya has defined as "the process by which newcomers adjusted to their new environment."[13] One of only three hundred Germans in Mexico City in 1865, Robert learned Spanish and Hispanicized his name to "Roberto" immediately after his arrival, but he returned to Germany after eight short years, leaving his brother in charge of the business. The success of the Casa Boker and the scarcity of cultural institutions that would have replicated German culture shaped Robert's and his brothers' attitudes toward Mexico prior to 1910. Not only did the business seldom require their presence after they became a partner (that is, partial owner) of the enterprise, but they also could not imagine raising children in a city without a German school.

Comprising Franz and Luise and their Mexican-born children, the next two generations showed signs of acculturation, a process defined by Jeffrey Lesser as "the modification of one culture as the result of contact with another."[14] Franz had planned to return to Germany before the Mexican Revolution forced him to stay, an event that turned him and Luise into permanent residents who became active in a multitude of civic associations. Born into an ethnic enclave that boasted a school as well as a large number of clubs, members of the third generation were natives of Mexico, yet still felt primarily German. With one exception, they married fellow German-Mexicans despite ample opportunities to find a spouse from Germany, and they began to make Mexican friends—facts that indicate that Mexico had become their point of reference.

After 1945, acculturation finally gave way to assimilation, according to Charles Price a multifaceted process resulting in the weakening and ultimate loss of the pre-migratory culture.[15] At the beginning of this still ongoing phase, the fourth-generation Bokers grew up between Mexican and German poles of identity. Amidst the coming of age of an entrepreneurial bourgeoisie; the arrival of a Mexican mass culture promoted through the new media; and the crumbling of a German community divided by class and ideology, this generation found out that it was possible to be German *and* Mexican. Two members of the fourth generation married Mexican spouses. Yet these Bokers and their siblings still imparted German language and traditions to their children. In the fifth generation, Spanish has replaced German as the first

6

language in the family, yet prolonged sojourns in Europe by several members of this generation have demonstrated that even the youngest Bokers still live "lives in between" the two cultures.[16]

The family's slow integration into Mexican society highlights the difficult process of nation building in a divided society that has attracted few immigrants and has succeeded in assimilating even fewer of them. For several reasons, postcolonial Mexico did not become a nation of immigrants like Argentina or the United States. The country offered immigrants little available farmland; Veracruz was not as easy to reach as New York and Buenos Aires; and a growing indigenous and mestizo population provided abundant cheap labor. As a result, Mexico was a desirable destination for adventurers, merchants, and professionals, but not for farmers and urban workers; thus, it encouraged elite and middle-class rather than lower-class immigration. At the high point of immigration to Mexico, the 1930 census counted a mere percent of the population as born outside the country.[17] Most importantly for this analysis, the prosperous Europeans and U.S. citizens who did come seldom blended in. As "trade conquistadors," most of the merchants plotted their return to their home country after accumulating enough capital in their overseas business to buy a partnership in the enterprise of their fathers.[18] Nineteenth-century representations of the Mexican nation encouraged such self-exclusion. While Argentine intellectuals such as Domingo F. Sarmiento propagated European immigration as a way of civilizing the pampas and stamping out gaucho culture, the Mexican thinker Justo Sierra conceived of Mexican culture as a blend of Spanish and indigenous components, to be improved by incorporating the "Indian" rather than by bringing in millions of immigrants. After the revolution, José Vasconcelos's idea that the amalgamation of Spanish conquistadors and the native population had created a "cosmic race" left out immigrants as well as Afro-Mexicans.[19]

Not surprisingly, the Bokers and other foreign merchants in Mexico City neither fit the stereotype of "uprooted" immigrants in the United States, who gave up ties to their ancestral country within a few generations, nor that of the rural ethnic enclave that once characterized German settlements in rural Argentina, Brazil, and Chile.[20] Instead, they typify a third type of immigration—the establishment of "trade diasporas" in Latin American cities.[21] These trade diasporas followed the ancient Greek rather than the Jewish model, as their members migrated voluntarily to improve an already privileged economic position, and not to escape persecution.[22] The formation of the German colony in Mexico City occurred in a context in which an underdeveloped nation welcomed wealthy immigrants and acquiesced in the efforts of these immigrants to avoid assimilation. Thus, like the Anglo-Argentine community in Buenos Aires, the German colony in Mexico City became an urban ethnic enclave in close contact with the host society that reproduced the culture of the sending society.[23] This enclave disintegrated only when the aftershocks of the Nazi dictatorship and the rise of a mass culture in Mexico lured young German-Mexicans out of their colony.

This study thus points a way out of the existing dichotomous notions of the German colony in Mexico. Relying on modernization theory, older accounts praised German merchants for their role in the modernization of Mexico. The authors of these accounts, often themselves members of the German community, practiced a hagiography of the colony, especially of its wealthiest and most influential members.[24] Influenced by dependency analysis, later scholars lambasted the German trade diaspora for its support of imperial and Nazi Germany, as well as for its role in the exploitation of Mexico. The self-conscious descendants of German immigrants who constructed this model portrayed the German diaspora as an outpost that merely served the interests of the sending society.[25] Neither of these models differentiated between foreign residents, who lived under local conditions, and foreign investors, who directed their faraway property from the comfort of their homes. As the example of the Boker family reveals, German entrepreneurs in Mexico refused to place the imperialist aims of the German state above their own commercial interests. Therefore, transnational theory comes closest to matching the German experience in Mexico City. Proponents of this model—which has thus far only been applied to poor migrants—have argued that immigrants and their descendants undermine nation-states by forming transnational networks.[26] As merchants, the Bokers were business people first and German second, and they often thought and acted like Mexican capitalists. As a family, however, they long clung to the Germany of their ancestors and refused assimilation.

Sources and Organization

This study primarily relies on the extensive archive of the Casa Boker. Previously unavailable to historians, this archive includes business records, letters, memoirs, diaries, newspaper clippings, and photographs. British, German, Mexican, and U.S. government records also contain much of interest about the family business, as it found itself the target of German imperial schemes as well as U.S. economic warfare. The notary archive of Mexico City and the Archivo General de la Nación contain valuable information about the business. I have also used foreign travel accounts, especially to learn about shopping and consumption in Mexico

8

City. Finally, oral history interviews with family members, friends, and employees provide important data on national identity in the most recent generations. Because of the pitfalls of oral history, especially in a case where the interviewer had a previous personal relationship with many of his interviewees, I have used it primarily as a source of anecdotal evidence. In addition, the interviews have allowed me to understand the surviving Bokers' own perception of the story told in the succeeding pages—and, in some cases, that of the Mexicans who knew them—and to learn about their personal preferences regarding language, friends, entertainment, and food.[27]

This book is divided chronologically into three parts, each containing two or three chapters. Sections within each chapter follow and link the three main interpretive threads: the Mexican and global contexts; the history of the Casa Boker; and the history of the family. Part One, "At the Vanguard of Modernization, 1865–c.1900," comprises the first two chapters. Chapter 1 outlines the establishment of the German trade diaspora in Mexico City and the founding of the Casa Boker. Chapter 2 examines the rise of the "Sears of Mexico" in the context of Porfirian modernization, and the emergence of the German colony. Part Two, "Between Revolution and Global War, c. 1900–c. 1948" consists of Chapters 3 to 5. Chapter 3 analyzes the business during the Mexican Revolution and World War I and the beginning of the family's acculturation. Chapter 4 delineates the efforts of the Casa Boker to withstand economic nationalism and the rise of urban labor in the postrevolutionary era, as well as the first Mexican-born Bokers. Chapter 5 discusses the struggle against U.S. economic warfare in the context of Nazi diplomacy and World War II. Finally, Part Three, "Neither Coffee nor Milk, c. 1948 to Present," makes up the last two chapters. Chapter 6 analyzes the crisis of the Casa Boker in the heyday of import-substitution industrialization and the incipient assimilation of the Boker family, and Chapter 7 provides a discussion of the present-day Bokers and their company.

Part One

At the Vanguard of Modernization, 1865–c. 1900

> With people bound for Latin America, Fate somehow seems
> more actively occupied, on more intimate, more intrusive
> terms than it is with people on the way to somewhere else.
> —Charles Flandrau, *Viva Mexico!*

I

A Trade Conquistador Comes to Mexico

On May 28, 1865, an unbearably hot and humid day, an anxious young merchant arrived in Veracruz. Robert Böker immediately realized that he had come to what a contemporary traveler called "one of the world's most unhealthful places. The yellow fever rages for eight long months, diminishing the ranks of the poor Europeans and . . . Mexicans from the highlands . . . who see themselves obligated to spend time in that dreaded port town."[1] Dilapidated facilities, buzzards circling unidentifiable cadavers, oppressive heat, and dark swarms of disease-bearing mosquitoes—in every way, Robert was far from home.

Not surprisingly, Robert looked forward to only a brief stay in Mexico. Unlike lower-class European immigrants of the time who left their home countries for a brighter future, he regarded his experience overseas as an apprenticeship. His destiny remained in Remscheid, located 20 miles northeast of Cologne in the Bergisches Land region, where his father owned a company that produced sheet metal, blades, and knives and sold hardware to importers throughout the Americas. During the previous two years, Robert had completed an internship in a hardware store in New York, and he had even acquired U.S. citizenship in order to make life easier for him in a war-torn country. Nevertheless, he had maintained psychological residence in Prussia. He had not looked to marry in the United States, he had rejected an offer to become a partner in a hardware store there, and his circle of friends had consisted primarily of fellow expatriate Germans. Therefore, he expected his stay in Mexico to be temporary as well, and he had the narrowly defined mission of looking into the state of affairs of Reichmann and Holder, a small hardware firm located in downtown Mexico City that owed money to his father's business. What he believed would be a short stay turned into eight years, and when the store became his own, he made destiny for some of his descendants.[2]

In the Wake of the German Columbus

Böker had witnessed sizable immigrant communities in New York City, but sleepy Veracruz introduced him to a far less desirable target for most immigrants. Tropical diseases aside, the Mexico he entered was nearing the end of a protracted time of troubles that had lasted more than fifty years. The Wars of Independence had ruined what had been the foremost economy of the Spanish Empire, especially many of the precious silver mines, and left central authority severely weakened. Between 1821 and 1861, the Mexican economy had experienced a prolonged crisis compounded by a poor infrastructure, high internal tariffs, and protectionist duties. Political instability worsened these problems. Mexico had also suffered four major foreign invasions due in no small measure to the fact that caudillo warlords successfully disputed central authority.[3]

Not surprisingly, Mexico lost more people to migration to the United States than it gained through immigration, making it "a country of emigration rather than immigration."[4] With a few important exceptions, farmers did not express interest in Mexico. Regionally diverse but predominantly dry and mountainous, the country possesses precious little farmland of the kind that encouraged European rural people to stream to Argentina, Brazil, Canada, and the United States. The mountain ranges, deserts, steppes, pine forests, and tropical jungles that mark the country's unparalleled natural beauty make up more than 85 percent of the truncated Mexico that remained after the war with the United States (1846–48). Much of the arable land requires irrigation to yield enough crops, and by the coming of independence, the best lands were in the hands of landed elite. In addition, the Mexican government did not grant assistance to rural colonization projects. A prospective farmer who came to Mexico without financial resources therefore found himself doomed to compete for jobs with the Mexican peasantry and, more often than not, a life of material deprivation. Further limiting the total number of immigrants, the 1824 Constitution had imposed Roman Catholicism as the state religion.[5] Workers found low wages; artisans, a glut of skilled crafts people; professionals, the lack of opportunity in a country with a tiny middle class; and merchants, political chaos and economic crisis.[6] As Table 1 shows,

Argentina, Brazil, Canada, the United States, and even Cuba dwarfed Mexico as destinations of European immigrants.

Among the sparse foreign-born population of nineteenth-century Mexico, four specific groups deserve a more detailed discussion: Spaniards, U.S. farmers, Guatemalan refugees, and European trade conquistadors (see Table 2). All of these immigrants either came from neighboring countries or counted on effective protection by family networks. Even more strikingly, the presence of the first three of these groups markedly increased the anti-immigrant tendencies of the Mexican elites. These tendencies by far outweighed sporadic efforts to encourage European immigration.[7]

The case of the Spaniards is particularly instructive in this regard. Peninsulares had followed on the trail of conquistador Hernán Cortés for almost three centuries, and their descendants had formed the creole elite that owned much of New Spain's most precious land. Excluded from the high colonial offices, the creoles had grown to resent the native Spaniards. Nonetheless, the Bourbon Reforms of the late eighteenth century had brought in ten thousand Spaniards. Many of the peninsulares became colonial officials. Others, along with their creole relatives, dominated the consulado, the guild that organized merchants and moneylenders. These great families of Mexico City not only controlled international and wholesale commerce, they also played important roles in provincial Mexico as mine- and landowners.[8] The chaos that began with the Wars of Independence, however, toppled many of the great families from their lofty perch. Anti-Spanish sentiments served as one of the causes of the Hidalgo and Morelos revolts that marked the first years of the conflict, and they intensified as government forces suppressed the revolts. The achievement of independence

Table 1: Mexican Immigration in Comparative Perspective, 1820–1932

Country	Number	Percentage of total European overseas immigration
Argentina	6,501,000	11.6
Brazil	4,361,000	7.8
Canada	5,073,000	9.0
Cuba	1,394,000	2.5
Mexico	270,000	0.5
Peru	300,000	.05
United States	32,564,000	57.9

Source: Adapted from José Moya, *Cousins and Strangers: Spanish Immigrants in Buenos Aires, 1850–1930* (Berkeley and Los Angeles: University of California Press, 1998), 46.

Map 1. Mexico

Table 2: Selected Foreign Nationals in the Mexican Censuses
(in thousands)

	1895	1900	1910	1921	1930	1940	1950	1960	1970	1980
British	3	3	5	4	5	4	2	2	1	2
Canadians	—	—	—	—	8	*	6	5	3	3
Chinese	1	3	13	14	19	7	6	5	2	*
French	4	4	5	4	5	3	3	4	3	4
Germans	2	3	4	4	7	4	5	7	5	5
Guatemalans	14	5	22	14	17	8	8	9	7	4
Japanese	—	—	2	2	4	2	2	2	2	3
Lebanese	—	—	—	—	4	4	5	4	2	2
Spaniards	13	16	30	29	47	29	37	50	31	32
U.S. citizens	12	15	21	11	12	19*	83	98	97	157

* Misleading or missing census data

Source: Census Records.

signaled the hour of payback, and in 1827, the Mexican government decreed the expulsion of the peninsulares and the abolition of the consulado. Over the next two years, this measure and Spain's failed attempt at a reconquest led to the exodus of more than 7,000 Spaniards—the lion's share of the country's merchants. The departing peninsulares contributed to an unprecedented capital flight. Only during the 1840s did a new group of Spaniards once again seek their fortune in Mexico.[9]

U.S. immigration proved even more ominous. Recognizing the specter of U.S. territorial expansion, late-colonial authorities had invited English-speaking Roman Catholic settlers to live in the sparsely populated northeastern province of Tejas. In 1824, the national government renewed this invitation, despite an unregulated influx of Protestant immigrants from the southern United States. By 1833, the situation had gotten out of hand. More than 30,000 English speakers in Texas, a majority of whom did not respect Mexican law, confronted approximately 9,000 Spanish speakers. Not only did these settlers outnumber the Mexicans, but U.S. citizens also accounted for the majority of foreign-born residents of Mexico. The Texas secession and the subsequent war with the United States demonstrated that the threat of U.S. land grabbing outweighed any possible benefits of immigration. Ironically, the annexations also demonstrated the viability of immigration. After the war, hundreds of thousands of people, many of them immigrants, settled in the old Mexican northwest. As Mexicans realized, these areas constituted the promising frontier that could have invited widespread immigration.[10]

The presence of a Guatemalan minority in the southeastern state of Chiapas constituted the mirror image of the Texas question. The westernmost province of the old Captaincy of Guatemala, Chiapas had not joined the United Provinces of the Center of America [sic] upon their 1823 secession from the Mexican Empire of Agustín Iturbide. While the other provinces had joined Guatemala City in forming the new federation, the creoles in the highlands of Chiapas had requested annexation by Mexico. Encouraged by this show of support, the Mexican government incorporated Chiapas against the wishes of the elite of the state's largest city, Tuxtla Gutiérrez. After a protracted conflict, the Mexican government imposed its will with military force in 1842, five years after the disintegration of the United Provinces. For decades thereafter, many Chiapanecos still thought of themselves as Guatemalans. Subsequently, tens of thousands of Guatemalans fled to southeastern Mexico to escape repression and even greater poverty than that found in Mexico, a pattern that has persisted to the present. In the first national census of 1895, 14,000 inhabitants classified themselves as Guatemalans, then the single largest group of foreigners.

Many of them worked on coffee plantations in Chiapas, often for fellow foreigners, especially Germans and North Americans.[11]

Robert belonged to the fourth group of immigrants in Mexico—the trade conquistadors, who acquired an influence disproportionate to their small numbers. Seeking to advance the economic interests of their families, most of the trade conquistadors came from the bourgeoisie of France, Germany, Great Britain, and Spain. Armed with investment capital, they soon filled the void left by the peninsulares. By 1850, a small group of British investors owned most of the mines. Moreover, the Europeans took advantage of their own family ties to bankers and manufacturers to seize control of high finance and commerce as well. Whereas investors from London and Paris founded Mexico's first modern banks, Frenchmen, Germans, and Spaniards owned the *almacenes,* the warehouse stores at the hubs of extensive wholesale networks.[12] Offering smaller profit margins, a large part of the retail business fell into the hands of newly arrived peninsular merchants. Since many of these Spaniards married Mexican women, their ability to seek naturalization (in addition to the payment of old-fashioned bribes) defied periodic attempts by the government to outlaw foreign ownership of retail stores.[13] According to one estimate, foreigners owned 81 percent of the 212 overseas merchant establishments in fin-de-siècle Mexico City.[14]

Joining a smattering of exiles and professionals, these entrepreneurs outnumbered the "typical immigrants"—peasant farmers and industrial workers—who dominated the migrant statistics elsewhere in the Americas. European immigration to Mexico, then, resembled a trickle of prosperous fortune seekers rather than a stream of poor immigrants in search of jobs and land. Although Mexico also received some lower-class immigrants and exiles, it never looked the part of the "promised land" that offered a chance to the downtrodden and persecuted. Instead, it remained a forbidding place for most newcomers, one where opportunity only beckoned with money or fortuitous family ties.[15]

Thus, like the Andean and Central American countries, Mexico represented a case of "qualitative" rather than "quantitative" immigration, that is, a pattern in which a relatively small number of immigrants had a disproportionately large impact on the receiving society.[16] Most immigrants to the United States and the Southern Cone were migrants of need, as they came to the Americas in order to flee either persecution or poverty in their home country. Trade conquistadors, by contrast, were migrants of choice, because their objective was to get rich quickly in order to return home to become a partner in the business of their forebears.

Such quick riches, however, were hard to come by in nineteenth-century Mexico despite the unique chance afforded by the departure of much of the country's peninsular merchant elite. During the 1830s and 1840s banditry threatened overland trade. The turmoil brought a constantly changing legal framework, which, along with double taxation at the federal and state levels, further scared off foreign investors. Not surprisingly, both foreign trade and internal commerce declined precipitously. Due to the widespread crime and instability, most wholesale merchants operated only on a commission basis, a practice that limited them to doing business with trustworthy retailers in larger Mexican towns. In addition, Mexico lacked a base of customers for foreign goods. A majority of the population consisted of peasants and indigenous villagers who did not spend their scant income on foreign-made goods, and the urban middle class remained too small to stimulate imports.[17] Retail commerce in Mexico remained characterized by the open-air market, where people haggled over prices for goods ranging from food to clothes to household items, and where human interaction mattered more than sales volume. As Joel Poinsett, the first U.S. emissary to Mexico, observed in 1823, "the mass of the people here will not for many years consume foreign manufactures."[18]

Although Mexico had disappointed many merchants, its well-advertised potential tempted the imagination of venturesome Europeans. As members of a nation without a state or overseas colonies, Germans expressed particular interest in Mexico. Before the Wars of Independence, Prussian geologist Alexander von Humboldt had depicted the country as a land of great mineral riches and astounding agricultural opportunities. A radical liberal for his time, von Humboldt had traveled through colonial Latin America at the turn of the century and identified the Spanish Crown and the Catholic Church as the two main obstacles to the fulfillment of the region's potential. Based on his travels in 1803–4, his *Political Essay on the Kingdom of New Spain* described a colony at its fullest economic bloom following a surge in silver production in the late 1700s. Mexico, von Humboldt believed, was a sadly mismanaged treasure that could reach its potential only through European immigration and the application of Enlightenment ideas. He argued that the future wealth of New Spain lay in its agriculture rather than mining. Von Humboldt's ideas had a special impact among his compatriots who watched as the British and French accumulated colonial possessions until a strong German state acquired colonies of its own in the late 1800s.[19] In their imagination, "von Humboldt metamorphosed into a German Columbus, an explorer who by conquering [Latin America] intellectually took on the legacy of the conquista, changed its nature, and opened up the continent for renewed exploration and colonization."[20] As Mexico descended "down from colonialism," and as the post–1821 crisis exposed the weakness of mining as the principal base of a national economy, his ideas were just gaining their fullest popularity.[21] At school, children of the mercantile bourgeoisie including Robert Böker were exposed to a curriculum that taught the gist of von Humboldt's work, which also included seminal studies of South America. If the United States was the country of unlimited possibilities, Mexico was the "country of unlimited impossibilities"—a nation kept by corrupt and inefficient governments from realizing its potential.[22]

In 1854, the triumph of the Reforma Liberals swept into power a faction that sought to put ideas such as von Humboldt's into practice. Like the contemporary Argentine Liberal Juan Bautista Alberdi, who had postulated that "to govern [was] to populate," Benito Juárez and his allies favored immigration from Europe.[23] Following on the heels of the U.S. annexation of millions of square miles of sparsely populated Mexican territory, the Liberal victory inaugurated an attempt to make Mexico a nation of immigrants. Seeking to emulate the U.S. economic success that the Liberals believed came from yeoman farming, the Liberals disentailed the lands of the Catholic Church and invited Europeans to colonize these vast territories. Opposites on the ethnic scale, the creole Miguel Lerdo and the Zapotec Indian Benito Juárez agreed that Protestant immigrants would infuse Mexico with such virtues as thrift, the love of hard work, and discipline. At a time when the Know-Nothing movement revealed mounting xenophobia in the United States, the Liberals hoped to exploit this opportunity to invite more immigrants to come to rural Mexico. Nonetheless, they could not persuade more than a few thousand immigrants to make Mexico their new home, as civil war and foreign intervention again ravaged the country in the following ten years. From 1858 to 1861, a civil war between Liberals and Conservatives again brought Mexico to the brink of ruin. No sooner had Juárez prevailed in this conflict than French Emperor Napoleon III sent troops to Mexico in 1862, ostensibly to collect overdue debts in concert with Great Britain and Spain. In reality, Napoleon was on a mission of reestablishing France's lost empire in the Americas. With the help of the Conservatives, the French occupation forces drove the Liberals out of the capital the following year, and in 1864, this coalition installed the young Habsburg prince, Maximilian, as emperor of Mexico, leaving Juárez and his troops to wage a protracted guerrilla war.[24]

Ironically, Maximilian, an idealistic ruler who sadly misjudged the precarious nature of his foreign rule, continued the Liberal program during his first eighteen months as emperor, when the French occupation troops appeared to guarantee his rule in Mexico. Surrounded by a circle of advisers influenced by French positivist ideas that emphasized material progress, secular rule, and rational administration,

Maximilian supported the reform laws in defiance of the Conservatives who had helped him to power. In a step certain to alienate rural elites, he even abolished debt peonage: a form of serfdom in which a debt, continually augmented through usurious interest rates or other means, formed the bond between master and peon. The emperor also actively encouraged European immigration and hoped that foreign and investment could build up the country's infrastructure.[25] The rule of Maximilian appeared the best opportunity yet to fulfill the colonial fantasies that von Humboldt's glowing descriptions had evoked among the German bourgeoisie. Apparently on the verge of breaking the cycle of violence that had impeded the process of modernization compared to other Latin American countries, Maximilian's Mexico offered great opportunities for the propertied immigrant. Consequently, it attracted a modest number of German merchants.[26]

Even as economic modernization proceeded at a snail's pace, merchants like Böker therefore found new opportunities. The nineteenth-century almacén sold not only household goods but also tools, machinery, agricultural and mining implements, carriages, and sewing machines; in sum, the equipment necessary to build up the Mexican economy. Despite the fact that the politically disunited German states had arrived belatedly on the industrial stage, German merchant houses such as Ketelsen and Degetau, Gutheil and Leffmann (later Sommer, Herrmann), and Korff and Honsberg dominated hardware sales in Mexico. These companies fell into two categories based on regional origin: those from the Hanseatic cities of Hamburg and Bremen (like Gutheil and Leffmann) and those from the Bergisches Land (like Korff and Honsberg). Experienced in overseas sales and transportation, the Hanseatic clans initially had the upper hand over their competitors from western Germany, accounting for forty out of the fifty German wholesale stores in Mexico. However, the Remscheid merchants, who hailed from an area close to the Rhein and Ruhr District, one of Europe's future industrial powerhouses, held the advantage of family ties to German producers.[27] Occurring at the precise moment when Maximilian attempted to create favorable conditions for immigrants in general and German-speaking merchants in particular, Robert Böker's 1865 trip to Mexico City followed these new developments.

The Making of a Trade Conquistador

When Böker boarded the stagecoach that took him toward Mexico City in an arduous journey from the port of Veracruz, the history of one of the foremost families of the Bergisches Land region south of the Rhein and Ruhr District weighed on his shoulders. First documented in the late sixteenth century, the Bokers had long been associated with manufacturing and trading hardware.[28] Farmers who owned large tracts of forest, Robert Böker's ancestors worked metal on wood fires. One generation later, they gave up farming to dedicate themselves to the manufacturing and servicing of tools. In the process, they overcame the powerful guilds in the Remscheid area that unsuccessfully attempted to restrict their right to service the tools they had made.[29]

The rise of the Bokers to prominence began in earnest with the first merchant in the family, Robert's great-grandfather Gottfried Böker. Gottfried commenced a pattern typical of middle-class families in areas in which the tradition of partible inheritance threatened to scatter family wealth: he married a member of a competing merchant clan. He took up the manufacture of sheaths and blades, products in great demand in the era of the Seven Years' War (1756–63). A self-taught man and devout Christian, he also learned the export business from his father-in-law, who already possessed important contacts in the German states, the Netherlands, and Scandinavia. By the time of Gottfried's death in 1795, the Bokers exported their products to nearby states amidst the chaos of the international conflict following the French Revolution.[30]

Presaging a future pattern that would see the Bokers benefit from most major wars, the era of the French Revolution and Napoleon Bonaparte witnessed the emergence of the clan as merchants on an international scale. The advancing French armies broke down trading barriers and opened opportunities for aspiring capitalists. In 1805, Napoleon invaded western Germany, established the "Rheinbund," and made his brother-in-law the archduke of the newly created Duchy of Berg. Although the Bokers resented the imposition of French rule and what they viewed as the corruption and "loose" morals brought by the foreign armies, they readily took advantage of the new situation. When Gottfried Böker's second son, Gottlieb, won election to the first democratic Remscheid town council, his election reflected the rising status of the bourgeoisie and the ability of his family to adapt to a rapidly changing political order. The position also reflected Gottlieb's growing stature in the community as one of the directors of "Johann Gottlieb Böker und Hilger," a business that gave up manufacturing to dedicate itself to commerce. Gottlieb's marriage illustrated the above-mentioned tendency of the bourgeoisie to stick to its own circles in order to keep capital together. His bride was not only the aunt of his partner but also his own first cousin. Managed thus by merchants linked by strong ties of family and friendship, "Böker und Hilger" began to export hardware to Belgium, France, the Netherlands, and Russia during the Napoleonic Wars. While many overseas exporters foundered due to Napoleon's blockade against Great Britain, this business survived because continental Europe had emerged as their principal market.[31]

Although the Bokers had thus taken advantage of the changes wrought by the French Revolution, they found the political climate of postrevolutionary Europe equally to their liking. When the Congress of Vienna awarded the Rhineland and Westphalia to Prussia, Germany's preeminent Protestant state, it eliminated tariff barriers that had thus far delayed the capitalist development of western Germany. Having thus far considered themselves Remscheiders, the Protestant Bokers now became patriotic Prussians. In 1815, during Napoleon's brief return to power, Gottlieb gave money to the Prussian authorities to help cover the costs of the war against France. Shortly thereafter, the onset of the Biedermeier era, in which the new authorities rigidly enforced law and order, convinced the Bokers that Prussia had indeed brought peace and stability to the area.[32]

This affinity to the new Prussian order manifested itself in a new ideal that would take on the utmost significance in the self-perception of Robert Böker: the ideal of the "kingly merchant." A kingly merchant was an honest-to-a-fault, modest entrepreneur who combined a gen- uine commitment to public service with a capitalist spirit. Public service indeed became a tradition among the Bokers, as many of them served on the city council, benevolent organizations, and, later on, in the most important associations and institutions of the German colony in Mexico City.[33] Frugal living would remain one of the Bokers' hallmarks into the twentieth century, as those who enjoyed material comfort found themselves the target of ridicule and criticism. Most importantly, the ideal of the kingly merchant served to construct a distinction from what they saw as the selfish, money-grubbing Mediterranean merchant, not to mention Jewish entrepreneurs, long-time victims of this stereotype.[34]

During the years of reaction, the family business endured a turbulent period. The economic stagnation of the 1820s and early 1830s negated the commercial opportunities afforded by the Rheinbund-era economic restructuring and the collapse of the competitors of "Böker und Hilger" during the Napoleonic Wars. Unable to move aggressively into the export market, the company resumed manufacturing. After a modest beginning, the company's sabers and blades became well known throughout Europe. By 1832, the company was so successful that Böker and Hilger parted ways in order to make room for their numerous sons. Five years later, with the export business rebounding, the Bokers were ready to take their business overseas. In 1838, Gottlieb Böker's eldest son, Hermann, founded his own trading house in New York City.[35]

Soon thereafter, industrialization began to transform the Bergisches Land and the adjacent Rhine and Ruhr District, a coal-rich area populated by middle-class farmers, small merchants, and manufacturers operating modest cottage industries. Beginning in the 1840s, railroads began to link the region's principal cities and towns, and steam engines allowed the mass manufacturing of steel products. In the formerly pastoral setting of the Bergisches Land, the exhaust from the new coal-powered machinery blackened the homes, trees, and people in the vicinity of railroads and industrial plants. Furnishing the technology, the infrastructure, and the demand for the exponential expansion of hardware production, the Industrial Revolution constituted a great opportunity for the Bokers.[36] Eventually, it changed the character of their hometown. Formerly a remote town, Remscheid became the *Seestadt auf dem Berge,* or port city on the hill: a city that rivaled the old trading centers of Bremen and Hamburg in its exports of German hardware.

When two of Gottlieb's younger sons, Robert and Heinrich ("Roberto's" father), took over their father's business, they faced some difficulties in taking advantage of these new opportunities. German industrialization came belatedly, and British and French industrial producers already shipped their goods overseas when the Germans finally got started. To make matters worse, Remscheid lay just off the main railroad lines: the Cologne-Dortmund line ran a few miles south of the town, while the Ruhr line lay 20 miles north. Since transportation other than by train was slow and expensive, many would-be manufacturers awaited the construction of a train station in Remscheid.[37] Moreover, the abortive Revolution of 1848 paralyzed production throughout the Bergisches Land, although the conservative Remscheid region was spared the worst of the unrest. At the low point of the crisis, workers greeted Heinrich with the question: "What should we do when there's nothing left to eat?" Heinrich answered, "Then we will eat each other."[38] Nonetheless, in 1854, the two brothers built a steam-powered grinding plant just outside the town. This investment constituted a considerable risk, as the Bokers faced stiff competition from the neighboring town of Solingen, a town with a train station. What enabled the two brothers to attempt such a venture were their marriages to women from families wealthier than their own, women who contributed significant dowries to the enterprise.[39] When the new operation proved unprofitable, these dowries allowed the Bokers to transform the grinding plant into a rolling mill and to add a small factory that produced blades as well as table and kitchen knives. In 1860, the two brothers divided the family business. Robert got the lucrative trade routes to Russia and the German states. Heinrich, meanwhile, took over the factory and sold hardware in the United States and Canada with the help of older brother Hermann in New York, who became his partner in what was renamed "Heinrich Böker."[40]

Born May 27, 1843, Robert (who became Roberto) Böker, the second of Heinrich Böker and Elisabeth Scharff's nine children, grew up in the Spartan environment characteristic of a kingly merchant. He was raised with few social pretensions, as his childhood friends were working-class children, and he often came home from his play dirty or soaking wet. The food he ate resembled that of his working-class friends: buttered black and white bread three times a day, and vegetable soup with potatoes and a little meat for a noontime dinner. The family home in Vieringhausen, a village just outside Remscheid, was small for a family of eleven, and the children slept two to a bed and all in the same room. His father's business was next door, and his mother only needed to play the flute to have her husband scurry home in order to either eat or discipline the children. Nevertheless, one thing distinguished young Böker from his friends: abundant educational opportunities, which manifested themselves in eleven years of rigorous schooling, including the last three years in Cologne. After graduation in 1860, Robert joined his father's company as an apprentice.[41]

Reflecting this background, Robert came to epitomize the kingly merchant: educated, but not academic; stingy in his expenditures; secular in outlook; patriotic and conservative in his political convictions; and committed to public service. As a prospective merchant, Robert did not study for the *Abitur* (high school) degree. Nonetheless, his education had equipped him with knowledge of English and French, along with mathematics, composition, history, arts, science, and literature. Although he attended church occasionally, he did not raise his children as devout Christians: for him, faith served a social, and not a spiritual purpose. Robert expressed deep loyalty to the Prussian king and state; he considered himself Prussian first and German second, even after the unification of Germany in January 1871. He had no sympathy for the failure of democracy in his home country, but he was a Liberal on economic issues. Public service consumed most of his life.[42]

Robert belonged to the patrician entrepreneurial class, the *Wirtschaftsbürger,* which had come to the forefront of German society in the middle of the nineteenth century. The formative experiences of this era included burgeoning industrialization and a rapidly growing nationalism in a country soon to be unified with what Prussian (and later German) Chancellor Otto von Bismarck called "blood and iron." The self-confident bourgeoisie of this generation expected greatness of itself and its home country. The only emotion that tempered this unbridled confidence was a fear of social dissolution, a threat manifested in trade unionism and the rise of the Social Democratic Party. Influenced by social Darwinism, the Wirtschaftsbürger saw themselves as the vanguard of progress, called on to bring order, technology, and Western values to the rest of the world. They cheered the Prussian defeat of Austria in 1866 that tore down customs barriers all over Germany; they were even more ecstatic when the German states defeated France five years later; and they rejoiced when the resultant unification of Germany made Prussians into proud Germans.[43]

During Robert's three-year stint in "Heinrich Böker," his uncle Hermann's arms deals with the Civil War-era United States made him the point man in Remscheid. In his function as Hermann's partner, Heinrich spent most of his time in New York City, leaving the day-to-day operations of his business in his son's young hands. In comfortable retirement in Bonn, Hermann sold used sabers to the Abraham Lincoln administration through his sons, who operated his hardware store in New York. Encouraged by the healthy profit from these deals (a margin of more than 200 percent), he signed several large-scale contracts with the Lincoln administration for combat arms manufactured in the Bergisches Land. By the end of 1862, however, when the U.S. government found itself unable to pay a debt of a few million dollars to the two Böker brothers, the saber venture threatened to bring down the entire family business. Ultimately, the Lincoln administration paid up, minus a deduction of a million dollars that resulted in fruitless lawsuits.[44]

These arms deals led to Robert's first trip to the United States, a trip that his father thought would provide international experience before his eldest son could become a partner in the family business. On March 20, 1863, Robert embarked for New York aboard the steamer *Bavaria,* a vessel offering only minimal comfort in the rough weather on the North Atlantic. In New York, he began an internship with a U.S. hardware store on Cliff Street. The fact that his father and his cousin helped him adjust to a very different environment did not save Robert from culture shock. As he reported, when the draft was held for the first time in New York City, "the rabble got angry, set fire to all locations where the draft was held, shamelessly pillaged the uptown, and hung a large number of Negroes from lantern posts. . . . It was a great fortune that the Northern [victory] . . . at Gettysburg . . . freed the militia in Washington to return to New York. When the militia arrived, . . . they shot four or five hundred of the mob, and the affair was over. But I had got an idea of what it meant to be at the utter mercy of an unbridled rabble."[45] The city mob in New York City had therefore proven quite a different matter than his poor childhood friends in Remscheid, and Robert had received his first lesson in dealing with other cultures. This

lesson did not encourage him to mix with "the rabble," and he chose
friends from his own social context, mostly fellow German residents
and immigrants.[46]

As the Civil War abated in the North, Robert came to enjoy his stay
in New York. Over time, he became involved in the entire scope of
Hermann's import business and spent what he later called the "greatest and most carefree years" of his life.[47] He acquired U.S. citizenship
in 1864, and one of his cousins offered him a partnership in his hardware store in the city. But Robert rejected this opportunity because he
wanted to "see something of the world."[48] In winter 1864–65, he traveled to Montreal several times to check on the family's commercial outpost in that city. By the time he returned to New York from the last of
those trips in April 1865, he received another opportunity to quench
his thirst for adventure. His next assignment was a trip to Mexico City
to look into the condition of "Reichmann and Holder," a small almacén
in which his uncle Hermann had invested money.[49]

Difficult Beginnings

Once en route to Veracruz, however, Robert learned that New York had
not prepared him to deal with life in Mexico. Although Wilhelm
Reichmann, one of the partners of the almacén and a veteran of the
French Foreign Legion, accompanied him along with his family, his first
days taught him always to expect the unexpected. While the party spent
three days in the tropical heat of Veracruz waiting for the train, which
in those days ended near the town of Paso del Macho, Reichmann
became delirious.[50] The trip to the Mexican capital served notice of the
conditions that Robert would encounter during the coming years. Even
though he—unlike Isabel Reichmann, the daughter of a Spanish
mother—did not speak any Spanish, he held full responsibility for the
entourage as the only healthy adult male. During the first day spent en
route to Orizaba, Wilhelm Reichmann became so sick that Robert
feared his business partner might die before they reached the capital.
At the end of the second day near Puebla, Robert spent the night sitting on a chair in his hotel room, chased from his mattress by an army
of fleas and bugs. On the third day, the party finally reached the forest
of Río Frío, a place notorious for its banditry, where Austrian hussars
met them to guide the party to Mexico City. As Robert related, "When
the three stagecoaches drove through the deeply worn out trails, and
[all] the . . . horses . . . whirled up the dust, I was sometimes not able
to see the person facing me in the stagecoach. . . . Days afterwards, my
throat was still sore and raw from all the swallowed dust." After three
days of hard travel, Robert felt lucky to have survived the trip.[51]

As the memories of this journey faded, however, the prospect of spending time in Mexico City seemed more appealing. To be sure, fifty years of political instability had taken their toll on the capital. Many inhabitants lived in abject poverty. Gas lamps, not electrical lights, illuminated the capital at night; electricity had not yet arrived in Mexico. The unpaved roads beyond the Centro Histórico, the historic downtown area hereafter referred to as Centro, turned into swamps during the rainy season, and flooding from the nearby Lake Texcoco occurred frequently.[52] But Mexico City was not a sleepy, dingy town like Veracruz; by 1865, more than 200,000 people lived there. The climate was pleasant all year, tropical diseases quite rare, and the landscape breathtaking, especially during the dry season, when the crisp mountain air permitted a clear view of two majestic volcanoes, Ixtaccíhuatl and Popocatépetl. To top it off, Maximilian and his wife, Charlotte (known to Mexicans as Carlota), desired to bring a city that already boasted great architectural beauty up to par with European capitals. Charlotte had made plans to construct a beautiful Belgian-style avenue from downtown Mexico City to Chapultepec Castle (today, the Paseo de la Reforma), and her husband planned to have the lake drained and the Centro furnished with electricity.[53] These renovations stood to benefit foreign merchants' stores, many of which were located in the Plateros District between Alameda Park and the Zócalo, the main square of the capital. Reichmann and Holder operated two separate stores; one at the corner of Espíritu Santo and Plateros (today, the intersection of Isabel la Católica and Madero), and the other one—which later became the main store—two blocks south at the corner with Cadena (today, Venustiano Carranza).[54]

The relative tranquility of the capital, however, did not mean that Robert's start as a Mexico City entrepreneur would be easy. Maximilian's rule began to disintegrate, bringing xenophobia, increasing unrest, and crime while Mexico lacked a government that could exert effective sovereignty. To make matters worse, Reichmann and Holder was in bad shape. This small wholesale and retail store offered a random assortment of goods such as wheels, soap, glassware, and crinolines, and it sold very few of them. Reichmann and Paul Holder had purchased these goods "without knowledge of what the country consumed," and they had paid tax on many of these items twice, once in New York and again in Veracruz.[55] As if these problems were not bad enough, Reichmann died from his illness two months after their arrival. His death gave Robert two options: quit and lose the investment, or take Reichmann's place in the partnership.[56]

Thus it was that on November 1, 1865, the same day Maximilian outlawed debt peonage, Robert became a partner in what was renamed "Holder, Boker y Cía," a small firm with a capital of U.S. $40,000.[57]

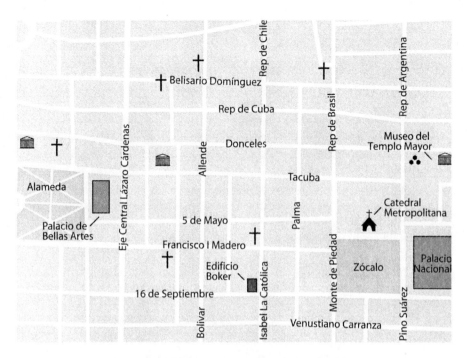

Map 2. The Centro Histórico of Mexico City.

Shortly thereafter, Holder departed for New York, never to return. New to the country and the Spanish language, Robert had to rely on his only assistant, the Frenchman Louis Drommel. Initially, they sold only a few pesos worth of merchandise every day, mostly to French and Spanish retailers.[58]

Thieves who took advantage of the political instability in the waning days of Maximilian's empire did not help Robert's efforts to make his father's investment pay off. The fading government could not protect merchants, and Mexican justice was slow by Prussian standards. Robert's own words well describe his impatience with the system of justice: "Since cases of theft that involved the police brought about annoyances such as interrogations etc., we sometimes preferred to take justice into our own hands."[59] In 1866, Böker hired a German veteran of the French Foreign Legion, Hermann Stiegler, to help him confront the "riffraff" hanging out at his store. Stiegler proved most effective: on one occasion, he took a revolver and a club to the home of an employee who had stolen from the store, and he thrashed the culprit mercilessly. With Holder in New York City, Robert now had two foreigners working for him in midlevel positions (Stiegler and Drommel) as well as several Mexican employees.[60]

Ultimately, however, neither petty crime nor a floundering economy could stop Robert from succeeding at a time when many trade conquistadors returned home in failure. Unlike many of his colleagues, Robert came equipped with international business connections and a U.S. passport. His apprenticeship in New York had made him aware of the enormous potential of the latest U.S. consumer goods. His decision to become a partner in Holder and Reichmann was based on the future rather than the present of the company: it held the exclusive rights to sell Singer sewing machines in Mexico. One of the newest items available in Mexico, sewing machines promised to eclipse all other goods the company offered, as they dramatically raised the productivity of tailors and textile manufacturers. Robert used the living room of his apartment right above the store on Plateros as a sales room.[61]

With the help of a shrewd sales strategy, the Singer sewing machines soon pulled the company out of its doldrums. Well aware of the shortage of cash that existed in war-torn Mexico, Böker allowed buyers to lease the machines, which remained the property of the company until paid in full. A Mexican employee collected 5 pesos a month

Figure 1: Boker building in Calle Cadena, ca. 1890
(Archivo Boker, Mexico City).

from each purchaser, kept records of these payments, and reclaimed machines if their owners had defaulted on their leases. The income from the sewing machines put Holder, Boker y Cía on track to make a profit, and the company soon added hardware and household articles to its list. As early as 1867, the sales volume had increased to 378,000 pesos.[62]

The sewing machines formed the most important source of income for the fledgling business, but arms deals constituted another. The Union had purchased arms from Robert's uncle Hermann during the U.S. Civil War. With that conflict past, the victorious Northern leaders turned their attention toward helping Juárez defeat Maximilian, which offered another opportunity for the Bokers to cash in on a military conflict. Although the U.S. government did not send troops into Mexico, two generals from Indiana, Lew Wallace and the German-born Herman Sturm, became secret agents for Juárez. A naturalized U.S. citizen like his acquaintance Robert Böker, whom he had known since his days in New York City, Sturm procured U.S.$2,000,000 worth of weapons in the United States. This was not only an astonishing feat, given that Sturm could only offer a promise to pay, but also a tremendous risk given the uncertainty of the political situation in Mexico.[63] After Juárez's victory in June 1867, these arms purchases gave Robert a chance to collect a hefty commission, as Sturm charged him with collecting more than U.S.$200,000 of overdue debt for the weapons. Although Robert was not successful in recovering the entire debt from a government deep in obligations, he did earn a commission of 5,000 to 6,000 pesos.[64] He also used the resulting connections to sell a large order of swords (likely used as ceremonial arms) to the Juárez government.[65]

These events also demonstrated Robert's ability to stay out of the political fray, yet profit financially from the turmoil. He hedged his bets initially, when Maximilian looked dominant. As the emperor's fortunes declined, however, Robert quietly cultivated ties to Liberal leaders while professing loyalty to Maximilian and taking advantage of the protection by Austrian cavalrymen for his trips through Mexico City's violent surroundings.[66] This attitude corresponded to political expediency. Whereas foreign merchants would ideally have preferred to live under an Austrian emperor, they considered Juárez the better bet to achieve political stability in Mexico. Ultimately, Robert pursued a cautious strategy. In contrast to his uncle's deals with the U.S. government at the beginning of the decade, he did not sell arms to either side until Juárez had won. Better yet, as a U.S. citizen with German roots, he benefited from the interruption of Mexico's diplomatic relations with Britain, France, and Spain following Maximilian's death, which allowed

German merchants to pick up much of the business that French merchants had controlled up to the mid-1860s.[67]

The final element in Robert's success came in 1869, when his father founded the cutlery factory "Heinrich Böker and Company" in Solingen (not to be confused with Heinrich Böker in Remscheid). Known for a tree motif that still serves as its insignia, this company came to fame as "Arbolito" in Latin America and as "Treebrand" in the United States. Even today, "Arbolito" razor blades and knives remain the signature merchandise of the Casa Boker, which continues to import these goods under exclusive license. The real Arbolito, however—the tree in front of the factory that provided the motif—was set ablaze during World War II.[68]

Robert soon became successful enough that he bought out Holder's share in the business. The two partners had not worked well together, and Robert had blamed Holder, whose expertise in gold and jewelry did not complement his objectives, for the early difficulties of the company. Holder's marriage to Isabel Reichmann, whom Robert may have secretly adored, compounded the problem. The buyout of Holder entailed a name change, and the business became a sole proprietorship known as "Roberto Boker." In 1870, Stiegler and Robert's brother Max became directors in the renamed company, a step up from the role of an "assistant."[69] This reorganization put his company on track to reap the fruits of Liberal modernization as a specialty store that carved out a niche for itself in the expanding Mexican market for imported goods.

Living in an Expatriate Community

As Robert's time in Mexico City demonstrates, most of the trade conquistadors were expatriates rather than immigrants. Since most of them expected a limited stay in Mexico, they sent their profits to their home country rather than commit significant capital investments to the host society. They seldom took families with them; instead, the typical merchant arrived as a bachelor in his early to midtwenties. Sharing the predominant view that "whiter" was better, he consorted primarily with fellow merchants from the country of his birth, segregating himself from the society around him in the process.[70] The Protestant German entrepreneurs expressed little interest in intermarrying with the Catholic Mexican elite. However, there were exceptions to this trend, such as the Hagenbeck and Pöhls families from Hamburg, who intermarried with the Mexican bourgeoisie. At a 1998 meeting of the descendants of the original Pöhls immigrant, only one-third of those present spoke any German at all.[71]

This self-segregation assumed three forms. Most importantly, the foreign resident avoided private contact with Mexicans, and often even with residents from countries other than his own. In addition, he stuck to people from his own social class, religious denomination, and profession. Finally, the resident did nothing to make his stay in Mexico appear permanent. He usually did not marry while overseas, he did not invest in local production or manufacturing, and he did not seek Mexican citizenship. Giving up his native citizenship would have deprived him of the recourse of diplomatic protection, which was quicker than going through Mexican courts.[72]

There were good reasons for foreigners not to seek assimilation into Mexican society. Many of them enjoyed considerable power and wealth precisely due to their status as outsiders, that is, their connection to overseas producers. Paradoxically, both xenophobia and xenophilia played important roles as well. Popular xenophobia resulting from European and U.S. interventions in Mexico helped immigrants justify their self-segregation. At the same time, centuries of colonial rule had imbued Mexicans with an inferiority complex with respect to Europeans and, later, white North Americans. Even many elite Mexicans thought of Europeans as representing the highest level of civilization.[73] According to popular lore, they held the French and the Germans in particularly high regard: in the words of twentieth-century U.S. novelist Katherine Anne Porter, the Mexicans "loath the Americans . . . hate the Spaniards, distrust the English, admire the French, and love the Germans."[74] As the nineteenth century progressed, the influence of positivist and social Darwinist thought only accentuated this trend.[75] As the Porfirian-era adage "Mexico: mother of foreigners and stepmother of Mexicans" indicates, foreign merchants enjoyed a high social prestige.

Moreover, creole efforts at maintaining their dominance in a multiethnic society encouraged constructions of identity that were not conducive to the assimilation of immigrants. Although a castelike division between the Spanish and Indian worlds had marked early New Spain, miscegenation soon produced a growing group of mestizos who did not fit into the established division between the *república de españoles* and the *república de indios*. As the mestizos grew in number over centuries of Spanish colonial rule, class and cultural distinctions began to replace racial categories (as one of Mexico's oldest adages goes, "money whitens"). In the absence of a rigid system of racial categories, the creoles asserted their superiority over both mestizos and Indians by imagining themselves as the representatives of a Spanish, Roman Catholic nation on Mexican soil as embodied in the Virgin of Guadalupe.[76] Even as the creoles defied the political power of the peninsulares in identifying themselves as "americanos," they recognized the perils of relinquishing the association with the Spanish heritage.[77] In this view, all those not of Spanish culture ("Indians" as well as foreigners) remained outsiders, while some mestizos gained acceptance by rising to economic and military significance during the bloody history of the nineteenth century.

Linguistic conventions further discouraged acculturation, as the Spanish language does not easily lend itself to describing hyphenated identities such as the ones common in English or German.[78] In Spanish, a woman may be either a "francesa" or a "mexicana," but never a "francesa-mexicana," and even the more graceful "franco-mexicana" sounds more cumbersome to Mexican ears than "franco-mexicaine" does to French ones. Likewise, the son of a German immigrant would refer to himself as a "Deutschmexikaner," or German-Mexican, in German, but he would face the stark choice between "alemán" and "mexicano" in Spanish. When foreign immigrants came to Mexico, they thus faced a cultural divide: one was either a Mexican or a foreigner, but not a hyphenated product of both worlds. This dichotomy between "Mexican" and "foreign" extended to succeeding generations, so that most children of non-Spanish-speaking parents still considered themselves foreign.[79]

Interestingly, the same language that discouraged hyphenated identities encouraged the Hispanization of names, especially where a German *Umlaut* was involved. Robert Böker became Roberto Boker in Mexico City. His brother Heinrich became Enrique, and his son Franz became Francisco, all without any paperwork. Unlike Portuguese-speaking Brazil, where one of Getúlio Vargas's chiefs of police never lost the Umlaut in his last name, Müller, Mexicans did not tolerate such oddities. In 1899, when workers embossed the name "Edificio Böker" [sic] above the portals of the new, grandiose Boker building, they therefore violated linguistic practice. For their part, the Bokers switched between Spanish and German versions of their names strictly as a matter of convenience.[80]

Not surprisingly, the foreigners in nineteenth-century Mexico City formed expatriate communities. Made up of well-to-do, temporary migrants with a limited personal stake in the host society, these communities were transient and male-dominated. Most of their members remained in Mexico less than a decade, and bachelors and young couples outnumbered families. The social life of the expatriate communities took place in males-only clubs. In the absence of other associations such as schools, churches, athletic clubs, and beneficent associations, these communities did not fulfill the functions of ethnic enclaves until the turn of the century.[81]

Instead, the word "colony," used by Mexicans to denote all close-knit communities of foreigners, best elucidates the condition of Germans and other foreigners in nineteenth-century Mexico. In the Latin American context, the word "colony" dates back to the Italian

Renaissance, where outsiders (for example, Genoese merchants) lived in a determined area of a city such as Florence or Venice. These merchant colonies remained separate from the elites but, in contrast to the Jewish ghetto, interacted socially with them. Thus, members of colonies were outsiders rather than outcasts. Borrowing from this Mediterranean tradition, Mexicans use the term *colonia* (aside from its more conventional meanings) to denote a neighborhood of a city, or a close-knit group of outsiders.[82] In the words of a U.S. sociologist, a colony consisted of "those who seek to maintain their own racial and cultural integrity although living in an alien land which has an independent government."[83] This effort to preserve the home culture involved a sense of superiority over the host society, membership in a close-knit community, and a "territorial consciousness": the notion that the colony constituted a part of the home country.[84]

About three hundred strong at the time of Robert's sojourn, the German colony serves as a good example of such an expatriate community.[85] Three out of four of the Germans were male, most were Protestant, and almost all of the women were married. Although deep social divisions marked the German community, merchants dominated the scene. Because most of these merchants had made plans to return to their native country before starting a family, their interest in social life remained slight. Their only significant social club, the Casino Alemán, or German house, was founded in 1848 in an effort to unify German expatriates divided in their political loyalties and became the central meeting point of all Germans in Mexico City. In this club, members could enjoy German food and drink and socialize with their compatriots.[86] Thus Robert lived his life among German and U.S. expatriates, isolated from Mexican society and largely ignorant of the life outside Mexico City.

Whenever Robert did venture outside the capital, the banditry and violence commonplace in the countryside reminded him of the safety of the small German community. One of these trips in particular highlighted his fear of a society that became increasingly xenophobic as Maximilian's stay in power drew to a close.[87] In March 1867, he traveled on business to the nearby town of Toluca. On his way there, he saw a Liberal cavalry regiment and came away impressed with their garb: "The fellows wore only white cotton pants and shirts, and a serape around their shoulders . . . they had strapped long spurs on their naked feet."[88] During his return trip, he suddenly felt a cold rifle barrel pressing against his cheek. The bandits took all valuables from the passengers of the stagecoach, and one of them even made Robert take off his shoes: "There were," he said, "people impertinent enough to hide money" there. When everything was over, Robert noticed that the bandits had left one of his fellow travelers a small amount of money. Surprised, he asked one of the bandits to return a peso "because I have not had breakfast, and, as a German, I would like to drink a glass of beer, too." This request offended the bandit, who tossed him a coin with the gratuitous advice that the money would buy him a few tortillas with enough spare change for a beer.[89] It is doubtful, however, that Robert enjoyed eating this most basic of all Mexican staple foods, as his choice of words indicated contempt for Mexicans. The German word for eating that he used in association with "tortilla" is *fressen* (to devour), a derogatory word that denotes an animal's way of taking food.

A few weeks after this incident, his first return trip to Germany further accentuated the emotions of adventure and estrangement that the young merchant felt during his first two years in Mexico. The trip to Veracruz usually took three to four days. By March 1867, however, Juárez's armies had encircled both Mexico City and Veracruz, and the collapse of a bridge had interrupted train service between Paso del Macho and the coast. Therefore, Robert needed twenty-five days to reach a ship to take him to Europe. The journey included travel by stagecoach to Otumba, by train to Apizaco, again by stagecoach to Orizaba, by carriage to Paso del Macho, again by train to Medellín, by boat down the river to the coast, and by steamship to Veracruz. When he finally reached the port city, his face was so badly sunburned that the "skin hung down [his] face in shreds."[90] The description of this voyage manifests the typical mind-set of a trade conquistador. Robert's memoirs depicted Mexico as an exotic land of adventure populated by semisavage rabble—a country where doing business constituted a merchant's baptism by fire.

Once Juárez's return to power restored peace to Mexico in June 1867, however, Robert adapted to his surroundings. As his business benefited from the sale of sewing machines, Arbolito cutlery, and a growing number of other products, he took steps that indicated that he considered himself a part of a larger, albeit foreign, community. He perfected his Spanish, and he cultivated ties to the increasingly important "American colony" in the capital. Later on, he even figured among the founders of the American Hospital.[91]

Ultimately, it was family rather than business considerations that made Robert return to Germany. During his 1867 trip to Germany, he had met his future wife, Auguste Günther. A fellow native of Remscheid, Auguste was the daughter of a well-heeled export merchant, a perfect match for Robert. Only eighteen at the time, she waited for three years until Robert married her and took her to Mexico City immediately after their wedding on October 1, 1870.[92] Once married, Robert's days in Mexico were soon numbered, as Auguste never felt comfortable in Mexico City. The couple had but a small circle of friends that included

Adolf Schmidtlein, who had served as Maximilian and Charlotte's private physician.[93] Even more importantly, fate dealt Auguste cruel blows that would make her describe her years in Mexico as "the saddest of our marriage."[94] Shortly after their arrival, her consumptive sister died. The following year, the couple looked forward to the birth of a child in October, but their daughter was stillborn. With the help of a doctored birth certificate, which stated that the daughter had been born alive, they buried her in the English cemetery of La Tlaxpana, near the present suburb of Tacuba.[95] To top it off, Auguste recovered slowly from the birth, only to finally come down with a severe bout of malaria. According to her diary, only Schmidtlein's "conscientious care" saved her from death.[96] Delirious with fever, she suffered a miscarriage, upon which Robert buried the fetus in a cigar case. Coupled with Robert's father's failing health, these tragedies soured the couple on living in Mexico City. In 1873, Robert and Auguste returned to Remscheid just in time to see Heinrich Böker on his deathbed.[97]

With his business on track to grow under the supervision of his brother Max, Robert returned to a comfortable life. Barely thirty years old, he became a partner in his late father's export firm and henceforth devoted himself to building up the BSI (Bergische Stahlindustrie, or Steel Industry of the Bergisches Land). The BSI combined the industrial ventures of the Böker family in Remscheid area into one corporation. Due to his extensive overseas experience, he also spearheaded export ventures in Buenos Aires and Melbourne, Australia, where family members had established businesses much like Roberto Boker y Cía in Mexico City.[98] Robert's most strenuous years, however, already lay behind him, which permitted him to pursue a career in public service. In 1877, he won a seat on the city council and henceforth dedicated himself to local and regional politics. To assure the supply of drinking water in rapidly growing Remscheid, he raised money for what became the first fresh water reserve in Germany. For these efforts, he was later named an honorary citizen, and an oversize bronze likeness of his head still graces the dam that Robert helped build. So important was his work for Remscheid to him that he used an entire room in his relatively small house as his public service office.[99]

Although Robert found the area of public service far more captivating than his investments in Mexico, his departure did not mean that he disappeared from the scene. He returned to Mexico four times to attend to changes in partnership. In addition, he remained involved in buying the goods his company sold. So far as his personal life was concerned, however, Mexico became a distant memory for Robert once he and Auguste settled down in Germany. They had four healthy children: Clara, Elisabeth, Franz, and Gertrud, who all grew up with scant knowledge of

Figure 2: Robert and Auguste Böker and their grandchildren
(Archivo Boker, Mexico City).

their father's Mexican connections. In Franz's words, his father "thought
little about Mexico and talked even less about it."[100]

Robert Böker's years in Mexico City marked not only the beginnings
of his business but also the pattern of immigration into a society
characterized by stark social and ethnic differences. Lacking both a
commercial elite and incentives for lower-class immigration, postcolonial Mexico offered opportunities to the privileged member of transcon-
tinental family networks rather than to the poor immigrant in search of
a better future. These conditions facilitated the establishment of a hardware store by a temporary immigrant and discouraged his contact with
Mexican society. Therefore, young, male entrepreneurs dominated the
foreign diasporas in Mexico City—investors who remained isolated
from what they considered a temporary host.

The young Robert was typical of foreign merchants in nineteenth-
century Mexico, yet he possessed important comparative advantages
over most of his peers. He was young and single when he arrived; he
returned home to find a spouse; his friends and associates were fellow
Prussians, and he came endowed with business connections that gave
him a head start. He also shared the conservatism and patriotism of the
other foreign merchants in Mexico, even though his patriotism did not
stop him from affiliating with the "American" colony as well. His business interests and his experience in the United States made him a
transnational merchant. Once Mexico emerged from its prolonged

period of troubles, this merchant and his partners would enjoy comparative advantages that would allow them to transform a tiny store into one of Mexico's most important wholesalers.

Times such as the ones my father witnessed . . .
will not return any time soon.
—Franz Böker

2

The Rise of the Casa Boker

On July 3, 1900, President Porfirio Díaz inaugurated a grandiose department store built at the enormous cost of 1.5 million gold pesos, or approximately 700,000 U.S. dollars. Located two blocks west of the Zócalo, at the intersection of the streets known today as Isabel la Católica and 16 de Septiembre, the "Edificio Boker" epitomized transnational capitalism in fin-de-siècle Mexico. An imposing three-storied structure, the building represented the collaboration of three nations. It was the property of German entrepreneurs, the design of U.S. architects, and the work of hundreds of underpaid Mexican laborers. The Edificio Boker housed a company that sold millions of dollars worth of hardware every year, thus serving as a vital cog in the process of modernization. Flanked by Finance Secretary José Y. Limantour, Foreign Secretary Ignacio Mariscal, and two other cabinet members, Don Porfirio praised Roberto Boker y Cía in the highest terms.[1]

Only one minor hitch marred the proudest moment of the company. The president was supposed to enter the building through an entrance graced by a floor mosaic of the Mexican national emblem, an eagle with a snake in its beak sitting on a cactus. Such displays of national symbols on the floor were acceptable in Germany, but they offended Mexicans. In keeping with the traditions of his country, Díaz refused to step on the national insignia. Although hampered by his age and girth, he squeezed into the building without treading on the mosaic, visibly upset by this affront to the national honor. General Director Carl Friederichs temporarily solved the problem by placing a rug on the emblem; soon thereafter, following an outcry in the Mexico City press, he had the mosaic removed.[2]

This incident not only typified the lack of cultural sensitivity common among foreign merchants in Porfirian Mexico; it also demonstrated the tension between an international business strategy and a German family identity. The Díaz-era rise of the Casa Boker that culminated in the construction of the Edificio Boker presents three important questions. First, what was the role of foreign merchants in general and the Casa Boker in particular in the Porfirian modernization project? Second, to what extent did the Bokers think in national terms, and to what extent did they cooperate with and learn from other foreign investors? And finally, how did the Casa Boker respond to the incipient consumer culture that emerged in Porfirian Mexico City?

At the Vanguard of the Porfirian Strategy

On June 19, 1867, the sound of gunshots over the city of Querétaro marked the execution of Emperor Maximilian, an event that at last ended Mexico's half century of civil and foreign wars. During the next five decades, returning President Juárez and his successors sought the answer to their country's problems in foreign investment. Initially, nine years of oligarchic parliamentary rule known as the Restored Republic witnessed the beginning of a campaign against banditry with a rural police force, as well as a boom in tropical agricultural exports.[3] The Restored Republic also saw the construction of the Veracruz-Mexico City railroad line, a major achievement that had been decades in the making. No longer did voyagers need at least three days to travel the distance; when Heinrich Böker and his young wife moved to Mexico City, the train covered the distance in fourteen hours.[4] In 1876, General Porfirio Díaz, a mestizo of Mixtec origins, seized power. Until the outbreak of the Mexican Revolution in 1910, Díaz steered a process of Liberal modernization, and he became ever "whiter" and more authoritarian as time went on. Just as liberal amounts of facial powder coated Díaz's bronze complexion, so the Porfirians covered Mexico with a veneer of modernity during this heyday of North Atlantic economic and political expansion.

Porfirian modernization responded to momentous changes in the global economy. The rapid expansion of industrial production in North America and Western Europe and a revolution in transportation assigned to Mexico the role of a raw material producer in an emerging global division of labor. Raw material producers furnished the new industries with minerals, agricultural products used in industry, and foodstuffs. The efficient production and transportation of raw materials required investment capital and the import of manufactured hardware and machinery such as that sold by Roberto Boker y Cía. Swept into power by a coup funded in part by South Texas investors, Díaz seized the opportunity afforded by the rapid industrialization of the United States. Believers in export-led development, the Porfirians introduced a Liberal framework emphasizing private property and limited government regulation. Financed by U.S. and British capital, a network of railroads soon connected the mining centers and Mexico City to the U.S. border, and the United States emerged as the major market for Mexican products, as well as the country's principal source of foreign capital.[5] Better communications led to a revival of the mining industry and the rise of dynamic agribusinesses. The international division of labor, however, did not preclude the emergence of the first industries in Mexico. For example, Governor Bernardo Reyes and the Garza-Sada and Prieto clans, among others, promoted the industrialization of the northern city of Monterrey. These clans owned the Cuauhtémoc brewery and Mexico's first steel foundry, the "Fundidora de Fierro y Acero," and later formed the nucleus of the Monterrey Group. The largest steel mill south of the U.S. border, the Fundidora became the first Mexican purveyor of the Casa Boker. By 1910, its iron bars and pipes accounted for almost 10 percent of the company's purchases.[6]

Economic growth helped Díaz put an end to the cycle of instability in Mexico. The dictator left power in 1880, only to return four years later to a presidency he did not leave again until 1911. Combining co-optation with ruthless repression of dissent, he tamed bandits, regional warlords, and metropolitan elites alike, and the railroads soon allowed him to deploy the army in remote areas. Thus began the *Pax Porfiriana*, the Porfirian "peace" made possible by coercion and persuasion. By linking economic progress with centralist rule, the Porfirians provided an authoritarian, Mexican version of the French Third Republic that had followed the demise of Napoleon III.[7]

Modernization and political stability contributed decisively to the growth of the urban middle class, the *gente decente*, who were the most important retail customers for merchants like Robert Böker. Hardware merchants had long found themselves at the cutting edge of building the infrastructure of a presumed "prosperous Mexico," as many of them sold mining equipment and agricultural and building supplies.[8] During the Porfiriato, the growth of a middle class—by 1900, 20 percent of the population of Mexico City—led to burgeoning demand for household goods such as cutlery, hand tools, and kitchenwares offered by Roberto Boker y Cía and other hardware merchants.[9] Even more importantly, as elsewhere in Latin America, a bourgeois search for social identity created a desire to consume foreign-made items, and an individual's claims to "modernity" rested on the consumption of imported goods.[10]

Modernization transformed Mexico City and exacerbated its spatial divisions. Most foreign travelers who visited the western half of the Centro came away impressed. The roads were paved, a draining project had eliminated the worst flooding, and electric bulbs illuminated the Plateros District. Most wealthy Mexicans and foreign merchants lived in apartments or mansions in and around this district. Impeccably manicured public spaces such as the Alameda and the Paseo de la Reforma gave the illusion of universal prosperity. Here, women in beautiful European dresses ambled leisurely in the shade of trees; there, an audience listened to an impromptu concert; and in the distance, a group of men in business suits discussed the stock market and the political gossip of the day.[11] This was the Mexico City of the elite and the gente decente. Travelers who looked more closely, or those who ventured past the Plateros District to the east of the Zócalo, however, saw another city: a poor crescent populated by what the elites callously called léperos (lepers). In this nether world, every day was a struggle for survival. Populated by the urban workers who eked out a living on miserable earnings, the other Mexico City did not have electrical lighting, drinkable water, or a sewer system. Growing daily through the influx of poor migrants from the countryside, it consisted of "barrios full of squat, dirty, and cracked houses that reek[ed] of misery and putrefaction," and the open drainage ditches contributed to a mortality rate that made the capital one of the world's most unhealthy cities.[12] Even though the urban poor were part of both parts of the capital, whether as workers, as servants, or as so-called vagrants, this other Mexico City existed far away from the consciousness of the elite: vilified and criminalized as an aberration from the norm.[13]

Not surprisingly, Robert held a favorable view of Porfirian Mexico. Informed through sporadic visits and the impressive balance sheets of the Casa Boker, his writings gush with praise for Díaz. He marveled at the swift progress of railroad construction and at the "ruthless energy" with which the dictator suppressed revolts against his regime. As late as 1904, Robert even insisted that Díaz's iron-fisted rule made revolutions impossible.[14] Robert's praise indicates that he, like other merchants, had bought into what one historian has called the "Porfirian persuasion": the notion that modernity had arrived with Díaz and his advisers, and the optimistic idea that Mexico would come to share the limelight with the world's most "advanced" nations.[15]

Yet this optimism was exaggerated, as material progress failed to improve the living conditions of the majority of Mexicans. Although the second half of the nineteenth century witnessed land acquisitions by the rural middle class, the rancheros, the redistribution of church and Indian village land furthered the enrichment of wealthy hacendados while exacerbating the misery of the Mexican peasantry. Likewise, the incipient industrialization of Mexico created an impoverished proletariat in the cities—a group growing faster than the urban middle class. Therefore, Porfirian modernization did not produce the type of internal market that supported mass consumption in the United States and

Western Europe. Instead, the Mexican economy rose and fell with demand from abroad; a small number of financier-industrialists and hacendados dominated the economy, and merchants remained restricted to a limited circle of customers.[16]

Without a doubt, however, foreign residents of Mexico City reached their high point in the Porfirian era.[17] Foreigners and their descendants were well represented in Díaz's inner circle. Finance Secretary Limantour came from a French family, and Foreign Secretary Mariscal and Matías Romero, Díaz's ambassador in Washington, had married women from the United States.[18] The Spaniards married into Mexico City's most distinguished creole families, and their number increased to almost 30,000 nationally.

Part of the reason for this still modest influx of foreigners was that the Díaz regime belatedly adopted the favorable immigration policies in place in the Southern Cone countries. Advertising Mexico as a land of unlimited opportunities, the Porfirians hoped that immigration would help attract the foreign investment needed to build up Mexico's infrastructure. Moreover, they believed that immigrant farmers could limit potential U.S. designs on the Mexican north, an underpopulated, mostly arid expanse with tenuous links to the capital. Finally, Díaz joined his colleagues in Argentina and Brazil in viewing immigration as a way of "whitening" a miscegenated and partly indigenous population. A Juarista Liberal still influential in Porfirian days believed that the sole remedy for the underdevelopment of the "Indians" lay in their "transformation" through European immigration.[19]

As applied to a process of whitening, the term "transformation," however, had a different meaning in Mexico than in the United States. North of the border, whitening involved the biological "improvement" of the racial stock, that is, the marginalization of nonwhite elements by European immigration. The Anglo-Saxon concept of whitening followed the social Darwinist thought of Herbert Spencer: the notion that race and sex, as determined by physical differences, determined an individual's fitness in the struggle for survival. In Mexico, whitening promised the infusion of European capital and culture into a countryside populated by supposedly indolent and ignorant indigenous people. French positivism played a role along with social Darwinism in formulating the racial thought of the Mexican elite. Hence, to the *científico* group—a positivist faction that increasingly dominated the Porfirian inner circle and whose ranks included Limantour—being white was both a stage of civilization and a biological condition. According to Education Undersecretary Justo Sierra, a leading científico, immigration helped civilize the "Indians." Immigrants could not only teach them Western values, but they could also fuse with them into a new, miscegenated race. Rather than an end in itself, immigration was thus a tool to achieve the integration of the "Indian" into Mexican society.[20]

The Díaz regime pursued a three-pronged strategy in order to lure immigrants. The first strategy consisted in the promotion of rural colonization projects, an effort for which Porfirian agents traveled to Europe in order to promote a sanitized version of Mexican reality. The most important of these agents, the German-born Heinrich Lemcke, advertised Mexico at the 1898 World's Fair in Paris as a country with wide-open spaces.[21] The second strategy entailed the recruitment of foreign workers and professionals. Foreign companies brought their own engineers and overseers, individuals paid many times as much as the Mexicans working next to them.[22] Finally, legal reforms that suited the needs of foreigners constituted the third strategy. In 1883, legislation allowed foreigners the right to own land and subsoil resources. The infamous "Law of Baldíos" permitted investors to scoop up land declared "public," much of it taken from indigenous communities. Three years later, the "Law of Foreignness and Naturalization" allowed male immigrants to pass their citizenship on to their children even though a provision in the 1857 Constitution mandated Mexican citizenship of all those born on Mexican soil. Under the new law, both the father and his children became Mexicans unless the father declared the intention to retain his original citizenship. Most foreigners, including the Bokers, made such a declaration.[23] What was thus absent from the Porfirian strategy was a plan to assimilate foreign nationals and to make them into what an influential politician called "the new creoles."[24]

Despite these efforts, the immigration project resulted in disappointing numbers. While direct foreign investment into Mexico grew by a factor of twenty between 1880 and 1910, this flood of new capital did not presage immigration, as the owners of much of the money remained in Europe and the United States. As land and work remained abundant in what Philip Curtin has called the neo-Europes of North America and the Southern Cone, newcomers continued to flock to these traditional targets of immigration, beckoned by relatives and friends who already lived in those areas.[25] By contrast, immigrants founded only thirty-seven rural colonies in the Díaz era, and most of them failed due to lack of government support, indigenous resistance, and poor crops. Aside from continued migration to the coffee region of Chiapas, where producing a coveted export product opened an avenue to a comfortable life, only a few hundred Germans followed the call for rural immigrants.[26] The failure of the rural colonies demonstrated again that Mexico was not a nation of immigrants, but instead a country in which a select few newcomers could make a great impact.

Moreover, the crowd that chose Mexico as their destination proved different from the prosperous group that had arrived during Mexico's time of troubles. Many of the newcomers from Mediterranean countries came from lower social backgrounds than the trade conquistadors. Kinship and friendship ties among these immigrants produced regional and even local communities within these colonies. Spaniards organized in Basque, Catalan, and Galician clubs, among others. The case of the French Barcelonnettes is particularly interesting in this regard. Beginning in the 1830s, members of a beleaguered middle class left the small Alpine town of Barcelonnette for Mexico. Descendants of these Barcelonnettes such as Finance Minister Limantour numbered among the great bankers and merchants of the Porfirian era. A second wave of Barcelonnettes that arrived after 1880 found upward social mobility harder to achieve.[27]

At the same time, Asians became Mexico's fastest-growing immigrant group. While the number of Europeans grew from about 26,000 to 47,000 between the 1895 and 1910 censuses, the number of Asians catapulted from 1,500 to 20,000. Seventy percent of this dramatic increase was due to Chinese arrivals diverted south in an age when the U.S. government adopted increasing restrictions on Asian immigration. Having worked in railroad construction in the United States, thousands of coolies moved south to work on the Mexican railroad projects and then stayed on. By the turn of the century, the Chinese played a pivotal role in northwestern Mexico, where they came to dominate retail and money lending. Sonora alone was home to an estimated 4,486 Chinese in 1910—the largest foreign colony in that state.[28] Meanwhile, Lebanese immigrants flocked to cities such as Mérida, Yucatán, where their role as traders earned them the label *casta beduina* (Beduine caste), an allusion to the creole *casta divina* that owned the surrounding henequen plantations.[29]

Although "whitening" therefore resembled the sprinkling of powdered sugar onto a multilayered cake, enough immigrants entered Mexico City to occasion an important change in the foreign colonies. To make their years away from home easier, prominent members of the largest expatriate communities—and especially the burgeoning "American Colony"—established institutions such as schools, churches, and athletic clubs.[30] Correspondingly, the wall that separated these communities from Mexican society grew higher while middle-class immigration made them more socially diverse. In the process, they became ethnic enclaves. The members of these enclaves remained alienated from the host culture; they expected an eventual, but not imminent return to their home country, and they developed institutions designed to preserve the home culture for the benefit of their children.

By the turn of the century, the German colony in Mexico City had become such an ethnic enclave. According to a head count by the German consul, its population numbered 1,236 people, not counting Austrian or Swiss citizens and a small handful of naturalized Mexicans. Thirty-two percent of the adult population was female, and, even more importantly, 407 German children lived in Mexico City. Although the census still counted 323 bachelors—but only 21 unmarried women— the nuclear family had increased in importance within the community.[31] In addition, the German colony, although to a lesser extent than its counterparts from France, Spain, and the United States, became more socially diverse, as an increasing number of middle-class professionals came to Mexico City. These changes spawned the emergence of a host of new institutions. A 1912 German travel guide to Mexico listed fourteen associations: sporting clubs devoted to rowing, horseback riding, swimming, and gymnastics, two Masonic lodges, a women's association, and a German school.[32] By 1910, the German colony in Mexico City looked like a smaller version of the one in Buenos Aires, which had become an enclave thirty years earlier.[33]

The foundation of the school in 1894 constituted the defining moment in the transition from loose diaspora to enclave. In 1886, the French colony had founded a primary school in Mexico City, an institution that grew over time until it awarded the high school degree. Not to be outdone by their French rivals, the German community opened the "Deutsche Schule von Mexico/Colegio Alemán de México," a school financed by tuition, German businesses in Mexico City, and a subsidy from the German Empire. In the absence of the Bokers, Carl Friederichs, who would later enroll his son at the school, donated start-up funds and served on the school council. From 1901–3, he even presided over the *Aufsichtsrat,* the equivalent of a board of trustees.[34] The school initially offered instruction in the first six grades only, but it soon expanded into secondary and preparatory education. In 1919, the first high school class graduated from the Colegio Alemán. The Casa Boker and its owners took an important part in this expansion, as Robert's son Franz followed Friederichs in serving on the administrative council. Among German companies, only rivals Sommer, Herrmann gave more to the school than the Casa Boker did.[35]

The Colegio Alemán pursued the twofold mission of educating German children in the tradition of their ancestors and acquainting Mexicans with German culture. As a result, it offered two different tracks: one for native speakers, and one for Mexicans who studied German as a foreign language. Teachers imparted knowledge of both cultures, despite an obvious assumption of the superiority of German ways. After 1905, students in the Mexican track outnumbered those in the German track, because there were not enough German students to keep the school running.[36] Unlike its French and U.S. counterparts that drew from larger colonies, the Colegio Alemán therefore acquired a material stake in its bicultural mission. Its mission statement promised that "the School will . . . impart an education to the children of German parents . . . equal to the one in Germany" and "preserve these children for German culture."[37] However, the mission statement also emphasized the "befriending of foreigners" with German culture.[38] Moreover, the school administration understood the need to educate all students about Mexican history and society. Essay topics for a comprehensive examination included "Mexican customs and habits," "The influence of Porfirio Díaz on the development of Mexico," and "What captivates Germans about Mexico."[39]

Efforts to establish German Catholic and Lutheran churches— another indicator of the development of an ethnic enclave—experienced greater difficulties than the school. A minority among the Germans in Mexico City, Catholics worshipped regularly under the direction of a priest sent from Germany if they did not exercise the option of attending services in Mexican churches. Representing the merchant elite as well as a two-thirds majority of the colony, the Lutherans congregated under the leadership of a German pastor in a variety of buildings, including a monastery, the British Episcopal Church, and the American Methodist Church.[40] Neither of the two denominations, however, formally organized until after the Mexican Revolution.

The case of the church illustrates that the foreign ethnic enclaves operated in harmony with one another. In particular, the colonies dominated by Protestants—that is, the "American," the British, and the German—cooperated broadly. The French, by contrast, generally steered clear of the Germans in the wake of the Franco-Prussian War. Although the principal newspapers of the two colonies, the *Deutsche Zeitung von Mexico* and *Le Courrier du Mexique,* stoked this incipient antagonism, it did not preclude social contact. Nonetheless, Robert and his brother Max had experienced this tension firsthand when Louis Drommel, their most trusted French assistant and expert on sewing machines, resigned after the Prussian victory in 1871.[41]

It is therefore not surprising that the Bokers identified with both the "American" and the German colony in Mexico City. Although many of his friends were German, Robert had cultivated his U.S. connections. He had served as one of the founders of the American hospital. His brother Max cosponsored an effort by the Deutsches Haus to collect money on behalf of the veterans and widows of the Franco-Prussian War of 1870–71, but he also included himself in the U.S.

expatriate community when it suited his purposes. In 1877, for example, he signed a petition of "American residents" to the U.S. government that protested the recall of the U.S. consul from Mexico City, an action that threatened importers of U.S. hardware such as Roberto Boker y Cía.[42] Under the leadership of Robert's younger brother, Heinrich, the Casa Boker even became a conduit for financial transactions of the U.S. consulate.[43]

On June 22, 1884, the birth of Heinrich's oldest son, Alexander, marked an important milestone in the history of the Boker family that epitomized the emergence of the German colony. Alexander was the first member of the family born alive in Mexico City, and his mother, the young Luise Böker née von der Nahmer, had pushed away the shadow that the failed pregnancies of Robert's wife, Auguste, had seemed to cast on this German family. Although she did not like Mexico City much more than Auguste had, Luise enjoyed close friendships with other German women during her almost six years there.[44]

Entering the Age of Consumption

A great part of the reason for Luise and Heinrich's satisfaction lay in the astounding success of the Casa Boker in the Porfirian era—a success rooted in large part in the decision to diversify its merchandise in terms of national origin. The company achieved its best results selling products from the United States, Britain, and Germany under exclusive representation (see Table 3). By the time Singer decided to sell through their own agents in Mexico, the Casa Boker sold Remington typewriters, Studebaker steam cars, fire insurance policies from the North British and Mercantile Insurance Company, cutlery from Heinrich Böker and Company, and many other products. The company sold so many products from other countries that the German minister to Mexico once complained vociferously to his superiors about the small percentage of German goods in its catalog.[45] Ignoring these complaints, the company took advantage of its connections in Anglo-Saxon countries to emerge as one of the country's main suppliers of hardware, machinery, and carriages. While the strategy of successful German merchants in Latin America had long included the sale of British goods, the number of U.S. products offered by the Casa Boker far exceeded those of its competitors.[46]

Despite its international sales strategy, Roberto Boker y Cía remained a German family business throughout the last decades of the nineteenth century, albeit one independent from the family's ventures in Remscheid and Solingen. In contrast to branch offices, which formed part of an overseas corporation, and the semiautonomous

Table 3: National Origin of Merchandise in
Catalogs of the Casa Boker

1900	40% Germany 20% rest of Europe (mostly Great Britain) 34% United States 6% Mexico
1911	42% Europe (Germany and Great Britain) 40% United States 18% Mexico
1935	45% Germany 15% rest of Europe (Belgium, France, Great Britain) 30% United States 10% Mexico
1960	50% Germany 1% rest of Europe 9% United States 40% Mexico
1975	30% Germany 10% United States 50% Mexico 10% Brazil and others
1997	16% Germany 16% rest of Europe (Spain, Sweden) 7% United States 53% Mexico 8% Brazil and others

Sources: AB, Fondo Catálogos; AB, Fondo Asambleas; estimates by Pedro Boker.

"free-standing companies," the Casa Boker was legally a Mexican company.[47] However, its partners were Germans, and after 1873, the most senior partner—Robert Böker himself—lived in Remscheid. As manager of the export firm Heinrich Böker in Remscheid, Robert continued to make important decisions for the Casa Boker and hence unified in his person the concerns of the "mother company" and those of Roberto Boker y Cía.[48]

The Casa Boker operated as a general partnership, the rough U.S. equivalent of the Mexican *sociedad* and the German offene *Handelsgesellschaft*. Partners shared earnings and liability in proportion to their investment, and liability extended to their personal property. This structure emphasized accountability, yet allowed partners to return to their home countries. It provided the perfect fit for the life plans of the typical merchant, who entered as a young intern; saved enough money to buy out his father; returned home assured of comfortable earnings, and finally sold his share in the business to a son. Because of its flexibility, this structure was perfect for profitable and well-capitalized family businesses.[49] A general partnership, however, could only work so long as all partners trusted each other—and was hence feasible only so long as close family ties bound a majority of them together.

Thus, only between 1888 and 1899 (the decade between Heinrich's departure and the arrival of the second generation) did Robert entrust the management of the company to people not of his family. He and his brothers Max and Heinrich also inserted important safeguards in the partnership agreements to protect their interests: they received a special status as owners, or *propietarios*, while others entered as partners, or *socios*. This status granted the Boker family important advantages. A propietario remained with the company indefinitely; a socio could be bought out at the conclusion of each partnership agreement (usually five years). After Robert's departure, Max joined him as an owner of the business, and long-time associate Hermann Stiegler became the first partner of what was renamed Roberto Boker y Cía. Four years later, Heinrich came to Mexico and subsequently became an owner, and in 1884, Carl Friederichs replaced Stiegler, who eventually served as honorary Mexican consul in Karlsruhe, Germany. Finally, in 1893, Hamburg native Rudolf von Lübeck became the company's second partner.[50]

The administration of Roberto Boker y Cía followed this hierarchy predicated on family ties and seniority. Until his departure, Robert served as senior owner, while Max, as the person in charge of purchases, had precedence over Stiegler.[51] Thereafter, Max became the point man in Mexico. In 1884, after Max had joined Robert in Germany, the management fell to Heinrich Böker and Carl Friederichs. Although Heinrich had the deciding vote in case of a disagreement, Friederichs stood to garner an increasing share of the earnings. Robert and Max took care of the import business, and Robert had the final vote in decisions regarding merchandise. Apart from a modest allowance, an owner or partner could not take out his yearly dividend, fixed at 6 percent until he had invested at least 300,000 gold pesos. In 1885, the total capital amounted to more than 600,000 pesos at a time when the Mexican currency was still close to parity with the U.S. dollar.[52] Indeed, the Casa Boker had prospered despite Robert's absence—a fact that demonstrated that the handsome earnings of import businesses allowed merchants to leave the operation of their enterprise to junior partners.

Due to a paucity of sources, it is unfortunately impossible to reconstruct the labor force and organizational structure of the Casa Boker in the Porfirian era. An enumeration of the top twenty employees contained in von Lübeck's memoirs does permit the conclusion, however, that a quite international group of people managed the business. Along with Germans from Remscheid recruited by Robert Böker, who had reacquired Prussian citizenship in 1874, were several Spaniards, Mexicans, and U.S. nationals. The sales department also featured a number of U.S. citizens who served as the agents of purveyors such as Remington and Studebaker. In 1903, a business guide listed thirty-eight English-speaking staff members, including several with Anglo-Saxon names. All of the lower-level employees were Mexicans.[53]

Only one testimonial has survived that yields some insight into the life of the employees, and that source originated with a member of the elite. The memoirs of Eduardo Iturbide, a distant relative of Emperor Agustín Iturbide and the future prefect of Mexico City under dictator Victoriano Huerta, contain some anecdotes from his apprenticeship in Roberto Boker y Cía in the early 1890s. Knowing well that the German leadership demanded strict discipline, Iturbide's father wanted them to "tighten up" a son whom he considered slack and lazy. The Casa Boker lived up to its reputation. As a trainee, young Iturbide earned only 20 pesos a week, and his workday started with picking up the mail at 7:30 a.m. and ended at 8 p.m. In between these hours, he cleaned desks, copied letters, and did countless other menial chores that he deemed beneath him. He sardonically remarked that the only thing his bosses did not ask of him was to stick out his tongue to moisten the back of stamps. After a few months, he attempted to use his typing skills to get a better salary. He convinced a typist who made 70 pesos a week to leave the firm, expecting to be named as his replacement. Unfortunately, the scheme worked out better for the typist than for Iturbide. While the typist soon found better-paid work, this young trainee typed away the next three years without receiving a pay increase. The directors of the business enforced a strict hierarchy among their staff. Only when Iturbide's time as a trainee expired was he offered a raise.[54]

By contrast, a scattering of sources provides a sketch of the wholesale and retail operation, if not reliable figures and statistics. According to von Lübeck's memoirs, the wholesale business proved a resounding success due to its low cost, generous profit margins, and ambitious geographical scope. Unlike its greatest competitor, the Hanseatic hardware store Sommer, Herrmann and Cía, the Casa Boker never opened branch offices in provincial capitals such as Guadalajara, Puebla, and Veracruz.

Instead, it relied on agents as well as on yearly visits by out-of-town merchants. Armed with fat catalogs, the agents of the company visited merchants in the cities and towns, taking orders for prompt delivery and generous terms that allowed up to eight months for payment. Rewarded by attractive commissions, these agents—who generally knew their territory like the backs of their hands—constituted the mainstay of success. Many of them were Spaniards with family ties to retail merchants in the territory in which they operated. Occasionally, unsuccessful agents quit the business, invoices remained unpaid, and the legal proceedings to recover debts in distant states could take many years. In general, however, nationwide trading had become relatively easy and safe: twice a year, trains accompanied by armed soldiers (*conductas*) even ensured the transportation of money from the outlying states.[55] The insurance business was also a success, although the directors of the Casa Boker failed to persuade Limantour to buy fire insurance for the dozens of marble and stone palaces owned by the national government in Mexico City.[56]

Culturally informed notions of how German merchants ought to conduct their business initially hindered the retail operation, which faced the transition toward a new era of consumption. As most of the almacenes had for many decades, Roberto Boker y Cía seldom sold over the counter. Instead, clerks usually took the merchandise to the carriages of their wealthy customers if they did not deliver them to their home. In the 1880s, however, U.S. traveler Fanny Chambers Gooch noted that while "the mercantile establishments do not generally possess in their exterior the attractions of those in our own cities [. . .] a few of the leading merchants have . . . recourse to show windows." These merchants, she observed, primarily sold jewelry and garments. Once inside the stores, she maintained, "the activity and agility of the clerks, in their eagerness to wait upon you, are equaled only by their lack of system and business management."[57] This transition from expert customer to casual shopper posed new challenges to the Casa Boker. With small windows, the main building did not attract passers-by—and following the fashion of the Mexican open-air market, those who entered often attempted to negotiate lower prices. In addition, Mexicans were not used to the idea of paying for their purchases immediately and asked for generous loan terms.[58] While showrooms in other buildings displayed the company's carriages, large tools, and agricultural implements, these were scattered over several different blocks and did not invite customers to check out other merchandise the company offered. The Bokers initially resisted the new age of advertising by display, believing that it did not behoove a kingly merchant to hector for the attention of anonymous customers. As von Lübeck put it, "A cordial relationship prevailed between salesman and client that made work easier for both sides. The more extensive the circle of friends [of the businessman], the more successful his endeavors."[59]

It was "Don Carlos" Friederichs, general manager after Heinrich's departure, who moved the Casa Boker beyond the limited vision of the kingly merchant. Although Friederichs, like the owners, hailed from the Bergisches Land, his background differed from that of the Bokers. The son of farmers, he was a first-generation merchant without capital of his own who began his training in Heinrich Böker before visiting Africa and Australia on behalf of that company. He came to Mexico in 1881 and remained there for twenty-three years; almost as long as the three Boker brothers taken together. Like Heinrich's, his children were born in Mexico City, but unlike the youngest Boker brother, who left Mexico City early enough that his children could attend a German school, Friederichs was able to send his son "Carlitos" to the brand new Colegio Alemán. Married to a German-French woman, Friederichs was not a kingly merchant. Rather, this Francophile entrepreneur understood that elite Mexicans were absorbing European and North American modes of shopping in department stores at fixed prices, and he sought to emulate the success of U.S. and French capitalists in Porfirian Mexico.[60]

Most importantly, the Friederichs era witnessed the rapid growth of U.S.-Mexican trade. Before railroads connected Mexico City with the northern border, 60 percent of Mexican imports had come from European countries, and especially Great Britain, and only 30 percent of Mexican imports had originated in the United States. After 1880, however, U.S.-Mexican trade increased by leaps and bounds. In fiscal year 1900–1, the U.S. share amounted to two-thirds of all Mexican imports.[61] As Friederichs and other merchants well knew, the U.S. challenge did not imply the ruin of European importers, but instead called on them to diversify their merchandise to include a balanced assortment of European and U.S. goods. The Europeans were fortunate in that many U.S. producers preferred to sell through them as intermediaries, rather than setting up a network of distribution in Mexico. Moreover, increasing demand for finished products allowed both the United States and European countries to expand exports to Mexico. German exports, for example, more than held their own in the hardware sector. In fact, hardware became a virtual German monopoly during this time. By 1905, it amounted to 68.5 percent of all German exports to Latin America, compared to 29 percent in 1890.[62]

In addition, Friederichs could not fail to recognize the enormous advances of the Barcelonnettes. While many of the German stores had benefited from the interruption of Mexico's diplomatic relations with Britain, France, and Spain after the French Intervention, this advantage had proven of short duration. By the 1880s, French merchants had recovered their previous share of the market and contributed to the disappearance of two-thirds of the German import businesses.[63] Even more ominous for German merchants was the fact that the Barcelonnettes—many of whom enjoyed personal and family ties with French producers—dominated the garment sector. The largest French retailers signed exclusive agreements with the major textile producers in Mexico that kept out their own weaker compatriots. Moreover, a group of those French merchants that had been left out of these agreements formed a conglomerate that became Mexico's first and largest industrial garment producer in Orizaba, Veracruz. Within two decades, the new industry produced undergarments, shirts, and other textiles that dropped the imports of such articles to 15 percent of their 1888 level.[64] In the succeeding decades, Ernest Pugibet, the founder of Mexico's largest cigarette factory, El Buen Tono, created a trust that included several different industries as well as utility companies. With slick advertisements, El Buen Tono pioneered tobacco use and consumerism in the cities.[65] By 1910, French investment amounted to 55 percent of foreign investment in manufacturing, and the Tron clan, among the capital's foremost textile barons, set up sweatshops at the outskirts of Mexico City that employed six hundred seamstresses.[66]

Taking advantage of growing demand for consumer goods, the Barcelonnettes established the city's first department stores and left their German rivals in a bygone era. Evidenced by the Trons' 1891 construction of the famous Palacio de Hierro—the first monument to modern consumerism in Mexico City—these stores catered to the rich with fancy imported clothes and to the gente decente with Mexican textiles.[67] Frequented by the Francophile Porfirian elite, the Palacio de Hierro ostentatiously displayed its luxurious wares in gleaming windows. The French rivals of the Palacio, such as the Puerto de Liverpool, built their own palaces of consumption a short while later, as the market for consumer goods expanded exponentially. This growth was due in large part to the emergence of women as consumers. For centuries, well-to-do women had sent their servants to buy groceries at the La Merced market southeast of the Zócalo, and few husbands allowed them to venture out alone to buy clothes. Beginning in the 1880s, however, bourgeois women began to travel unaccompanied to the department stores in the Centro.[68] Meanwhile, the staid German importers pitched their wares to an all-male crowd, seemingly impervious to the sweeping changes in consumer culture. Believing that tools, unlike textiles, were not objects of desire, they left their inconspicuous goods behind tall counters in dusty boxes, away from the eyes of curious consumers.[69]

The Palacio de Hierro represented the Mexican version of the department store that revolutionized retailing in Europe and North America during the last decades of the nineteenth century. Department stores emerged from dry-goods stores during a period of rapid industrial growth that resulted in the mass production of textiles, which responded to a skyrocketing demand. This mass production "required a retail system far more efficient and far more expansive than anything small shopkeepers had to offer."[70] The first department stores, Le Bon Marché and Macy's, sprang up almost simultaneously in Paris and New York City during the 1870s. As in France and the United States, the first Mexican department stores sold textiles to an upper- and middle-class clientele that practiced, as historian William Beezley paraphrased Thorstein Veblen, "ostentatious consumption . . . that . . . demonstrate[d] their personal, if not Mexico's wealth and reputation."[71] But as an important difference, until 1900, they did not devote much attention to marketing beyond the showrooms and the newspaper, until Pugibet's pioneering ad campaigns opened their eyes to the possibilities of advertising.[72]

As Friederichs knew, German hardware merchants could learn from the Palacio de Hierro because they offered goods that were equally suitable for display: cutlery, hand tools, and household items. Friederichs sensed that the demand for household items offered an opportunity to take advantage of an incipient consumer culture in Mexico, a strategy that required the company to become a department store. Therefore, Roberto Boker y Cía acquired a warehouse located in the north part of the Centro, a transaction that opened up display space in the store. The directors also purchased carts and mules to transport goods from the warehouse to the store, and they even established a delivery service for their customers in the capital.[73] As had become evident in the architecture of the Palacio as well as in that of the new palaces of consumption in rapidly modernizing cities such as Monterrey, however, the business needed an imposing storefront—an impossible change in a rented building.[74] Thus, the partners decided that they needed a department store of their own.[75]

Before this idea could come to fruition, however, the world recession of 1893 delayed Friederichs's plans. After the British government responded to the crisis by decreeing the free minting of silver in their Asian colonies, the price of silver fell to 50 percent of its 1892 level, causing the peso to plummet. This decline cost Roberto Boker y Cía and other importers dearly.[76] Since outstanding balances on imported goods were payable in gold currencies while revenues remained in the silver

54

peso, the "Mexican dollar," the company lost 70,000 pesos in one year.[77] Despite this crisis, however, Friederichs and von Lübeck remained convinced of the need for a department store building, as the rent on the company's principal building quadrupled within a few short years.[78]

When the late 1890s witnessed another boom period for Roberto Boker y Cía (see Table 4), Friederichs and von Lübeck decided that the time had come to invest in a permanent home for the company. In 1897, the two directors purchased the Hotel de la Gran Sociedad and the adjacent building, amounting to a total area of 19,000 square feet. Located only two blocks from the southwest corner of the Zócalo, at one of the busiest street corners in the Plateros District, the site appeared perfect for the Edificio Boker.[79]

The White Elephant

It took three more years before the Edificio Boker opened its doors. After unsuccessful negotiations with German and Mexican architects, the leadership of the Casa Boker agreed on a design proposed by the New York architectural firm DeLemos and Cordes. Recommended by Robert's nephew, this company later became famous for designing Macy's in New York City as well as the present-day building of the Banco de México. Construction began in 1898 and lasted fifteen months. The digging yielded more than just soil and stones, as the Edificio Boker literally arose on Aztec and Spanish foundations. Construction workers unearthed two Aztec artifacts and a Spanish coat of arms. The partners donated these objects to Mexican museums.[80]

A palace of 20,000 square feet, the Edificio Boker represented a new departure for a hardware business. Constructed in the mold of the department stores in Chicago and New York City, the building rivaled the Palacio de Hierro in both glamour and presentation of merchandise. Not surprisingly, the Bokers called the building the "white elephant," a

Table 4: Earnings of Roberto Boker y Cía, 1895–1899
(in thousands of gold pesos)

Year	Earnings
1895	463
1896	501
1897	484
1898	478
1899	546

Source: "Finanzlage und Rentabilitaet des Hauses Roberto Boker y Cía in den Jahren 1895–1909," AB, FFLB.

name referring to the Art Nouveau design of the building. Three entrances led customers into a large air well, where a huge round display case surrounded by a circular counter featured the famous Arbolito cutlery. Toward the walls on the first floor, customers found kitchen supplies, lamps, and leather goods. An imposing staircase (made of marble imported duty-free due to the collaboration of the Díaz regime) ushered them to an upstairs level well lit by large windows. From there, a set of smaller stairs led to the third floor. Each floor had high ceilings between 14 and 16 feet high. The second floor housed office furniture and accessories as well as art supplies, while carriages and agricultural machinery were displayed on the third floor. To haul the heavy merchandise to the upper floors, Friederichs had even installed an ornate elevator, one of the first of its kind in Mexico.[81] In striking fashion, the company had left behind the conservatism of the German kingly merchant and embraced French and U.S. strategies of consumerism. If customers sought the famous cutlery, many other goods enticed them along the way to the center of the ground floor.[82] Predictably, the building met with the acclamation of the Porfirian elite. Finance Secretary Limantour expressed these favorable sentiments when he told von Lübeck that "you are making the city beautiful."[83] The official press chimed in with similar accolades.[84]

Figure 3: The Edificio Boker at its inauguration
(Archivo Boker, Mexico City).

Figure 4: The great staircase (photo by Guillermo Kahlo).

Figure 5: The Arbolito cutlery (photo by Guillermo Kahlo).

Figure 6: Machinery on the third floor (photo by Guillermo Kahlo).

Not everyone, however, applauded the architecture of the Edificio Boker, which offended the sensibilities of traditionalists and nationalists alike. For example, Nicolás Mariscal, a noteworthy Mexican architect and a relative of the foreign secretary, labeled the Edificio Boker a "commercial pump" and criticized the stylistic syncretism reminiscent of U.S. buildings. After praising the Palacio de Hierro for its "well-proportioned" design, he characterized the Boker building in the following words: "It gives me the impression of a worker wearing a coat and a white tie with his blue work shirt showing and the hard hat on his head. This carnevalesque mixture costs it its character. When passers-by see the building, they will go on exclaiming: my money should buy what I need rather than pay for this superfluous luxury."[85] The building also found critics in the Liberal and the Conservative opposition, the newspapers of which joined in lambasting the placement of the Mexican national seal on the ground as an act repugnant to the nation. The Liberal *El Popular* headlined a brief story "The national seal on the ground: An offense that must be corrected."[86] The story pointed out that the law prohibited the use of national symbols for commercial purposes, and it demanded the relocation of the emblem to a place where it would not be trodden on by thousands of people. The Conservative *El Tiempo* called on the company to move the mosaic as well.[87]

When Díaz and his coterie appeared at the inauguration of the Edificio Boker, they went to a celebration that marked a new era in Mexican commerce—the first department store that did not sell textiles. Looking back, the old dictator knew that the Casa Boker had registered a significant impact on the Mexican economy. Although hard to quantify, that impact was impossible to overlook. With the Singer sewing machines, Roberto Boker y Cía had furnished technology instrumental to garment manufacturing. In addition, it had sold much of the hardware used to build the railroads between Mexico City and the U.S. border and many of the agricultural implements used in the tropical plantations that boosted the Porfirian economy.[88] Therefore, fifteen years after the French had pioneered the modern department store in Mexico, the Casa Boker came to represent the Anglo-German response in the hardware sector. For the old dictator, the new building also represented a welcome European commercial presence that disguised what opponents of the Porfiriato labeled the "Pacific Conquest" of Mexico by U.S. investments. When Díaz raised his glass of champagne along with Carl Friederichs and forty-five other guests and employees, he was celebrating the success of his own regime.

Friederichs's toast played on these sentiments: "The new building," he announced, reflected conditions that "all of us . . . who live in this hospitable country have enjoyed for many years. . . . And indeed, how would it have been possible for these columns to rise, or for these ceilings to vault, without . . . fast modes of transportation, without the relief of liberal laws, without the protection of reasonable authorities, and—above all else—without peace and security in this country?"[89] The company, Friederichs concluded, owed its success to Díaz, who had demonstrated a keen understanding for the situation of merchants. Clearly flattered, Don Porfirio returned the compliment. Asserting that his government had done nothing except create the conditions for economic growth, he said that only the initiative of "pioneers" such as Robert Böker could help Mexico realize its potential. He expressed the hope that the Edificio Boker, "one of the great ornaments of the capital and a testament to its culture," would serve as a fountain of wealth not only for its owners but also for the country in general.[90]

An expensive ceremony that included the consumption of almost five hundred bottles of champagne, the inauguration of the Edificio Boker showed the Casa Boker at its pinnacle.[91] Robert Böker and his partners had put their company in the position of taking advantage of the Mexican *belle époque*. Although the investment of a modest 20,000 gold pesos into a tiny almacén would not have led one to expect it, the formation of Holder, Boker and Cía in 1865 had marked the birth of the fastest-growing hardware store in Mexico. The main reasons for its success were the directors' international business connections, their flexibility in dealing with political change, and a long-range vision that emphasized future successes over short-term gains. Evidence of this approach was the conspicuous absence of Robert and Max at the ceremony. Both considered the long trip a waste of time and money and thus sent Heinrich as the only representative of the German socios.[92]

The construction of the grandiose building gave the Casa Boker enough visibility that Friederichs decided to experiment with extending the circle of customers through aggressive advertising. In the early 1900s, the Casa Boker issued a monthly pamphlet entitled *Anunciador Boker,* a serial catalog sent to the company's customers throughout Mexico. At first, this catalog was printed in Buffalo, N.Y., before Mexican printing facilities improved enough to produce a volume of up to 40,000 copies locally at a low cost.[93] The company also produced a beautiful, leather-bound catalog in Spanish and English that contained more than 1,000 pages, as well as a calendar sent to the company's most important customers each Christmas season.[94] Unlike Sears, Roebuck and other large department stores in the United States, however, the Casa Boker did not add a mail-order department. Although mail ordering was revolutionizing the distribution of merchandise in the United States, Friederichs knew that it could not easily catch on in Mexico, where customers still preferred to buy on sight and shipping remained relatively slow and expensive.[95]

Thus, the "Sears of Mexico" had not and could not become a genuine counterpart to the new U.S. commercial giants. By 1910, almost 70 percent of the Mexican population still lived a peasant existence on the countryside, and half of all urban residents were destitute. In other words, twelve million Mexicans could not afford goods such as the expensive Arbolito knives, and the Casa Boker remained restricted to a relatively small circle of customers. This social reality marked a sharp difference from the United States, where millions of rural middle-class consumers eagerly perused the catalogs of Sears, Roebuck and other mail-order department stores. To be sure, the construction of the Edificio Boker went a long way toward bringing the company up to speed with modern commercial capitalism. Nevertheless, while the United States became the land of desire where conspicuous consumption announced the arrival of mass prosperity among the middle class, Mexico remained the land of necessity for most of its inhabitants.

Moreover, this giant in the hardware business appeared a dwarf when compared to the French department stores. Although these businesses dealt with the same limits to their marketing capabilities, they greatly exceeded the Casa Boker in capitalization, political clout, and connection to domestic industry. The Palacio de Hierro employed 1,600 workers, including seamstresses; the Casa Boker never had more than 170 people on its payroll. Unlike the Palacio, the Casa Boker had not invested in manufacturing.

Even more ominously—and an issue that would greatly distress Friederichs's successors—the building had cost 1.5 million pesos, too much money for a company like the Casa Boker. The company, capitalized at slightly more than 2 million pesos, was far smaller than the French department stores. Relative to its capital, it also had a far more expensive inventory, which it turned over a maximum of 1.5 times per year.

Indeed, the capital buried in real estate and inventory left the Casa Boker with a liquidity problem that would affect the company for the next seventy-five years. The cost of the building (triple the estimates of the architects) amounted to 75 percent of the firm's capital, forcing Roberto Boker y Cía to borrow against its expensive inventory worth another 1 million pesos. During the first three years of the twentieth century, the company's debt amounted to 58 percent of its assets. To make matters worse, the Edificio Boker was too large for the company's assortment of goods.[96] To address this problem, the partners increased the number of goods the Casa Boker offered, a solution that only aggravated the lack of capital. Therefore, in 1904, Robert made one last visit to Mexico City to organize the liquidation of 40 percent of the company's wares. This move freed up almost 900,000 pesos, but it again made the store look empty. Only during the 1910s did the management definitively address this problem by converting parts of the Edificio Boker to office and store space, a solution that brought the company a modest income in rent.[97] By then, the directors had recovered some of the funds spent on the building by selling the giant marble staircase to the state government of Veracruz, which installed it in the governor's palace in the state capital of Xalapa. This decision recognized the fact that the Edificio Boker was too large for its customers, as few of them had ventured up to the top floors. It also removed one of its most ostentatious amenities.

The Casa Boker succeeded through the adoption of a transnational business strategy. In a departure from the ethos of the kingly merchant, Friederichs had embraced U.S. notions of commercial capitalism. The partners' involvement in the U.S., British, and (in Friederichs's case) French communities, their promotion of U.S.-made products, and their acceptance of U.S. and French methods of marketing and distribution showed that they considered economic nationalism to be incompatible with commercial success. To be sure, all of the partners returned to live in Germany, and they raised their children as Germans. But so far as their business was concerned, foreign merchants in late-nineteenth-century Mexico did not think primarily in national terms. Entrepreneurs distinguished between their business lives spent in cooperation with Mexican and other foreign business leaders and their private lives, which they lived in a segregated ethnic enclave. By 1900, there was no doubt that the Böker brothers and Friederichs had adapted to their environment.

Europeans rather than North Americans spearheaded the consumer revolution that began to transform Mexico City at the turn of the twentieth century. The rise of the Casa Boker and other department stores challenges recent analyses that have stressed the role of U.S. capitalists in the modernization of Mexico to consider the important role of European intermediaries such as the Boker family and their business.[98] During the Porfiriato, German merchants became the prime marketers of hardware, while U.S. producers utilized the efficient system of distribution that their German partners had set up for imported merchandise. At least in this sector, then, the Americanization of Mexico required the concomitant growth of European influence—and particularly the help of transnational German merchants such as Robert Böker and Carl Friederichs.

Finally, this German import business faced fundamental cultural and economic limitations that would stunt its further growth in the far more difficult era for foreign merchants that dawned with the new century. Although Friederichs had successfully fought the ethos of the kingly merchant, the Bokers' hostility to consumer culture had not disappeared, and the cash flow problems caused by the construction of the Edificio Boker did not endear another generation to the idea of emulating the Palacio de Hierro. Even more significantly, the owners of the Casa Boker could not even think of challenging the French monopoly on the sale of garments and textiles—items indispensable, along with jewelry and other luxury goods, for the success of a department store. Despite its glamour, the Casa Boker primarily remained a store for specialized male customers, and it did not create dream worlds like the real Sears, Roebuck, or even the Palacio de Hierro. The adversity that came with the twentieth century would leave the Casa Boker fighting for its survival, and its owners in the vortex of the Mexican Revolution and global war.

Part Two

Between Revolution and Global War, c. 1900–c. 1948

> [His] idea that his fortune and success was over—an inner truth
> rather than an idea founded on external realities—had placed
> him in a state of such suspicious despondency that he . . . began
> to save money . . . in a miserly fashion. He had cursed the day his
> new house had been built a hundred times; [a house] that had, it
> seemed to him, brought him nothing but disaster.
> —Thomas Mann, *Buddenbrooks*

3

In the Business of Imperialism and Revolution

In the late evening of September 8, 1899, a train from Nuevo Laredo on the Texas border made its approach to Mexico City. After a long journey, only eight more hours of travel separated the passengers from their arrival in the capital's fancy Buenavista train station. As the train rumbled through the darkness, the first-class passengers prepared their pullout beds for the final night in their plush compartments, while the less fortunate passengers braced for another night of sleeping propped up in overcrowded cabins. Back in first class, Franz Böker was drinking a beer with a fellow German traveler when the train suddenly plunged into water several feet deep and turned over. Soaking wet, the travelers spent the night in a small town, from where they continued their trip the next morning.[1]

This incident constituted a bad omen for the second-generation Bokers in Mexico City and a business then in its golden age. Franz witnessed the end of an era in which most observers had long taken the Pax Porfiriana for granted. Within years after his arrival, the financial consequences of the construction of the Edificio Boker as well as a serious economic crisis forced Franz and his peers to restructure the business into an enterprise less likely to expand in the future. After 1910, the Mexican Revolution and World War I threatened the very survival of this and many other businesses and hence induced merchants to stay in Mexico to protect their investment rather than return home. Although Franz did not know it at the time, what he had intended as a stay of several years turned into lifelong residence in Mexico.

The years 1900 to 1920 marked the beginning of a new era for the Casa Boker and its owners: one in which the business consolidated rather than expanded, while the Boker family embarked on a long-term process of acculturation. Franz Böker, who assumed leadership of the company at the beginning of this period, was an intellectual forced to follow in his father's footsteps. At the same time, the Mexican Revolution and World War I not only threatened the Casa Boker but also dragged the Boker family into world politics and reshaped the attitudes of the family toward their German and Mexican worlds.

Dark Clouds over the Second Generation

Born in Remscheid on March 24, 1877, Franz Böker was his parents' only son, the heir apparent whose life path appeared charted from the beginning. Robert and Auguste had been happy enough to see the birth of his two older sisters, but they celebrated Franz's birth with plenty of champagne. Merely two years old, Franz stood in for his absent father when he laid the first stone for the remodeling of the family residence. His mother, whose Mexican experiences had contributed to a lifelong obsession with sickness, constantly fussed over the frail yet mischievous child. Using a walking aid until school age, Franz did not play with the lower-class children of the neighborhood as his father had done. Therefore, he grew up as a relatively lonely child, and his studies came easier to him than making friends—so easy, in fact, that his work habits suffered. Innately "lazy" in his own words, Franz had to learn that the German bourgeoisie valued discipline and obedience above all other things. Each dinner conveyed to him the meaning of hierarchy: Franz and his sisters ate standing up, while the parents dined sitting down in an adjacent room.[2]

Raised in the same Spartan fashion, Franz continued the work of his father in many ways. After he arrived in Mexico at twenty-two years of age, he demonstrated a commitment to public service, particularly to institutions that furthered the cooperation among German merchants, U.S. investors, and Mexican elites. Together with U.S. entrepreneurs and Porfirian notables, Franz served on the board of directors of the Banco Mexicano de Comercio e Industria.[3] He was also one of the founding members of a committee that supported the activities of the YMCA.[4]

Franz also shared his father's positive opinion about Porfirio Díaz: "How without a care in the world was our life in fin-de-siècle Mexico!"

he reminisced years later. "Don Porfirio was firmly entrenched in the saddle; the country was so safe that [a woman] could travel through the remote South all by herself. . . . The traffic was so light that . . . [what is today Calle Madero] was blocked off in front of the Jockey Club each day at noon to allow Secretary of War General Mena and his friends to drink champagne on plush easy chairs."[5] Franz even cast his vote for Díaz in 1904, in one of his proudest moments.[6] He never commented on the dark side of Porfirian modernization, visible in what a Mexican newspaper article called the "muddy pigsties . . . of our sickening tenements on those open sewers we call streets."[7] Not surprisingly, Franz deeply lamented the passing of the Díaz dictatorship, the "era that feigned an orderly Mexico."[8] As late as 1958, he wistfully recalled the days of Don Porfirio, when order and progress allowed foreign entrepreneurs to accumulate wealth without state intervention.[9] Like his father, Franz therefore belonged to the patrician entrepreneurial class, the Wirtschaftsbürger, transplanted to Mexico.

However, quite in contrast to his father, Franz shared many of the values of a group that many historians have portrayed as the opposite of the Wirtschaftsbürger: the *Bildungsbürger,* or educated bourgeoisie.[10] The first member of his family to finish the *Oberschule,* the university preparatory school, Franz was an intellectual rather than an entrepreneur, and he often bemoaned the fact that his father did not read books.

Figure 7: Franz (second from right) and his fellow directors in the Porfirian "Golden Age" (Archivo Boker, Mexico City).

Even without a university education, he possessed an encyclopedic knowledge of "high" culture, including art, literature, and music, as well as a reading knowledge of English, French, and Latin (he learned Spanish only after his arrival in Mexico). His experiences in Mexico—experiences that included a series of global and national catastrophes in rapid succession—drove him toward the writings of the cultural pessimists Friedrich W. Nietzsche and Arthur Schopenhauer. Over time, he became an introverted skeptic who shared these authors' rejection of Christianity, which he practiced as a ritual rather than in faith. As an older man, he followed Schopenhauer's quasi-Buddhist notion that true happiness required defeating one's desires and lived a life of self-abnegation. Not surprisingly, the older Franz looked the part of an ascetic: tall and gaunt, with long legs that appeared as thin as reeds. One needed to live frugally, he believed, in order to avoid the moral decadence that he saw as the primary reason for the decline of civilizations. Accordingly, Franz liked all that was simple, functional, and modest, and he abhorred ostentation, frills, and conspicuous consumption. He preferred Neoclassicism to Art Nouveau, the restraint of Johannes Brahms to the pomp of Richard Wagner, and Johann von Goethe's philosophical, brooding *Faust* to the same author's lyrical, Romantic *The Sufferings of Young Werther.* Above all else, he valued an unflinching dedication to one's obligations to work, family, community, and country. In spite of his wealth, Franz saw himself as an average man, a pawn of the great waves of the twentieth century.[11] His antimodernist, ultraconservative attitude rejected the noisy progress of his era in favor of an idealized, simpler past.

Franz grew up in a world very different from that of his father: one that was German rather than Prussian, and one that was rife with imperial rivalry. He was born in the newly unified German Empire, and his formative years coincided with the reign of Emperor William II, an impetuous, boastful ruler who represented the very pomp that Franz abhorred. Franz cringed at William's lack of tact and frequent verbal infelicities. Fearing that the emperor might offend the Mexicans, he reportedly edited a speech delivered by William's brother, Prince Henry, at the lavish celebration on September 16, 1910 that commemorated the centennial of the struggle for independence.[12] At the same time, as an ardent nationalist, he agreed with William's efforts to expand German power worldwide in an era that brought imperialist rivalry to Latin America. While India and most of Africa had fallen under colonial rule, informal structures of empire preserved the political sovereignty of the Latin American republics in a context of increasing U.S. influence. The War of 1898 had resulted in the beginning of a small U.S. overseas empire, and soon thereafter, a "promotional state" encouraged U.S. investments as strategic assets.[13]

The rising imperialist tide pitted German commercial and geopolitical interests against growing U.S. influence in Mexico. German industrialists, who aspired to become the world's main suppliers of industrial goods, forged an alliance with the influential Alldeutscher Verband, or All-German Confederation, which promoted territorial conquest.[14] For the imperial government, the goals of economic and territorial expansion therefore merged into one. Although the German government did not pursue the aggressive goals of the Alldeutscher Verband, it did formulate a "Reichsmark Diplomacy" that combined government monitoring of foreign investment with efforts to promote the sale of German products abroad.[15] Just like the "Dollar Diplomacy" of U.S. President William H. Taft, Reichsmark Diplomacy promoted private profit abroad as a means of expanding political influence. Although this effort remained half-hearted, Reichsmark Diplomacy, along with the rise of the German navy, and William's boastful rhetoric that made him appear the greatest imperialist in a world full of imperialists, contributed to U.S. fears about German influence in Latin America. These fears began during the near-clash between U.S. and German naval forces in Manila Bay during the War of 1898, and they increased through German attempts to enforce debt collection from Venezuela and schemes to politicize German immigrants in southern Brazil.[16] As historian Friedrich Katz has related, Mexico became a major focus of the emerging German-U.S. rivalry. Although Germany could not compete with the growth of U.S. economic influence, its trade with Mexico became increasingly important.[17] By 1910, the United States absorbed 75 percent of Mexican exports and had become the source of more than half of the country's imports. The same year, however, Germany surpassed Britain for second place among Mexico's importers: with almost 13 percent of the import market, it was second only to the United States.[18] The imperialist vogue therefore complicated the precarious position of the Casa Boker as a German company selling an international assortment of products.

Considering these circumstances, Franz's career could not resemble that of his father. Franz did not share Robert's passion for commerce. As the only son, he could not determine his own professional future. Instead of studying architecture—the field that he saw as his true calling—Franz interned for two years in his maternal grandfather's firm, followed by an obligatory stint in the military and two additional internships in Remscheid and in Wolverhampton, England. He went to Mexico City without enthusiasm, believing that he would follow the pattern of the previous generation in returning home after a decade overseas.[19] This lack of interest remained constant throughout his life. Many years later, as director of the Casa Boker, he left the day-to-day operations to his senior employees. Once, he even had to ask his son Gunther to find out the name of the Mexican bank that managed the company's financial transactions.[20] As someone who followed in the footsteps of a trade conquistador, Franz regarded his life in Mexico as his duty rather than an opportunity for adventure. It was ironic that the adventurous and pragmatic Robert lived the rest of his days in Remscheid, while the cautious intellectual Franz remained in Mexico throughout a revolution, the Great Depression, and two world wars.[21]

In contrast to Robert, who had lived in Mexico eight short years, the man Mexicans knew as "Don Pancho" and his wife, Luise, began a lifelong journey toward acculturation. During his sixty-six years in Mexico City, Franz not only dedicated himself to helping the institutions of the German colony, but he also became active in historical preservation efforts. The couple's circle of friends gradually grew to include other foreigners, and—after the Spanish Civil War—even progressive Spanish refugees and their Mexican friends. Unlike his father, Franz owned a large number of Spanish and Mexican books, cherished the Mexican landscape, and developed a genuine appreciation for the Mexican people. Finally, he shared the fears of many Mexicans about the United States.[22]

Franz also differed with his father as far as the Edificio Boker was concerned. During his first year in Mexico, he saw a building go up that he considered ugly and unnecessary. Like the Mexican architect Nicolás Mariscal, Franz disliked the great legacy of Robert's generation for what he considered the bombastic syncretism of Art Nouveau and a functional U.S. design. Even more importantly, however, the younger Böker regarded the "white elephant" as an expensive millstone that weighed down the company's fortunes. He believed that a less pompous and less costly building would have better served the needs of his company, and he scoffed at Friederichs's vision of the Casa Boker as a great department store.[23]

Thus, after he became a partner of Roberto Boker y Cía in 1902, Franz managed the business only half-heartedly and without a clear vision for the future. He was ill suited to oversee the further growth of a Mexican department store. Franz saw the Casa Boker as a company that dealt in items of necessity rather than luxury, and his pessimism closed his mind to the opportunities of the twentieth century. Similarly, however, his frugality and financial conservatism made him shun unnecessary risks—a quality that assured the survival of the business in the difficult years that lay ahead. At the very least, Franz endured in his task, unlike his cousins. Max's eldest son, Robert, left Mexico within a few years after becoming a partner in Roberto Boker y Cía in 1902, and Heinrich's son Alexander returned to Germany after one year as an intern.[24] Thus ended the involvement of the families of Franz's uncles Max and Heinrich in the management of the Casa Boker.

Fortunately for Franz, his wife (albeit grudgingly) came to terms with life in Mexico. Julia Luise Pocorny, whom he met during a trip to Remscheid in 1903, was a diminutive, but highly energetic person who blended optimism with a radiant charm and social acumen. The daughter of an immigrant from Poland, she grew up with the mentality of a social climber. Her father had risen from humble origins to become a wealthy merchant and never let his four daughters forget that fact. In contrast to Franz—and most other Bokers, for that matter—Luise was a devout Christian. Her abundant social graces smoothed off many of her husband's rough edges and made life easier for her in a context that welcomed female immigrants. For many years, Luise served as the president of the Deutscher Frauenverein, or German Women's Association. She surrounded herself with a social circle large enough that her husband tired of her social engagements. Unlike her husband, she enjoyed living in a world of luxury and leisure. In a letter to her mother, Franz once complained that Luise did not consider nine Mexican servants sufficient for running a household of eight people. By 1918, the couple had two daughters and four sons: Gabriele, Liesel, Günther, Helmuth, and the fraternal twins Klaus and Peter. Unlike her husband, she was proud of the Casa Boker and often dismissed Franz's gloomy predictions. As events during the next two decades would reveal, the optimistic Luise proved a good match for her pessimistic husband, as she saved him from succumbing to the doom that he feared for the entire world.[25] Had she had any say in the affairs of the Casa Boker, Luise would have expressed some degree of appreciation for Friederichs's ambitious vision. However, she did not— and thus could only look on as Franz pulled his company back from the vanguard of modernization.

Beginning his work in the accounting department once under the leadership of the photographer Guillermo Kahlo—whose daughter Frida would enjoy global fame as an artist—Franz found a company in deep trouble. Roberto Boker y Cía had spent beyond its means, and the excessive cost of the building had created an acute cash flow problem.[26] In 1907, a global recession and the concomitant decline of the price of silver (Mexico's principal export product) compounded this problem. In a significant blow to the Porfirian system, the crisis sent hundreds of thousands of Mexicans into unemployment and drastically reduced the earnings of countless others. With reduced demand came cutthroat competition among the several German hardware merchants that led to the formation of a short-lived cartel, the Unión de Ferreteros, that vainly attempted to sustain healthy profit margins. By 1908, sales of the Casa Boker had plummeted to their lowest level in more than ten years,

Figure 8: Franz and Luise Böker wedding photo (Archivo Boker, Mexico City).

which forced the company to borrow 600,000 marks (300,000 pesos) from a German bank.[27] The company's earnings during the first decade of the twentieth century—down 70 percent from those of the 1890s—demonstrate its precarious situation (see Table 5).

In 1909, these difficulties led to the decision of ending the partnership that had served the company well since 1865. Partnerships could only succeed so long as a firm generated enough surplus to attract a new generation of partners. By the time the 1907 economic crisis hit Mexico, these conditions no longer existed. Although the three Böker brothers, Friederichs, and von Lübeck were all ready to sell their shares, only Franz made a permanent commitment to the Casa Boker. Other members of his generation such as Max's and Heinrich's children and Friederichs's son Carlitos did not express any interest. They knew about the dire situation of the company and understood that the Casa Boker could not have survived the withdrawal of

Table 5: Earnings of Roberto Boker y Cía, 1900–1909
(in thousands of gold pesos)

Year	Earnings
1900	74
1901	-48
1902	112
1903	133
1904	178
1905	123
1906	171
1907	211
1908	-62
1909	-10

Source: "Finanzlage und Rentabilitaet des Hauses Roberto Boker y Cía in den Jahren 1895–1909," AB, FFLB.

one of the partners. Therefore, they remained in Germany to pursue careers there.[28] As a result, upon the expiration of the 1904-09 contract of Roberto Boker y Cía, Franz and the other partners formed a joint stock company named the Compañía Ferretera Mexicana (Mexican Hardware Company, or CFM). The new contract was for thirty years, and it divided the capital of the new company into 2,250 shares of 1,000 pesos each, for purchase only by the partners and their heirs, creating a closely held corporation.[29] This corporation could survive the withdrawal of any of its owners, as anyone who wished to sell his shares needed to find somebody to buy them.

The bland name of the CFM, which never replaced the term Casa Boker in popular usage, reflected legal as well as political concerns. Most importantly, Mexican law would have held the Bokers personally liable for bankruptcy if the name Roberto Boker y Cía had remained. In addition, the name Compañía Ferretera Mexicana paid homage to economic nationalism. A phenomenon confined largely to the Mexican middle class, economic nationalism appeared in the late Porfiriato to target the privileges of foreign investors and workers.[30] This effort to Mexicanize the economy presaged, in Franz's words, the "nationalist wave" that constituted an "outgrowth of the inferiority complex of underdeveloped societies."[31] That same concern contributed to the naming of Mexico's foremost breweries, Moctezuma and Cuauhtémoc.

The creation of the CFM marks an important step toward the "Mexicanization" of the Boker family business. Until 1900, the company had remained a typical trade conquistador venture despite its legally Mexican nature. It was designed to allow each partner to retire in Germany after a relatively short period of working in Mexico. Its owners invested profits in Germany, they did not own Mexican real estate, and they could sell their share to a new partner. As a result, the partners made business decisions based at least partially on their plans in Germany, and the senior partners who had returned home played important roles in the company's decisions. The Edificio Boker, however, had tied up capital crucial to the generational succession in Mexico. Since 1909, the directors of the Casa Boker have always lived in Mexico, and they have kept most of their capital invested locally in real estate and inventory. Although the majority of the shares remained in the hands of Böker and Friederichs family members resident in Germany, the directors in Mexico made all important business decisions. Despite the fact that these directors were native Germans, they lived amidst Mexican economic realities and thus followed the logic of a Mexican, and not German, business. As the principal concession to the German shareholders, the statutes of the CFM created an advisory board of directors in Germany, the Consejo Consultivo. However, this body could not overrule the Consejo Administrativo, the board of directors based in Mexico.[32]

Despite its advantages, the establishment of the CFM mortgaged the future growth of the Casa Boker, thus marking the turning point from expansion to stagnation. Since the CFM shares were not publicly traded and thus had a book rather than market value, the shareholders' primary interest in them lay in the annual dividend payment. Responsive to the wishes of the shareholders, Franz and his fellow directors therefore paid a high dividend rather than reinvesting profits, which would have increased the capitalization of the Casa Boker. The high dividend drained capital that might otherwise have been used to invest into manufacturing or to keep the CFM competitive in the long run. In addition, the restructuring raised the possibility that the directors of the CFM, as managers rather than privately liable partners, might not have a personal stake in the success of the Casa Boker.[33] If other department stores in Mexico such as the Palacio de Hierro and the Puerto de Liverpool had also become closely held corporations, that was primarily due to the fact that their garment-manufacturing operations had given employment opportunities to distant branches of the Tron and Michel families. The Bokers alone chose this business model to avoid the consequences of their debt.[34]

These concerns, however, were long term rather than immediate. Only one year after the founding of the CFM, the Mexican Revolution swept away the Díaz regime that had proved such a good host to the Bokers and other foreign investors. In this upheaval, the CFM fought for its survival, leaving little opportunity to ponder the consequences of the momentous step that the creation of the closely held corporation entailed.

Doing Business in the Fiesta of Bullets

The Mexican Revolution sowed paranoia among foreigners. Accompanied by calls for an end to the privileged status of foreign nationals, the revolution reminded the blond, blue-eyed Bokers of their status as outsiders. As such, they became a target of social movements that (despite the many differences among them) agreed on limiting foreign influence in Mexico. Whether or not one concurs with John M. Hart's claim that the revolution was a war of national liberation against the gringos and associated outsiders, the Bokers regarded it as just that.[35] Following a warning by the German minister—a former rear admiral of the Far Eastern Squadron—that conditions would resemble those of the Chinese Boxer Rebellion, they braced for a xenophobic war to drive all foreigners out of Mexico.[36]

The revolution brought together several major opposition movements. Díaz's retraction of a 1908 promise not to run for reelection cost him the support of important members of the northern elites and, especially, of Francisco I. Madero. Peasant leaders such as Emiliano Zapata had long seen their village lands usurped by large landowners, who had enjoyed not only the backing of Porfirian legislation but also that of the Mexican army and law enforcement. Meanwhile, peasants who had lost land and political independence during the Porfirian push to develop the Mexican north rallied around leaders such as Pancho Villa. A final group led by northern elite and middle-class leaders such as Venustiano Carranza and Alvaro Obregón forged a new national vision for Mexico that included limiting the privileges of foreign residents and investors. This group called for equal pay and employment opportunities for Mexicans and an end to the diplomatic protection of foreigners.[37]

Madero carried this uneasy alliance of diverging interests to victory in May 1911, but his triumph did not bring peace to Mexico. As president, Madero failed to address the complex social and economic issues that his allies had brought to the table. The ensuing agrarian revolts brought a counterrevolutionary alliance onto the scene. General Victoriano Huerta's coup d'état of February 1913, a coup supported by most of the foreign diplomats and, especially, U.S. Ambassador Henry L. Wilson, betrayed the Madero regime to this alliance. After Madero's assassination later that month, Huerta established a military dictatorship in Mexico, before a new coalition under First Chief Carranza defeated him in July 1914. The victors then turned to fighting among themselves, a struggle that did not end until 1920. When the smoke had cleared, Carranza, Madero, and Zapata were dead, and assassins would kill Villa and Obregón within the next eight years. Aside from destroying much of the Bokers' network of rural customers, many of whom had suffered severe damages, the conflict virtually shut down the wholesale operation and, in its 1915 climax, retail as well. Authored by allies of Carranza and Obregón, the revolutionary Constitution of 1917 left a specter of nationalist legislation designed to put Mexicans and foreigners on an equal economic footing.[38]

As a staunch supporter of the Díaz regime, Franz opposed the revolutionaries. Writing in retrospect, he charged Madero with stealing from the full coffers of the Porfirian treasury to supply an endless list of relatives with power, wealth, and political positions. In his view, the idealist zeal of the new president to create a democratic Mexico only fed the appetites of the underdogs, such as, for example, the poorly paid workers of the Casa Boker.[39] Nonetheless, after Madero's triumphant entry in Mexico City, an event ominously accompanied by a strong earthquake, Franz enjoined his fellow Germans to avoid friction with his government. In 1912, he even spearheaded a collective letter asking the editor of a German weekly that had printed diatribes against Madero to temper his criticism.[40] Later that year, the Bokers were confident enough of political stability in Mexico that they visited Germany to order the affairs of Franz's late parents.[41]

When Huerta deposed Madero, Franz initially welcomed what looked like the restoration of the Porfirian oligarchy. However, the new strongman plunged Mexico into chaos, and Franz later observed that "the dictatorship of Huerta was the most baroque type of political rule we have ever seen in Mexico. The seventy-year-old was the prototype of the Mexican bandit: unscrupulous, impervious to pressure, asleep on a powder keg."[42] He ignored the mounting pressure around him, threatened Mexican elite figures and foreign business leaders with execution unless they loaned him money, and regularly got drunk in full view of the public.[43]

As Franz found out, the collapse of the Huerta regime did not improve conditions either. Although foreign residents faced few threats to their personal safety, they did become targets of retribution by the revolutionaries. For example, foreign merchants, particularly those who sold food and other items of primary necessity, incurred the wrath of General Obregón for their practice of price gouging as well as for their support of Huerta. In February 1915, Obregón imposed a special tax on all capital investments in Mexico City. In response, the foreign merchants locked the doors of their stores and affixed consular seals to prevent forced entry. Obregón reciprocated by ordering those entrepreneurs who did not pay the tax to sweep the Zócalo in front of the National Palace.[44] As the war between the factions raged farther north, that winter brought hunger and starvation to a city that had thus far avoided the worst of the fighting. In April, a British resident described Mexico City as a "silent sepulcher" in which "peons were eating horseflesh and cat flesh and rat flesh."[45] Lamented Franz decades later:

> Toward the end of this period of terror, all haciendas and railway stations in the interior had been burned; all but one restaurant in the capital had been closed; sales of import businesses had decreased to 1 percent of their 1910 level; endless series of paper money were imposed at gun point, only to disappear; the market women no longer came to sell their tomatoes, which they had eaten . . . or bartered for other necessities; to make firewood for tortillas, trees had been felled in the parks and rolled through the streets; corpses doused with petroleum smoldered in the streets and were carted off without a coffin; and human life was as worthless as paper money.[46]

As this account relates, propertied Germans like Franz felt under a state of siege in revolutionary Mexico. For his daughter Gabriele, however, a nine-year-old child at the time, the entry of the Zapatistas into Mexico City that same winter caused more wonderment than fear. Eight decades later, she still remembered that she had seen "a procession of dark-skinned *indios*. Some of them were clad in a strange combination of barbarism and wealth. Women wore dresses they had stolen from the *hacendadas*, yet they walked barefoot."[47] The foreigners were so frightened that many of them kept their children out of school. To keep the school open, Franz rented a bus that took the German children to the Colegio Alemán.[48]

Beyond a doubt, Franz and Luise disliked the revolutionary factions. Although Villa and Obregón were mere bandits in their opinion, Zapata, an "idealist Indian," encountered a bit more sympathy, if not understanding.[49] Although the Carrancistas enjoyed the backing of both the United States and imperial Germany, foreign residents found many reasons to oppose them as well. Luise loathed the Carrancistas, and she actually rejoiced when the Villa/Zapata alliance occupied Mexico City in March 1915. Her letters to her mother in Germany portrayed Carranza as a venal bandit who "sucked the people dry," a politician who could only rise to power over a people like the "indolent and obtuse" Mexicans.[50] Although she recognized the danger that Villa and Zapata's agrarian coalition posed to merchant interests, she praised them for allowing food to enter the capital.[51] Franz was not enamored with the Carrancistas either. When they began their final triumphant march through the city, he saw "men in rags and women full of lice, the animals loaded with prey such as typewriters and rugs, with stolen heron feathers on [their] hats."[52] Not surprisingly, Franz and Luise reportedly sympathized with the counterrevolutionary faction of Don Porfirio's nephew Félix Díaz.[53]

Although few sources have survived from this turbulent time, the year leading up to Obregón's defeat of Villa in June 1915 was no easier for the Casa Boker than for the family. The fighting in the countryside confined the wholesale operation to Mexico City and eliminated markets that amounted to 25 percent of the company's income.[54] The unrest also complicated retail sales. During this chaotic year, each faction that occupied Mexico City flooded the capital with paper money that became worthless with the triumph of the next revolutionary leader. In September 1914, a Carrancista general attempted to impound the Casa Boker's supply of spurs and only backed off upon the intervention of the German chargé.[55] The following summer, retail sales hit rock bottom: on July 24, the day when Franz's son Helmuth was born, the Casa Boker sold 1 peso worth of merchandise.[56]

These events forced foreigners in Mexico City to work together despite the fact that their sons had begun to kill each other in the trenches of eastern France. British, French, German, and Italian businessmen cooperated with merchants from thirteen other countries in forming the Comité Internacional, a committee that coordinated the response of foreign entrepreneurs to the demands of revolutionary leaders. A leading figure in this committee, Franz later remarked that "unlike our fellow countrymen in Europe, we did not sit on our own national islands, each one walled off from the next, but instead together in the Mexican conundrum. We had common enemies who made us forget our national differences . . . until the Americans joined the war and polluted the atmosphere."[57] Together, the European merchants established a courier service to Veracruz run by a U.S. citizen. Whenever an invading army attempted to force its paper money on merchants, the Comité Internacional organized a boycott, in which the members of the committee closed down their shops until they were once again allowed to request payment in gold or silver.[58] When the revolution claimed the life of a prominent Englishman, the Germans mourned his death by placing a wreath with the German imperial colors on his grave.[59]

In this, the most violent phase of the Mexican Revolution, the problems of the Casa Boker remained minor compared to the widespread destruction elsewhere—and, indeed, even to other businesses. Although hundreds of thousands of Mexicans either died or emigrated, the Boker business did not incur any major losses. By contrast, Sommer, Herrmann and El Palacio de Hierro suffered fires caused by arson, and in October 1914, one of the capital's first great strikes shut down the Palacio de Hierro after a foreign-born manager struck a seamstress. As the textile workers of the great garment emporium, organized by the anarcho-syndicalist Casa del Obrero Mundial (House of the Global Worker) demanded higher wages, better working conditions, and the right to unionize, entrepreneurs in Mexico City understood that urban labor could no longer be taken for granted.[60] The workers of the Casa Boker did not strike or take other labor action during this period—for lack of sources, we unfortunately do not know how the CFM management kept them under their control.

Indeed, the Casa Boker quickly recouped its losses after the definitive triumph of Carranza and Obregón, who—with Carranza in the presidency—ultimately proved "the least bad of them all" to the Bokers and their peers.[61] The end of the fighting in Mexico City produced a pleasant surprise for the CFM. When the paper peso became worthless in late 1916, the customers began to spend the gold pesos that many of them had stashed away during the period of violence. With its warehouse full of imported goods irreplaceable during this time of revolution and global war, the CFM charged high prices for these items; prices often twice or three times as high as before the revolution. To Franz's astonishment, the company realized a profit of 600,000 gold pesos in 1917 at a margin of more than 60 percent. Although the Casa Boker could never replicate this result, profit margins remained well over 50 percent during the next three years (see Table 6).[62]

At least in the short term, the Casa Boker had emerged unscathed from the revolution. Like several other German companies, the Casa Boker profited from the scarcity of imported European goods in Mexico, and the resultant higher profit margins after Carranza's reestablishment of central authority made up for the severe depression in sales between 1913 and 1916.[63] In the long term, however, the revolution spelled trouble for the Casa Boker and other foreign merchant houses. The Constitution of 1917 made a theoretical commitment to social justice and Mexican ownership of the economy and contained

Table 6: Earnings of CFM, 1915–1920	
Year	Earnings (in thousands of gold pesos)
1915	5
1916	44
1917	598
1918	538
1919	299
1920	236

Source: Compañía Ferretera Mexicana, Memorias de Asambleas Ordinarias, 1915–21, AB, FA.

provisions that ended the relatively free rein of foreign investors. In addition, workers were learning that the new constitution gave them the right to resist their continued exploitation. Finally, Mexicans both rich and poor emerged with a sense of pride from what Mexican intellectual Octavio Paz has labeled a "fiesta of bullets."

The Casa Boker and World War I

A blood bath that showed the savage underside of the so-called civilized world, World War I contributed to this process by giving Mexicans a good reason to question the supposed superiority of Europeans—and it came to constitute yet another challenge to the Casa Boker.[64] Seen from Latin America, the U.S. declaration of war on Germany in April 1917 divided World War I into two distinct phases: the European war and the global war. The first phase of the war affected German merchant houses such as the Casa Boker only to a limited extent. While the British naval blockade made German trade with Latin America difficult, U.S. neutrality assured German capitalists of virtually complete freedom of operation. In the second phase, however, the U.S. participation in the war threatened the German entrepreneurs by subjecting German interests to novel methods of economic warfare.

In the first phase, imperial rivalry benefited the Casa Boker by giving the revolutionaries an incentive to protect German economic interests as a counterweight to the United States. As Friedrich Katz has demonstrated, the governments of Britain, France, Germany, and the United States intervened in the Mexican Revolution at each step of the way. In particular, the United States and Germany pursued wide-ranging plans. In 1913, the U.S. embassy in Mexico City brokered the agreement that brought Huerta to power in part because Madero appeared too pro-British. In 1914, the U.S. navy seized Veracruz within gunshot of a German warship carrying weapons for Huerta. Finally, in 1916, Wilson sent the Punitive Expedition into Chihuahua to catch Pancho Villa, who had earlier made known his German sympathies. Likewise, the German interest in Mexico focused chiefly on its position as a neighbor of the United States. Decried by Franz as a serious blunder, the infamous Zimmermann Telegram of 1917 offered Carranza the four southwestern U.S. states in exchange for an alliance with Germany. Although Carranza rejected the overture, he did keep Mexico neutral in the war and protected the interests of German businesses.[65]

More ominously, however, the early years of World War I produced economic warfare that targeted not only nation-states but also their overseas diasporas. In particular, the British and French blacklists of enemy nationals sought to eliminate German trade with neutral countries. The blacklist was a British invention used to countervail Napoleon's continental blockade. This first blacklist aimed to prevent inadvertent economic assistance to the other side and discouraged British citizens and companies from trading with the French and their allies. The decree that authorized the list not only included war materiel but all transactions with the enemy. Since free trade benefited the British Empire, the British did not use the blacklist again until German submarine warfare put them in a position in many ways analogous to the Napoleonic era. In 1915, claiming that submarines could not easily distinguish between belligerent ships and neutral vessels, the German admiralty declared the waters around the British Isles and France a seat of war. As British captains often flew the U.S. flag, the German navy also threatened to sink neutral merchant ships along with military craft. In retaliation, the British and French governments issued blacklists that asked their nationals not to trade with individuals and businesses of enemy nationality in neutral countries.[66] By December 1915, moral suasion had turned to prohibition. Because of the British dominance in transatlantic trade, the blacklist could severely damage German interests in the Americas, even in neutral countries such as Mexico, where both sides operated freely.[67]

As a firm owned by Germans, the Casa Boker faced two problems as a result of its inclusion in the first British and French blacklists. Most importantly, the lists prevented the Bokers from ordering from their British suppliers. Thus, the Casa Boker lost some of their most important business partners, including the North British Mercantile Insurance Company. After continuing to allow the CFM to underwrite its fire insurance policies until 1916, the company regretfully informed Franz that it could not continue its business relationships with German firms.[68] Of secondary importance, the blacklist banned purchases by British and French citizens from the Casa Boker, a virtually unenforceable provision.

However, the U.S. government, even though it was concerned about German espionage in Latin America, defended the rights of neutral powers to free trade.[69] Even the Anglophile Secretary of State Robert Lansing vociferously opposed the blacklists as undue interference into the internal affairs of neutral countries. Lansing remarked in his reaction to the British blacklist that the act was "pregnant with possibilities of undue influence with American trade."[70] The principle of the blacklist infringed on the sovereign rights of states as then interpreted in the United States: of global reach, the list affected German-Americans in Milwaukee as much as German-Mexicans in Mexico City. The U.S. government worried about the establishment of a blacklist of U.S. citizens and pressured the British and French into abandoning their plans for a comprehensive list of enemy interests in the United States. Consequently, the Casa Boker landed on the blacklist, while its New York counterpart, Hermann Boker and Co., remained free to trade with the Allies.[71] Finally, U.S. policymakers knew that blacklists could prove counterproductive to their country's economic interests. As a British diplomat in Guatemala who was critical of the blacklist put it: "Our German competitors . . . excel in identifying themselves with the people of the country, and this undoubtedly leads to success in business. . . . The fear that the German importer in neutral countries will bar British goods out of hatred may easily be exaggerated, judging, at least, by the care for his self-interest shown during the heat of the war."[72]

Indeed, the Allied effort to destroy German commerce did not stop British, French, and German merchants from coordinating their efforts to keep Mexican revolutionaries at bay. Although Franz exaggerated when he claimed that "despite our love for our Fatherlands, the war did not cause excitement among the Europeans" in Mexico City, his observation demonstrated the lack of enthusiasm among the foreign merchants.[73] Even as many Europeans in the Mexican capital joined their nations' armies or signed up for war loans, they focused on their own situation rather than the war. As the formation of the Comité Internacional demonstrated, foreign merchants emphasized local over global interests, and their class and profession over their nationality. In the words of the British consul, they displayed a "ludicrous inability to realize the bitter realities of the situation in Europe."[74] It was only after Carranza's definitive triumph that this cooperation—which was no longer so sorely needed—began to give way to open hostility along the lines of the war.[75]

Until that point, which coincided with the U.S. entry into the war, the Bokers therefore privileged their need to cooperate with other foreigners over their desire to help the German war effort. Reports to the contrary rely on a misinterpretation of confusing evidence. For example, in September 1915, the British consul in New York City reported that a shipment of weapons of U.S. origin, destined for the Casa Boker and other German firms, had arrived in a Mexican port. These "weapons," however, consisted of items such as steel bars and barbed wire that had long figured among the company's merchandise.[76] Similarly, one scholar read a British report from 1916 as claiming that the Casa Boker served as a conduit of weapons to the nationalists in British-held India.[77] A careful look at this document, however, exonerates the Casa Boker, pointing instead to the New York firm H. Boker and Company. Founded by Franz's grand-uncle and owned by U.S.-born relatives, that company was not on the British blacklist, not entwined in a revolution, and hence—unlike the CFM—in a position to sell arms to distant rebels.[78]

The cooperation among foreign entrepreneurs, however, did not imply harmony. Quite to the contrary: among the members of the German colony—and particularly in the Colegio Alemán—shrill nationalist rhetoric dominated social interaction. Even before the guns of August sounded, the Colegio Alemán had begun to serve the purposes of German imperialism. Principal Max Dobroschke, a career school administrator who knew nothing about Mexico until his arrival, saw the school as a mouthpiece for German propaganda rather than as a bicultural institution. This view echoed the perspective of the German legation, which paid a large annual subsidy to keep the school afloat. By 1915, Dobroschke had firmly integrated the school into the war effort. In a speech to the school's board of directors, he enjoined those present to "remove everything within us that is not German, and to resist the internationalist disintegration of our thoughts."[79] Final examinations reflected such efforts: for example, an English essay asked students to "Describe all that has been done by the German colony in Mexico to help their native country in the European War."[80] Four years later, Dobroschke wrote a new mission statement that proclaimed the intent to "practice German discipline, to impart a thorough scientific education, and to open eyes and minds of its charges to the German character and German knowledge."[81] When Franz and Luise's eldest daughter graduated with her high school class of four in 1922, she therefore left a different school than the one she had entered in 1911.

In April 1917, the U.S. entry into the war reversed the conditions in which the Casa Boker existed. In the context of increasing U.S. fears of German influence in Mexico after the publication of the Zimmermann Telegram, German merchants could once again count on a friendly Mexican government. Afraid of the possibility of a German-Mexican alliance, Wilson withdrew the Punitive Expedition in order to focus on securing access to Mexican strategic resources such as oil and precious metals. His government also began a hunt for German spies and agents in Mexico.[82] U.S. Ambassador Henry P. Fletcher labeled the 1917 Constitution the work of German agents, notwithstanding the fact that this constitution threatened German economic interests just as it did those of the United States.[83] He became agitated when Carranza rejected U.S. demands to rein in German espionage, propaganda activities, and economic influence. In light of the recent U.S. military interventions, Carranza showed no inclination to harm Germans, citizens of a country that had never violated Mexican sovereignty. Instead, he sought greater economic ties with Germany, and only the Allied victory prevented the making of an agreement that would have given Germany a major stake in the Mexican economy.[84]

Carranza's pro-German tendencies allayed Franz's opposition to the new order in Mexico, and they make it unlikely that he aided the efforts of Félix Díaz to unseat his government as implied in a June 1917 article in the *New York Herald*. According to this article, Mexican authorities had seized a cache of weapons in a box labeled "Roberto Boker y Cía" destined for the Díaz faction, which operated primarily in southern Mexico. Despite Franz and Luise's sympathies for the counterrevolution, it is hard to believe that they would have alienated the revolutionary government at a time when they most needed its assistance. Two possible explanations fit this isolated and circumstantial source into the interpretation presented here. The first is that the CFM no longer owned the box, which bore the name of its defunct predecessor. The second is that the U.S. newspaper attempted to stir up fears of German activities in Mexico by reporting old news: at the height of factional conflict, Franz had indeed rooted for the Felicistas.[85]

Whatever the case, the outbreak of hostilities between Germany and the United States subjected German businesses in Mexico to U.S. economic warfare, as the Wilson administration broke with its earlier policy and developed a blacklist of enemy nationals. In July 1917, Wilson submitted a "Trading with the Enemy Act" to Congress that sought to block trading with "enemy aliens." The act stipulated a wide range of criteria for blacklisting a company that included, among others, the ethnic origins of its owners, its banking connections, as well as the origin of its merchandise. Hesitant in the face of isolationist and pro-German critics, the U.S. Treasury Department did not compile the list until it realized that many U.S. producers continued to sell to German businesses in Latin America.[86] The first *Enemy Trading List* appeared in December 1917, a list revised several times until the signing of the Versailles peace treaty in June 1919. The retired von Lübeck appeared in the first version of this list, and Franz and the CFM followed suit in July 1918. While the U.S. government thus did not include the Casa Boker until late in the war, it made up for lost time. In May 1919, the CFM was among the last thirty entries that remained on the *Enemy Trading List* for Mexico.[87]

Like other German merchant establishments, however, the Casa Boker remained impervious to U.S. efforts to eliminate German commerce. Since the Carranza regime remained neutral in the global conflict, the blacklists never attained any legal force in Mexico. While Latin American governments that had declared war on Germany seized the property of German residents, Mexican neutrality allowed German merchants to continue their operations. The Casa Boker and other

German firms acquired Allied goods through intermediaries, and the U.S. participation in the war proved too short to create a serious supply problem. With an inventory worth 2.5 million pesos, the Casa Boker was well equipped to survive and even profit from the Allied boycott.[88] Since other German businesses constituted its main competition, the blacklists allowed the CFM to charge high prices for its wares. To most disgruntled customers, the difficulty in substituting these goods during times of war served as a sufficient explanation. In addition, the Bokers and other German merchants sought Mexican items that could substitute some of the imports from Allied countries and even invested in local manufacturing. By 1918, the Casa Boker obtained one-sixth of its purchases from Mexico. The CFM also continued to sell U.S. and British products from their warehouse throughout the years during which they could not legally obtain them. In the long term, the black lists proved irrelevant: once the Wilson administration lifted its embargo against German firms in 1919, the Casa Boker resumed its purchases from Britain and the United States.[89] Ironically, then, U.S. economic warfare made the Casa Boker a stronger enterprise.[90]

Encouraged by the resurgence of their company's fortunes and by Carranza's victory in the revolution, Franz and his associates finally followed their hearts and supported the German war effort. In late 1917, the CFM signed up for a German war loan. Although no exact figures are available, the amount likely came close to matching the rival firm Sommer, Herrmann's contribution of 100,000 marks. Franz also allowed the Germans to install a wireless station in the tower of the Edificio Boker. According to U.S. military intelligence records, the German legation used this wireless station for espionage and conveyed sensitive information to the German Foreign Ministry through the harmless-looking commercial telegrams of the CFM.[91] Eager to have ready cash available in Germany to resume purchases after the war, Franz and other German entrepreneurs also lent gold currency to the German legation to keep it afloat after Wilson's declaration of war. Ultimately, these cash loans came to harm the enterprise, as the German defeat and postwar inflation rendered the Weimar Republic unable to repay them.[92]

Even more significantly, as agents of the "Transocean" news service, Franz and von Lübeck played important roles in German war propaganda.[93] Housed in the Edificio Boker, the Verband Deutscher Reichsangehöriger (VDR, or German Reich Citizen's Association) spread German propaganda in an effort to keep Mexico neutral and to increase anti-American feelings among the Mexican population. With a membership estimated at close to six hundred, the VDR subsidized two widely circulating newspapers, *El Demócrata* and *La*

Defensa and distributed pro-German coverage of the world war to many other mass publications.[94] It also maintained close ties to pro-German elements within the Mexican army. Under the eyes of U.S. Ambassador Fletcher, VDR members trained Mexican boy scouts in the goose step made famous by the Prussian army. Until July 1918, this organization even operated in Central America despite the fact that Costa Rica, Guatemala, and Nicaragua had all entered the war on the side of the United States. The CFM gave this ultranationalist organization free headquarters. None other than von Lübeck himself served as president of the VDR, and Franz, just like many other German merchants in the capital, worked as an important agent. Throughout the war, the Edificio Boker thus served as a meeting place for Germans in Mexico City.[95]

When German and Allied representatives met in a railroad car in the woods of Compiègne, France, on November 11, 1918, to formalize the German surrender, a violent and paradoxical chapter in the history of the Boker family came to a close. Although Franz and his family reacted with consternation to the German defeat, his company had benefited from the global conflict. Despite a concerted effort to eliminate German trade, the U.S. government had not succeeded in displacing German hardware products. In the last two years of the war, the Casa Boker had profited from the scarcity of European imports. Although the continued growth of U.S. trade at the expense of Europe had seemed an ominous foreboding, the Casa Boker had adapted by seeking Mexican purveyors. The only lasting legacy that troubled the business was the U.S. blacklist. To be sure, this time Carranza had prevented its effectiveness in Mexico. What would happen, however, if a future Mexican government decided to be less neutral in another global conflict?

At Home in Mexico

As a principal shareholder and director of the CFM, Franz personally benefited from the recovery of the Casa Boker during the late 1910s. Augmented by sizable bonuses, his dividend income put Franz in an unexpected position. As Germany struggled to rebuild itself, and as inflation ate away at wages, profits, and bank accounts, he discarded the traditional mode of investing profits in the home country. Incensed by the U.S. participation in the war, he dismissed the obvious alternative of investing the money in the United States. The only remaining option was to keep the funds in Mexico, which implied a greater commitment to his host society. In the last years of the revolution, Franz invested the money in Mexican manufacturing and, much more importantly, in a private residence. In the process, Mexico became home for him and Luise, while the memory of a powerful German Empire made it difficult for them to love their defeated, depressed, and newly democratic homeland.

In investing in Mexican manufacturing, Franz put his money where the Casa Boker needed a supplier. In 1917, with trade between Mexico and Europe practically nonexistent, Franz and two other German merchants founded the stoneware factory El Anfora, to this day a major producer of sinks, toilets, and other stoneware used in house construction. Initially a modest venture, El Anfora was an instant success at a time when the war prevented expensive stoneware imports. Even after the end of World War I, the company successfully competed with importers.[96]

In 1919, the architectural aficionado Franz built what henceforth became the social center of the Boker family, a home in Tlacopac near San Angel. At the time, Tlacopac was a sleepy village separated from Mexico City by 8 miles of cornfields. For years, his family had lived for rent in the suburb of Colonia Roma, the neighborhood of choice for wealthy foreign residents. After buying and selling several properties there in order to invest the profits of the late 1910s, however, Franz and Luise decided to flee bustling Mexico City with its increasing automobile traffic.[97] Moreover, the revolution had contributed to a process that drove the Mexican bourgeoisie away from the city center toward the southwest of the Federal District.[98] For these reasons, Franz and Luise bought an area totaling 1.5 acres in Tlacopac.[99] Amidst adobe huts and a small colonial church arose a building of approximately 6,000 square feet, a house the Bokers affectionately call the "Casa Amarilla," the yellow house. Later, the family added two more residences and a tennis court to form a residential complex. Even today, Franz's grandsons who manage the Casa Boker live in this compound.[100]

The new house and its furnishings constituted a unique blend of German and Mexican culture. Franz had not attempted to re-create a patrician German *Bürgerhaus* in Mexico: instead, he had designed a home in Spanish colonial style that fit into its surroundings. Before the age of skyscrapers and air pollution, the family enjoyed a magnificent view of the Ixtaccíhuatl and Popocatépetl volcanoes from the patio at the southeast corner of the house. The inside of the home, the intimate sphere of the family that one might have expected to resemble a patrician German home, also marked the coexistence of cultures. In the grandiose living room with 20-foot ceilings, a grand piano, on which Luise played classical music in her leisurely moments, represented the European upbringing of the owners. Most of the furnishings came from the Casa Boker, and to Franz's chagrin, Luise bought freely and expensively from her husband's company. The furniture came from Austria

Figure 9: The Casa Amarilla (Nachlass Gabriele Buchenau).

or from the United States; and the china and cutlery, from Germany. Although many of the paintings on the walls were of European origin, Franz and Luise had also acquired magnificent landscape paintings of the renowned Porfirian painter José María Velasco. Finally, the sole surviving picture of the inside of the house—a photograph unfortunately too damaged to reproduce in this volume—shows that the family displayed Mexican tapestries and other handicrafts in the living room. In the rear, or western part of the house, of course, the servants' quarters displayed a much more Mexican appearance.[101]

Thus, the Casa Amarilla highlights the emergence of Mexico as the psychological home of the Bokers. Like other German private residences that followed in the 1920s, the house represented a departure from the ways of the old trade conquistadors, who lived for rent and remitted almost all of their earnings to their home country. The Bokers, by contrast, owned two expensive buildings in Mexico City: the Edificio Boker and the Casa Amarilla. In addition, their choice of location indicated that they intended to stay for the long haul. Miles away from their peers in Mexico City, and years before Tacubaya, Polanco, and Lomas de Chapultepec became havens for affluent foreigners, the Bokers lived in a pastoral setting between two old haciendas that would have discouraged most potential buyers.[102]

The decision to invest money in Mexico in the uncertain years of revolution highlighted Franz's aversion to the new order in Germany and his alienation from his home country more generally. Indeed, he and most other Germans in Mexico City operated almost as a counterpoint to the reality in their home country, thus demonstrating that Franz trusted his future in Mexico. While the Bokers and their peers enjoyed prosperity and a high social status, most of Germany saw the aftermath of 1918 as a time of hunger and national humiliation. In lieu of the German Empire, the Weimar Republic administered what had once been a great power. In its early years, this first democracy was under close scrutiny by the victorious Allies and beset by coups d'état from the Left and Right, runaway inflation, economic failure, and, most of all, desperation. To this Germany Franz did not desire to return.[103]

In fact, Franz's private ranting about German politics reveal that he saw the establishment of the Weimar Republic as the result of an Allied, Catholic, and Jewish conspiracy. In a 1919 telegram to his sister Elisabeth, he lambasted the influential Catholic democratic politician Matthias Erzberger, a man later assassinated for his signature in Compiègne. He described Erzberger as a "hell of a crook [*Mordslump*]." Franz went on: "Why don't you just throw out the whole Jewish gang? What is your national holiday: July 14, the day of the Pope's declaration of infallibility, or the Sukkoth? We celebrate January 18 [the national holiday of the empire] with the old flag."[104] According to Franz, democracy bred sycophants and demagogues, and he continued to consider William II the legitimate ruler of Germany.[105]

These views mirrored those of the vast majority of the German colony in Mexico; theirs was an ideological conformity best demonstrated in the community's attitude toward the *Flaggenstreit,* or the debate over the German flag. The official flag of the Weimar Republic was black, red, and gold, the colors of the student movement during the wars against Napoleon, and since, the flag of democratic Germany. Throughout Latin America, right-wing enemies of the Weimar Republic refused to recognize these colors, preferring the old black, white, and red flag of imperial Germany, while the Communists displayed their internationalist red flags.[106] Although German diplomats steadfastly propagated the new colors, a vast majority of Germans all over Latin America continued to fly the black, white, and red flag. The results of a poll administered by the VDR claimed that Germans favored the imperial flag by a vote of 1,800 to 2.[107] In 1920, Franz gave expression to such sentiments when he sparred with Berlin over the flag. Invoking his right as the owner of a building rented by the German consul, he lowered the Weimar flag and hoisted the imperial one instead. Frustrated, the consul moved out of the building.[108]

Ultimately, however, Franz and Luise came to terms with the new realities. As his relatives witnessed mounting strikes and violent clashes between Marxist Spartacus partisans and the armed forces in Remscheid,

Franz became more opposed to the leftists who tried to end the Weimar Republic than to the republic that had replaced the monarchy. He likened the situation to the Mexican Revolution: "In our opinion, it had to come to this. When the working masses, ignorant of the world and therefore unaware of the limits of economic possibilities, hear sermons for thirty years about a utopian state and exploitation, then the end can only look like what we have experienced here. . . . Those who are second overthrow the first; those who are third overthrow the second. . . . Within a decade, all of the wonderful demagogues will live blissfully outside Germany, and the government and the bourgeoisie will struggle to coexist with a revolutionary working class."[109] Franz and Luise therefore grudgingly accepted the Weimar Republic as an imperfect bulwark against socialist agitation and accepted democratic Weimar Germany as the only fatherland they had.

This pragmatic attitude found its greatest expression in 1921, when Mexico celebrated the centennial of its independence. On that occasion, each of the foreign colonies in the capital agreed to dedicate a piece of art to Mexico. As the leading representatives of the German colony discussed an appropriate present with their country's legation, Franz suggested a statue of the great composer Ludwig van Beethoven—a figure above political and partisan rank. The German minister to Mexico was most pleased with this idea, opining that the statue could not raise any objections "from our former enemies."[110] With his endorsement, Franz traveled to Germany to seek an appropriate artist and ultimately selected Theodor von Gosen, a renowned sculptor from the city of Breslau (today, Wrocław, Poland). He paid for the manufacture and transportation of this statue, and the statue spent several months in the Edificio Boker.[111] Since 1925, the statue has looked out of Alameda Park toward the Palacio de Bellas Artes. Perhaps not coincidentally, Beethoven looks east, toward the Zócalo and the Edificio Boker.

The turbulent first decades of the new century had brought unintended and paradoxical results to the Casa Boker. Weighted down by the construction of the Edificio Boker, the company had suffered through the last years of what other foreign-owned businesses experienced as a golden era. After 1910, the revolution had virtually shut down sales, but the Casa Boker rebounded in better shape. In 1914, a world war broke out that did not stop the revolution-era cooperation of the foreign diasporas in Mexico City. After 1917, U.S. economic warfare targeted the Casa Boker as a German business in Mexico, but only contributed to the further consolidation of its position. In turn, the rising fortunes of the company allowed the Casa Boker to help the losing German cause in the last eighteen months of the war.

However, the positive outlook of the Casa Boker in the late 1910s could not make up for a problematic legacy that would only come to fruition in the next three decades. The reorganization of the company as a closely held corporation that paid out a high dividend threatened future projects that required a reinvestment of profits. The Mexican Revolution left the unfulfilled promise of redress for a plethora of grievances directed against foreign entrepreneurs. The German defeat in World War I severely weakened German influence in the Western Hemisphere and elevated the United States to superpower status: a combination that did not bode well even for a company offering an international assortment of products. Finally, the turbulent events of the early twentieth century contributed to Franz's cautious, defensive, and pessimistic attitude toward the world in general and the future of the Casa Boker in particular. Although this attitude had helped his business through difficult times, it highlighted the beginning of an era in which the Bokers defended their position rather than seeking to expand it.

Franz and Luise's life in Mexico was just as paradoxical as the fortunes of their business. They had come with the expectation of going home after several years, but the revolutionary turmoil made them a part of Mexican society. Once the violence had subsided, they could not easily leave what had taken much time and energy to protect. Equally important, the Germany they had known had disappeared. Although Mexico had lost Don Porfirio's guiding hand, its social reality still corresponded more closely to their expectations than Germany. As Franz and Luise founded a new family amidst the turmoil of revolution and war, Mexico became their home, and a long and complex process of acculturation was under way.

The Germans own the hardware stores
The Spaniards own the hotels
The Americans own the railroads
And the Mexicans . . . stand in the streets
Shouting "Viva México"
　　　—Arthur Ruhl, *The Central Americans*

4

In the Eye of the Storm

In the summer of 1920, the family of eight moved into the stately Casa Amarilla with a German maid and seven Mexican servants. Projecting an illusion of serenity to a family that sought refuge from an increasingly chaotic world, Tlacopac's pastoral charm made it seem like a place in which time had stood still for centuries.[1] What Fanny Calderón de la Barca had said about nearby San Angel in the 1840s still held true in the 1920s: "All that might be dull in any other climate brightened and made light and gay by the purest atmosphere, and bluest sky, and softest air, that ever blew or shone upon a naughty world."[2]

But that naughty world was never far enough away. Six days a week, Franz took El Rápido, a tram that stopped at Alameda Park west of the Edificio Boker. Despite its name, El Rápido stopped every few blocks to pick up or drop off passengers, many of them in coat, tie, and well-shined shoes. As the tram fitfully and noisily made its way to the Centro, Franz overheard conversations about workers' strikes and regulation of foreign-owned businesses. Ford and General Motors automobiles zoomed past roadside billboards, reminding him of the precarious position of European-born entrepreneurs in a society marked increasingly by U.S. influence. The ride in El Rápido was comfortable, but the outside world scared the conservative, middle-aged German entrepreneur passenger.[3]

Franz's life spent between the seclusion of the Casa Amarilla and the bustling Centro epitomizes the schizophrenic era in which the Bokers lived during the 1920s and 1930s. While their businesses profited from the reestablishment of political stability, Mexican revolutionary nationalism and growing U.S. influence forced European merchants to reconsider their business strategies as well as their private lives. If the years of revolutionary violence had already raised the hackles of Franz and Luise, they were even more appalled to find that Mexicans questioned the privileges to which foreign investors had grown accustomed. These attacks on their status reminded Franz of the Bolshevik Revolution, which had just ended the foothold of a branch of the Boker family in St. Petersburg.[4] Complicating the success of the business, the postrevolutionary governments placed fetters on foreign investments, and new labor unions reshaped the relationship between entrepreneurs and their workers. Meanwhile, U.S. corporations raised the expectations of consumers by molding their needs with help of the new mass media. In their effort to shield their Mexican-born children in a German enclave, the Bokers confronted not only a cultural nationalism that inculcated a greater sense of self-confidence in the Mexican people but also the increasing influence of U.S. popular culture. The Bokers adopted a defensive response to these challenges that demonstrated the precarious position of German merchants between Mexican nationalism and U.S. influence. Against this backdrop, Franz and Luise raised their children as patriotic Germans in a community marked by increasing internal divisions.

Facing the Enormous Vogue of Things Mexican and "American"

Postrevolutionary Mexico City had changed drastically from the city Franz Böker had entered at the turn of the century. The capital had grown to more than 700,000 inhabitants, and the advent of motorized transportation had transformed it into a bustling, noisy city. The influx of thousands of peasants who had fled the ravaged countryside accelerated a long-term process of in-migration that blurred the boundaries dividing space among the wealthy and the poor.[5] As some formerly upscale neighborhoods became lower-class barrios, the wealthy built new homes further west and south, in Polanco, Lomas de Chapultepec, and San Angel. Even the posh business district around the Edificio Boker, in which the propertied bourgeoisie had long attempted not to notice the poor whose work sustained their enterprises, could no longer pretend to be Paris amidst hamlets. Rural Mexico had invaded the capital, and the foreign colonies floated like bubbles on the surface of a steaming cauldron.

Instead, Mexicans from a variety of social strata felt that an opportunity for profound change had arrived. As eyewitness Anita Brenner wrote, there was "a lift, a stirring feeling . . . a sense of strength released: . . . everything at the beginning."[6] The Constitution of 1917 contained great promises: collective bargaining for workers; land for peasants; national control over resources for nationalists; and democratic rule for old-fashioned Liberals. To be sure, revisionist historians (with the considerable benefit of hindsight) have pointed out that a new bourgeoisie allied with foreign economic interests came to dominate the new state.[7] Nevertheless, recent research has demonstrated that the postrevolutionary state was the malleable object of a multifaceted interplay among a new national elite, regional power brokers, foreign and domestic capitalists, and popular movements. The reconstruction of state authority involved a complex process of negotiation in which peasants, workers, and the middle classes played crucial roles. Revisionist arguments also fail to capture the great emotions of the era: the sense of excitement prevailing among ordinary Mexicans, and the elites' fears of a Bolshevik transformation of the kind that Vladimir I. Lenin had initiated in Russia.[8]

To the chagrin of the Bokers, revolutionary rhetoric and pressure from below continually redefined the Mexican state and its relationships with entrepreneurs. Although Mexico remained on a capitalist path of development, the Bokers and their peers viewed the 1917 Constitution as the sword of Damocles: ready to injure their interests at any time. Specifically, they feared an implementation of Articles 27, 33, and 123. Article 27 declared land and mineral resources the patrimony of the nation. In the vein of the Drago Doctrine, the article also required all foreign investors to forsake the diplomatic protection of their governments that had given them advantages over Mexicans in the Porfirian years. To give this provision some bite, Article 33 threatened recalcitrant foreigners with expulsion. Article 123 guaranteed labor unions the right to collective bargaining as well as the right to strike. In addition, foreign entrepreneurs and Mexicans alike worried that the victorious revolutionaries would line their own pockets instead of helping ordinary Mexicans. Not surprisingly, Franz and his associates foremost feared the possibility of outright expropriation and, secondarily, the prospect of debilitating strikes, protracted labor disputes, high taxation, and stifling government regulations.[9]

Although these fears might appear exaggerated today, they seemed realistic at a time when a succession of revolutionary generals in the presidential chair gave at least rhetorical (and sometimes actual) support to economic nationalism and labor causes. Even Venustiano Carranza, a wealthy landowner who profited from his ties with foreign business interests, lambasted what he called the asphyxiating foreign economic influence in Mexico. The next great strongman, Alvaro Obregón, who ruled Mexico from 1920 to 1924, worked hard to reassure foreign investors at a time when the U.S. government had severed diplomatic relations with Mexico. Nonetheless, the tenure of what Franz called a "rough-and-ready saber hero"—a reference to Obregón's clashes with foreign entrepreneurs during his 1915 occupation of

Mexico City—witnessed the rapid growth of syndicalism.[10] His successor, Plutarco Elías Calles, whose support for labor causes had earned him the undeserved reputation of a firebrand radical, revived Carranza's nationalist rhetoric. He imposed government regulation on the oil industry, faced off with the United States over U.S. intervention in Central America, and pursued a campaign to eliminate the influence of the "foreign-controlled" Catholic Church in Mexico. Even during the Maximato (1928–35), when Calles, as so-called *jefe máximo*, orchestrated the formation of a ruling party that sought to control rather than empower workers and peasants, the Mexican government responded to pressures from below. For example, the Labor Law of 1931, implemented at the height of the Great Depression, led to the unionization of the Casa Boker. Finally, just as the Casa Boker began to dig out from the effects of the Depression, along came Lázaro Cárdenas (1934–40), in the Bokers' opinion a dangerous Communist. Building a populist state with the support of workers' and peasant organizations, Cárdenas embarked on a reform program that ended with the distribution of 42 million acres of hacienda land to peasants. He also implemented many of the pro-labor provisions of the 1917 Constitution, and, in March 1938, he expropriated the foreign-owned oil industry. The strikes and demonstrations that became commonplace in the Cárdenas years alienated the conservative Bokers, as did the president's opposition to Nazi Germany.[11]

In response to the emergent alliance between the postrevolutionary state and organized labor, the Bokers joined other German merchants in founding a German chamber of commerce that (unlike individual entrepreneurs) could appeal for diplomatic protection.[12] In contrast to the British, French, and U.S. colonies, the Bokers and their German peers had long resisted the creation of a chamber of commerce because, as the German trade attaché surmised, they feared that such an institution would foster upstart enterprises that could emerge as potential competitors. As late as 1920, Franz and his colleagues tried to dissuade his legation from the plan of establishing a German chamber of commerce. Facing the specter of economic nationalism, however, the German entrepreneurs finally supported the venture. In 1929, the Cámara Mexicano Alemana de Comercio began its operations, and a director of the CFM served on its board of directors.[13]

It did not help assuage the worries of the Bokers that an explosion of artistic creativity promoted Mexican cultural and racial nationalism. Writers and artists alike discovered the heritage of Mexico's indigenous populations and questioned the supposed superiority of U.S. and European ways. It mattered little to the Bokers that the goal of the *indigenismo* movement was the incorporation of the "Indian" population into Mexican society, and not the redemption of the indigenous peoples at the expense of privileged capitalists.[14] To them, indigenismo and other forms of cultural nationalism smacked of xenophobia. Franz cringed when Secretary of Public Education José Vasconcelos talked about a "cosmic," mestizo race, a race superior to both its European and indigenous components. He winced when muralist Diego Rivera painted a Marxist interpretation of Mexican history on the walls of the Palacio Nacional only four blocks from the Casa Boker. Among other representations, brooding, angry peasants and workers threatened to jump out of the mural to attack the avaricious capitalists and conquistadors who served as the object of the artist's fury. And he scoffed at the frequent invocation of the revolutionary tradition by Mexico's leaders; it was a discourse that would become a stale ritual in post-1940 Mexico.[15] Although this cultural nationalism was, in the words of historian Daniel Cosío Villegas, "a nationalism without a trace of xenophobia, . . . not anti-something, but above all, for Mexico," these efforts to redefine the nation could only reinforce the foreigners' existing fears.[16]

Efforts to naturalize the children of immigrants and to constrict immigration highlighted these fears. Porfirian law had deferred to the fact that most immigrants did not wish to obtain Mexican citizenship. As most foreigners, including Franz and Luise, declared against naturalization, their children hence acquired the citizenship of their father. Although Carranza and Obregón had promised to end all legal vestiges that gave foreigners a special status, it took until 1933 until a law established *ius soli*—the notion that the place of birth determines one's nationality—as the principle of Mexican citizenship. This law inaugurated a series of measures to regulate further immigration. While propertied Europeans and U.S. citizens continued to enjoy an open door, the new legislation sought to keep out poor newcomers, who after 1918 made up the bulk of immigration to Mexico.[17] These measures did not promote assimilation, however. Mexico remained a diverse quilt of unhyphenated identities, in which one was either "Mexican" or "German." Until decades later, the privileged foreign colonies remained separate from Spanish-speaking Mexico, and in the absence of a hyphen, the road to assimilation led only over the chasm defined by the dichotomy of *mexicano* and *extranjero*. Indeed, the revolutionary rhetoric encouraged the foreign colonies to reinforce self-segregation.[18]

Compounding these anxieties, an unrelated event, the Great Depression of 1929, challenged virtually every business in Mexico, including the Casa Boker. In Mexico, the Depression came three years early, following a plunge in the price of silver and other mineral exports; it deepened as oil companies began to shift their operations into other countries, and it culminated after the infamous Black Friday of October 1929 inaugurated the collapse of the U.S. economy. Between 1926 and 1932, real per capita GNP fell by almost 31 percent, reflecting a severe contraction of demand for consumer goods and to a prolonged crisis in the manufacturing sector. Having hovered at a parity of 2 with the U.S. dollar for more than twenty years, not counting paper money, the peso declined to 3.60 in 1934, and to 5.19 five years later. Fortunately for the Casa Boker, demand for producer goods such as tools and machinery remained relatively stable, as President Calles and his successors continued spending on roads and other infrastructure projects, which in turn benefited the company's large clients.[19] Although the Casa Boker sold many consumer goods, the resilience of a producer goods market supported by government spending helped the company weather the Great Depression—and even more so, in a growing city. In an ironic twist, Mexico's degree of underdevelopment also helped, as the very shallowness of the market that had limited the potential of the Casa Boker in good years protected it from the trough of the Great Depression. In a country in which only an estimated 5 to 10 percent of the population bought industrial products, the market did not react dynamically to the highs and lows of the economy, and most of those who bought from the Casa Boker in 1920 continued to do so in 1930.[20]

Amidst postrevolutionary turmoil and economic crisis, U.S. influence in Mexico City continued to increase. The American colony in the capital more than doubled, with the wealthiest members buying mansions in posh new subdivisions such as Lomas de Chapultepec, a new development far west on the Paseo de la Reforma.[21] Along with affluent investors and professionals, a plethora of U.S. intellectuals came to Mexico to view a revolution from up close. These "political pilgrims" included progressive journalists such as Carleton Beals and Ernest Gruening as well as eminent writers such as Katherine Anne Porter and John Steinbeck. They joined Rivera and his fellow Marxist muralists David Alfaro Siqueiros and José Clemente Orozco in forming a left-leaning community in the quaint, colonial village of Coyoacán, about 2 miles east of San Angel and 6 miles south of the city center. Sneered at by the Bokers and their peers, this community became a counterpoint to the foreign ethnic enclaves dominated by conservative entrepreneurs. Unwittingly, the U.S. radicals played an important role in the building of the new state, as their public critique of imperialism and capitalism lent legitimacy to a government that promoted nationalism. In synergy with cultural nationalism, they promoted a national, simplified vision of Mexico that helped the government's attempt to impose such a national vision on Mexico's many *patrias chicas,* or "little fatherlands."

They also provided a new vision of Mexico in the United States—one that portrayed Mexico not as a semisavage nation à la Jack London, but as a country with a rich heritage whose indigenous and mestizo inhabitants were engaged in a quest for justice and national redemption.[22] In turn, this vision helped attract a wave of U.S. tourists. Both radicals and tourists contributed "to the nationalization of cultural expression in Mexico and its projection outside of the country."[23]

These newcomers promoted U.S. popular culture in Mexico City. Although the Porfirians had already embraced recreational activities such as baseball and bicycle riding, U.S. cultural influence had been limited to a relatively thin veneer of society.[24] After the revolution, however, the advent of mass communication and transportation lifted the United States into the role formerly occupied by France.[25] Marketed cleverly by corporations, U.S. popular culture permeated Mexico City. As one historian has described, "the bob was replacing the classic braid of the Mexican woman. Jazz and chewing gum became popular, as did English-language phrases, expensive cars, weekends, the beach and women's sports."[26] In this desire to emulate gringo culture, not even the traditional salon, a prominent symbol of the French cultural influence prevalent in the Porfirian capital, escaped unchanged, as "waltzes and mazurkas gave way to the saxophone playing the hit parade."[27]

Mexican cultural nationalism, economic crisis, and the "Americanization" of popular culture were all in large measure by-products of closer commercial relations that also deepened the process of industrialization in Mexico. The revolution had not tempered the flow of U.S. investments: by 1920, U.S. direct investment in Mexico had at least doubled from the level of 1910.[28] Despite stormy relations between the U.S. and Mexican governments, this trend continued into the 1920s, a decade that witnessed the "consolidation rather than expansion" of U.S. investments.[29] These investments changed in quality rather than quantity: while many U.S. citizens sold their rural properties, U.S. corporations invested in utility companies and infrastructure. In particular, Ford, Colgate-Palmolive, and other U.S. corporations took advantage of an oil-financed boom earlier in the decade—a boom that had increased the spending power of middle-class Mexicans—to invest into new industries. The first phase of industrialization had led to the domestic mass production of beer, "heavy" hardware, and textiles; this second phase focused on chemicals, drugs, dyes, and household goods.[30] The involvement of foreign investors in import-substitution industrialization demonstrated that U.S. corporations and the Mexican government had found common ground in an effort to fuse "Mexican nationalism and capitalism into the patriotic project of Mexican development."[31] Neither the Great Depression nor the oil expropriation, two events that led to capital flight out of Mexico, could reverse this trend. The Bokers, of course, could ill criticize the move toward import-substitution industrialization, as Franz remained a principal shareholder in El Anfora.

In turn, industrialization spurred the further development of Mexican consumer culture. The emergence of a limited internal market for consumer goods had begotten the Mexican department store, and Friederichs had built the "white elephant" to capture these new opportunities in retail capitalism. During the postrevolutionary decades, these opportunities vastly increased through rural electrification; road building and the coming of the automobile; new mass media and the rise of advertising; and the repatriation of thousands of Chicano workers. U.S. travelers observed that consumerism had even penetrated many Mexican villages: Eyler Simpson, for example, heard the St. Louis Blues played by a rural band. In Mexico City, members of a small, but growing entrepreneurial bourgeoisie bought imported cars; white-collar employees acquired radios; even many of the working poor consumed toothpaste and soap from Colgate-Palmolive.[32] The Great Depression slowed this trend only briefly.

The emergence of a consumer culture challenged entrepreneurs like Franz Böker, who favored strategies of advertising and distribution that targeted a limited circle of male insiders. Significantly, Franz concentrated on serving its existing customers rather than finding new ones through the new media.[33] With some justification, he banked on the fact that the Casa Boker had achieved renown as the preeminent hardware store of the nation: according to an employee based in Chiapas, Tzotzil people who hardly spoke Spanish used the word "Arbolito" to mean "knife" or "razor blade."[34] So synonymous was the Casa Boker with hardware that the company gained notoriety for reportedly selling the pick ax used to kill Soviet exile Leon Trotsky in his Mexico City home.[35] These vignettes suggest that the CFM succeeded in promoting the products of the Casa Boker by means of their network of agents, who sold exclusively to retail and wholesale merchants, and they explain why Franz and his associates saw little need to advertise more aggressively. The Bokers therefore differed markedly from French and Spanish entrepreneurs as well as U.S. direct marketers. There was no Ernest Pugibet in their family who promoted his products with sexy billboards and glossy advertisements.[36]

This reluctance to feed the culture of mass consumption was also rooted in Franz's opposition to the United States. From the time of his first visit en route to Mexico City, Franz disliked the country that Mexicans call the northern colossus. He believed that the United States lacked the cultural sophistication of Europe, and he viewed "Americans" as materialists who worshipped the god of conspicuous consumption. This critique resembled the assessment expressed in *Ariel,* written by the Uruguayan writer José Enrique Rodó. Interestingly, Franz applied it primarily to the U.S. North, the very area that had helped his father rise to prominence. In his perspective, "money [had] won out over culture" in the Civil War, and he bemoaned the fall of the Old South, which he romanticized as a positive alternative to what he considered an increasingly materialist world.[37] After 1917, President Wilson's declaration of war on Germany accentuated this aversion; in fact, Wilson became the bogeyman due to his policies toward *both* Germany and Mexico.[38] Like many Germans, Franz opposed the United States (and Wilson's Democrats in particular) due to its entry into World War I on the side of the Allies.[39] Like nationalist Mexicans, he identified the new mass market with a pernicious, modern "Americanism" that represented U.S. hegemony. He and Luise did anticipate the crucial importance of the English language in a globalized economy. Therefore, they retained a U.S. maid, and both of their daughters spent several months as au pairs in Canada.[40]

In the long term, Franz's rejection of consumerism limited the opportunities of the Casa Boker. Franz considered himself frugal and modest, immune to the wasteful ways of the twentieth century. As someone who had brought the ethos of the kingly merchant back to the Casa Boker after Friederichs's flirtations with consumer culture, he had always considered advertising a superfluous expense. He was confident that the existing customers of the Casa Boker, many of them professionals and resellers, would remain loyal. Franz also believed that his company's products constituted "necessities" rather than luxurious frills such as the expensive clothes available at the Palacio de Hierro. In addition, the Casa Boker found unspectacular, but steady success in the postrevolutionary era—success that offered little reason for drastic changes in the operation of the Casa Boker other than the need to give the company a more "Mexican" appearance.

The "Mexicanization" of the Casa Boker

The Casa Boker found steady success in the postrevolutionary era. With the exception of the worst years of the Great Depression, the CFM managed to realize such handsome earnings that Franz, in hindsight, called them the "fat" years of his time with the company.[41] The wholesale operation of the Casa Boker eclipsed that of its main rival, the venerable Sommer, Herrmann y Cía. Not only had Sommer, Herrmann's net of provincial branch retail stores operated by that company suffered far more than the Mexico City businesses from the violence of the revolutionary years, but that company was also handicapped by its failure to offer U.S. merchandise. The mainstay of the business since the construction of the Edificio Boker, the retail department did even better. After the Great Depression wiped out many establishments that sold consumer goods, the Casa Boker offered Chrysler vehicles, Rosenthal china, dolls, paints, and toys, as well as kitchenware.[42] These items replaced the heavy steel products of the Fundidora de Fierro y Acero de Monterrey, the sale of which ceased after a government decree prohibited large trucks in the Centro. As a result, in 1935, only 10 percent of all products sold in the Casa Boker came from Mexico, down from 18 percent in 1911 (see Table 3).

Although it had consolidated its position in Mexico, the Casa Boker was not impervious to the vicissitudes of the economy. Before the Great Depression, the CFM employed almost 150 people, including 25 Germans and German-Mexicans as well as more than a dozen traveling agents. By the early 1930s, the effects of the global economic crisis drastically lowered earnings: in the four years from 1931 to 1934, the CFM only reported profits totaling 75,000 gold pesos (see Table 7). The crisis led Franz to reduce the personnel and the space that the CFM occupied within the Edificio Boker. By 1935, only 130 employees remained. Having replaced machinery and agricultural implements with smaller items such as toys and china, Franz rented out space in the building to tenants and small companies, and eight apprentices from Germany lived in small rooms under the roof.[43] In the late 1930s, the company experienced another slump in the wake of the expropriation of the oil industry, before rebounding in the initial phase of World War II. This expansion led the CFM to add more than 30 employees to the payroll to bring the total up to 165.[44] As Table 7 demonstrates, the success of the Casa Boker remained closely tied to the volume of Mexico's foreign imports. The two troughs corresponded to the Great Depression and the oil controversy, respectively, and when imports recovered, so did the Casa Boker.

The strategy of the firm during these years combined a defensive and pessimistic general orientation with a flexible response to the everyday challenges of doing business in postrevolutionary Mexico. The three directors of the Casa Boker, which included two fellow Remscheid natives along with Franz Böker, remained in the world of the nineteenth century, an era when kingly merchants responded to consumers' needs rather than creating them. Fear of change and pessimism conditioned Franz's actions. During good years, he predicted a downturn; during bad ones, he predicted disaster. Instead of putting surplus capital to work in the new industries as he had done in El Anfora, Franz invested in real estate. Rather than aggressively trying

Table 7: Earnings of CFM, 1920–1940,
Compared to Value of Mexican Imports

Year	Reported Earnings (in thousands of pesos)	Mexican Imports (in millions of pesos)
1920	236	397
1921	301	494
1922	285	400
1923	302	315
1924	201	321
1925	244	289
1926	320	391
1927	373	364
1928	385	358
1929	505	383
1930	335	350
1931	10	217
1932	−9	180
1933	30	245
1934	44	331
1935	175	407
1936	335	457
1937	397	617
1938	133	460
1939	183	680
1940	364	961

Sources: Asambleas Ordinarias, 1920–1929, AB, FA; folder 37, AB, FFLB; Nacional Financiera, "Statistics on the Mexican Economy," 385.[45]

to expand market share, he remained content to defend the commercial niche of the Casa Boker. Nonetheless, the business adapted well to the rapidly changing Mexican environment. In particular, Franz and his lawyers designed schemes that minimized the effects of postrevolutionary legislation and labor activism on the Casa Boker. Most importantly, a series of reforms to the CFM statutes gave the company a more "Mexican" and less "German" appearance, an aspect that would assume crucial significance in its struggle for survival during and after World War II.[46] In August 1919, the shareholders of the CFM eliminated the Comité Consultivo. Composed of the most significant shareholders who resided in Germany, this board had become a liability in an era when the law required Mexican nationality of the owners of family businesses.[47] In 1932, another amendment stipulating that the company considered itself Mexican and that it would not invoke

German diplomatic protection brought the CFM into compliance with a new Mexican law.[48]

As a further and even more important step, the Bokers created a secret holding company, the Fondo A, that helped them camouflage the fact that the Casa Boker continued in German ownership. Comprising the total assets of the Casa Boker, the Fondo A became a convenient tool to hide the nationality of the shareholders from nosy government authorities and allowed the directors to assemble a war chest of hidden funds. The fund initially contained only the CFM, then it gradually acquired other assets excluded from official bookkeeping, including stocks, bonds, cash, and gold coins. Franz kept a detailed ledger on the Fondo A, as each of the 2,250 shares of the old CFM amounted to a corresponding share in the new fund. Franz's trick created two different sets of owners. On the one hand, there were the *ostensible* shareholders of the CFM, in their vast majority Mexican citizens. On the other hand, there was the *actual* share-owning majority of the Casa Boker, which, as reflected in the Fondo A, still resided in Germany.[49] In 1933, for example, 2,171 of the CFM shares were in the hands of a Mexican-born employee of the company, while only 73 shares remained with Franz.[50] Yet, in reality, the Casa Boker continued in majority German ownership. To begin with, Franz's three sisters had each inherited 25 percent of Robert's shares. Upon his father's death in 1912, Franz owned 437 shares, including some of his uncles' shares that he had purchased, while his sisters owned 853. Moreover, Friederichs's interest had passed to his son Carlitos. On the eve of World War II, individuals other than Robert's descendants still owned almost 40 percent of the Fondo A.[51]

Far from mere camouflage, however, the Fondo A was also a mechanism to funnel money to Germany and, thus, a good example of a culturally determined business decision. Reflecting Franz's notion that rewarding the German "shareholders" was more important than the growth of the company, the Fondo A paid out a dividend as high as 12 percent in good years. Although the dividend kept Franz's German relatives happy during the chaotic early Weimar years, the capital outflow forestalled any possibility of expanding the position of the Casa Boker in El Anfora or other Mexican industrial ventures. Indeed, Franz used his own dividend income (as well as his share of the 39 percent of net profits that went to the directors) toward a gradual buyout of the German "shareholders," which became increasingly difficult as the Germans realized that their stake in the Fondo A was an excellent investment safe from taxing authorities. Shortly before World War II, Franz and Gunther even transferred a large amount of money to a German bank that paid the dividend throughout and after the war.[52]

The CFM also confronted the Labor Law of 1931, a law that forced midsized firms to allow unions. Before this legislation took effect, individual labor contracts had regulated the relationship between the company and its workers. Employees had virtually no negotiating power, and the CFM could fire workers who participated in strikes or pickets.[53] When the Labor Law prohibited such practices, Franz and his lawyers created a mechanism to prevent pickets of the Edificio Boker. They established the Compañía de Inversiones La Esperanza, S.A., a real estate company with a capital of 100,000 pesos that subsequently purchased the Edificio Boker from the CFM. This new structure prevented pickets of the Edificio Boker by CFM employees, as the law allowing pickets only applied to buildings owned by the company that employed the workers who desired to express a grievance. Leasing living and office space to more than a dozen individuals and small companies in addition to the CFM, La Esperanza employed only a handful of janitors, a workforce so small that many of the benefits of the Labor Law did not extend to them.[54]

As it turned out, Franz need not have worried, as the new labor union, the Unión de Empleados y Trabajadores de la Compañía Ferretera Mexicana (UET), proved a pliant collective bargaining partner. Founded in 1932, the UET organized 103, or about two-thirds of the employees.[55] Twenty Mexicans in managerial and midlevel positions dominated the union, and one of them, José Arturo Pliego, became the first Mexican to rise to the rank of director.[56] As its first labor contracts illustrate, the UET had very limited negotiating power, because all important personnel decisions remained in the hands of the directors. The CFM gave the UET the bare minimum: the constitutionally mandated forty-eight-hour workweek, six days of vacation time, and basic health insurance. But as Table 8 shows, the UET did negotiate pay raises for its lowest-paid workers: while the cost of food increased 65 percent, between 1933 and 1939 wages rose 81 percent.[57] For the higher-paid employees, the CFM instead implemented an informal profit-sharing scheme that gave them a stake in the success of the Casa Boker. Between 1930 and 1941, upper- and midlevel employees received between 35 and 50 percent of official earnings as their share of the profits.[58] As a result, the UET leadership cooperated with management until declining profits and inflation put pressure on real pay after 1942.[59]

Given this co-optation of labor, it was not surprising that Cardenismo proved harmless to the Casa Boker. While Cárdenas fomented the centralization of labor under the CTM (Confederación de Trabajadores Mexicanos, or Mexican Workers' Federation), the "white" UET remained outside the CTM. For example, in February 1936, the

Table 8: Maximum and Minimum Wages in the CFM, 1933–1939

Year	Maximum Monthly Pay (in pesos)	Minimum Weekly Pay (in pesos)
1933	300	13.50
1937	325	18.00
1939	370	24.50

Source: Contratos de Trabajo, AB, FS.

UET disobeyed a strike called by a CTM affiliate organization against the Casa Boker. The reason for this strike was a labor dispute in the El Anfora stoneware factory, which the strikers connected to the Casa Boker by way of Franz's stake in that company. Much to the Bokers' surprise, the Mexico City Justice Department ordered the CTM affiliate to end their strike.[60] Two years later, a youth organization organized an anti-Fascist vigil at the Casa Boker and two major Japanese and Spanish firms in Mexico City. The Bokers mobilized support from the National Chamber of Commerce, and Mexican authorities ended the vigil after a few days.[61]

Life and work in the Casa Boker in this second heyday of the company resembled that of the Porfirian era, with its emphasis on order and discipline, and sharp distinctions between German and Mexican employees. As the most apparent difference, there were no U.S. citizens on the payroll: the directors and the twenty highest-ranking employees were Germans. With the exception of a handful of German apprentices, the rest were Mexican. These apprentices cycled through all departments, including those requiring menial tasks. They initially spent months in the unpacking room before moving up to the floor of the department store. For working forty-eight hours per week including Saturdays, they received 350 pesos per month: seven times as much as the lowest-paid Mexican employee, but less than one-tenth of the pay of one of the directors. In that fashion, the apprentices, who usually were from wealthy merchant families and served a stint of three to four years before returning home, learned humility in the Casa Boker. Only toward the end of their time in the Casa Boker did the apprentices get the chance to learn about the business aspects of the company. The directors even made Franz's oldest son, Gunther, take the same route, although the heir rose all the way from the packing room to general director in four years. The apprentices' exposure to the lowliest work, however, did not mean that Franz encouraged the social interaction between them and their Mexican colleagues, or that he promoted their contact with Mexican culture. To feed them, the directors hired a German cook, who alternated traditional German dishes with an occasional taco or enchilada; meanwhile, a cantina served the Mexican workers. Franz even reprimanded a young German intern who wanted to join the CFM soccer team, made up of only Mexicans. In his view, a "respectable" German in Mexico pursued his recreation with compatriots and practiced rowing or horseback riding rather than this proletarian British game.[62]

Growing up Under the Bell Jar

These vignettes of everyday life in the Casa Boker yield important clues about Franz and Luise's attitude toward their Mexican-born children (see Table 9). Although they both had come to know Mexico much more intimately than the elder generation, they were adamant about limiting the Mexicanization of their offspring. Like many Germans in Mexico, they not only displayed a defensive attitude so far as their business behavior was concerned, but they also sought to stall the natural and inevitable process of acculturation that they themselves had begun during more than two decades of residence in Mexico City. As with the Casa Boker, the results of these attempts were mixed.

In their efforts to isolate their children from Mexican influences, Franz and Luise first raised them under what their eldest daughter, Gabriele, called "the bell jar."[63] Until 1926, the Bokers used the existence of German cultural institutions as a shield from Mexican influences. Most importantly, all six of them attended the "German track" of the Colegio Alemán. Apart from communication with the

---

Table 9: Franz and Luise Böker and Their Children
(Casa Boker employees in bold)

Franz Böker b: Mar. 24, 1877, Remscheid, Germany; d: Aug. 18, 1965, Mexico City.
∞ Julia Luise Pocorny b: May 9, 1882, Lennep, Germany; d: Sept. 11, 1977, Mexico City.
  1. Gabriele Boker b: Apr. 27, 1905, Mexico City; d: Feb. 27, 1995, Warleberg, Germany.
  ∞ Franz Wilhelm Buchenau b: Sept. 29, 1900, Torreón; d: Mar. 13, 1969, Mexico City.
  2. Elisabeth Boker b: Sept. 18, 1906, Mexico City; d: June 21, 1933, Wismar, Germany.
  ∞ Alfred Vermehren b: July 18, 1906, Torreón; d: 1987, Tuxpan, Mich., Mexico.
  3. **Gunther Boker** b: Apr. 11, 1909, Mexico City; d: June 6, 1993, Mexico City.
  ∞ Margot Trauwitz b: Feb. 25, 1919, Mexico City; d: Feb. 16, 2001, Mexico City.
  4. **Helmuth Boker** b: July 24, 1915, Mexico City; d: Feb. 11, 1995, Mexico City.
  ∞ Ruth Schwartzkopff b: July 30, 1924, Kassel, Germany.
  5a. Johann Peter Boker b: May 21, 1918, Mexico City d: June 19, 1940, France.
  5b. Klaus Boker b: May 21, 1918, Mexico City d: January 24, 1942, Tobruk, Libya.

family's servants, the children were not allowed to speak Spanish inside the home. Life in the posh Casa Amarilla and in German institutions engulfed the young Bokers to such an extent that German, and not Spanish, became their first language. Although they spoke Spanish fluently and idiomatically, a slight German accent betrayed the existence of the bell jar into their old age. Far from embracing the type of assimilation expected of the children of German immigrants to the United States, Gabriele and her siblings clung to their German heritage. Their life under the bell jar typified the efforts of the foreign colonies in Mexico City to preserve the home culture. With the exception of the Spaniards, these colonies continued to cultivate a sense of separateness, both from one another and from the host society. Their members acquired a "colonialist consciousness" that emphasized their sense of superiority over the host society and that, especially for women, limited everyday contacts with Mexicans other than servants.[64] During the late 1920s, German families formed a veritable "Little Germany" in the suburb of Tacubaya that even included a German butcher and deli store.[65]

It was not surprising that this ethnic self-segregation elicited criticism in postrevolutionary Mexico. In 1935, the Bokers and other German *ferreteros* became the target of such criticism in a Mexican melodrama filmed under the direction of the famous Fernando de Fuentes. *La Familia Dressel* features a zealous German woman, her son, and his Mexican wife, who finds herself vilified by her mother-in-law because she is not German. Although shots of a hardware store in 16 de Septiembre and a villa in a posh suburb strongly suggest the Bokers as a point of reference, the Dressel family does not resemble them either physically or in terms of the story described in the film. As press reviews of the film show, however, many Mexicans considered *La Familia Dressel* an allegory of the Bokers. The fact that de Fuentes used the German colony for his sketch of the relations between the native and foreign-born bourgeoisie of the capital demonstrates that he viewed the German colony (and, presumably, the Bokers as some of its most visible exponents) as the epitome of the segregated foreign communities of the capital. At the same time, the film—and particularly its happy denouement—demonstrates de Fuentes's admiration for supposed German virtues such as discipline, industriousness, thrift, and loyalty.[66]

Just like Frau Dressel, Luise noticed that the German bell jar did not work well enough to suit the purposes of raising her children exclusively in German traditions. Most importantly, it could not keep out Mexican influences. Mexicans continued to make up the majority of the students at the Colegio Alemán, and a growing number of children from mixed marriages, many of whom spoke Spanish as their first language, blurred the boundaries between who was German and who was Mexican. Even the young Bokers playfully mixed German and Spanish in a unique and idiosyncratic blend typical of a bilingual environment.[67] Finally, the bell jar also failed to nurture an emotional and intellectual connection of German-Mexicans with an organic, changing culture in the faraway home country.

Instead, Franz and Luise's strenuous efforts to raise Germans in Mexico led to what one might call "deculturation," a process of disconnection from the ancestral culture. Their point of reference was the German Empire, a past episode in history that they increasingly idealized as their years in Mexico went by.[68] When the family visited Germany in 1922 after ten years in revolutionary Mexico, Franz and Luise noticed that the culture they transmitted to their children no longer corresponded to the realities of the 1920s.[69] Moreover, life in isolated Tlacopac had spoiled Gabriele and her siblings, as servants catered to their every need. Nothing describes the situation of the young Bokers better than the following firsthand observations about the typical Mexican-born child of U.S. parents:

> His contacts with Mexicans seldom exceed those of his parents. He usually attends the American school; if he does find Mexican playmates they speak English and are learning his ways. . . . He is cared for by a maid over whom he soon learns to assume authority; he is not required to do anything for himself and becomes dependent upon servants for his needs. So long as he remains in Mexico he is not in a position between the two cultures and there is little conflict in his situation. It is when he leaves Mexico that he finds conflicts because life there has not equipped him to meet the conditions which he finds in the United States. It is when he leaves Mexico that he finds himself in a marginal position.[70]

By weakening the ties with the real Germany, the deculturation of the Bokers had created the conditions for their eventual acculturation into Mexico. This situation left Franz and Luise with two choices: accept the gradual hybridization of their children, or transplant them to Germany. In the case of their teenage daughters, Gabriele and Liesel, the decision was easy enough: both moved to Germany after their graduation from the Colegio Alemán. The four younger boys, however, who ranged in age from thirteen to four, returned to Mexico City. Franz had come to feel at home in their host society, and he did not believe that the Casa Boker could survive his absence.[71]

Figure 10: The first "Mexicans:" Gabriele and
Liesel Boker (Archivo Boker, Mexico City).

Figure 11: Little masters and their servants (From left: Gunther Boker, two
unidentified servants, Helmuth Boker) (Nachlass Gabriele Buchenau).

Figure 12: Returning home as a "foreigner:" Gunther Boker's immigration permit (Archivo Histórico de la Secretaría de Relaciones Exteriores, Mexico City).

Back in the Casa Amarilla, however, Luise had second thoughts. For twenty years, she had experienced firsthand that it was easier for a male merchant to live in Mexico than for his wife. While Don Pancho consorted with social equals in the workplace, Luise made conversation with her servants and children, relying only on an extensive network of other German women in Mexico to find friendship. Meanwhile, Franz had developed a genuine affection for his host country: after scarcely a week in Germany, he missed "the dust of Mexico" as well as the wide-open spaces of the Mexican landscape and the hospitality of its people.[72] Mexican fatalist philosophy struck a chord with this deeply pessimistic man: he may well have said with Octavio Paz that "a realist is always a pessimist."[73]

Equally important, the German colony continued to evolve from a merchant diaspora to a more diverse community. After World War I, as immigration restrictions diverted traditional migrant flows from the United States to Canada and Latin America, Mexico—although still a relatively unpopular destination for most lower-class migrants— became the new home of tens of thousands of immigrants. In addition, following the lead of Ford and Colgate-Palmolive, German corporations such as a chemical consortium that included BASF, Bayer, and Hoechst sent their agents to Mexico.[74] Thus, the 1930 census counted more than 2,325 Germans in Mexico City, an increase of 650 over the 1921 figures. Families connected with merchant establishments only made up 24 percent of the colony, down from 61 percent in 1910, and many of the new arrivals were poorer than the established families.[75] Correspondingly, their outlook on their new country differed from that of the Bokers. Many of them optimistically viewed Mexico as a Promised Land of golden opportunities. Those who were more critical seldom shared the Bokers' perspective on Mexican society. The most famous of the German-speaking critics, the mysterious B. Traven, hardly endeared himself to the Bokers when he wrote impassioned novels that attacked the exploitation of workers and indigenous peasants.[76]

Franz and Luise joined other Porfirian-era immigrants in resenting the new immigrants. As Luise wrote, they were of the "worst sort, with hair-raising ideas. They will soon be surprised about this country, [and, in particular] the difficulty of making money. They should rather go back immediately, because the Indio will scoff at their pretensions."[77] Of course, Luise did not include in her harsh judgment the thousands of German-speaking Mennonites who arrived in the northern states of Chihuahua and Durango. The Mennonites did not shun hard work and established themselves in arid rural areas. In procuring the implements necessary for planting and irrigation, they became some of the most important customers of the Casa Boker. Moreover, the Bokers benefited from the influx of Germans: by 1940, they had hired several of them to bring the total number of German speakers up to around thirty.[78]

Not surprisingly, increasing disagreements divided the German colony. The old merchant families (and the professionals and white-collar employees who had arrived during the Porfiriato) were well established financially and had acquired an intimate knowledge of Mexico through their experience with the revolution. The poorer new-comers knew little about Mexico and often intended to use the country as a stepping stone to the United States. Moreover, the Germans diverged widely in their political views. A majority of the "old colony" supported conservative parties such as General Paul von Hindenburg's DNVP (German National People's Party) that dreamed of restoring the German monarchy. The more recent arrivals reflected the same broad range of political opinions that had elected representatives from more than twenty different parties to the Reichstag. Over time, however, pressure from employers and the realization that almost all Germans in Mexico were relatively wealthy compared to their host society prompted a rightward shift in many newcomers. This shift was manifested in the burgeoning membership of von Lübeck's ultraconservative VDR, one of the primary vehicles of German propaganda during World War I. A rival, avowedly democratic organization, the Vereinigung Deutscher Republikaner (Union of German Republicans) attracted but a few dozen adherents.[79] Even before Hitler's triumph, the stage was set for the Nazification of the colony.

The ongoing difficulties to establish a Lutheran Church illustrated some of these differences between "old" and "new" Germans. Most of the old colony remained indifferent toward the church, considering it one of the least important of the German associations. In large part for lack of tithes from the most solvent sector of the German colony, the Lutherans worshipped in a concert hall during the 1920s, where, as Pastor Johannes Reichardt reported, "lewd decorations featuring Venus and lovebirds threatened the quiet devotion of . . . visitors."[80] In light of widespread support from middle-class Germans, however, Reichardt received financial backing for the construction of a church building from the Lutheran umbrella organization in Berlin as well as a subsidy for the pastor. Due to the continuous squabbling among the colony, the building project languished until 1957, when the German Lutheran Church finally found a home in the suburb of Mixcoac.[81] The Bokers stayed aloof from the Lutheran Church and even waited until Luise moved the family to Germany to have their three youngest children baptized.[82] Before the end of World War II, the family did not consider as one of its obligations helping the church. In this regard, the Bokers were typical of the merchant elite. Not even the fact that the U.S.-based Missouri Synod began to woo German Lutherans in the mid-1920s could encourage the Bokers and their peers to give up their indifference toward the church.[83]

The German experience in postrevolutionary Mexico City resembled the situation of the French, but not that of the Spanish colony. Like the Germans, the Barcelonnette community distinguished between old and new arrivals. While department store owners such as the Michel clan that owned the Puerto de Liverpool continued to prosper, migration from Barcelonnette to Mexico City was no longer a pipeline into the commercial elite. Instead, it became a path to respectability in the best cases, and at worst, a ticket back to the French Alps.[84] The Spanish colony, by contrast, remained more unified. As Clara Lida has demonstrated, the conservative Spanish colony accepted and even welcomed thousands of left-leaning refugees during and after the Spanish Civil War.[85]

In 1926, Franz and Luise reluctantly decided to break up the family in order to raise their children the way they wanted. Playing her gendered role as primary transmitter of German culture, Luise moved herself and her four sons to Lennep, her hometown near Remscheid. Two years later, the family moved to Bonn, and in 1936, the Bokers built a large house in nearby Bad Godesberg. Added to the value represented by the Casa Amarilla, the construction of this expensive house was further evidence that Franz put his money in relatively unproductive real estate rather than reinvesting it into the company. He visited his family whenever his schedule permitted: between 1926 and 1938, he crossed the Atlantic twenty-four times, devoting several months each summer to his family.[86] But the children did not visit him there: as his son Helmuth later explained, "Mexico . . . was kept away from [the] children. One almost had the impression that our father worried that one of us might consider returning to the land of our birth. We were supposed to finish our education in Germany and avoid falling into the hands of a nice little Mexican woman."[87]

Not surprisingly, life in an ethnic enclave and the subsequent move to Germany engendered deep contradictions in the formation of identity among the children. Each in their own way, the six children sought to resolve these contradictions as they grew into adulthood. A sketch of two of these children—Gabriele and Gunther—demonstrates important differences of personality, education, and gender in a process of acculturation that affected primarily the elder children who had grown up in Mexico. These differences shaped the first into a German nationalist who resented Mexico, and the second into someone who felt German but often thought like a Mexican.

Born in 1905, Gabriele completed the entire curriculum of the Colegio Alemán up to her Abitur in 1922. Shy and unassuming by nature, she allowed her parents to make her into a surrogate mother to her four younger brothers. After a short stay in Canada, where she became fluent in English, she moved to Berlin. The first university student in the family, she studied preschool pedagogy at the Humboldt University. In 1928, she married a fellow German-Mexican, Franz ("Pancho") Buchenau, whom she had met in the "Antares" rowing club in Xochimilco south of Mexico City. Together with his father-in-law, Julius Vermehren, Buchenau's father had established a highly successful agricultural implements store that owned large tracts of land near Torreón, Coahuila. Franz Buchenau later became the manager of Heinrich Böker and Company in Solingen, where the couple had five sons, including this author's father. Although Gabriele and Franz obtained German passports, they did not notify the Mexican government and thus left open the option of seeking Mexican citizenship later in life.[88]

Gabriele embraced her father's values and moral standards. She shared his asceticism as well as his disdain for pomp and ostentation, and she resented her mother's penchant for luxury and consumption. Gabriele had low expectations of what life had to offer, but high expectations of what she owed to others. She regarded her life as a set of duties: to her father, to her husband, to her children, and even to her grandchildren. Stoic and prudish, she rejected pleasure as a fleeting source of satisfaction, instead finding fulfillment in serving her family. Her outlook was anachronistic: she once remarked that the Enlightenment, which took place 150 years before her birth, marked the beginning of the decline of Western civilization into decadence, corruption, and arrogance. At the same time, however, her studies in Berlin nurtured a progressive attitude toward children. As much as she held fellow adults to a strict yardstick of Prussian discipline, she believed that children needed to explore their individuality with minimum strictures.[89]

With the possible exception of her grandmother Auguste, Gabriele was the one Boker who most disliked Mexico, to the extent that her sons absorbed these prejudices "with [their] mother's milk."[90] She considered the country dirty, its government corrupt, its people superstitious and untrustworthy, and its climate unhealthy. Although she lived more than forty years in the country of her birth, she considered herself a German born abroad. The items she left her heirs upon her death in 1995 demonstrated this identification with Germany: her library was almost entirely German, and her handwritten cookbook contained only one Mexican recipe. Gabriele's dislike of Mexico came from several different sources. Perhaps most importantly, her family expected her to serve as another transmitter of German culture. Like her mother and thousands of other daughters of foreign immigrants, Gabriele did not have any opportunity to interact with Mexicans from a social class that corresponded to her own. As unequal relationships, the contacts she did have only deepened Gabriele's contempt for Mexican society. Moreover, as a woman, she could not freely move around as her brothers did. Finally, the older Gabriele never experienced the kind of luxury known by the other Boker women of her time. When she returned to Mexico in 1948, she lived in austere conditions, and unlike her mother and sisters-in-law, she did not have servants to tend to her needs. The following decades gave her another reason to connect Mexico with bad memories: Pancho's ongoing affair with a woman of mixed German and Mexican ancestry.[91]

Nevertheless, the country of her birth had shaped Gabriele more than she would have liked to admit. In fact, a closer examination of her life reveals hidden transcripts of a subtle rebellion against the exclusive German identity expected of her.[92] As the presence of a dozen books on the Aztecs and Mayas in her personal library attests, she admired Mexico's ancient civilizations. She also treasured the country's unique ecology. When she moved back to Germany in 1969, she brought dozens of cactus plants with her. Until her death, she frequently used typical Mexican expressions such as "ni modo" (a way of saying "it doesn't matter") among her family. Finally, even her culinary choices were more diverse than her cookbook would suggest, as she enjoyed cooking black beans and spicy sauces along with German fare.[93]

Gunther, by contrast, cast his lot with Mexico. Battling a lifelong stomach ailment, he was a frail, kindly, and timid individual rather than the tough merchant Franz desired in his successor. Born in 1911, Gunther shared his father's plight in that his parents chose a profession for him that did not match his own aspirations, or even his talents. In his dreams, he directed a symphony orchestra or studied history, and he viewed his call to the Casa Boker as an obligation rather than a privilege. He attended the Colegio Alemán but completed his schooling in Bonn. After an apprenticeship in an export firm in Hamburg, he returned to Mexico in 1933 to begin work in the Casa Boker. Within four years, he had become director of the CFM, which allowed his father to retire. Like Gabriele, Gunther married a German-Mexican, the former Margot Trauwitz, with whom he had five children. Unlike Gabriele, however, he never claimed German citizenship. His failure to opt for Mexican citizenship upon adulthood forced him to apply for a visa on his return to Mexico in 1933; he thereafter obtained a "Certificate of Nationality" that identified him as a Mexican citizen by birth.[94]

Gunther's choice of spouse manifested that the soft Gunther and his spry older sister were polar opposites in many ways. Margot Trauwitz was loquacious, fun loving, and extroverted; Franz Buchenau appeared taciturn, workaholic, and inscrutable. Margot was the first member of the family who showed visible signs of acculturation. The daughter of a mine owner, she lived her earliest years in Zacatecas, before her family moved to the capital. Her only experience living in Germany came during the late 1930s, when she trained as a neonatal nurse in a hospital. Deeply rooted in Mexico, she learned impeccable Spanish and took on Mexican mannerisms, and only her husband's chronic illness kept her from asking her maids to cook spicy Mexican fare. Franz Buchenau, by contrast, moved to Germany at the age of seven, served in the German army during World War I, and remained in Germany until 1940 except for a two-year stint in New York City.[95]

As a man who interacted with the Mexico City bourgeoisie, Gunther felt at home in the country of his birth. He loved Mexico's natural beauty; he treasured the politeness and etiquette of its inhabitants, and he studied its history. As an executive, he acted the part of a Latin American *patrón*. He threw a blanket of paternalistic benefits over his most important employees, including personal loans and serving as a godfather at baptism ceremonies, and unlike most German employers, he proved more than willing to bend the rules to mete out rewards and punishments to his workers.[96] Moreover, despite the fact that he often derided Mexican politicians, he cultivated ties to national leaders. Unlike his father, Gunther knew how to flatter the *políticos,* and his innate desire to please fit into a political culture that valued unctuousness.[97]

Nevertheless, Gunther fashioned himself a German, albeit one from another era. As someone who only spent seven years of his life in Germany, he cultivated a self that no longer corresponded to the nation of which he considered himself a member. His image of Germany resembled the anachronistic and idealized mirage that characterized the mind-set of many members of the old German families in Mexico City. The Germany that he and his family loved was an orderly, socially stable country in which the elite enforced their rules, not one rife with social upheaval and nasty political conflict such as the one that he had witnessed between 1929 and 1933. Reflecting this chasm between the Germany in reality and the one in his head produced by deculturation, Gunther considered himself an *Auslandsdeutscher,* or a German born abroad. In the words of his younger brother Helmuth, an Auslandsdeutscher was somebody of German culture who, due to his or her birth in another country, remained above the fray of the political factions of the mother country.[98] True to Helmuth's characterization, Gunther had much stronger opinions on Mexican and even U.S. politics than on the German political scene. In fact, however, the separation of the Auslandsdeutscher from his home country transcended the realm of politics. Gunther never entertained the idea of moving to Germany, and he is the only one of the six children buried in Mexico. His library was much more diverse than Gabriele's. Along with works on Prussian king Frederick the Great—his favorite historical figure— he owned hundreds of books on the American Civil War as well as many titles on Mexican history and culture. He also did not share Franz and Gabriele's dislike of the United States, making several close friends on his numerous trips to "El Norte."[99]

Of the other four siblings, Liesel's path most resembled Gabriele's, while their three younger brothers fell into a different category altogether. Liesel also married a German born in Torreón, Franz Buchenau's first cousin Alfred Vermehren. Vermehren moved his bride to a farm in the Mecklenburg region, where Liesel died in June 1933 following childbirth. Following the expropriation of farmland in the Soviet zone of Germany, Vermehren later returned to Mexico, and his descendants still operate a farm in Tuxpan, Michoacán.[100] In the youngest children, Franz and Luise's goal of maintaining German culture met with its greatest success. Since these boys moved to Germany between the ages of eight and eleven, they considered Germany their home. Believing that he would never return to the country of his birth, Helmuth, who studied medicine before joining the army, did not face the alternative of rejecting or accepting Mexico that consumed his older brother.[101] Klaus and Peter never did see Mexico again; both died on the fronts of World War II.

Despite the differences among them, the Boker children shared assumptions that defined their generation of German Auslandsdeutsche in Mexico as one that clung to a lost past. The gospel of this generation was Oswald Spengler's *The Decline of the West,* a popular book that predicted the end of Western dominance and the eventual triumph of the non-European cultures. After a social revolution and a lost world war, this book gave meaning to their constructions of their national origins. Along with most other children of European and U.S. immigrants, the Bokers considered their parents' culture far superior to the Mexican. At the same time, they remained aware of the growing nationalism that threatened the established privileges of foreign investors in Mexico. Hence, they did not formally renounce their claim to Mexican citizenship. They also absorbed their father's ultraconservative political ideology marked by a deep mistrust of democratic institutions and staunch opposition to revolutionary nationalism and socialism. In this regard, the first creole Bokers shared the sentiments of many elite Mexicans, whether born to immigrant parents or not.[102]

During the 1920s and 1930s, Franz Böker confronted the legacy of the Mexican Revolution, the transformation of Mexico City in an age of rapidly increasing U.S. influence, and an evolving consumer culture that brought new and aggressive schemes of marketing and distribution. The Casa Boker had acquitted itself well in the first challenge. At a time when protectionism did not yet accompany the nationalist rhetoric, German import firms could still prosper if they camouflaged themselves as Mexican businesses. Firms like the Casa Boker that adapted to the constantly changing legal framework of postrevolutionary Mexico could still rake in profits comparable to those of the Porfirian era. While political conflict and economic crises affected almost all other sectors of the economy, the retail business remained profitable. There were, however, limits to the growth of the Casa Boker, as Franz's defensive rather than proactive management kept the company in a phase of consolidation. At the same time that the Casa Boker shook off its German competitors, Franz failed to expand his company's customer base by means of the emerging consumer culture, and he did not make additional investments into Mexican manufacturing, an area of great future potential.

The Bokers' process of acculturation manifested significant ambiguities. As Franz strove to defend his business against Mexican nationalism, and as he and Luise attempted to inoculate their children against both Mexican and U.S. influences, they lived lives in between that, contrary to their wishes, led to the emergence of hyphenated identities.

Franz and Luise fought the acculturation of their children, natives of Mexico whom their parents desperately wanted to be Germans, and they largely succeeded in their atavistic attempts to keep their Mexican-born children within their own German culture. However, Gabriele and Liesel had married fellow German-Mexicans; Gunther provided a good example of a partially acculturated Boker, and all of the children considered themselves Auslandsdeutsche rather than native Germans. As the Bokers would soon find out, Nazi ideology provided a solution to their dilemma. The implementation of this solution, however, brought about far greater difficulties than they had ever imagined possible.

> Happy families all resemble each other.
> Unhappy families are each unhappy in their own way.
> —Leo Tolstoy, *Anna Karenina*

5

Between the Swastika and the Eagle

The end of the rainy season near, Mexico City was at its most verdant on September 1, 1939. When the sun rose on a beautiful day, the flowers in the garden of the Casa Amarilla radiated a mellow happiness that reflected the prosperity and good fortune of the owners of the garden. This late summer spectacle, however, belied the mood of Franz and Gunther. Alone in Mexico, with the rest of the family scattered throughout Germany, they could not focus on their environment. During the night, Adolf Hitler's troops had mounted a vile attack on Poland that would soon provoke France and Great Britain to declare war on Nazi Germany. While those in Germany—bamboozled by Hitler's press—hoped for a quick end to the war, Franz and Gunther braced themselves for blacklists and millions of deaths.[1]

The Bokers assumed an ambivalent position in the conflict that unified the United States and Mexico as wartime allies against the Axis powers. Franz and Gunther shared in the euphoria provoked by the Nazi triumph in 1933 among the majority in the German colony that had long pined for renewed imperial greatness. Yet they were more concerned about their position in Mexico than about German politics. Sure enough, during the war, the Germans in Mexico got caught between Hitler's aggression and U.S. measures of hemispheric defense. In June 1942, the Mexican declaration of war provoked the government takeover of the Casa Boker. For the Bokers, the seizure of the Casa Boker not only marked the end of their commercial heyday, but also the close of an era in which the family had successfully resisted its integration into Mexican society.

The position of the Bokers between the Nazi swastika and the U.S. eagle yields new insights into Mexican international history in the World War II era. It demonstrates that the Franklin D. Roosevelt administration treated so-called enemy aliens in ways that resembled the subsequent hemisphere-wide hunt for Communists in the cold-war era. The U.S. government placed many Axis nationals—even Mexican descendants of German and Japanese immigrants—without regard to their political convictions, on a blacklist that barred those listed from commercial activities and financial transactions. Not surprisingly, the Mexican government was a reluctant and self-interested ally. It not only resisted U.S. entreaties to extradite Nazis, but it also used the pretext of the Nazi threat to seize much of the wealth of the German colony.

Nazi Strategies and the German Colony in Mexico City

In 1940, the former mayor of Danzig, Hermann Rauschning, published a book in exile that caused a great stir in Mexico. Purporting to contain authentic conversations with Hitler, the book claimed to reveal the grand plans of the führer in the Americas. Fueling U.S. fears of a Nazi "fifth column" in the Western Hemisphere, Rauschning claimed that Latin America occupied an important place in Hitler's war plans. Hitler reportedly believed that Latin Americans would eagerly seize the opportunity to befriend a strong European power capable of military victories over the United States, the much-feared leader of the Western Hemisphere. According to Rauschning, Hitler intended to impose his own hegemony over Latin America. He quoted Hitler as saying: "Mexico is a country that calls out for a capable master. It is perishing under its leaders. Germany could be great and rich with the help of its mineral resources. . . . We could have all of Mexico for a few million [marks]. Why should I not conclude an alliance with Mexico, a currency agreement, a customs union?"[2] This book contained numerous inaccuracies and was based partially on hearsay.[3] As Hitler well knew, President Cárdenas was an unlikely ally. Despite his nationalist policies, the lingering effects of the Great Depression made him increasingly aware that he needed U.S. assistance in order to achieve economic growth. Even as Cárdenas nationalized Mexico's foreign-owned oil industry, he moved toward cooperation with the United States in other areas. Moreover, Mexico had been the only country besides the Soviet Union to give military aid to the Spanish Republicans, the enemies of Hitler's ally Franco.[4] Aware of the failure of the Zimmermann Telegram and other World War I-era schemes to use Mexico as a tool against the United States, Hitler expressed, as Friedrich Katz has put it, "practically no interest" in Mexico.[5]

Nazi diplomacy therefore pursued relatively modest goals in Mexico. Represented by Baron Rüdt von Collenberg, a second-rate diplomat whose highest previous post had been that of consul in Shanghai, the Nazis limited themselves to the promotion of trade, the control of the German colony, intelligence activities, and a propaganda campaign.[6] Although relatively insignificant in the grand dreams of world domination, these strategies dramatically changed the context in which the Bokers and other members of the German colony in Mexico lived.

Designed to secure access to strategic commodities, the economic offensive was Hitler's most important goal. When the führer reappointed the financial wizard of the Weimar Republic, Hjalmar Schacht, as Reichsbank president, he set the stage for an aggressive promotion of German trade interests overseas. Following the disastrous hyperinflation of 1923, Germans of all political colors had credited Schacht with saving the German currency, and he had engineered impressive German successes in Latin America by targeting new, capital-intensive sectors of the economy. For example, he had played an instrumental role in the attempted building of a German monopoly over commercial aviation in the Andean republics of Bolivia, Ecuador, and Peru in the late 1920s. Schacht did nothing to disappoint Hitler. In 1934, he developed a trade policy that allowed the Germans to overcome their Depression-era lack of cash for purchasing Latin American goods. Aside from barter trade—his preferred method of trading—Schacht created an artificial currency, the ASKI-mark, a compensation currency redeemable only on his terms and frequently devalued. At a time when Latin American exporters faced closed markets and high tariffs in the United States, Schacht's schemes boosted German trade with Latin America. By 1938, goods from Germany amounted to more than 16 percent of total Latin American imports, as compared to 12.2 percent in 1913 and 7.9 percent in 1934.[7]

The oil controversy between Mexico and the United States gave the Nazis an unexpected and quite welcome opportunity. As early as January 1937, when the oil companies in Mexico clashed with their unions over labor rights, the Nazi commercial attaché proposed a trade pact that bartered German machinery for raw materials. After Cárdenas expropriated the sixteen largest foreign oil producers on March 18, 1938, the German government quickly followed up on these earlier contacts. When the oil companies imposed a boycott on Mexican crude, renegade oilman William R. Davis brokered a secret agreement that swapped Mexican oil for German manufactured materials and the construction of two power plants. During the next year, these deals brought 1.5 million tons of Mexican oil—or two-thirds of all Mexican oil exports—to the German navy at a low price.[8]

The German colony in Mexico was another important target, as Hitler sought to subordinate all *Volksdeutsche* (people of German culture) to his party. According to the inflated estimates of Rüdt von Collenberg, Mexico was home to 17,000 individuals of "German character and language."[9] However, many of these "Germans" were either

Mennonites or Austrian and Swiss nationals who felt no connection to the German nation-state. Even "real" Germans were far from united in their attitude toward the Nazis. Most significantly, more than a thousand German-speaking exiles, among them many extraordinary intellectuals and artists, entered Mexico, from where they attacked Hitler's totalitarian state.[10] In addition, the German colony in Mexico City remained divided politically: a right-wing majority that welcomed strongman rule confronted a small, but vocal group of supporters of the Weimar Republic. Nonetheless, Nazi ideology found fertile ground in the colony. With its institutions devoted to the promotion of German culture, and its effort to seal itself off from Mexican influences, the colony had long operated as a microcosm of what the Nazis desired to accomplish among all Volksdeutsche. Many Germans in Mexico held their host country in low esteem and justified their attitude with racist arguments. Finally, open anti-Semitism had existed in the colony at least since the late 1920s, and Germans of Jewish descent had never held prominent positions in its institutions.[11]

Therefore, von Collenberg had little trouble bringing the German colony into line. In 1935, the Nazis founded the Deutsche Volksgemeinschaft (German People's Community, or DVG) that soon came to serve as an umbrella organization for all the ethnic German associations under its control. In addition, the Nazi Party flourished: between 1932 and 1945, the membership of the party in Mexico mushroomed from 68 to 411, or 10 percent of all adult Germans in Mexico. Affiliate organizations of the NSDAP such as the Hitler Youth and the Association of German Girls (BDM) also grew.[12] Most importantly, the Colegio Alemán emerged as the centerpiece of Nazi efforts. By 1938, Hitler's *Mein Kampf* had become required reading; all Jewish students had been forced out of the school, and exams included essay topics such as "racial thought as a pillar of National Socialism."[13] Von Collenberg also disposed of effective measures to quiet dissent among the Germans in Mexico. Before the war, the dependence of the merchants on German imports made them think twice before opposing Hitler in public. Moreover, most of the Germans in Mexico had close relatives at home, a fact that made them vulnerable to blackmail. This type of leverage increased during the war: speak up against the Nazis, some feared, and one's brother or son might be heading to the killing fields on the Eastern Front. Von Collenberg never had any hesitations about extorting money from wealthy Germans, and he collected "voluntary" contributions often exceeding 100,000 pesos.[14]

Support for the Nazis was one thing; wholesale cooperation proved another. For example, Franz and other Germans dealt von Collenberg a symbolic setback in the naming of the new school building. In January 1940, the Colegio Alemán moved into a new building in Tacubaya, a building designed by Franz on land purchased in Gunther's name. Prevailing over von Collenberg, who desired to honor World War I "hero" von Hindenburg, Franz persuaded the board of directors to rename the school Colegio Alemán Alexander von Humboldt (CAAH). The new name honored the German connection to Mexico rather than the man who had handed Hitler the reins of power on January 30, 1933.[15]

Even more importantly, the German merchants resisted those Nazi initiatives that threatened to place them at a commercial disadvantage. Companies like the Casa Boker refused to cut ties with those few Jewish merchants who still bought from German wholesalers, and they also continued to sell British, French, and U.S.-made goods.[16] Moreover, the Bokers and many other merchants would neither proclaim their allegiance to the Nazis nor lay off their Jewish employees. Whether or not they did business with U.S. exporters, they knew that overt support for the Nazis would guarantee their inclusion in U.S. blacklists in case Hitler's aggressive policies led to war. Therefore, the Bokers retained their two Jewish associates, including the head of the retail department, Ysser Kalb.[17] In general, the greater an individual's stake in the Mexican economy, the less he or she complied with the dictates from the German legation. As one British diplomat put it, "The German business community are quietly conducting their own affairs, and are endeavoring to maintain their business without laying stress on their national sympathies."[18]

These trends led to a further "Mexicanization" of the Casa Boker. The CFM and many other companies began to require Mexican or Allied citizenship of all of their owners and shareholders. By 1939, both of the directors of the Casa Boker—Gunther and Julio Carstens Alcalá—carried Mexican passports, not only to comply with recent Mexican laws of company ownership but also as protection against any future blacklists.[19] Moreover, the Bokers' camouflage against revolutionary nationalism paid further dividends. Keeping track of the real ownership in the Fondo A, the Bokers deposited all CFM shares with Mexican-born shareholders such as Gunther, Carstens, and Franz Buchenau; only La Esperanza remained in Franz's hands. To countervail a possible freezing of their bank accounts, they also made sure that a slush fund would be available in cash. They buried gold coins, certificates of deposit, and stock in milk containers in the yard of the Casa Amarilla, and they bought 500,000 pesos worth of shares in breweries through Mexican straw men.[20] By early 1942, the Bokers and other wary merchants had also resigned their offices in the German-Mexican organizations that were now under Nazi oversight.[21]

German intelligence efforts, potentially that aspect of the Nazi strategy most detrimental to U.S. interests, focused primarily on espionage. Reluctant to commit resources to an uncertain venture, the German *Abwehr* established a spy ring in Mexico run mostly by amateurs. This spy ring made Mexico the focal point of a continent-wide network that gathered information on U.S. economic activities and joint U.S.-Latin American defense. Rather than sending their messages in vulnerable and cumbersome code, these spies smuggled the information to Germany with the help of microdots, microscopic reductions of pages of text that appeared like a dot on an ordinary personal letter. After 1941, however, the U.S. involvement in the war thwarted the efforts of this spy ring. By the time Mexico entered the war in May 1942, the German government had abandoned most of its intelligence activities.[22]

The final aspect of the Nazi strategy in Mexico consisted of a propaganda campaign. Even before the war, the press attaché of the German legation, Arthur Dietrich, had begun sponsoring selected Mexican newspapers. This propaganda operation was first designed to improve Germany's image abroad, and later, during the war, stepped up to help ensure Mexican neutrality. For example, the German legation subsidized *Timón,* the right-wing newspaper of former Mexican education secretary Vasconcelos, a publication that constantly printed pro-Axis and anti-U.S. articles and editorials. Dietrich answered directly to Ernst Bohle, the boss of the Auslandsorganisation (Foreign Organization), who in turn reported to Hitler's propaganda minister, Joseph Goebbels. Dietrich also coordinated the activities of the local branch of the NSDAP and helped with the intelligence operations mentioned above.[23]

Nazi policies in Mexico therefore hardly resembled the concerted strategy of subversion and domination depicted by Rauschning. Unlike in the European countries and in Argentina, Brazil, and Chile, Hitler's agents never seriously attempted to influence national politics, let alone bring down the Mexican government. Apart from their desire to control local Germans, Nazi diplomats sought modest gains that corresponded to Mexico's distance and relative lack of significance to the German strategy.[24]

The Bokers and the Nazis

Like the majority of the German colony in Mexico City, the Bokers supported Nazi rule. Their opinions were rooted in their conservative German-National ideology that supported the idea of a greater Germany. No one in the Boker family shed a tear for the Weimar Republic when Hitler dismantled the democratic state. The humiliation of Germany after World War I; the desire to reduce U.S. influence in Mexico; fears of Communism in both Mexico and Germany, and the "idealism of the expatriate German" all convinced the Bokers that Hitler's seizure of power was a change for the better.[25] During the war, when the three younger Boker brothers fought in Africa, France, and Norway, the family obtained a personal stake in the success of the German offensive that deepened this support. They admired Hitler and agreed with his virulent nationalism; however, they resented the more plebeian, base aspects of Nazism, such as Hitler's brash and ostentatious demeanor. This patrician family thus considered the Nazis useful allies in their position as Germans in Mexico.[26] This attitude bred a dangerous hubris toward a monstrous regime that claimed millions of lives: Franz Buchenau explained after the war that he had joined the NSDAP "out of concern over the type of people that dominated the party."[27] Despite such endeavors to improve Nazism by participating in it, the Bokers were used by the Nazis and not the other way round.

However, beyond this general support, individual family members reacted in different ways to the reality of Nazi rule. These differences primarily reflected a discrepancy between those who lived in Germany and those who lived in Mexico. As entrepreneurs vulnerable to U.S. pressure, the Bokers in Mexico City did not make their views public, while their relatives in Germany (with one exception) openly supported Hitler. However, the generational change from foreign-born to Mexican-born, and differences in personality played important roles as well.

In Mexico, both Franz and Gunther rooted for the victory of the German armies during the war. They also applauded each of Hitler's major decisions from the 1939 pact with Soviet leader Joseph Stalin to the declaration of war on the United States in December 1941, which Gunther believed would lead to the destruction of U.S. influence in Latin America.[28] Similarly, Gunther's wife, Margot, had worked as a clerk in the German legation, although she discontinued these activities after their marriage in July 1940. But contrary to U.S. reports, none of the three became NSDAP members, and they did not publicly support the Nazis.[29]

Of the family members residing in Mexico, Franz was most supportive of the Nazis' efforts to redraw the map of Europe. During the Weimar Republic, he had voted for Hindenburg's ultraconservative DNVP. He regarded Hitler's offensive as the "second half" of World War I, a chance for revenge. After World War II cut him off from Luise and most of his children, he wrote them hundreds of letters that passionately defended German aggression. Although these letters reveal an astonishing degree of pathos in a man who prided himself on his rational thinking, they also demonstrate that Franz's well of chauvinistic nationalism fed from a different source than Hitler's. Acquired in his years as a destitute artist in Vienna, anti-Semitism—and hatred of diversity generally—was the führer's primary motivation for his desire for world domination. Franz, however, saw the war as a chance to pay back the "perfidious" United States for its entry into World War I. In blind faith in the German war effort, he anticipated the imminent decline of the United States. "The Yankees," he wrote, "are . . . on top, but broke, and hopelessly outmoded—they stand for all that is over-due and obsolete in this world."[30] He thus viewed the United States as the antithesis of Western civilization, and he lambasted U.S. President Franklin D. Roosevelt as a cowardly, yet shrewd tactician bent on the pacific conquest of Mexico.[31] If Franz therefore displayed his agree-ment with the one element of Nazi ideology that made most sense to him as a German living abroad, he was not a typical Nazi supporter in other ways. An earlier outburst had demonstrated his own anti-Semitic sentiments, but the same Nazi-era writings that predicted Germany's victory eschew any mention of Jewish people. After the war, Franz accepted German responsibility for the Holocaust more easily than the Bokers in Germany, who continued to make excuses.[32] Moreover, as Franz's choice of friends demonstrated, his personal life did not mirror the battle lines of the war. A strong Hispanophile, Franz Böker befriended several Spanish Republican refugees—ardent anti-Fascists and the very people that Hitler's ally Franco had driven into exile. Not only did he consider them cultivated people; many of them also shared his dislike of the United States. In 1943, one of these refugees, the noted artist José Bardasano, liked Franz enough that he painted a por-trait with dark hues that capture the mood and personality of the patri-arch of the Boker clan.

By contrast, Gunther and Margot's support for the Nazis reflected their own everyday experiences in Mexico City, and, hence, their accul-turation into Mexico as well as their self-image as Auslandsdeutsche. In many ways, their sentiments resembled those of Mexican right-wing movements of the day. Feeling threatened in his position among the elite of a multiethnic society in the Cárdenas era, Gunther found much to like about Nazi racial thought. In 1939, on one of his frequent trips to the United States, he discovered the Jim Crow solution to the prob-lem of race. In New Orleans, he got firsthand experience with strict, legalized segregation and institutional racism. To his satisfaction, Gunther concluded that Southerners understood the Nazi point of view better than any other U.S.-Americans. As another example, Gunther's diary of the war years reveals that he and the largely apolit-ical Margot were less caught up in the European war than Franz, and much less hostile to the United States. Although Gunther scanned the airwaves for news of the war, his diary lacks the diatribes against the

Figure 13: José Bardasano's portrait of Don Pancho (Archivo Boker, Mexico City).

western Allies that mark Franz's letters. Instead, it shows a greater pre-occupation with the implications of the war for the Casa Boker and his family.[33] Finally, Gunther differed from his father in that he saw some positive aspects in the Weimar Republic—the Germany he had known during his residence there from 1926 to 1933. Five decades later, Gunther and Helmuth still argued endlessly about the reasons for the failure of the Weimar Republic under the doomed Brüning, von Papen, and Schleicher cabinets. Their estates own huge sets of published primary documents from those years. It is thus debatable whom Gunther and Margot resembled more: Mexican right-wing opponents of Cárdenas, or Nazi supporters in Germany.

Franz and Gabriele Buchenau were such Nazi supporters. During the 1930s, this couple lived in Solingen, where Franz served as manager of Heinrich Böker and Company. According to NSDAP records, both joined the party in 1937. They enrolled their eldest son, Jürgen, in the Adolf-Hitler-Schule, an elite academy near Bonn designed to train future party leaders. Franz Buchenau's support for the Nazis did not stop at party membership, as he became an important member of the German espionage network in Latin America. Recruited by Reichsbank president Schacht, whom he had met at a meeting of industry representatives, he was an ideal agent for the Abwehr. Buchenau spoke fluent English and Spanish, and his position as head of a German export firm gave him an intimate knowledge of the Latin American economies. In addition, he often traveled to Latin America on legitimate business and hence possessed the ideal cover for his activities. Thus, the Abwehr put him to work on the microdot affair. He traveled to Rio de Janeiro in November 1940. After trips to Argentina and Chile, he arrived in Mexico City in June 1942, where he reportedly hid in the house of a Jewish (!) friend until the police arrested him in October. He spent four months interned in the fortress of Perote, Veracruz, along with other German agents as well as the crews of several German ships impounded by the government. As the FBI reported, he was released in February 1943 on the payment of a bribe. Kept under surveillance by the Mexican government, he raised chickens on a farm in the village of Ixtapaluca east of Mexico City until his death in 1969.[34]

For lack of sources, the three younger Boker brothers are hard to characterize in their position toward the Nazi dictatorship. Drafted into military service as university students, Helmuth and his twin brothers enthusiastically went to war for the führer. As "anti-American" as his father and Gabriele, Helmuth became an NSDAP member in 1938 while in medical school in Munich. But the harsh experience of war soon sobered him. He joined the navy, the one branch of the German armed forces in which some muted criticism of Hitler persisted throughout the war. Stationed in Norway, far away from the heat of battle, Helmuth acquired a critical distance from the horrors of the front, and he understood the futility of Hitler's enterprise before its apocalyptic conclusion.[35] When he returned to Germany in 1948 after three years as a British prisoner of war in Norway, he found himself disillusioned with the career he had chosen. Based in great part on his experiences during the war, he no longer believed that the study and practice of medicine contributed to the progress of humanity. As he later often remarked, "every step forward brings a step backward"—a pessimistic attitude that remained with Helmuth through his two subsequent careers as a partner in Franz Buchenau's chicken operation and as a Casa Boker sales representative.[36] For their part, his twin brothers, Peter and Klaus, never saw the end of the war. On June 19, 1940, Peter died during the German invasion of France, and Klaus fell on January 24, 1942, near Tobruk, Libya. This dual tragedy heightened the remaining Bokers' support for the German side.[37]

Figure 14: Marching to their deaths: The twins Peter and Klaus Boker (Nachlass Gabriele Buchenau).

Even less is known about Luise's attitude—and her steadfast refusal to write about politics leaves interviews with her friends and descendants as the primary historical sources. Luise reportedly combined strong support for the war with compassion for the victims of the Nazis. While she applauded Hitler's efforts to curb unemployment and restore the national greatness of Germany, she opposed the führer's anti-Semitic and xenophobic propaganda.[38] Much of her opposition might have owed to personal issues: Luise could not be sure of her Aryan origin. According to the *Ahnenpass,* the genealogical document that the Nazis prepared for all Germans, her father Theodor Pocorny was born in the city of Czenstochova to parents of thoroughly Polish names and baptized a Catholic. Although eager to separate Aryan from Jewish ancestors all the way back to the seventeenth century, the Nazi genealogists could not find out anything more. Likewise, the detailed chronicle of the family of Luise's German mother does not clarify Pocorny's origins.[39] To this day, the subject provides lively debate among his descendants. One of Luise's grandsons believes that he was a Catholic descendant of Volga Germans. Married to a woman partially of Jewish descent, another grandson surmises that his ancestors were Jewish.[40] Whatever the case, Luise did not join the NSDAP, and she reportedly even sheltered a Jewish refugee.[41]

Like the vast majority of the German "colony," which excluded the anti-Fascist refugees, the Bokers thus supported Hitler's effort to make Germany the foremost power in Europe. Like their peers—and many Mexicans, as well—they hoped that Hitler would defeat the Anglo-Saxon powers that, in their opinion, had brought misery to both Germany and Mexico. However, the very significance of the United States for the success of the Casa Boker stopped the Mexican residents, Franz and Gunther, from even considering membership in the NSDAP. Aware of their vulnerability in a country bordering the United States, they did not make the mistake of resuming their World War I-era role as agents of the German campaign. In the words of a member of the Barcelonnettes—a foreign community unlikely to underestimate the German threat—the Mexican Bokers "were not Nazis, but Germans who went about their business."[42] Instead, they navigated carefully between the Scylla of the German legation and the Charybdis of U.S. efforts to eliminate Axis influence in Mexico.

Confronting the Emerging U.S.–Mexican Alliance

The specter of Axis influence affected U.S. policy toward Mexico as early as the aftermath of the oil expropriation in 1938–39. While Secretary of State Cordell Hull argued for punishing Mexico, and while FBI Director J. Edgar Hoover blasted Cárdenas for his supposed "anti-American" attitude and friendship with the Nazis, the German barter for Mexican oil helped U.S. Ambassador Josephus Daniels prevail over these more hard-line officials. As Daniels pointed out, Cárdenas had demonstrated his opposition to Fascist movements by his support of the Spanish Republicans, and his resolute stand against the annexation of Austria. In the end, widespread fear of Axis activities contributed to prodding U.S. President Franklin D. Roosevelt toward Daniels's position. Cárdenas, however, did not unequivocally support U.S. efforts to eliminate German influence in the Americas even though he personally loathed the Nazis. Unwilling to alienate the numerous sympathizers of Hitler in his country and aware of the economic importance of Germans in Mexico, he discontinued the provision of oil to Hitler's navy but did not interfere with activities within the German colony.[43]

The outbreak of war greatly accentuated U.S. fears of the Nazi threat in Mexico. Daniels wrote in his memoirs: "Hitler's Fifth Column arrived early . . . [and] spread their poison assiduously. . . . We were vigilant to detect any Nazi infiltration . . ., to make a complete Blacklist of concerns aiding the enemy, and to obtain from Mexico [a] rich variety of war materials."[44] As early as September 1939, Hoover dispatched agent Gus T. Jones, who had gained knowledge of Mexican affairs as an investigator of Pancho Villa's 1916 raid on Columbus, New Mexico. In the following years, Jones intercepted messages to and from the German embassy and developed an intimate understanding of the German colony and its organizations. The FBI agent not only monitored Axis activity, he also tracked Communists, whom—in the era of the Hitler-Stalin Pact—he suspected of cooperating with Axis agents.[45]

While German aggression in Europe thus speeded up U.S. anti-Nazi activities, it did not make an immediate difference in the Mexican posture. In fact, the Cardenistas viewed the U.S. fear of Nazi "penetration" as a potential problem for their country's sovereignty. In particular, they took exception to sensationalist U.S. press reports that Axis agents had infiltrated their government. In May 1940, Cárdenas declared that his government was not worried about a fifth column in Mexico. A few weeks later, a memorandum by a secret agent concluded that presidential candidate Juan Andreu Almazán posed a much greater threat than German infiltrators. The memorandum did lead to the expulsion of German press attaché Dietrich, who had directed the Nazi propaganda campaign in Mexico.[46]

After the German defeat of France in June 1940, however, the Mexican government moved toward greater cooperation with the United States, as the specter of Axis influence helped convince the U.S. government to settle all outstanding disputes with Mexico. In December 1940, U.S. Vice President Henry A. Wallace (whom Franz dubbed "Váyase," or "go away") attended the inauguration of new President Manuel Avila Camacho in December 1940 and began negotiations about a joint defense commission with the president-elect. Wallace recommended aggressive propaganda measures to counteract Nazi influence in the Mexican press, a recommendation that contributed to the establishment of the Office of Inter-American affairs under the direction of the young Nelson Rockefeller.[47] Vested U.S. economic interests invoked the German threat in Mexico to advance their own agendas during Wallace's visit. As a representative of the U.S. Chamber of Commerce told Wallace, U.S. businesses in Mexico suffered from German competition, which had been fueled recently by the Nazis' willingness to provide generous loans to German businesses abroad. Moreover, Wallace reported, Mexico remained in dire need of investment capital, which the Germans and Japanese would supply if the United States did not. In return for Mexico's pledge to support the coordination of hemispheric defense, the U.S. government brokered a comprehensive settlement of the oil controversy.[48]

Despite the emergent U.S.-Mexican alliance, the first two years of the war brought relatively few difficulties to the Casa Boker. While the war in Europe interrupted direct trade, it again increased the company's profit margin by driving up prices of hardware and imported goods. Moreover, officials in the U.S. embassy in Mexico City recognized the usefulness of German merchants such as the Bokers for their country's exporters. As late as November 1940, a memorandum of the commercial attaché stated that German firms "constituted the best media for introducing manufactured [U.S.] products throughout the republic" and singled out only sixteen firms—but not the Casa Boker—for activities detrimental to the United States.[49] In addition, the Bokers stocked up on German items by obtaining merchandise through intermediary countries. Until March 1941, the company received several shipments of German cutlery via Russia and Japan. The last of these shipments was large enough that a U.S. official estimated that it would meet the needs of Mexico City residents for approximately ten years.[50]

By the time the last shipment arrived at its destination, however, the U.S. government had identified German merchants as an integral part of the Nazi strategy in Latin America. In February 1941, a State Department memorandum portrayed German merchants in Latin America as "cogs in the [Nazi] economic machine." "The interior parts of many countries," the report went on, "are serviced commercially only by Germans, and . . . the whole commercial structure, private and official, is an open book to German commercial agents . . . allied to native financial and political personages. It is a web of influence, from the water's edge to the far boundaries of practically every state."[51] Although the report proved hyperbolic in light of the willingness of Latin American leaders to cooperate with the United States, it signaled that the Roosevelt administration would bring back World War I-era methods of economic warfare.

Sure enough, on July 17, 1941, the U.S. government published the *Proclaimed List of Certain Blocked Nationals.* Similar to its World War I predecessor, this second blacklist disregarded many changes in ownership since the last war. Just as Wilson's *Enemy Trading List,* Roosevelt's *Proclaimed List* lumped Axis nationals with Latin American natives of German, Italian, or Japanese descent. As in 1917, ethnicity, and not citizenship, determined inclusion on the blacklist, and U.S. officials maintained that culture rather than a passport determined who was an enemy alien.[52] The new blacklist ruined many small businesses. For example, the Division of War Trade Intelligence recommended the addition to the list of a German photographer in Mexico City on the basis that he had *requested* German film for his studio. In Ecuador, the blacklist even included a Jewish Social Democrat, who despite repeated attempts did not succeed in getting his name cleared.[53] Considered "highly suspect" by the British Board of Trade, the CFM unsurprisingly was included in the *Proclaimed List*.[54]

Still, the Bokers did not lose sleep. Unable to procure U.S. imports directly, they bought them through Mexican intermediaries, including several of their most trusted wholesale customers.[55] Moreover, Mexican neutrality had blunted the effects of a similar blacklist in World War I, and the Bokers remained hopeful that the Mexican government would once again assume an attitude that would allow them to continue operations. As they knew, Avila Camacho resented U.S. attempts to eliminate companies controlled by Mexican citizens.[56]

Initially, events proved the Bokers correct in their hope. While fifteen Latin American countries handed over some 4,000 ethnic Germans, Avila Camacho (like the leaders of Argentina, Brazil, and Chile) refused to punish Mexican citizens whose only sin was to speak, look, or act German. He also did not deport German agents like Franz Buchenau to the United States, choosing instead to intern them in Perote, where they were treated relatively well.[57] This lack of cooperation irritated State Department officials. As late as May 1942, Assistant Secretary of State Sumner Welles labeled Mexican steps to curb Axis activity "wholly inadequate." In particular, he criticized the fact that the Mexican government did not crack down on nationals of "Germanic extraction whose known sympathies are pro-Axis."[58]

Statements such as this one demonstrated that Welles was determined to use a sledgehammer where a fly swatter would have sufficed. In what became a dress rehearsal for the Cold War, legitimate interests of national security gave rise to a strategy that treated every German in Mexico as a potentially dangerous Nazi.[59] The campaign against the Germans was at least partially the result of an intelligence operation based on shoddy research that produced inaccurate information. On the basis of a denunciation contained in an FBI report, for example, Ambassador Daniels concluded that Gunther Boker was a member of the NSDAP.[60] In 1943, another such report stated that the Bokers had housed their German interns in the Casa Boker just so that they could indoctrinate them with Nazi ideology.[61] As a final example, the FBI erroneously reported in 1945 that Franz Böker was a naturalized Mexican citizen and a Nazi party member.[62]

Meanwhile, the Avila Camacho administration steadily drifted toward the Allied camp. Many Mexicans identified with the smaller nations of Europe gobbled up by the German war machine, and the war offered enormous incentives to the Mexican government in an era of rising U.S. demand for raw materials. Although this increase in trade with the United States further accentuated Mexico's dependence on the U.S. economy, it proved a significant windfall that allowed Mexico to accelerate its program of import-substitution industrialization.[63] The Japanese attack on Pearl Harbor destroyed what was left of the Mexican resolve to remain neutral: on December 9, Avila Camacho declared in a radio broadcast that the war pitted democracies against dictatorships. As he explained, "The republics of our hemisphere are bound together by bonds that no menacing ideology can ever sever."[64] Two days later, he broke relations with the Axis powers. Soon thereafter, Avila Camacho froze the assets of Axis nationals as well as Mexicans who still traded with the Axis, creating, in the words of the British minister, an "unlimited opportunity for graft."[65] Finally, in May 1942, German submarines torpedoed two Mexican tankers, the *Potrero de Llano* and the *Faja de Oro*. Amidst the vain claims of many Axis nationals that the U.S. navy had sunk the tankers, this action precipitated Avila Camacho's declaration on May 28 that a state of war existed between Mexico and Germany.[66]

Even at war with the Axis powers, Mexico became but a lukewarm ally of the United States. Avila Camacho set limits to its cooperation with the United States. Resisting entreaties of the U.S. embassy, he did not formally expropriate German property. Although the president agreed to participate in hemispheric defense measures, he did not consent to giving control of strategic Pacific airstrips and ports to the U.S. armed forces. The president also refused to allow U.S. troops to use Mexican territory and insisted that he would only allow Mexican authorities within the limits of Mexican law to take steps against Axis nationals.[67] A joke Gunther liked to tell made light of the Mexican attitude toward the war: it was said that the new U.S. ambassador, George S. Messersmith, had asked Avila Camacho for ten thousand troops to assist the Allied invasion of Italy. The Mexican president reportedly replied, "We do not have ten thousand soldiers to spare, dear Mr. Roosevelt, but may we send you ten thousand generals?"[68] As it turned out, the reverse was true: 250,000 Mexican residents of the United States fought as conscripts in the U.S. army.[69]

Ultimately, however, the decision of the Mexican government to cooperate with U.S. efforts to eliminate Axis commerce had calamitous consequences for the Casa Boker. Since the company had never intervened in Mexican political affairs, the Bokers had always expected the Mexican government to protect them. In June 1942, they found these hopes hanging in the balance despite the exclusively Mexican appearance of their company.

The "Intervention" of the Casa Boker

Early that month, Gunther Boker and other representatives of the German colony attended a private meeting in Avila Camacho's office. The president began the meeting by praising the German entrepreneurs for their contribution to Mexican economic development. Regrettably, he stated, the war with the Axis powers forced him to limit the activities of ethnic Germans in Mexico. "I will do everything I can to protect you," he said, "but what is about to happen follows the wishes of others rather than my own."[70] Following this advance warning, on June 13 the Mexican government placed the Casa Boker under the control of the newly formed Junta de Administración y Vigilancia de la Propiedad Extranjera (Council of the Administration and Surveillance of Foreign Property). Responsible for as many as 381 companies worth more than 100 million pesos, the Junta took over all those businesses that the Mexican government labeled enemy property.[71] Reflecting U.S. satisfaction, Ambassador Messersmith applauded the Mexican enforcement of U.S. currency controls and blacklists. The ultimate reward came five months later with the Suárez-Lamont agreement, which drastically reduced Mexico's foreign debt by canceling 90 percent of the nominal value of 500 million dollars worth of Mexican bonds.[72]

Fortunately for the Bokers, Mexican cooperation in the blacklist matter proved half-hearted. Avila Camacho had planned to move exclusively against known Nazis, and only under U.S. pressure did he sign a blanket decree covering all Axis property.[73] The Mexican president also refused to leave the surveillance of Axis nationals up to U.S. agents. Throughout the war, he "protected" the Bokers by stationing two security guards in front of the Casa Amarilla, who followed Gunther everywhere he went.[74] Avila Camacho knew that the Casa Boker and other German businesses played an important role in bringing much-needed foreign technology to Mexico, and he realized that the seizure of Axis property would increase Mexican dependence on trade with the United States. Not surprisingly, many Mexicans, while supportive of their country's entry into the war, opposed the takeover of the property of Mexican nationals of foreign descent.[75] In part to appeal to such sentiments, the Mexican president appointed as head of the Junta the aging Carrancista and noted anti-U.S. intellectual Luis Cabrera, who considered his agency a trustee for the national good rather than a vehicle of war.[76]

As a further mitigating factor, Gunther could count on valuable personal connections with a government friendly to business interests. When Avila Camacho was secretary of Gobernación under President Cárdenas, Gunther had reportedly once "filled him up with champagne" at a private party at his house.[77] Before the attack on Pearl Harbor,

Foreign Secretary Ezéquiel Padilla had unsuccessfully petitioned the U.S. government to remove the CFM from the *Proclaimed List* because of the company's "Mexican" character. Finally, the appropriately named secretary of Gobernación, Miguel Alemán Valdés, actively protected the interests of ethnic Germans and assured the merchants that their property would be returned once the war ended. Alemán's attitude toward the war followed the Mexican adage "obedezco pero no cumplo" (I obey but I do not comply).[78]

Encouraged by these signs, Gunther presented a legal case to Avila Camacho that asked the president to release the Casa Boker from Junta supervision. As he pointed out, Mexicans owned the enterprise, and the Casa Boker had never formally appealed for German diplomatic protection.[79] Despite its merits, however (and apart from the fact that Avila Camacho could not reverse his decision) the case was far from convincing. Gunther left clues that he still identified with Germany. For example, the FBI gleaned from U.S. immigration records that Gunther held a German passport as well as a Mexican one, and he sent more than 2,000 CARE packages to relatives and friends after the war.[80] Franz Böker, a German, still owned La Esperanza in the early 1940s. In addition, while U.S. agent Gus Jones had erred in identifying Margot as the head of the BDM, her former membership in that Nazi organization for teenage girls did not help her husband's argument.[81] One of the shareholders, Franz Buchenau, engaged in Nazi espionage. Finally, U.S. intelligence somehow got wind of the existence of the Fondo A. With customary imprecision, an embassy dossier reported that Franz Boker and his three brothers [sic!] held the majority interest in the Casa Boker. Indeed, it was common knowledge that blacklisted individuals put up Mexican fronts for their ownership of real estate, companies, and even automobiles.[82] Unbeknownst to U.S. intelligence, the CFM even distributed dividends from a German cash account up to March 1945—hardly the mark of a "Mexican" business![83]

As Gunther Boker soon found out, intervention by the Junta threatened not only the future of German employees in the Casa Boker, but also the very existence of the company. The Junta separated thirty-six German-speaking directors and employees from the Casa Boker, among them almost the entire management team. To add insult to injury, the Junta made its home in the Edificio Boker, without ever paying as much as 1 centavo in rent, and it forbade Gunther to enter the building.[84] He attempted to defy this ban until force and open threats made him back off. He spent the rest of the war working in the German-interest section in the Swedish legation, where he coordinated relief efforts for the prisoners in Perote as well as Germans impoverished by the seizure of their properties.[85]

Much more importantly, the Junta's management practices threatened the survival of the companies under its supervision. In its quest to extract the maximum short-term revenue, the Junta sold machinery and inventory irrespective of business considerations. In addition, the absence of the owners often led to careless financial management. Thus, the Junta published astonishingly modest profits of 9 to 12 percent per fiscal year and ended up auctioning off many of the companies when they had become worthless.[86] Even the Casa Boker ended up on the auction block in 1945, and only the high asking price and Gunther's pleading with prospective buyers prevented its public sale.[87] To make matters worse, U.S. companies that had competed with German businesses in Mexico attempted to take advantage of this situation. To their credit, however, U.S. diplomats did not help these companies take over the German concerns. In fact, Messersmith and his associates foiled a scheme by the American Cyanamid Company to acquire a monopoly in the confiscated pharmaceutical sector formerly dominated by German concerns.[88]

The financial situation of the Casa Boker therefore deteriorated throughout more than six years of Junta administration. During an era in which hardware once again became scarce, what could have been years of solid profits instead haunted the company for decades. The balance sheets from these years tell a sad tale. Between 1942 and 1947, while the peso lost half of its purchasing power to inflation, the annual revenues of the CFM decreased from 1,100,000 to 260,000 pesos; a real decline of 88 percent (see Table 10). Reserve cash decreased by 150,000 pesos; a 50 percent drop in real terms. At the same time, the Junta made the CFM contribute to its operating expenses, and by 1947, this contribution exceeded the net gain of the company. To top it off, the inventory lost one-third of its value in real terms, as the Junta replaced expensive imported items with cheaper domestic ones. As the inventory constituted the greatest asset of the company, this issue raises the question why the CFM was not able to show greater returns at a time when it liquidated a large part of the inventory. Although the Junta furnished no exact figures even after the return of the company, Gunther Boker later surmised that the Junta colluded with purveyors and the purchasing department of the Casa Boker in manufacturing artificial invoices with inflated prices.[89] Thus, the sorry state of the company owed primarily to the administration of a corrupt agency that milked "Axis firms" for easy money. It became clear that the Junta had little interest in the continued operation of the companies under its supervision beyond ensuring that money flowed into government coffers. The Junta reportedly even went so far as to take 269,000 pesos out of the CFM, money that Avila Camacho personally distributed among the 269 remaining Perote inmates on the day of their release.[90]

Table 10: Financial Situation of CFM, 1942–1948
(in thousands of pesos)

Year	Net Profit	Expenses Paid to Junta	Inventory
1942	1,173	25	3,697
1943	615	28	n/d
1944	911	182	3,427
1945	880	344	n/d
1946	655	53	n/d
1947	261	142	n/d
1948	351	194	4,980

Source: "CFM Reclamación Intervención," AB, FI.

Not surprisingly, in 1947, an economic crisis caused by a postwar slump in U.S. demand for Mexican products touched off the most serious crisis in management-labor relations that the company has witnessed in its many years of existence. Due in part to Junta mismanagement, the pay of CFM employees had lagged behind rising prices at a time of *carestía,* or high inflation.[91] For example, the lowest-paid workers made just 60 pesos a week—a 150 percent increase over 1939, but a decrease of 20 percent in real terms. Therefore, the UET called a strike after management had turned down its demand for a wage increase that would have compensated union members for inflation. Encouraged by Mexican labor boss Fidel Velásquez, whose sister worked in the Casa Boker, the UET went on strike for seven weeks and nearly forced the CFM into bankruptcy. In the end, management and labor resolved the crisis by restructuring the labor contract to give the union control over the hiring and firing of workers. The UET soon thereafter affiliated with the CTM, which protected it from pressure from management.[92]

This darkest hour of Gunther's career ironically signaled the impending end of the takeover. Three years after the German defeat, the Mexican government saw no further utility in administering "enemy property." In view of the sad economic state of most of the companies under its supervision, the Junta faced the choice of returning the companies to their former owners or selling their assets for a virtual pittance.[93] By 1948, the Casa Boker faced further trouble with its employees, and one of Mexico City's major newspapers called on the government to end the *intervención.*[94] On December 21, 1948, President Miguel Alemán released the Casa Boker and 144 other companies from Junta supervision.[95] Shortly thereafter, the Mexican government returned the Edificio Boker as well, although it had belonged to Franz, who later claimed that he was the first German national to have property returned to him.[96]

As it turned out, Franz's nemesis, the "white elephant," had paid dividends after all. The company's structure as a closely held corporation—which only existed as a result of a dearth of capital after the construction of the Edificio Boker—had allowed them to camouflage the actual ownership of the CFM. Without this camouflage, the Mexican government might have expropriated the Casa Boker. The Bokers' reticence displayed in the face of Nazi initiatives also helped them, as the U.S. embassy did not oppose the devolution of their company. Finally, the money from the brewery shares and the gold coins hidden in milk containers came in handy. The slush fund not only helped the Bokers restock the warehouse and fund the bribe necessary to obtain the return of the company, but it was the family's main source of income during the intervention.[97]

This relatively happy end could not disguise the damage that the Nazi period had inflicted on the Bokers and their company. The company never recovered from the *intervención*; likewise, the family would never be the same. Not until 1952 were the remaining Bokers reunited in Mexico. After long legal wrangling, Franz and Gunther succeeded in bringing Luise's and Gabriele's families to Mexico in 1948, and Helmuth arrived four years later.[98] This reunion, however, could not bridge the chasm that the war had opened within the family. Gabriele had not gladly traded a country in ruins for a nation in which her material and political well-being were assured. After the catastrophe of war, she and her family could not imagine living in a world in which employees and servants doted on the Bokers in "quasi-colonial" fashion.[99] The shared tragedy of the war had only reinforced her strong bond with Germany, and she believed that Franz, Gunther, and Margot could not imagine what their relatives had been through.[100]

At the same time, events had propelled Gunther Boker toward a greater involvement with Mexican society. The rise of the Nazis had made his company's position in Mexico much more difficult. Hitler's aggression had eliminated the support that the German merchant houses had always been able to muster, regardless of the nationalist rhetoric of the revolutionary regimes. World War II had accelerated the displacement of German businesses by U.S. and Mexican interests, and it had interrupted the Bokers' involvement in the Casa Boker for six years. This ordeal had left Gunther and Franz Boker bitter about what they perceived as Mexican impotence vis-à-vis the United States. But the negotiations that led to the devolution of the Casa Boker had also brought them into unprecedented contact with Mexican society.

In prompting the Junta's seizure of the Casa Boker, the global conflict provoked by the Nazi regime accomplished what the Mexican Revolution and other previous crises had failed to do. The *intervención* tore down the barriers the business had erected to protect itself from economic nationalism, and it forced the Bokers to use political connections to regain control of their company. The German defeat shattered their illusion that Germany was a world power that could challenge U.S. dominance in Mexico. It contributed to a weakening of Gunther and Margot's ties with Germany. If acculturation consisted in the modification of one culture as a result of contact with another, by 1948 the Mexican Bokers fit that definition. As bicultural individuals who shunned the self-segregation and German nationalism of their forebears, their descendants would take this process one step further.

Part Three

Neither Coffee nor Milk,
c. 1948–present

There was . . . nothing left to conquer; there was only the present
and its petty reality, no longer a future with its ambitious plans.
                                               —Thomas Mann, *Buddenbrooks*

6

At the Margins of the "Mexican Miracle"

With German and Mexican flags, the Edificio Boker hosted a grand gala
to celebrate the centennial of "Holder, Boker y Cía" on November 1,
1965. A two-page feature in the newspaper *Excelsior* showed smiling
executives and politicians in elegant suits and their wives posing in
expensive dresses. The five hundred guests included a veritable who's
who of Mexico City's business elite, the German ambassador, and several of his colleagues from the diplomatic corps.[1] Yet, the contrast to
the much smaller, but more eminent crowd that had attended the inauguration festivities of the Edificio Boker in 1900 could not have been
more apparent. While the Porfirians had gleefully celebrated the opening of one of the country's first department stores, President Gustavo
Díaz Ordaz did not consider the Boker centennial important enough
to ask even one of his cabinet members to attend. Evidently, the fact
that one of Mexico City's oldest firms had just completed a century of
existence was not important to the governing elite.

Appearances were not deceiving, as the Bokers operated in an
increasingly marginal context within the Mexican economy in the
period 1948–75. The process of rebuilding their business after World
War II had taken place at a time that did not allow the rapid commercial success of the kind enjoyed by sojourning trade conquistadors and
their descendants during the previous century. Mexico wanted industry rather than merchants, manufacturing rather than imports, and the
ample cash of U.S. investors and tourists rather than the spare pennies

Figure 15: Celebrating "El Centenario" (From left: Helmuth, Pedro, and Ruth Boker, Alexander Scharff, Gunther Boker, Gabriele Buchenau, Margot Boker) (Archivo Boker, Mexico City).

of the old trade conquistador families. The rise of an industrial mega-lopolis amidst more intimate ties between Mexico and the United States therefore ended the heyday of European merchants in Mexico City. At the same time, the Bokers faced a Mexican society that no longer coun-tenanced unassimilated foreign enclaves. Living at the margins of what has misleadingly been referred to as the Mexican miracle, the fourth generation grew up in a city in which foreign merchants played a steadily decreasing role.[2] Exposed to Mexican mass culture, this gen-eration finally began the process of assimilation of the Boker family.

When the Air Became Less Clear

The Bokers looked to recover from the *intervención* in an environment of rapid economic growth made possible in large part by political sta-bility under the leadership of a dominant party. After 1940, Avila Camacho had given closure to the postrevolutionary era by ending the feud with the Catholic Church and replacing the Marxist leader of the CTM with the moderate Fidel Velásquez. Avila Camacho's successor, Miguel Alemán, combined lip service to the Mexican Revolution with the construction of a corrupt, authoritarian state dominated by what was now called the PRI (Party of the Institutional Revolution). In theory a popular party composed of peasants, workers, and the middle classes, the PRI masked an alliance between the state, foreign investors, and a rapidly rising Mexican entrepreneurial bourgeoisie. Although other parties existed, such as the conservative PAN (National Action Party), the PRI ruled virtually unchallenged until the 1980s. The dominance of this party in Mexican politics does not mean that the "post-postrevolutionary" state was a monolithic Leviathan, as suggested in a popular U.S. textbook for Mexican history.[3] Instead, post-1940 Mexico—and the party that dominated its political landscape for the rest of the century—was the product of a process of negotiation between the "top" and the "bottom," and of the interplay between mass and popular cultures.[4]

While the Bokers and other entrepreneurs benefited from political stability, they remained alienated from this cynical political system. Franz aptly summarized his family's opinion about Mexican politics when he called the PRI "a creation of firmly entrenched ex-revolutionaries. Its program: realization of the ideals . . . of the great revolution of 1910–1917. Its true goal, however, is to keep its members in power."[5] He had a point: Alemán actively courted foreign investment and allowed his cronies to enrich themselves with lucrative government contracts and the unethical sharing of inside information on future infrastructure projects, all while claiming the mantle of the revolution for his party. After he left office, the administrations of Adolfo Ruiz Cortines (1952–58) and Adolfo López Mateos (1958–64) solidified the power of the PRI by alternately placating the Right and the Left. In this fashion, Ruiz Cortines's dour demeanor contrasted with the populism of López Mateos, who—in what led Franz to label him a "hot-air merchant"—verbally supported the Cuban Revolution while tacitly welcoming U.S. measures to isolate it.[6] Finally, President Gustavo Díaz Ordaz, a man often dubbed "Porfirio Díaz Ordaz" for his conservative policies, made his indelible imprint on history by presiding over the massacre of Tlatelolco. On October 2, 1968, on the eve of the inauguration of the Olympic Games in Mexico City, security forces killed hundreds of university students who were demonstrating for a more democratic Mexico. The carnage tore off the mask of the PRI as the torchbearer of revolutionary change.[7] Even Gunther, a strident anti-Communist who feared left-wing protest movements, opined that the government had gone too far in its brutality.[8] Had Franz Böker not died a few months before the centennial of the Casa Boker, he probably would have seen the shootings as an ominous foreboding. The Tlatelolco massacre not only exposed the flaws of the PRI but also marked the end of what observers later labeled the "golden decades" of Mexico City.[9]

While the Bokers could not share in such nostalgia, there was a reason for the "golden decades" label. Until 1970, the capital experienced rapid economic development, with yearly growth rates of up to 12 percent, as its population increased from 1.5 million to 8.5 million. An ambitious industrialization program promoted the domestic manufacture of precisely those imported goods that the Casa Boker sold at ample margins. Along with the metropolitan areas of Guadalajara, Monterrey, and Puebla, the valley of Mexico was home to a large part of the new industries.[10] In Franz's words, his adopted city came to enjoy "screaming prosperity,"—a description that reflected the coming of age of Mexico City's entrepreneurial bourgeoisie rather than a general improvement in living standards.[11] This growth transformed a compact Hispanic city into a sprawling metropolis that blended Mexican and North American ways in a new, uneasy syncretism. Even as most Mexicans continued to frequent taco stands, *pulquerías,* and open-air markets, the suburbs seduced the wealthy with new restaurants, shops, and finally even U.S.-style malls that competed with the staid downtown stores. The syncretism—which also included some influence from "socialist realism" as practiced behind the Iron Curtain—found its reflection in housing patterns as well. The government constructed huge Soviet-style apartment complexes for wage-earning workers, and the growing middle class moved into new suburbs, such as Ciudad Satélite, built according to the precepts of U.S. urban planners. As the famed poet and city chronicler Salvador Novo saw it, the Americanization of the urban landscape provided evidence of the growing sophistication of a city that offered its residents a choice between traditional Mexican culture and cosmopolitan flair. Of course, Novo knew that poor Mexicans could not but choose the *taquería* while their bosses enjoyed steaks and champagne at the San Angel Inn.[12]

Fortunately for the Bokers, the urban sprawl initially diminished neither the livability of the city nor the importance of the downtown district. During the 1950s, automobile traffic "was light enough so that middle-class people could make their way home for a . . . lunch break."[13] Had Franz and Gunther not lived so far from the city center, they could have continued their prewar tradition of spending the middle of the day at home in Tlacopac. Despite the emergence of the suburbs as an alternative for shopping, until the early 1970s the Centro remained the commercial heart of the city, and the Casa Boker its best-known hardware store.[14]

Begun under the Cárdenas administration and accelerated during the 1940s, the drive toward an industrial future followed a trend of the larger Latin American countries to ditch export-led growth in favor of domestic manufacturing. Alemán and his successors heeded the advice

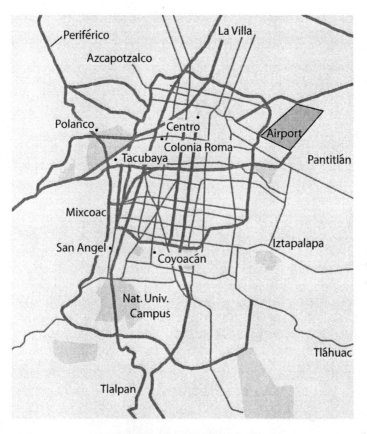

Map 3: Metropolitan Mexico City.

of Raúl Prebisch, the Argentine chair of the United Nations' Economic Commission for Latin America, to combat weakening terms of trade with accelerated industrialization. The roller-coaster ride that the Latin American economies had experienced since the Great Depression had shattered the liberal orthodoxy that exchanging raw materials for industrial products made economic sense. As the prices of Latin America's export products first hurtled downward, then ratcheted upward during World War II, only to fall back to earth, Prebisch argued that the terms of trade left Latin Americans shortchanged. Financed by an alliance of the state, national capitalists, and foreign banks, this most aggressive phase of industrialization was designed to decrease the dependence on the industrialized world and to retain a greater part of the capital generated in Mexico. It also addressed the problem of a shortage of industrial imports at a time when many European factories still lay in ruins and a large number of U.S. manufacturers produced for the cold war.[15] The overall results of this program were impressive: between 1950 and 1973, per capita gross domestic product doubled from $1,169 to $2,349 in 1980 dollars. This increase was not only 17 percent higher than the Latin American average; it approached the average of the OECD countries—the most "developed" nations of the world—and it was 11 percent greater than that registered in Mexico during the preceding fifty years.[16]

However, the program of accelerated industrialization contained serious flaws. In the first place, it increased rather than decreased the need for foreign, and especially U.S. capital. Accompanied by a growing neglect of rural development, the program necessitated the import of food and expensive capital goods. The immense cost of building new industries also required public and private borrowing, which in turn made Mexico vulnerable to inflation and monetary depreciation. Thus, the cycles of the global economy affected Mexico just as they had done before. For example, in 1954, just after a brief economic boom during the Korean War, the peso dropped from 8.65 to 12.50 to the U.S. dollar. This experience led to the policy of "stabilizing development," a hard-money stance that kept the peso at the fixed rate of 12.50 to the dollar until 1976.[17] In order to safeguard the country's fledgling industry from foreign competition, the Mexican government erected high protectionist barriers. By the mid-1960s, these barriers forced the Bokers to pay customs duties that often approximated the value of the imports, and virtually all imported hardware required import permits.[18]

Industrialization ultimately proved a mixed blessing for Mexico City. Although economic growth primarily benefited the entrepreneurial bourgeoisie and a burgeoning middle class, it also created increasing disparities of wealth along with rampant corruption and out-of-control urbanization. The statistics that showed steady improvement of living conditions obscured the fact that urban squalor increasingly marked the northern and eastern reaches of the nation's capital, as well as an explosion in real estate values that far outpaced official inflation figures. As the countryside remained undercapitalized in an era when advances in medicine allowed an annual population growth of 3 percent or more, millions of rural migrants streamed to Mexico City in search of work. Those lucky enough to find jobs that paid a few dollars a day lived in small, cramped apartments; the rest became squatters in a growing ring of *ciudades perdidas* (shantytowns) that resembled the *favelas* of Rio de Janeiro and São Paulo.[19]

The Mexican version of the industrial miracle gradually reduced the quality of life even for the bourgeoisie. The Bokers learned this lesson in graphic fashion in 1960, when a high-rise rose up just southeast of the Casa Amarilla to block the family's view of the volcanoes.

To this family, the ugly building provided a dramatic statement that the megacity had arrived in a quaint colonial village many miles away from the city center, and a reminder that even in San Angel, asphalt and the automobile had replaced dirt roads and the horse cart.[20] As the city grew, air quality also declined. As recently as 1963, novelist Carlos Fuentes had referred to the Valley of Mexico as the "region where the air is clearest."[21] A short decade later, industrial and exhaust fumes obscured the Bokers' view of their surroundings to such a degree that the hulking building did not make much of a difference.

Accelerated industrialization, then, completed a long-term process that left the Bokers at the sidelines of Mexican economic development. Along with other import businesses, the Casa Boker faced a concerted effort to industrialize Mexico that reflected the determination of both the state and the private sector to reduce the country's dependence on imports. While the CFM numbered among the first clients of the new industrialists, it did not become an exclusive customer as in the case of Arbolito and, much earlier, Remington and Singer. As a result, Mexican-made items offered smaller profit margins than imported ones. The "Mexican miracle" thus not only created Mexican competition for the foreign-made items that had made the fortunes of the CFM, but it also contributed decisively to the rapid growth of a city in which the Casa Boker played an ever decreasing role.

No Miracle for an Import Business

The postwar period proved to be a difficult time for the Casa Boker. After six years of Junta control, the Casa Boker stood on the brink of bankruptcy. The immediate legacy of that period—debt, a dearth of cash, a low inventory, and staffing problems—preoccupied Gunther for the first three years thereafter. The long-term consequences of the intervention (labor relations and a loss of market share) proved even harder to tackle. Under these conditions, it was almost a miracle that the Casa Boker returned to profitability far more modest than that of the Porfirian and postrevolutionary periods.

When he took over the CFM in late 1948, Gunther faced conditions that would have persuaded someone who did not value preserving a family patrimony to liquidate the company. Cash on hand totaled less than $1,000, and when wages came due two days later, Gunther did not have the money to pay them. Moreover, the document that authorized the return of the CFM imposed onerous terms. In addition to claiming for the Junta all profits from the preceding six years, it stipulated that the Bokers repay a "profit" of almost 1.8 million pesos that consisted of a nominally higher value of the inventory. A product of the carestía, these inflation gains were in fact losses, as the worth of the inventory had dropped in real terms. Many of the items that the CFM had bought during the intervention period were Mexican- and U.S.-made goods that were available at a lower cost at other stores. The years of decline had cost the Casa Boker the services of forty employees, in addition to the ethnic Germans fired by the Junta. Many of those who left departed to take advantage of more lucrative contracts with competitors. To top it off, the flooding of the Centro following heavy rains in July 1952—which gave the streets surrounding the Casa Boker the appearance of Venice—caused widespread damage.[22]

Not surprisingly, tackling the company's liquidity problem and finding staff at the management level constituted Gunther's first priorities. After long negotiations, the Mexican government reduced the debt by more than 1 million pesos, and Gunther and Franz used personal funds to cover the rest. Reestablishing a viable cash flow also forced the two men to dig up the milk cans in the yard of the Casa Amarilla and to liquidate their interest in the El Anfora stoneware factory. In April 1949, an infusion of 2 million pesos doubled the capital of the CFM.[23] The staff issue proved equally difficult. For the Bokers, improving personnel meant finding ethnic Germans, and most of the former German-speaking staff members had left the hardware business if not the country. Moreover, Mexicans had come to occupy the posts formerly held by German speakers. Not only did the terms of the agreement with the Mexican government forbid Gunther to demote these managers; he also remained grateful to them for keeping the company afloat despite the Junta's effort to bleed it dry. In fact, Gunther formally shared power with Arturo Pliego, who had steadfastly defended the Bokers' interests during the Junta administration. Ultimately, the CFM hired just five Germans, among them Carlos Seippel, who became head of the retail department, and Claus Schlenker, who was director of the wholesale department for most of his fifty years with the Casa Boker.[24]

If this matter had proven difficult enough for Gunther, relations with the union would cause him continuing headaches. In 1932, the workers of the Casa Boker had formed the UET, a pliant company union. The UET that greeted the Bokers in late 1948 bore little resemblance to this "white" company union, as three years of declining real wages and a distant, impersonal Junta had undone the paternalistic relationship that had existed before World War II. Following the strike of 1947, the union had negotiated a more favorable labor contract in exchange for accepting a smaller pay increase. Gunther particularly loathed the so-called *escalafón,* or staircase, a rule that stipulated the filling of staff vacancies with the most senior employee within the same unit. No longer could management promote a junior,

Figure 16: The great flood of 1952 (Archivo Boker, Mexico City).

but better qualified worker over a more senior colleague. The contract made it difficult for Gunther and Arturo Pliego to fire an employee and impossible to pare down a staff of 170 despite deteriorated business conditions. Moreover, the union hired all new employees except at the executive level. For its part, the UET regarded these provisions as nonnegotiable, their only victories during a long period of declining real wages.[25]

The most fundamental problem underlying these difficulties was a decline in market share. To be sure, the CFM remained the foremost German hardware store of the capital—and, in fact, the only one of note that had survived the tumultuous first half of the twentieth century. But new, formidable competitors claimed retail customers. Most importantly, Jewish and Spanish refugees had set up scores of small stores in Corregidora Street east of the Zócalo. These *tiendas* successfully vied with the Casa Boker for retail customers. The wholesale operation faced another problem: that of direct marketing. During the war, the blacklists had forced many U.S. manufacturers that had sold through German hardware stores to form their own distribution networks. Many of these producers learned that direct marketing proved more effective than they had expected. Likewise, Mexican producers

Figure 17: The weight of tradition: Gunther
Boker (Archivo Boker, Mexico City).

directly sold to retailers and, after 1970, signed large contracts with
new wholesalers in Monterrey, the cradle of the nation's hardware
industry. By 1975, that city boasted companies such as the Ferretería
Nacional de Monterrey that rivaled the Casa Boker in serving a nationwide web of wholesale customers.[26]

In addition, U.S. corporations reshaped the commercial landscape
of Mexico City. In February 1947, Archbishop Luis María Martínez
blessed a brand new department store on Avenida Insurgentes, several
miles southwest of the Centro. The real Sears, Roebuck had come to
Mexico, a corporation that demonstrated by way of comparison that
the Casa Boker was not prepared for the age of mass consumption.
Sears brought the first vertically integrated department store to Mexico,
a store that combined manufacturing, warehousing, and distribution
into one operation. Unlike the old-style department stores, it did not
focus on a set of product lines in order to offer specialized merchandise, but instead offered customers a wide range of common products
at low prices, many of them manufactured in Mexico. With the backing of a huge corporation, Sears de México aggressively marketed itself

as an affordable, middle-class, and "American" alternative to its aristocratic, upper-class, and European competitors such as the Casa Boker and El Palacio de Hierro.[27] Its success soon attracted imitators: in 1956, Woolworth opened two stores in the Mexican capital. Both Sears and Woolworth provided competition for the Casa Boker in the areas of toys, garden supplies, and kitchenware. They contributed to a decline in the percentage of U.S. products in the catalog of the Casa Boker from 30 percent in 1935 to around 10 percent in the 1960s (see Table 3).

Nonetheless, many purveyors and customers remained loyal to the Casa Boker. To begin with, the Arbolito cutlery from Heinrich Böker and Company had not lost its appeal. In fact, when the Allies forced the Solingen firm and all other West German producers to imprint their products with a "Made in West Germany" mark, the Arbolito merchandise became even more attractive to many Mexicans. As a barber told this author: "I bought this German razor in the Casa Boker ten years ago, and I still use it. An American razor would have given up long ago, let alone a Mexican one!"[28] The company regained the business of several important British and U.S. producers as well; for example, the toolmaker Stanley renewed its old relationship with the CFM as early as 1952.[29] Winning back wholesale customers also proved easier than expected. By 1963, capably guided by twenty traveling agents on a commission basis, the wholesale operation accounted for almost 50 percent of total sales, and the company enjoyed close ties to a number of industrial clients. Even the Jewish merchants bought merchandise from the Casa Boker.[30]

The surviving balance sheets of the CFM tell the tale of a modest recovery. As Table 11 reveals, the earnings of the company grew during the 1950s, especially after the stabilization of the peso in 1954, before displaying an erratic pattern over the 1959–70 period. In real terms, these earnings appear minuscule in light of the exchange rate of 12.50 pesos per dollar. Nonetheless, the unofficial figures of the Fondo A, which included the gains of La Esperanza as well as other profits kept outside the books, by far exceeded these numbers. In 1962, Gunther's official personal income was close to 600,000 pesos (50,000 dollars), and the sales of the Casa Boker amounted approximately 30 million pesos, or 2.4 million dollars in 1965. Although down almost 50 percent from the 1941 figures, these numbers suggest significantly higher profits than those exhibited in the official tables.[31]

The Bokers might well have been content with the recovery of their business if they had owned the Casa Boker outright. However, the CFM was operated, but not majority owned, by Mexicans. Franz, the son of one of five former partners of the Casa Boker, had not been able to acquire a majority. After the revolution, Franz had created the Fondo

Table 11: Official Earnings of CFM, 1949–1970
(in thousands of pesos)

1949	673
1950	1,182
1951	494
1952	491
1953	1,199
1954	1,746
1955	1,567
1956	1,015
1957	1,255
1958	680
1959	543
1960	935
1968	1,320
1969	1,717
1970	1,053

Source: Asambleas Ordinarias, CFM, 1950–1971, AB, FA.[32]

A, a secret holding company that left 58 percent of the shares with Carlitos Friederichs and the families of Franz's sisters, Elisabeth Lucas, Clara Böninger, and Gertrud Hentzen, while the official books of the CFM showed only Mexican citizens as shareholders. Not surprisingly, the principal interest of these Germans in the Casa Boker consisted of their annual dividend. This dividend varied between 6 and 12 percent after 1948, when the Bokers felt that their bombed-out relatives in Germany needed every possible penny.[33]

Therefore, the question whether to buy the interest of the German relatives in the Fondo A had occupied Gunther and Franz throughout the 1950s. Gunther desired to invest in domestic manufacturing as a solution to the problem of obtaining quality, Mexican-made products, while his father wanted to buy out the overseas "shareholders" to avoid further share dilution after his death. What ultimately tipped the scales in favor of Franz's position was a 1961 decree that required at least 51 percent Mexican ownership in each company, a law that ironically excluded multinational corporations. Although Mexican authorities did not know of the existence of the Fondo A, the Bokers would not risk expropriation by defying this decree. Instead, Gunther visited Germany in the fall of 1962 and purchased enough "shares" to increase his and Franz's interest in the Fondo A to 57 percent.[34]

Gunther's visit showed that the Mexican Bokers valued their extended family more than their German relatives did. While bidding for his relatives' shares, Gunther found out that the Germans had no interest whatsoever in the viability of the Casa Boker. Spoiled after decades of handsome dividends, the relatives demanded such exorbitant amounts for these shares that Gunther finally announced a drastic reduction in the dividend.[35] Due to the modest profits of the CFM, it took him eight more years until he bought out the final German "shareholder." Fortunately, Gunther did not face a further dilution of shares upon his father's death in 1965. Franz's pre-testamentary dispositions, as well as buyout agreements with Gabriele, Helmuth, and Liesel's son Dieter Vermehren, made him the owner of 100 percent of Franz's Fondo A shares.[36]

Franz and Gunther's favorable treatment of the German shareholders revealed the business ethics of a bygone era in both Germany and Mexico. Indeed, since the Germans could not produce actual shares that would have documented a legal claim, most people in Gunther's position would have forced a sale of the shares at deeply discounted prices. After all, it was the directors' clever camouflage that had rescued the CFM from confiscation during the war, and the devaluation of the peso had diminished the value of the shares. By paying a high price, Franz and Gunther did an honorable deed, but one that eliminated any possibility of expanding their position in an increasingly competitive market. Yet, the Bokers' sense of obligation to their German relatives also demonstrated the convergence of German and Mexican values in this respect. Just like the Gómez clan of Lomnitz and Pérez-Lizaur's study, which refused to take its company public in order to safeguard employment opportunities for family members, the Bokers subordinated economic gain to the interests of the extended family.[37]

Despite the differences between them, both Franz and Gunther ultimately demonstrated that they intended to continue on old paths: no debt, little reinvestment of profits, and no major initiatives to diversify the company and attract new customers. In particular, the long-standing reluctance to invest in industry came to haunt the company.

Although this attitude initially seemed appropriate due to the magnitude of the job of rebuilding the company, it cost the Casa Boker dearly in an age that historian Arnold Bauer has dubbed that of "consumer nationalism."[38] As new legislation required permits for most imported goods, Mexican-made items increasingly replaced imports on the shelves of the company's warehouse. As Díaz Ordaz told Gunther, it was "unpatriotic to import merchandise."[39] Even though it is difficult to measure the intrinsic attraction of Mexican-made versus imported goods, imports clearly lost ground in an era when they were punished by protective tariffs and undersold by cheaper Mexican products. The percentage of foreign-made goods in the CFM catalog dropped to 50 percent by 1975 (see Table 3). In general, domestically manufactured merchandise yielded no more than one-half the profit margin of imported products—a problem that could only have been solved by locally manufacturing some of these products under a Mexican brand name. In the absence of a stake in industrial production, the CFM stagnated at a time when the "Mexican miracle" was still in full bloom.[40]

It was thus not surprising that the already strained relations between management and labor deteriorated through this period. At a time when industrial wages increased an average of 8 percent per year, almost double the rate of inflation, the real income of employees in the Casa Boker lagged behind. As Table 12 illustrates, nominal wages increased at an annual average of 5.5 percent between 1956 and 1973 for a total increase of 150 percent. However, government estimates of the cost of living of Mexican workers show an average annual increase of 4.4 percent for these years, and historian Jeffrey Bortz has demonstrated that these official estimates of inflation are too low.[41] A profit-sharing scheme devised by outgoing president López Mateos in 1964 did not help matters much. While it gave 8 percent of net earnings to the employees, profits kept outside the official books eluded this effort to better the living conditions of Mexican wage earners.[42] In its demands for a just compensation, however, the union overestimated the financial health of the company and proved unwilling to agree to a more flexible labor contract that would have allowed the Bokers to reduce the workforce. If the directors had been able to downsize their personnel and increase efficiency, the UET might well have succeeded in negotiating larger wage increases. Because of the ironclad rule in the labor contract that each departing worker be replaced, however, they limited the ability of CFM to match national wage trends. Therefore, rising labor costs put pressure on the company's earnings without bringing relief to the workers. In 1971, the lowest-paid worker contractually received 281 pesos (22 dollars) per week, while the highest-paid worker, often a veteran of fifteen or more years, received 941 pesos, or 75 dollars.[43] Attempting to slice a pie that no longer grew in size, both the Bokers and their workers thus ended up unhappy with their share.

This situation grew worse between 1970 and 1976, when Luis Echeverría Alvarez presided over a significant economic downturn at the precise moment that the Tlatelolco massacre had left the credibility of the PRI in shambles. Gunther had initially harbored high hopes for Echeverría, whom he knew as a former partner in a law firm in the Edificio Boker, a golf partner, and a fellow parent at the CAAH. He supported the efforts of the former secretary of Gobernación to suppress an emergent guerrilla movement.[44] But the new president soon

Table 12: Weekly Wages in the CFM, 1956–1973

Year	Worker "H"	Elevator operator	Overseer of packing room
1956	134.50	194.00	402.00
1965	182.50	336.50	690.80
1971	280.85	480.80	941.40
1973	323.00	552.90	1,082.60

Source: "Contrato Colectivo del Trabajo," (1956, 1965, 1971, and 1973) AB, FS.

demonstrated his desire to co-opt the rest of the Left. He declared Mexico a nonaligned leader of the Third World and publicly scoffed at Western capitalism during photo ops with Cuba's Fidel Castro and Palestinian leader Yasser Arafat. Echeverría also expanded profit sharing and established housing subsidies partially funded by employer contributions; benefits that put further pressure on the balance sheet of the Casa Boker.[45] Gunther was not too disturbed at this rhetoric until 1973, when leftist guerrillas assassinated Eugenio Garza Sada, patriarch of the Monterrey Group and one of the wealthiest men in Mexico. That same year, a global recession led the national economy into crisis. At a time when the recession made credit tight, decades of state borrowing led to a revival of inflation. The government's attempts to sustain the peso left Mexican products vulnerable on the world market, and Mexico's balance of payments deteriorated further until 1976, when Echeverría allowed the peso to fall to half its previous value. As the crisis unfolded, he announced a return to the principles of the revolution in order to assuage the lower classes, the sector hardest hit by the recession. Most importantly, he raised taxes on the rich in order to finance ambitious new programs that sought to mitigate social inequality and regain popular support for the PRI. Together, Echeverría's populist response to the economic crisis and the murder of Garza Sada made Gunther paranoid about Mexican politics. Along with other entrepreneurs, he viewed the president as an authoritarian socialist who desired to abolish private property and suppress dissent after the Soviet model.[46]

Not surprisingly, Echeverría's rule witnessed a further deterioration of management-labor relations in the Casa Boker. When inflation topped 20 percent in 1973, these relations reached the breaking point. In September of that year, four months after the UET had won a 15 percent pay increase, Echeverría called for a nationwide 18 percent wage hike. During the ensuing negotiations, the UET demanded a further increase, and on October 1, the second strike in the history of the Casa

Boker began. Despite his contempt for Echeverría, Gunther personally called on the Mexican president to intercede. On the president's orders, an official from the Mexico City government brokered an agreement favorable to the Bokers on November 23. Stunned by the intervention of a supposedly pro-labor government, the UET leaders remained bitter toward what they saw as a stingy and exploitative CFM management. For his part, Gunther had to admit that Echeverría was not so hostile to entrepreneurs after all.[47]

Looking back on the past quarter of a century, the Casa Boker had successfully rebuilt itself from the Junta takeover, but it had lost crucial ground. Five factors had conspired to decrease the importance of the Casa Boker in the Mexican commercial landscape: the loss of capital and market share resulting from the *intervención;* increasing hurdles to the importation of foreign goods; the ongoing difficulties with the UET; the need to buy out the German shareholders, and Gunther's personality, which was no less averse to risk than that of his father. Hamstrung by dwindling profits and without optimism for the future, the leaders of the company did not invest in the government-sponsored industries that had made riches for a new Mexican bourgeoisie and its U.S. associates. If the leaders of the entrepreneurial bourgeoisie of postwar Mexico were, in the words of political scientist Roderic Camp, "competitive, innovative risk-takers, lacking in future orientation," Gunther Boker and his father worried so much about the future that they were no better prepared when it arrived.[48]

So Far from Germany and So Near the United States

While the Casa Boker became more marginal within the Mexican economy, the family that owned it confronted diminished European influence in Mexico during the cold war era. As U.S.-style consumerism made headway in Mexico City, defeated and divided Germany rose from the ashes only to ape its respective masters, the United States and the Soviet Union. To paraphrase the famous adage attributed to Porfirio Díaz, the Bokers realized that they lived "so far from Germany and so near the United States." This insight drove them to come to terms with the United States as the leader of the capitalist world, and to grapple with the disintegration of the German colony in Mexico City.

One important impetus for the Bokers' rethinking of their position in the world came from the endless negotiations with the German "shareholders," a process that had soured both father and son on their German relatives. In their view, these relatives had not reciprocated Franz and Gunther's charitable disposition toward their hungry kin in the immediate postwar period. The more the *Wirtschaftswunder* (West Germany's own economic and political miracle) elevated its citizens to new prosperity, the more the Germans demanded in payment for their stake in the Fondo A. As Franz and Gunther concluded, their relatives selfishly promoted their financial interests without understanding the situation of the CFM. Franz had to realize that his relatives saw the Casa Boker as a "blue flower" to be picked at the convenience of wealthy Germans.[49]

This disenchantment contributed to a process of alienation from Germany rooted in the defeat and division of their ancestral homeland, a process that had begun immediately after the war. Franz hid his sorrow about the German defeat by banishing all German books from his household. Surrounded by a small circle of friends composed primarily of Spanish refugees, he instead read Spanish literature. Perhaps appropriately, Miguel de Cervantes Saavedra's *Don Quixote* became his favorite book, followed by the works of *Generación del 98* authors such as Miguel de Unamuno.[50] For his part, Gunther reportedly showed his psychological distance from Germany during a visit to Bonn and Solingen in 1949, a visit that made him believe that his father's native country would never again see good times. Noting that Germans were only allowed to walk on the street, and not the sidewalk, he used the sidewalk along with the British occupation forces: "I am an Allied citizen," he proclaimed to all those who inquired.[51]

This response came naturally enough, as the United States had turned from foe to friend in the preceding four years. Whereas Franz had once looked to Germany to protect the virtues of Western civilization, the cold war fundamentally altered his family's ideological universe. Not only had the end of the war taken Germany off the map as a strong, unified country in the middle of Europe; it also left two superpowers and an ideological struggle between capitalism and Communism. As the specter of Communism emerged as the single greatest fear of foreign investors in Latin America, the Cold War significantly mitigated the Bokers' dislike of the United States and its allies. Although Gunther referred to the United States as "our so-called Allies," and even though his father railed against what he saw as the consummation of U.S. hegemony, both realized the need to let go of yesterday's anti-U.S. slogans.[52]

While the acceptance of U.S. leadership in the Cold War constituted a step in a new direction, history threatened to repeat itself when the German colony in general and the Bokers in particular failed to embrace democracy in Germany. In part, the colony's renitence owed to the fact that the Federal Republic constituted only the western half of the old nation-state. But at least as importantly, the Germans in Mexico City resented the close association with the Western Allies, an alliance that prompted Franz to call the rump country "Rheinbund Germany" in reference to the era of the Napoleonic occupation.[53] After the left-of-center

Social Democratic Party won the 1969 elections, Gunther and Margot opposed the progressive spirit that connected Germany with the other members of the new European Union. Finally, even the Wirtschaftswunder elicited concern among overseas Germans. As the Cold War neared its height, the rise of shopping malls and modernist cultural symbols emphasized what one critic has called the "Coca-Colonization" of Europe.[54] During a trip to Germany in August 1961, Helmuth observed that a "scary" degree of prosperity had made West Germans shallow and superficial. He would later insistently criticize what he called the "Mexicanization" of Germany—the decline of Prussian discipline in a more open and democratic society, and what he saw as a rise of corruption, which was in reality also a more honest and open accounting for the failings of government officials.[55]

Over time, however, the Bokers and their peers accepted the democratic, capitalist West Germany in light of the alternative—the Communist East Germany under Soviet control, not to mention the eastern areas incorporated into Poland and the Soviet Union.[56] The existence of the Iron Curtain was particularly painful for Margot, who, unlike Gunther, had friends and real estate in the East. The Bokers never accepted the German Democratic Republic as a sovereign state and referred to it as "Ostzone," or Eastern Zone, long after the 1972 signing of an agreement between the Federal Republic and the GDR had made the term politically incorrect.[57] Ironically, however, due to East German frustration about its exclusion from Western consumer culture, the conservative social values important to the Bokers survived to a greater degree in East Berlin and Dresden than in Hamburg and Remscheid.[58]

Not surprisingly, the Bokers and their peers found common ground in a strident anti-Communism that often defied a rational assessment of Latin American politics. As the Cold War progressed, Gunther opposed every Latin American experiment in social democracy, not to mention revolution. Guatemala, Bolivia, and Cuba in the 1950s; Brazil in the early 1960s; Chile and Nicaragua in the 1970s; and Grenada in the 1980s: Gunther saw Communism advancing throughout the hemisphere, with only U.S. intervention on hand to check it. In particular, Castro's Cuba caused him sleepless nights, as he feared the Communist contagion spreading from the Cuban "canker" through Salvador Allende's socialist government in Chile and the Mexican labor and student movements to Echeverría's government. By the time that a CIA-assisted coup put an end to Allende's presidency in September 1973, Gunther had concluded that the United States was an actual, and not just so-called, ally of conservatives all over the world.[59]

The recognition that the future of capitalism in Latin America lay squarely with the West did not stop Gunther and Helmuth from expressing similarly reactionary views of European and U.S. politics. After Willy Brandt, the Social Democratic chancellor of West Germany, signed agreements in the early 1970s that recognized Poland's post-war annexation of German territory and the existence of East Germany, he joined Castro on the Bokers' list of dangerous politicians. In Helmuth's opinion, one could not trust Brandt because he had left Germany during the war rather than help his country during a time of need, while Gunther loathed his "socialist" tendencies and his willingness to negotiate with Communist leaders.[60] Among U.S. politicians, Democratic presidential candidate George McGovern fell into a similar category because of his opposition to the Vietnam War, while President Richard Nixon enjoyed the accolades of the Bokers and other old German families in Mexico City.[61]

However, anti-Communism could not patch over the existing fissures among Germans in Mexico City. By the 1960s, no fewer than five different German communities existed in place of the former colony. The "old" Germans such as the Bokers, who had arrived before the Mexican Revolution, continued to live in the world of the German Empire. Disappointed twice by the failure of German arms and aware of the crimes of the Hitler regime, a majority of them disdained dictatorship and democracy alike, yearning for an enlightened despot to lead Germany. More numerous than the first group, the "interwar" generation still contained many Nazi supporters. As recently as the mid-1960s, many of these former Nazi Party members met in a coffeehouse just around the corner from the Edificio Boker.[62] Not surprisingly, when German author Günter Grass conducted a public reading of his anti-Nazi novel *The Dog Years,* the audience greeted his presentation with icy silence. The third group, the refugees from Nazi Germany, generally stayed aloof from both of these groups. Said Marianne Frenk-Westheim, a Jewish immigrant who considers herself German even after seventy years of residence in Mexico City: "The Germans in Mexico did not include us, and that really did not change after the war. Not that many of us wanted to be included, but the rejection still hurt."[63] The fourth group was the *Kindernazis,* or children Nazis, who had experienced the Third Reich as children only to experience a profound reorientation as young adults. Finally, as this author observed firsthand, the products of postwar democratic Germany who immigrated most recently cringed at the persistence of conservative and chauvinistic sentiments among groups one, two, and four. This group mostly consists of the so-called expats, the engineers and middle managers of multinational concerns such as Volkswagen that have begun production in Mexico since 1960.

Gunther and Margot's children grew up in a weakening network of German culture. For a variety of reasons, as a bitter disappointment to the "old" German families, the postwar era witnessed a blurring of the sharp lines between the German colony and Mexican society.[64] To begin with, changes in Mexican immigration law hindered the further development of the German colony. In 1947, the "Ley General de Población" emphasized the natural growth of the Mexican people and ended the last legal vestiges of the "whitening" ideology. The law stipulated public health and literacy programs designed to reduce the steep mortality rates of Mexican children, and it made immigration a secondary priority. It also contained incentives for Mexican workers in the United States—often called "lost sons" in their home country—to return to Mexico. The law therefore made a statement that Mexico was not a country of immigrants, and that it would increase its population primarily through natural growth. By 1973, it was precisely this growth that made the government clamp down further on immigration. After the immigration reform of that year, most newcomers only qualified for temporary visas, and obtaining permanent residency in Mexico became more difficult than receiving a "green card" for the United States.[65] Since only a continuing flow of permanent immigrants could make up for the loss of people to remigration and miscegenation, these changes threatened the foreign colonies, and particularly the German community. The immigration of German nationals remained suspended until the resumption of diplomatic relations in 1952, and Mexican law continued to curtail the activities of existing German residents. Not surprisingly, many Germans born in Mexico belatedly declared themselves Mexican citizens, a step that allowed them to bring family members from Germany.[66]

Just as importantly, the process of assimilation picked up steam. Industrialization finally produced a sizable urban entrepreneurial bourgeoisie. Not only did this group of *nouveaux riches* reject the artificial barriers existing between foreign enclaves and Mexican society; it also formed an entity equal in status to the foreign colonies, that is, an attractive point of reference for assimilation. Along with the growth of the bourgeoisie came a maturing of *mexicanidad*—an "attempt on the part of the state to create a mass media-based cultural nationalism" designed to co-opt popular cultures of resistance and dissonance with the PRI state.[67] Although this effort was only partially successful, the descendants of the old trade conquistadors progressively lost influence to the new bourgeoisie. As more Mexican families began to enjoy a higher income, more of them enrolled their children in the schools of the foreign colonies that enjoyed an excellent reputation for their stringent curriculum and their bicultural education. They also began to frequent the tennis and swim clubs of the foreign colonies. The German club in particular has become thoroughly Mexicanized. As of late 1999, among fourteen executive officers of the club, only four spoke German as their native language. A decade earlier, the Mexican tennis federation had even held its Davis Cup competition against Germany there, confident of a home-court advantage.[68] In addition, following the lead of the United States, the Mexican media began to produce culture appealing to the descendants of foreign immigrants. When young Mexicans used the new mass media to articulate their own version of the wave of counterculture made in the USA, their peers from foreign families discovered that it was "hip" to be Mexican.[69]

These changes played themselves out in the CAAH—as always the mirror of the German colony. After the Junta's takeover in 1942, the school did not offer instruction in German to new entrants, although Gunther and an amenable *interventor* convinced the Junta to allow current students to complete their German curriculum.[70] Consequently, the Mexican share of the student population increased to almost 75 percent, and Spanish became the language of currency among the students. Following the *desintervención* in 1948, new principal Rudolf Brechtel mandated the exclusive use of German in the first three grades. Consequently, German briefly regained dominance in the early 1950s. Since Brechtel could not dictate the language the children used on the school grounds, however, Spanish again began to trump German as the decade ended. A similar trend toward Spanish occurred even in the schools that had not suffered from the war, such as the American School. This era also witnessed an increasing number of mixed marriages between German and Mexican alumni of the CAAH.[71]

Not surprisingly, after 1950, Gunther, as a member of the board of directors, played an important part in promoting the German language in the school. Due in part to the difficulty of hiring German-speaking teachers, the faculty and staff included a considerable number of Nazis.[72] These Nazis played an important role in the instruction of the school. For instance, Gunther's youngest daughter, Barbara, born in 1954, related that she was taught "Fraktur" in elementary school— the arcane German script loved by the Nazis and outlawed in 1945 because most Allied censors could not read it. Moreover, Gunther vociferously defended the exclusive use of the German language. As chair of the board of the CAAH, he often showed up on the playground to exhort the students to speak German. Indeed, he visited the school as often as twice a day. At a time when the German nation-state lay in shambles, Gunther considered language the sole remaining unifier of all Germans, whether at home or abroad.[73]

Aside from his desire to preserve the German language, Gunther's campaign for the use of German in the CAAH followed pragmatic and financial considerations. Even with the Wirtschaftswunder in full bloom, the West German government did not fund the diaspora schools at nearly the same level as Adolf Hitler had done. Between 1959 and 1960, the subsidy amounted to 7.1 percent of the budget, in addition to the salaries of the teachers sent from Germany (about 13 percent of the faculty). This support represented a fraction of the assistance during the Nazi period, when Joseph Goebbels's Ministry of Propaganda had earmarked lavish funds to the education of Greater Germans.[74] When Gunther visited the German Foreign Ministry in 1960, he found out the explanation for this lack of support. In the view of the Foreign Ministry, the Colegio Alemán was not a German school because the majority of the students spoke Spanish. As one Ministry official pointed out, "In your school, German is not even spoken during the breaks!"[75] Despite its proclamations of international friendship, the Federal Republic wished to help educate Germans rather than Mexicans. Moreover, the level of corporate subsidies to the school reflected the dominant sector within the foreign community—the German corporations and their employees—at the expense of the old immigrant families. In the case of the American school, multinational corporations provided funding with the primary purpose of enabling the children of their employees to reenter their home schools after several years abroad. By contrast, they had little interest in financing bicultural schools in which the primary language was Spanish.[76]

During the late 1960s, the Mexicanization of the "foreign" schools in general and the Colegio Alemán in particular attained full force. The triumph of the Social Democrats in Germany ushered in a centralist policy designed to increase state control over semiprivate German schools abroad, as well as the arrival of progressive faculty who alienated the largely conservative German community. The German-Mexicans did not like either of these changes. According to the former secretary of the school, Blanca Huici, these smelly and "slovenly dressed Hippie teachers," who had attended German universities during the time of student protests in the late 1960s, provided a poor advertisement for German culture.[77] In fact, many of these teachers saw a political mission in an expensive school in which most of the students came from privileged backgrounds. To make matters worse, these teachers earned up to five times of the salary of their Mexican colleagues, and more than twice as much as bilingual German-Mexicans who possessed the best qualifications to teach in this bicultural school. Nonetheless, Mexican elite families continued to send their children to the CAAH, as they still believed that knowledge of German culture improved the moral fabric of their children. According to Huici, even Presidents Echeverría and José López Portillo, as well as the noted Mexican intellectual Daniel Cosío Villegas, enrolled their children there. Bolstered by

160

the influx of "hippie teachers" and a bicultural curriculum supported by the new left-of-center authorities in Germany, the school soon promoted a more progressive vision.[78]

The issue of the "hippie teachers" highlighted the crisis in confidence among the German colony. The citizens of imperial and Nazi Germany had held their heads high at a time when their country's military power jockeyed for world dominance, and they had often regarded the Mexicans as an inferior people. With the two successor states a pair of pawns on the Cold-War chessboard, however, self-segregation from Mexican society became hard to justify. Moreover, the already divided German colony fell to mutual recriminations. The Nazi past separated those who had actively participated in the dictatorship from those who had passively observed the situation, only to proclaim their anti-Nazi leanings as soon as the war was over. A further gap existed between these two factions and returnees from Germany such as Gabriele, who had lived through years of aerial bombings and bitterly complained about the materialist attitude of the Germans in Mexico. In Gabriele's view, the German colony had enjoyed an easy ride, relatively speaking.[79] Her son Ulrich bluntly decried the "insipid and superficial materialism" of the German colony that flew in the face of the millions of lives claimed during the war.[80]

Finally, a new wave of German immigrants once again overwhelmed the existing German colony. Between 1960 and 1990, almost 6,000 Germans came to Mexico City on temporary visas. "Industrial nomads," most of these newcomers worked for multinational companies such as Volkswagen and planned to return to Germany at the conclusion of a three- to five-year term. Better paid than most German-Mexicans, many of these "Kartoffeldeutsche" or "potato Germans"—a reference to their preference for boiled potatoes over the rice, black beans, and tortillas served at most German-Mexican dinner tables—proved more alien to the old colony than many Mexicans. Only a minority of the newcomers expressed an interest in the country where they worked and lived. Therefore, beyond the classroom, only tenuous links connected pre-1945 immigrants and their children to the German industrial nomads, who often showed little interest in Mexican society and culture.[81] Not surprisingly, where old and new Germans met, their cultural differences produced conflict. The Bokers and other conservative German-Mexican families resented the progressive politics of the "Kartoffeldeutsche," and particularly the "hippie teachers." They also opposed the soul searching that took place in a Lutheran church engaged with confronting its role in the Nazi past.[82] Therefore, if Gunther Boker had already exhibited marked differences in identity from his relatives, his children would not only differ from their German peers but also from the "Kartoffeldeutsche" in the Colegio Alemán.

Under the Broken Bell Jar

Living in a house across from the Casa Amarilla in the Boker compound, Gunther and Margot attempted to raise their children as traditional Germans. In what one of their daughters-in-law later labeled a "ghetto," they defended their heritage to a greater degree than most other old German families in Mexico.[83] Like Auguste and Luise before her, Margot taught her two Mexican servants to make German dishes, which her family ate in the dining room while the servants ate Mexican fare in the kitchen. Gunther and Margot gave their children German names, among them those of Gunther's brothers who had died in the war. They sent their children to the CAAH and discouraged the use of Spanish in their home. According to their daughters, Barbara and Renate, they even charged them 5 centavos (about 0.4 cents) for each Spanish word directed at a member of the family.[84] When the children grew into teenagers, their parents sent three of them to a boarding school in the small German town of Holzminden, one of the few schools that offered Spanish. Moreover, the German education fomented in their home followed traditions of a bygone era. Not only did "old" German families such as the Bokers pine for the lost greatness of their nation; Gunther and Margot's image of Germany corresponded to their personal experiences in the 1920s and 1930s.

Gunther and Margot's children therefore developed a hybrid identity, as they grew up in a world that increasingly demanded acceptance of and assimilation into Mexican bourgeois society. They also came to know a Germany that—quite in contrast to that of their parents and grandparents—no longer projected an imperial presence in Latin America. Moreover, they faced a pervasive U.S. cultural influence in Mexico that fundamentally shaped the attitudes of urban Mexicans. As might be expected, however, the four surviving children each came to terms with the shattered bell jar in their own way.[85] As they each remain alive today, which precluded a look at their personal correspondence and other written sources, the following discussion relies primarily on oral history interviews. In addition to important anecdotal evidence, these interviews reveal the self-perception of the four Bokers, complemented by the views of Mexicans who know them and this author's personal impressions.[86]

Born in 1941, Pedro/Peter, the eldest of these children uses both the Spanish and the German version of his name in order to express what he has fashioned as a bicultural identity. His ancestors had used

Figure 18: Margot and her children (From left: Pedro, Barbara, Margot, Klaus, Renate) (Archivo Boker, Mexico City).

"Roberto" and "Francisco" instead of "Robert" and "Franz" in order to facilitate the communication with Mexicans. Pedro/Peter, however, feels equally comfortable with the Spanish "Pedro" and the German "Peter." A congenial, sociable man with a temperament resembling that of his mother, Pedro has constructed the identity of a "Mexican of German descent" proud of his bicultural heritage.[87] Although he lived in Germany for six years, Pedro never felt at home there, and he considered many of the Germans he met uninterested in his opinions. After his return to Mexico in 1966, he demonstrated his affinity for Mexican culture by bringing the first person into the Boker family who spoke Spanish as her native language, Cecilia Regens Galvanduque, who is of Austrian, Czech, and Mexican extraction. Her father was one of the few prominent former Jewish members of the German colony and later president of the Club Alemán.[88] With her family ties to the Mexican bourgeoisie, Cecilia brought a new element into the Boker family. Strong-willed and independent, she was not in awe of the venerable merchant clan, and her marriage to Pedro served as a sign that the days of self-segregation lay in the past. She claims to have steered Pedro toward a greater identification with Mexico: in her words, "the

Pedro of today is no longer the Pedro of the past."[89] Ironically, Cecilia herself is hardly an average Mexican: according to her father, the "Mexican traditions in [her] family are not very strong."[90]

Pedro's and Cecilia's volunteer activities demonstrated that the couple did more than promoting the interests of the German colony in Mexico City. To be sure, Pedro followed the example of his forebears in serving on the board of the CAAH as well as that of the Club Alemán. Nonetheless, he also became active in associations such as the Asociación de Comerciantes del Centro (Downtown Merchants' Association), the Museo de San Ildefonso, and the Cámara Nacional del Comercio de la Cuidad de México. The latter awarded him the Medalla de Honoral Mérito Empresarial in 1998. He also became the first Boker to serve as a conscript in the Mexican army. For her part, Cecilia has served in civic organizations in San Angel, including, among others, a historic preservation society founded by Franz Böker.[91]

In predictable fashion, Pedro continued the tradition of the Boker sons of being drafted into the Casa Boker. Educated in the CAAH as well as in Holzminden, he was studying at the University of Aachen when his father recalled him to Mexico in March 1966 to replace one of the few remaining German employees. Frustrated with the unsatisfactory progress of his studies, Pedro began to work for the CFM two weeks later. Following family custom, he did grunt work for years, including haggling for import licenses in the Secretaría de Comercio, before becoming director responsible for purchases, pricing, and merchandise.[92]

Four years younger, his brother Klaus pursued a slightly different path. His quintessentially German first name did not lend itself to easy Hispanization, and the distant "Nicolás" never emerged as a Spanish version of his name. Klaus resembles his grandfather Franz both in appearance and in temperament; and just like his uncle Helmuth, a dry wit masks a skeptical if not pessimistic outlook on the world. He spent his high school years in Holzminden, followed by an internship at a private bank in Frankfurt. Yet in contrast to Pedro, Klaus thinks of himself as a "mix of German and Mexican," and by his own admission, the German element prevails. His Spanish retains some of the modulations of a German speaker. Unlike his elder brother, he married a Swiss-Mexican woman, Julie Muller Hoerig, whom he had known since his childhood and who later sought to preserve German culture in her own children. Of Gunther and Margot's children, Klaus is the one who most clings to his family's German heritage, and Julie is the only Boker spouse with extensive experience living in Germany.[93]

Not surprisingly, Klaus's public service has followed more closely along the lines of his ancestors. He dedicates most of his spare time to

German associations such as the German-Mexican Chamber of Commerce. He has become especially devoted to helping the Asociación de Ayuda Social de la Comunidad Alemana (Social Assistance Association of the German Community), the organization responsible for the operation of a German-Mexican retirement home. In June 2000, his successful effort to raise millions of marks for a new retirement home earned Klaus Boker the "Bundesverdienstkreuz am Bande," or Honor Cross, a distinction given by the German government for extraordinary accomplishments.[94]

Where Klaus's path has converged with that of Pedro is in his career. In 1970, he began work in the Casa Boker after receiving thorough training in banking and finance. After the customary apprenticeship, Klaus rose to join his brother in the executive ranks of the CFM, becoming the director responsible for finance and administration. The pragmatic Pedro and the cerebral Klaus came to form a good tandem, allowing each to concentrate on their strengths.[95] Pedro and Klaus also complement each other in their outlook on the future. In the words of their aunt, Ruth Boker, "if one asks Peter [about the Casa Boker] one will hear that things are going well; if one asks Klaus, one will learn that the situation is awful."[96]

Although Pedro and Klaus attribute Mexican traits to themselves, the Mexicans who work with them hold a different view—one that illustrates that Mexico has not yet become a "melting pot" despite the above-mentioned efforts to assimilate the foreign colonies. Between themselves, the two brothers communicate in German, a fact that has contributed to the judgment of several trusted Mexican directors and associates that the Bokers are still a German family. Even more importantly, some of their employees use ethnic and racial distinctions in order to describe the difference between themselves and the Boker brothers. In the words of one of the Mexican directors of the Casa Boker, they "have spent a lot of time in this country and . . . have sunk deep roots. . . . [But] they definitely look German, and their race and customs mark them as Germans."[97] Other Mexicans have stressed their German sense of humor, as well as the high level of punctuality and discipline with which the Bokers run their business; "they do everything as if they were in Germany," as one employee remarked.[98]

The employees of the Casa Boker would not have said the same thing about Renate, whose name translates to "Renata" in Spanish. Born in 1949, the highly intelligent and reserved Renate took the unprecedented step of marrying a wholly Mexican husband, Héctor Cirilo Hernández Valdés, albeit one educated in the CAAH. "More Mexican than German," she never spent time in Germany as anything but a visitor.[99] Against the wishes of her parents, Renate was already dating Héctor by the time she was supposed to go to Holzminden. When time came to pick an institution of higher education, her relationship with Héctor precluded devoting the five to six years necessary to obtain a degree from a German university. Renate paid dearly for her rebellion, as her parents virtually ignored Héctor up to their marriage. For a long time thereafter, they served the couple at a separate table during family dinners. Later, Renate studied chemistry at the National University (UNAM) and graduated as the first female Boker with a university degree. Not surprisingly, she also became the first family member with less than perfect mastery of German. Due to a combination of her sense of self-worth and Héctor's modest income, Renate served notice that she would never be the housewife that her father wanted her to be. She continued to work after the birth of her first child, thus reducing, as her father lamented, the baby's opportunities to learn German.[100] Nonetheless, she did attempt to teach her children the language of their ancestors.

Renate felt at home in Mexico City academic culture, with its own fundamental critique of Mexico that would have resonated with the skepticism of the Bokers if not for its left-wing orientation. As students at the UNAM in the wake of the Tlatelolco massacre, Renate and Héctor joined their fellow students, many of them from conservative elite families, in assailing the corruption and authoritarianism of the PRI state. Just like other students, they became disillusioned as Díaz Ordaz and Echeverría suppressed leftist dissent.[101] Renate's ties to the Mexican intelligentsia instead of the Germans from the CAAH showed that she had assimilated to a greater extent than her brothers, whose self-fashioned hybrid identities contrasted with Mexican perceptions of them as Germans.

Just as Renate has been "Mexicanized," however, her husband has been "Germanized," demonstrating that assimilation is not a one-way street. A light-skinned Mexican of humble origin who attended the Colegio Alemán on scholarship, Héctor professes to feel no more Mexican than Renate. The school not only weakened his emotional ties with his home society; it also instilled in him German habits and mannerisms. As the owner of a video store in Austin, Texas, where the couple and their baby daughter moved to escape the brunt of the 1982 debt crisis, Héctor found out how thoroughly the school had trained him in German culture. Standing erect in an impeccably clean and well-ordered store, he was once mistaken for a German by one of his customers. Although the family returned to Mexico City after five years, Héctor still feels alien in his native country.[102]

Five years younger than Renate, Barbara, whose name exists in Spanish just as it does in German, has advanced even farther on the path toward assimilation into the Mexican middle class. The most sensitive and independent-minded of the four siblings, the youngest child openly defied the ban on the use of Spanish in her home. She preferred the enchiladas and tacos cooked up by her family's servants to the European dishes offered at the dinner table. At her family's vacation home in Tepoztlán, Morelos, Barbara played with the local children rather than with the offspring of fellow vacationers. She hated her time in Holzminden, where drug use had become commonplace since Klaus's departure, and once home in Mexico, she met an Austrian-Mexican who showed a similar inclination to let go of his Teutonic heritage. Barbara married Roberto Hieber at the age of eighteen against the strenuous objections of her parents, who considered Roberto a Mexicanized "half-caste." Today, she works as the director of neonatal medicine in a Mexican hospital.[103]

If Klaus forms one pole of the German-Mexican continuum in the Boker family, Barbara stands at the other. Considering herself the "black sheep" of her family, Barbara remains the member of her generation who uses the most Spanish with her siblings, and unlike Klaus, Pedro, and Renate, she has few German-speaking friends. Moreover, unlike her older brothers and more so than her sister, she opposes the very existence of a German community in Mexico, a community that she believes should have vanished into Mexican society many decades ago. Barbara is the member of her generation most weighted down by a century of nationalism and ethnic segregation within the German colony. Thus, her actions and attitudes have reflected a desire to break down the boundaries between Mexican society and the German colony. Thus, Barbara's stance is in part a reaction against her parents' attempt to maintain the old bell jar, and in part an attempt to contribute to a new chapter in the history of the Germans in Mexico.[104]

Why have the two Boker daughters demonstrated a greater willingness to assimilate into Mexican middle-class society than their brothers, and particularly Klaus? Most importantly, gender defined the Bokers' career aspirations, with the sons joining the firm and the daughters limited to share ownership. The degree of involvement with the family business explains to what extent the fourth-generation Bokers have striven to maintain their ancestors' German culture. The daily interaction with the firm conveys upon Pedro and Klaus a perceived responsibility to uphold the bicultural identity associated with that business. Their status as directors of the oldest German business in the country also implies a prominent standing in the old German colony, and, hence, the obligation to serve various German-Mexican institutions. Both brothers live in the Casa Amarilla compound, a place marked by the aristocratic life of the German ancestors who built it. Renate and Barbara, by contrast, developed their identity less fettered by the strictures imposed by their family's pedigree, and they—like other ethnic German women—found leaving the bell jar of the German colony to be a liberating experience despite the relatively lower status of Mexican women.[105] Income also played a role in shaping identity. Although Gunther's four children inherited equal shares of his holdings, Pedro and Klaus enjoy a higher standard of living than their sisters. "We," as Renate put it, "travel by Metro (subway) . . . [and] eat tacos in street stands; but not my brothers."[106] As they might have added, they also needed to work for a living while their sisters-in-law did volunteer work.

In a striking role reversal from the acculturation phase, women have therefore stood at the vanguard of the assimilation of the Bokers—an observation further borne out in the case of Helmuth's family. Helmuth returned to Mexico in 1955 with a German wife, the former Ruth Schwartzkopff, and the couple raised three children there. While his eldest child, Isabel, spoke both German and Spanish with her brothers, Roberto and Joaquín preferred German. With the benefit of dual citizenship, two of them reside outside Mexico—Roberto, in Detroit, and Joaquín, in Russia—and Isabel recently returned to Mexico after two decades in Germany and France. Of the three, Isabel is the most Mexican, and during her years in Paris, she even retained a Mexican maid to ensure that her children learn Spanish along with their father's French and the German she speaks at home.[107] In light of the possibility that she may return to France, however, Isabel wants her children to think of themselves as French. She does not want them to follow her own example as a "mestiza": someone, in her mind, unsure of their national belonging.[108] While Helmuth overstated his case when he claimed that "women are more susceptible to Mexicanization than men," and that "Mexicanization begins in the womb," the case of his own family supports his hypothesis.[109]

The struggle of the Casa Boker to recapture its prominent position in the era of the "Mexican miracle" reflects the effects of import-substitution industrialization, urbanization, and corporate capitalism in postwar Mexico. As the United States had taken advantage of the war to displace German economic competition, the Casa Boker could not reclaim the position it had held before the war. During the 1940s and 1950s, Mexican producers filled the void left by German exporters, and the Mexican state came to play a pivotal role in steering the economy away from its dependence on imported consumer goods. In an age in which the state protected industry by high tariffs and import licenses, the Casa Boker faced drastically reduced profit margins and stiff competition. In turn, shrinking profits increased tensions between management and the UET and ultimately created a stalemate in which both the Bokers and their workers ended up as the losers. Despite these problems, Gunther Boker and his relatives could ultimately express some satisfaction with the performance of the business in the period 1948–75. They had built the Casa Boker back up from virtual bankruptcy; they had survived the ruin of every other German wholesale emporium in Mexico City, and they had even bought out the last German shareholders. To be sure, Gunther had shown that he was just as disinclined as his father to taking financial risks for future growth. But he had also demonstrated that he (like his father) was at his best when the survival of the business was at stake.

While the Casa Boker declined in importance, the German colony and its bell jar fragmented. By 1970, the colony had splintered into a poly-diaspora of Porfirian-era merchants, interwar-era professionals, anti-Fascist refugees, and the industrial nomads of the postwar period. To add to these trends, the postrevolutionary Mexican state made a concerted effort to assimilate its urban ethnic enclaves. The disintegration of the German colony was both inevitable and beneficial. In the words of Renate von Hanffstengel, the chair of German Studies at the UNAM and a prominent member of the present-day German community, "it opened the community and freed its members from the constraints and prejudices that a closed community . . . imposes."[110]

Therefore, the fourth generation of the Bokers abandoned their parents' attempt to identify with Germany. Perceiving themselves as a culturally miscegenated group, this generation began to turn toward Mexican society and, in some cases, marry Mexican spouses. This newly constructed identity became all the more important because the Casa Boker never recovered from the blow of the wartime intervention. The new generation of Bokers pointed in a different direction, a future in which the family began to assimilate into the Mexico City bourgeoisie.

> The Mexican assimilates without being assimilated.
>
> —Carlos Monsiváis

7

Cross-Cultural Bokers in an Urban Leviathan

On the morning of February 8, 1975, a CFM employee noticed smoke billowing out of the space between the packing room and the store. The fire in the Edificio Boker got out of control before anyone realized it had started. By noon, flames raged high into the azure sky of the Valley of Mexico, and the military blocked off the downtown area to protect drivers and pedestrians from the noxious smoke. The huge columns of fire and smoke made the evening news and the front page of the newspapers, and the embers continued to glow until early the next day.[1] The result of a short circuit, the fire destroyed most of the merchandise as well as the interior of the building, and the stockrooms looked like "large halls . . . covered with a layer of coal, soot, and molten iron."[2]

In graphic fashion, the conflagration signified the outward expression of the decline of the Casa Boker.[3] Once a showpiece of the Centro, the Edificio Boker underwent renovations that showed that the Bokers envisioned a much more modest future for their company. Workers covered the enormous air well that had given the inside of the building its grandiose, fin-de-siècle appearance, thereby creating additional floor space on the second level, and they reinforced the aging structures of the building. The changes in the layout allowed the family to rent out most of the Edificio Boker to Sanborns, the famous drugstore and restaurant chain. From its modest beginnings in the old Jockey Club building, Sanborns would become what the Casa Boker was not: a nationwide chain that sold, as a U.S. traveler observed in 1956, "almost everything under Heaven that a tourist could wish to buy."[4] Other companies such as the Banco Nacional de México rented office space on the second and third floors. The Bokers reopened their business in August 1978 on the south side of the building and accepted a greatly reduced visual presence. In the words of a member of the Barcelonnette community, "the Casa Boker looks greatly diminished. Most people on the street believe that it's not there anymore."[5] Nonetheless, this "diminished" business has survived in a bloated city afflicted by economic crisis and political upheaval amidst sweeping changes in the heyday of globalization, a process that has brought both intense competition and new opportunities. This era has also witnessed the ongoing assimilation of the Boker clan in its fifth generation in Mexico.

A Troubled Phoenix

When Gabriele, who had returned to live in Germany after her husband's death, visited the city of her birth in 1983, she expressed horror at what had become of Mexico City.[6] Indeed, since its days as the center of global attention during the Olympics and the 1970 soccer World Cup, the capital had become prima facie evidence of an economic miracle run amuck. It had become the world's largest metropolitan area with a population estimated at twenty million. Even more so than the natural growth of the Mexican population, the PRI's continuing neglect of the countryside contributed to the unchecked expansion of the city. The failure of the *ejido* structure of state-supported communal land holding coupled with official neglect drove millions of rural Mexicans away from their homes. If these migrants did not end up in the United States, they became residents of ciudades perdidas such as Ciudad Nezahualcóyotl, itself one of the country's largest cities and home to more than three million people. Not surprisingly, the ecology of the Valley of Mexico has collapsed under the weight of so many people. Composed of industrial and automobile exhaust as well as human waste in aerosol form, a coat of yellow smog covers Mexico City on most days. Health experts have likened the impact of life in the capital to smoking two packs of cigarettes a day. Both Renate and her cousin Isabel have cited air pollution as one of the reasons why they left Mexico City, although both returned to their native city later on.[7]

As Mexico City expanded, the Centro, and hence the Casa Boker, declined in economic significance. Unlike the centers of other Latin American metropolises, where U.S.-style skylines and broad avenues overshadow old structures, the Centro has remained a vestige of five centuries of Mexican history.[8] While the commendable decision to preserve the downtown district as a national historical patrimony earned it the distinction of being named a UNESCO World Heritage Site in 1985, the award did not create many new economic opportunities. Although the construction of two subway lines during the late 1960s made it easy to reach the Centro Histórico underneath the heavy traffic, many upper- and middle-class Mexicans stayed away. As most of them thought, *el metro* was for *pelados*, or have-nots. During the early 1970s, the first U.S.-style shopping malls with easy access and ample parking opened in Coyoacán and the distant, but popular Ciudad Satélite—a small operation at first, but soon a huge success. In the next decades, other malls followed in Polanco, Santa Fe, and other posh suburbs. Unlike the Palacio de Hierro and the Puerto de Liverpool, the old Barcelonnette emporium that offered fancy clothes and kitchenware, the Bokers did not open stores in these malls. The high rent in the new suburban shopping centers scared the Bokers, as did the idea of leaving a branch store to the management of an employee.[9] In addition, supermarkets such as Aurrera, Gigante, Comercial Mexicana, and, most recently, Wal-Mart franchises, each of which boasts sales volumes exceeding 1 million dollars per day, began to offer a wide range of products formerly available only in the city center.[10] Not surprisingly, retail sales suffered, as fewer affluent Mexicans went to shop in the Centro Histórico. Those who continued to frequent the Centro did so because they were looking for specific merchandise, such as "Arbolito" cutlery and hand tools, not available in either the malls or supermarkets.[11] Thus, the primary clientele of the retail operation became one that reached the Casa Boker by Metro or bus, while the status-conscious upper-middle class drove to the malls in their automobiles.[12] The 3.5 square miles that made up the territory of Mexico City around 1900 "comprise less than 1 percent of the metropolitan area of today."[13]

Figure 19: The storefront today (photo by Jürgen Buchenau).

Figure 20: The office floor (photo by Jürgen Buchenau).

These developments explain in part the decision to downsize the Casa Boker. By the time of the fire, the company still sold consumer goods such as kitchenware and toys.[14] Without a presence in the new malls, the company was no longer competitive in those areas. As Pedro explained in an interview with the newspaper *La Jornada,* "We were expected to founder because people no longer went to the city center to buy toilet paper and glassware."[15] Not surprisingly, once they had the chance to reconstruct the interior of their building, the Bokers decided to limit themselves to the product lines of hand tools and cutlery, the merchandise that had proved most profitable. This drastic reduction in offerings—from 40,000 products to just over 8,000—also entailed a prioritizing of the wholesale business over the flagging retail operation.[16] The changes had a dramatic psychological impact on Gunther, who was depressed at the prospect of a much smaller company than the one to which he had dedicated a lifetime of work.[17] His aging mother, Luise, remained upbeat, quoting an old

Figure 21: Inside view of the store (photo by Jürgen Buchenau).

Mexican saying that "nothing bad happens that does not also bring good things."[18]

Luise's instinct proved correct, as the fire gave the Bokers an opportunity to weaken the UET and dismiss more than one hundred employees. In the opinion of Claus Schlenker, the head of the wholesale department, "the union would have destroyed [the Casa Boker] if it had not been for the fire."[19] The destruction of part of the building forced the CFM to suspend retail sales immediately, and it soon became clear to the UET leadership that the company could not continue to offer 170 jobs, let alone at a time when the retail operation had shut down. As early as March 1975, union and management began negotiations about the termination of the collective-bargaining agreement. Both sides ultimately agreed to end the labor contract in exchange for severance pay for all laid-off employees. In addition to the amount stipulated by Mexican law (pay equaling ninety days plus another twenty days for each year worked), the CFM guaranteed another twelve days' pay per work year per employee. In November 1975, the CFM paid out approximately 12 million pesos, or almost 1 million dollars. As seniority determined how much an employee received, the lion's share of the money went to the highest-paid workers. With the buyout, the

Chapter 7

Bokers had rid themselves of almost 75 percent of their labor costs.[20] For their part, the employees had received some compensation, although inflation quickly diminished the value of the cash that they had received.

This agreement allowed the Bokers to start afresh. In 1977, they founded a new company, Boker, S.A., which issued new contracts to fifty employees, in addition to the eighteen remaining wholesale agents. The new labor contract once again put management in charge of the most important personnel decisions. The functions of the venerable CFM—in which the old rights of labor still survived in theory— were limited to holding the trademarks, the representations of imported merchandise, and the management of the warehouse in the Calle Jaime Nunó. The formation of Boker, S.A., finally led to the establishment of a holding company. Appropriately named Crisol Mexicano S.A. de C.V. (the Mexican melting pot), the new holding company included the bulk of the family's commercial assets. Capitalized at 2.9 billion pesos in 1987, or 1.2 million dollars, Crisol owned more than 95 percent of the CFM and La Esperanza, and almost 92 percent of Boker, S.A. de C.V.[21]

The national economy initially cooperated with this fresh start. By the time Echeverría left office at the end of November 1976, the economic crisis had bottomed out. A former partner of Echeverría's in the law office housed in the Edificio Boker, the new president, José López Portillo, began his tenure with a stroke of good luck, as the discovery of vast oil deposits in the Gulf of Mexico jumpstarted the country's economy. Between 1977 and 1981, Mexico's gross domestic product increased by an average of more than 8 percent annually, as the newfound wealth made López Portillo embark on a spending spree, financed by multinational banks at double-digit interest rates. In turn, public spending raised disposable income among the middle classes.[22]

This friendly economic climate allowed the slimmed-down Casa Boker to benefit from its reorganization. The reopening of the store attracted thousands of curious customers. One day during the 1979 Christmas season, the retail store grossed almost 10,000 dollars in its most successful day since World War II.[23] Nonetheless, the wholesale department, which had continued to operate throughout the aftermath of the fire, remained the mainstay of the Casa Boker. By 1982, two-thirds of its revenue came from wholesale transactions, which partially offset the loss of retail customers in the decaying Centro to the suburban shopping centers. The Casa Boker expanded their sales to the Jewish retailers in the Centro thanks to the efforts of Helmuth, who overcame his own Nazi past to become an effective agent. Moreover, the decision to give up the prime part of the building to Sanborns paid off in the form of a highly favorable rental contract. The "Sanborns Boker," an offshoot of its more famous counterpart in the former Jockey Club, attracted scores of customers who spent considerable sums on food, prescription drugs, and electronics; La Esperanza received a fixed percentage of net sales. Thus, after seventy-five years of weighing down the company, the "white elephant" finally paid some dividends.[24] The success of the Casa Boker led Gunther to attempt a small joint venture with the U.S. file maker Nicholson, which failed when Nicholson would not conclude an agreement on his timetable. Instead, Gunther invested in Hella, a German auto parts producer in Mexico, and served on the board of directors of Campos Hermanos, the most important Mexican tool producer. The Bokers also invested in Tubos Reed, the Mexican subsidiary of a U.S. firm.[25]

Not all was well, however. To begin with, López Portillo adopted a policy of hyperprotectionism, during which only a trickle of imported products reached the Casa Boker. Consequently, by 1981, Mexican-made products, which sold at smaller profit margins than imported ones, amounted to 80 percent of total sales volume. In addition, mounting inflation produced artificial gains on inventory, which greatly increased the company's tax burden. Between 1978 and 1981, inflation also eroded the purchasing power of Mexican workers by 9 percent, which came on top of a 12 percent loss the preceding two years (see Table 13). Over the long run, this decline of purchasing power threatened to offset the effects of increased public spending.[26]

Notwithstanding these problems, in 1982 the Bokers looked forward to better years ahead when Mexico experienced its most serious economic crisis since the Great Depression. The discovery of oil at a time of high crude prices had encouraged López Portillo to run up a large debt with foreign lenders. After oil prices fell in late 1981 and early 1982, the revenues of PEMEX, the state-owned oil company, dropped to the point that the Mexican government defaulted on its staggering foreign debt. Aided in part by rampant corruption at the highest levels of government, the default threw the Mexican economy into utter chaos. Between January 1982 and June 1983, the peso plunged from 4 to 0.66 U.S. cents. Irritated at Mexico's support of the Sandinista Revolution in Nicaragua, U.S. President Ronald Reagan

Table 13: Real Wages in Mexico, 1977–1982 (index 1976=100)						
Year	1977	1978	1979	1980	1981	1982
Legal minimum wage	110.0	125.5	146.6	172.5	230.4	309.2
Real wages	85.6	88.0	83.4	77.7	81.0	66.0

Source: Salazar, "Balance global," 48.

stood idly by while the Mexican economy collapsed.[27] The ensuing massive capital flight prompted López Portillo to take the ill-conceived step of nationalizing the private banks, a particularly cynical measure in light of the fact that he and his friends had already stashed away their wealth overseas. This step only compounded the crisis and cost the president, whom Gunther labeled a "corrupt pig," his remaining credibility.[28] Throughout the rest of the 1980s, Mexico experienced inflation of between 20 and 100 percent annually, economic growth was negative, industrial production decreased dramatically, and the peso continued to crumble. After three decades of economic growth, the country had entered the *década perdida,* or lost decade, a time of crisis throughout Latin America.[29] Only by 1988, with the peso at 2,500 to the U.S. dollar, had the disaster run its full course: Mexico had descended "from riches to rags."[30]

The economic collapse demoralized workers inside and outside the Casa Boker. While the peso plummeted against the dollar, prices of basic foodstuffs, rent, and public transportation skyrocketed. Pressured by the International Monetary Fund (IMF), the government relaxed the price controls that had kept many necessities within reach of working Mexicans. Nationally, real wages decreased by 40 percent between 1983 and 1988, and the minimum wage dropped a whopping 48 percent: calculated per hour, it fell to a bare 30 U.S. cents. As the pay of most employees, excluding managers such as Alvaro Gómez, was based on the minimum wage or its multiples, the runaway inflation had a devastating effect on the workers' real income.[31]

As personal income dropped, the aftermath of the debt crisis hit the Casa Boker hard. Consumer spending declined, credit tightened, and many customers could no longer afford imported items. For example, a top-of-the-line Arbolito pocketknife cost the equivalent of a month of minimum-wage work.[32] Even the Mexican-made products, which made up 80 percent of sales but only 50 percent of the catalog, were out of reach of many customers. Moreover, the currency controls instituted after López Portillo nationalized the banks made it practically impossible for the Bokers to obtain the U.S. and European currencies needed to pay their foreign creditors.[33] By the fall of 1983, retail sales had ground to a virtual halt, and the showroom employees bided their time with gallows humor. In the words of Carlos Seippel, the long-time head of the retail department: "In the morning, it is quiet around the store. In the afternoon, things calm down."[34] The wholesale sector did not fare much better. Although sales continued, obtaining payment proved another matter, as many of the Bokers' clients found themselves in dire financial straits. Moreover, an increasing number of the wholesale customers turned hyperinflation and a plummeting peso to their advantage by waiting several months before paying their invoices with depreciated money. Combined with overhead and labor costs, the delays and defaults wiped out most of the margin of 30 percent reflected in wholesale prices.[35]

As if these problems were not bad enough, a disastrous earthquake rocked Mexico City on September 19, 1985. The earthquake badly damaged the downtown area, much of which was built on former lake soil, and it left seventy thousand capitalinos homeless.[36] While the disaster did not damage the Edificio Boker, it led to a further decline in commercial activity in the Centro, and thus contributed to the crisis of the retail operation.[37] As Seippel remembered, the store was deserted for months following the earthquake, and he labeled the fall of 1985 the slowest period in his fifty years of service to the company, the two years after the fire excluded.[38]

Seippel's remarks demonstrated that the economic crisis and the earthquake had speeded up the decline of the Centro as a commercial district. As robberies and assaults increased in frequency, and as traffic and parking problems became more severe, many capitalinos no longer went to the Centro to shop and sightsee. To be sure, the downtown district did not experience the level of decay of many U.S. inner cities. Nonetheless, it took on the image of a lower-price alternative for shoppers who used public transportation rather than their own automobile. This image problem particularly affected the retail operation of a business like the Casa Boker, which sold quality, high-priced items.[39] It pained entrepreneurs like Pedro, who commented, "I . . . feel like I am a part of the Centro. It is fascinating to work in an office where every little piece means something."[40]

The growing number of street vendors illustrated the image problem that increasingly depressed commercial activity in the Centro. Hawking a wide range of low-end consumer goods from chewing gum to alarm clocks, they set up shop every morning on prearranged spots on sidewalks, plazas, and Metro entrances. Often poor migrants from rural Mexico, they formed the base of a pyramid of corruption, as they "leased" their street space from corrupt local politicians and paid kickbacks to police officers trying to expel them.[41] These vendors harmed formal merchant businesses for two reasons: their struggle for survival brought more crime to the area, and their stands posed physical and visual obstructions to pedestrians that made shopping in the Centro even less attractive to customers. Not surprisingly, Pedro regarded the removal of the street vendors as one of the most important goals of the Downtown Merchants Association, an organization in which he continued to play a prominent role. He could consider himself lucky that the Casa Boker suffered relatively little from the direct consequences of

178

street vending. As competition, the street vendors appealed to a different clientele than Boker, S.A. de C.V., and apart from a newspaper stand near the Sanborns entrance, they steered clear of the Edificio Boker.[42]

When they realized that the Mexican domestic market had collapsed beyond immediate repair, the Bokers attempted to use the weakness of the peso to their advantage by *exporting* hardware to the United States. For the first time in the history of the business, a female member of the family became the linchpin of a business venture. Renate and Héctor had moved to Austin, Texas, where Héctor operated a video rental store. In an effort to help their sister establish a more lucrative existence, in 1984 Pedro and Klaus joined Renate in establishing Stanimp, Inc. The company imported Mexican hardware into the United States and funneled Arbolito items into Mexico. Its most ambitious plan, however, was a joint venture with Heinrich Böker and Company, a company no longer in the hands of the family, to purchase the Treebrand trademark, a U.S. brand name that had fallen into U.S. hands during World War II. Obtaining this trademark would have enabled the Bokers and their German co-investors to manufacture the signature cutlery in the United States. This venture failed over a dispute regarding which of the two partners would obtain a majority in the venture. Eventually, Heinrich Böker and Company secured Treebrand for itself, shutting out the Bokers and poisoning the vintage relationship with one of their most important customers.[43] Nonetheless, the very fact that the Bokers had once attempted to gain a foothold in the U.S. market indicated their desire to tie their family's fortunes more closely to the United States. In a sense, Robert's transnational approach to business had returned after more than one hundred years.

If there was a positive aspect in the 1982 bust so far as the Bokers were concerned, it lay in the end of the Mexican experiment in industrial protectionism. As López Portillo handed over power to Miguel de la Madrid, the IMF prescribed a bitter austerity plan in exchange for a loan bailout package that allowed the Mexican government to refinance its foreign debt at lower interest rates. With the intention of forcing Mexican industry to become more competitive with its rivals, this plan mandated an opening of the borders to industrial imports. Soon after his inauguration, de la Madrid complied, and the Casa Boker and other companies again received permission to import merchandise. In October 1983, amidst the gloom and doom of the worst phase of the crisis, the Bokers celebrated the arrival of the first boxes of imported goods that had reached the Casa Boker that year. Over the next years, liberated from the fear that they could not replace any of the foreign-made items that they sold, the Bokers realized modest inflation gains on inventory that kept the cash flow at an acceptable level.

The Casa Boker in the NAFTA Era

The end of protectionism signaled the advent of neoliberalism in Mexico, a sea change in Mexico's political economy that provided new challenges and opportunities to the Bokers. During de la Madrid's tenure, the IMF and the World Bank had begun to pressure the Mexican government to privatize ineffective state-run businesses and lower tariff barriers with the most industrialized nations. It fell to the next Mexican president, the Harvard-educated Carlos Salinas de Gortari, however, to put this program into effect. During its tenure from 1988 to 1994, the Salinas administration renegotiated Mexico's debt, signed the North American Free Trade Agreement (NAFTA), and repudiated many of the nationalist and social reformist provisions of the 1917 Constitution. In this manner, Salinas helped U.S. President George H. W. Bush achieve two long-standing policy goals: he committed Mexico to free trade with its northern neighbor, and he officially ended the revolution. Although not nearly as comprehensive as the European Union treaty, NAFTA drastically lowered tariffs and committed Mexico to trimming the state-owned sector of the economy. Salinas also sought to reinvent Mexico as a politically stable, economically prosperous nation based on laissez-faire capitalism.[44]

Mexicans as well as foreigners saw the president's neoliberal policies as evidence that the country had indeed opened a new chapter in its history. Consequently, between 1989 and 1993, foreign investment helped the Mexican economy get back on track. Salinas soon became the darling of the world press and the Bush administration. To journalists and politicians alike, he represented the "new world order" after the fall of Communism: a neoliberal world in which the Left had been economically and ideologically discredited. Once again, consumption of imported items became the rage. However, neoliberal consumers craved not German hardware or fancy French clothes, but the popular material culture of the United States: coke, burgers, and sneakers.[45] Nonetheless, relieved that Salinas was rolling back decades of protectionism and state intervention in the economy, the younger Bokers supported him as well. In contrast to Helmuth, who railed against the "Americanization" of Mexico, and who argued that privatization provided Salinas and his cronies with new opportunities for corruption, Pedro and Klaus saw him as the key to a better Mexico.[46]

Unfortunately, Helmuth's Cassandra predictions proved accurate, as the NAFTA era started most inauspiciously. On January 1, 1994, the day NAFTA went into effect, the Ejército Zapatista de Liberación Nacional (Zapatista Army of National Liberation) began its insurrection in Chiapas. Reflecting the dismal social conditions in southeastern

Mexico, the rebellion protested against what its leader, the enigmatic Subcomandante Marcos, labeled the pillage of rural Mexico by avaricious landowners and multinational corporations. Widely advertised over the Internet, the Zapatista rebellion tarnished Salinas's carefully cultivated image.[47] The Boker family was divided on the Zapatistas: Cecilia condemned the uprising; Margot, and to some extent Helmuth, expressed sympathy for a rebellion caused by nearly five centuries of oppression.[48] In March, the assassination of Luis Donaldo Colosio, the president's handpicked successor, rocked Mexico amidst rumors that Salinas himself had masterminded the murder after learning of Colosio's intentions to break the power of the PRI bosses. Investors responded immediately by taking money out of Mexico, pulling down the country's foreign currency reserves by more than 10 billion dollars, or more than one-third of the total, in the matter of one month. September brought another politically motivated slaying, that of PRI Secretary General José Francisco Ruiz Massieu. Brought on in part by rising U.S. interest rates, the ensuing capital flight undermined the Mexican currency, which had remained relatively stable since 1990. On December 19, the new president Ernesto Zedillo allowed the peso to fall 15 percent against the dollar. The devaluation turned into a free fall, and the currency continued to decline for a few years until it leveled off at 10 new pesos to the dollar (10,000 old pesos): one-third of its 1994 value. Just as in 1982, the Mexican government stood at the brink of default. It was only after U.S. President Bill Clinton put together an emergency loan package that it averted even more serious consequences. To top it off, Mexicans found out in the ensuing years that Salinas had presided over the most corrupt administration in Mexican history. These crises plunged Mexico into another recession, and the country's GDP declined 7 percent in 1995.[49]

Like the rest of the commercial establishments in the Centro, the Casa Boker could no more escape the effects of the peso crisis than it had been able to fend off the consequences of the 1982 crash. Although the Mexican economy recovered relatively quickly, the aftermath of the crisis brought more humbling disappointments for the Bokers. Once again, the fallen peso put the prices of European products out of reach of ordinary Mexicans, all the more so because the dollar, in an unrelated development, fell to historic lows against the Deutsche Mark. Among the employees, real wages, which had not fully recovered from the 1982 crisis, sank another 30 percent.[50] While the percentage of foreign-made merchandise in the Bokers' catalog remained close to 50 percent, imported products amounted to a shrinking share of total sales volume. Moreover, the new crisis brought yet another wave of crime to Mexico City. As in the 1980s, this trend has disproportionately affected the Centro and further depressed retail sales. By 1998, the retail operation—once the pride of the Casa Boker—only netted 15 percent of all sales. Already burdened by almost 830,000 dollars in outstanding accounts before the crisis, the wholesale operation again experienced problems with payment collection from its 6,000 clients. "Selling," as Schlenker remarked in 1998, "is no problem, but getting the money is difficult."[51] This issue also highlighted the increasing disparity between north and south in Mexico; Schlenker cited his clients from southern states as particularly prone to defaulting on their debt.[52]

Not surprisingly, this most recent disappointment soured the mood of Pedro and Klaus as well as that of their employees. "We like our work because we are continuing a tradition," Pedro remarked in a 1995 interview. "But we realize that we could make much more money elsewhere," he added in an obvious allusion to the multinationals.[53] For his part, Klaus stated that "German corporations like Bayer enjoy the backing of a worldwide company. We are on our own."[54] These sentiments not only echoed the concerns of many Mexican entrepreneurs in the peso crisis; they also showed a lingering identification with the Bokers' German heritage. For their part, most employees soldier on stoically, but frustrations have mounted since the 1994 crisis: as one former employee stated, "The company can survive, but not the staff."[55]

While it is too early to judge the long-term effects of NAFTA on a business that no longer serves as a major importer of U.S. merchandise, the short-term verdict is therefore less than encouraging. The lower tariffs have helped large retailers that import directly in great quantities, thus undercutting their smaller competition that makes up the majority of the wholesale customers of the Casa Boker.[56] Capitalized at just under 13 million pesos (less than 1.5 million dollars) in 2001, Boker, S.A. de C.V. has bobbed and weaved with the Mexican economy, a movement that has entailed more downs than ups in the last two decades.[57] Moreover, as NAFTA has allowed Asian exporters to use the United States as an intermediary to the Mexican market, the treaty has signaled the growth of Chinese and Japanese imports at the expense of European and Mexican commodities. In Pedro's words, "Chinese junk" inundated Mexico's street markets and replaced most handmade Mexican items.[58] When Salinas enrolled his children in the Japanese school rather than the Colegio Alemán as Echeverría and López Portillo had done, the symbolism of his choice was clear. Under Salinas, Mexico had become a Pacific country; beyond its intimate relationship with the United States, it no longer looked primarily at the Atlantic market.[59]

Nonetheless, as of today, the NAFTA era looks better to the Bokers than what they experienced the preceding four decades. To Pedro and

Klaus, the most encouraging aspects of contemporary Mexico lie in the codification of free trade and the democratization of Mexican politics. With a treaty framework in place, sudden swings of the Mexican political pendulum to the populist policies of the past have become less likely. Even more importantly, the Bokers applauded Mexico's democratic opening under Zedillo. As supporters of Vicente Fox Quesada's conservative PAN, Pedro and Klaus loudly cheered Fox's defeat of the PRI in the July 2000 presidential elections. Finally, the recent signing of a trade agreement with the European Union makes European-made hardware more competitive. Realizing that Salinas had neglected Mexico's relationship with Europe, Zedillo drastically slashed tariffs on European imports, and thus put them on a more equal basis with their Asian and U.S. competition.[60]

Moreover, the Casa Boker maintains market share in the niche it has carved out for itself, and it proudly continues its business decades after the demise of the other German hardware stores. Even though its competitors from Monterrey boast nationwide networks of distribution that far surpass that of the Casa Boker, the company stubbornly holds on. As of 1999, Boker S.A. de C.V. commanded 6 percent of the national market share for cutlery. Although Spanish merchandise has replaced the Stanley products, the Casa Boker also sells 0.5 percent of all hand and power tools in the country.[61] Finally, Pedro and Klaus have combined effective cost-cutting measures with promotional efforts such as a Web site and a much-publicized mission statement. After the 1994 crisis cost La Esperanza several tenants of the Edificio Boker, they also invested in a small software company housed in the Casa Boker as well as in other minor ventures. The rumors of the demise of the Casa Boker, therefore, have been greatly exaggerated, as Pedro and Klaus have adjusted to changing conditions. They also sold the warehouse, a decision that reflected the location of the Casa Boker in an area without easy automobile access. Since most Metro-borne retail customers bought only small items that they could carry on to public transportation, the Casa Boker needed far less space than before to accommodate bulky merchandise. Accordingly, in the latest of a series of organizational adjustments of the family business, the Bokers folded the old CFM—the owner of the warehouse—into Boker, S.A. de C.V. on February 7, 2001 (see Table 14).[62]

Whatever the future may bring for the Casa Boker, two recent marketing studies—one by Pedro's daughter Alexandra and the other by a German intern—identify the challenge before the business. As both studies point out, among the middle and upper classes, most capitalinos over forty years of age still associate "Boker" with the hardware business, whereas the name has lost meaning for younger Mexicans.

Table 14: The Changing Names of the "Casa Boker"
(most significant)

Name and Dates of Existence	Organization
Holder, Boker y Cía (1865–69)	General partnership
Roberto Boker (1869–73)	Sole proprietorship
Roberto Boker y Cía (1873–1909)	General partnership
Cía Ferretera Mexicana (1909–2001)	Closely held corporation (import and sales)
Cía de Inversiones "La Esperanza" (1931–)	Closely held corporation (rent and real estate)
Boker, S.A. de C.V. (1975–)	Closely held corporation (import and sales)
Crisol (1983–)	Closely held corporation (holding company)

In addition, women make up no more than 11 percent of the retail customers. As a consequence, the clientele of the store is predominantly middle-age and male, a fact that not only reflects the product lines of the Casa Boker, but also the flight of younger, automobile-oriented Mexicans to the suburban shopping malls. Unless the company finds a way to exist without the retail operation, or to sell to intermediaries in the malls, both studies argue, the Bokers will need to strengthen the name recognition of their business.[63]

Finally, Pedro and his siblings will one day face the issue of handing over the business to the next generation. This issue will not be an easy one, as the generational transition once again led to the diffusion of shares among Gunther's and Margot's four children. As a fifth generation of Bokers has come of age, it is not yet clear whether one or more of them will express an interest in taking over the family firm. Apart from the fact that Pedro and Klaus (unlike their forebears) have not exerted any pressure on their children to follow in their footsteps, the younger Bokers' reluctance stems from the prospect of buying out other family members.[64] After several purchases of shares and the injection of additional capital, Pedro and Klaus each own 40 percent of Boker, S.A. de C.V., reducing Renate's and Barbara's stakes to 10 percent each. Pedro has already indicated that he will pass on his entire interest in the firm to whichever of his children expresses an interest in taking his place. Even if Klaus follows suit, however, any heir interested in the Casa Boker faces the specter of minority ownership, unless two cousins can agree to work together just as Pedro and Klaus did. This scenario has virtually eliminated Renate's and Barbara's families from consideration. Among the children of the Boker executives, Pedro's eldest son,

Francisco, is the most serious candidate to enter the firm. This second Pancho not only has a background in business administration but also has developed tangible ideas about the future of the Casa Boker, including investing in tool production.[65] The author of the above-cited marketing study, his sister Alexandra is another possible candidate, as is Klaus's daughter Susana. Neither of the two, however, has expressed much interest in managing the Casa Boker. The other two children, Pancho's younger brother Jan, a lawyer, and Susana's brother Andrés, a physician, appear unlikely to join the Casa Boker. Regardless of the macroeconomic parameters, the question of succession likely holds the key for the future of this family firm.

Cross-Cultural Bokers

In light of this unsettled question, the fifth Boker generation in Mexico City has recently claimed the spotlight. In apt symmetry with the name of their family's holding company, Gunther's grandchildren represent a melting pot of identities and visions. Unlike their German-Mexican parents, these nine Bokers unequivocally see themselves as Mexicans. Nevertheless, since their German background still confers advantages on them, and since many Mexicans still cannot overlook their Germanic physical attributes, the process of assimilation has not yet reached its end point in a family described by a German scholar as cross-cultural brokers.[66]

Differences in personality, income, gender, and professional goals have spawned a variety of ethnic identities among the youngest Boker generation. In particular, Gunther and Margot's grandchildren followed the lead of the previous generation in that their place of residence and degree of connection to the Casa Boker shaped their identity. The other significant factor is their parents' own identities, which influenced the upbringing of the children. Thus, the Tlacopac Bokers (the families of Pedro and Klaus, who live in the San Angel compound) contrast with the "diasporic" Bokers (the families of Renate and Barbara, who live in condominiums in southern Mexico City). Among the Tlacopac Bokers, Klaus's family is more German than Pedro's, and among the diasporic Bokers, Barbara's family is more assimilated than Renate's.[67]

Both the Tlacopac Bokers and the "diasporic" Bokers had strong reasons to continue their journey into assimilation, albeit for different reasons. Pedro's and Klaus's families were better off than those of their sisters, which made their children appreciate the material benefits of life in Mexico. In the words of Pedro's son, Pancho, they "lived in the 'Boker Suites,' a really nice five-star hotel."[68] With servants catering to their daily needs, Mexico—unlike Germany or the United States, where household help is much less affordable—appeared like a paradise to their children. What kept the Tlacopac Bokers connected to Germany was their proximity to Gunther and Helmuth, who also lived in the compound, as well as their relationship with the Casa Boker, which still epitomizes German influence in Mexico.[69] The Tlacopac Bokers have consequently retained more of an interest in German culture than their cousins. By contrast, the "diasporic" Bokers are more assimilated into Mexican society, but acutely feel the strain of the series of economic crises that have buffeted Mexico in the past twenty years. Although few of them continue to travel to Germany, they know firsthand the hardships faced by Mexico's middle class since 1982, as well as the comparatively good times experienced by many Germans and North Americans. Therefore, their assimilation remains limited to a comparatively greater degree than that of their cousins by their awareness of Mexico's ongoing crisis.[70]

As a final important difference, the fall of the Berlin Wall and the subsequent reunification of Germany allowed the Bokers to become German-Mexican dual citizens. Paranoid about the remote possibility that the Allies would pressure the Mexican government to seize the Casa Boker in case Germans managed the firm, Gunther had long insisted on Mexican citizenship for all members of the family. It was not until September 1990 that the signing of a peace treaty between Germany and the Allies, which preceded German reunification, gave Pedro and his siblings the opportunity to override their father's wishes. In yet another display of convenient citizenship, they invoked their grandparents' nationality to obtain German passports that gave their own children the opportunity to live in Europe if they desired.[71] Klaus, Julie, and their children took advantage of the Mullers' background to obtain Swiss documents as well.[72]

Pedro and Cecilia's children are the ones most comfortable with their bicultural existence. For Pancho, the most likely candidate to join the family firm, being German as well as Mexican has distinct advantages. As a child, he established strong friendships with fellow German-Mexicans in the Colegio Alemán, and he learned German well. When he realized that his future lay in the business world, and possibly in the Casa Boker, he cultivated this bicultural image because he viewed it as befitting someone associated with a venerable German-Mexican import business. Consequently, he completed a long internship in Germany, followed by an MBA at a French business school.[73] He is married to a German-Venezuelan. Pancho's brother Jan, the youngest of the three children, expressed a similar desire to combine Mexican and German traits. "In Mexico," he reported, "I feel German, and in Germany, I feel Mexican."[74] Like Pancho, Jan spent a year in Germany, and he speaks

Table 15: Gunther and Margot Boker and Their Descendants

Gunther Boker b: Apr. 11, 1909, Mexico City; d: June 6, 1993, Mexico City.

∞ Margot Trauwitz b: Feb. 25, 1919, Mexico City; d: Feb. 16, 2001, Mexico City.

  1. **Pedro Roberto Boker** b: Sept. 9, 1941, Mexico City.

  ∞ Cecilia Regens b: Sept. 25, 1948, Mexico City.

    1.1. Francisco (Pancho) Boker b: Mar. 14, 1971, Mexico City.

    1.2. Alexandra (Sandra) Boker b: Sept. 26, 1973, Mexico City.

    1.3. Jan Roberto Boker b: Dec. 23, 1977, Mexico City.

  2. Brigitte Boker b: Aug. 1, 1943, Mexico City; d: Aug. 30, 1944, Mexico City.

  3. **Klaus Boker** b: Aug. 8, 1945, Mexico City.

  ∞ Julie Muller b: Nov. 5, 1945, Mexico City.

    3.1. Susana Marianne Boker b: June 11, 1973, Mexico City.

    3.2. Andrés Boker b: Aug. 31, 1974, Mexico City.

  4. Karin Renate Luise Boker b: May 23, 1949, Mexico City.

  ∞ Héctor Hernández b: Jan. 6, 1947, Mexico City.

    4.1. Vanessa Hernández b: May 13, 1979, Mexico City.

    4.2. Claudio Hernández b: July 31, 1984, Austin, TX.

  5. Barbara Boker b: Oct. 27, 1954, Mexico City.

  ∞ Roberto Hieber b: Jan. 1, 1947, Mexico City.

    5.1. Barbara Hieber b: Sept. 24, 1975, Mexico City.

    5.2. Roberto Hieber b: Sept. 11, 1977, Mexico City.

---

almost flawless German. Nonetheless, he dislikes the German qualities of discipline and organization and feels more at home in Mexico. Finally, Alexandra, or "Sandra" as she is commonly known, is the most Mexican of the three. She does not speak German well despite her CAAH degree, and her circle of friends consists almost entirely of Mexicans who do not speak German, including her husband.[75] Nonetheless, Fernando's career took the couple to residence in Brussels before moving to Panama.

Following the lead of their parents, Klaus and Julie's children are the least Mexican of the Bokers. They attended the Swiss school, an institution that Klaus portrayed as less "Mexicanized" than the CAAH. Not only had it avoided the fate of the German school during World War II, but the school also enjoyed more generous subsidies from the Swiss government than the CAAH received from the German one. Andrés, or "Andy," left Mexico for Miami years ago. Initially, he enjoyed the freedom that life in another country gave him: in December 1999, a journal published on the Internet identified him as a "South Beach paparazzi" surrounded by other socialites from the Miami Beach area. Written in Spanish, the article describes a glitzy group of Spanish-speaking North Americans and English-speaking Latin Americans, and hence offers a clue about Andy's identity.[76] For Andy, the main attraction of living in the United States lies in the possibility of living in a bicultural city with strong Latin American influences. Today, he is a successful physician and researcher in Miami, and he does not entertain any plans to return to Mexico. Susana, or "Susi," is proud of her German heritage, although she identifies more with Mexico. With a business degree, she, like Pancho, completed an internship in Lippstadt. Recently married, she lives in the city of Puebla and plans to speak German to her own children.[77]

Renate and Héctor's children remain the most difficult to categorize. Not only are they the youngest of their generation, but Vanessa and Claudio have also been marked by their family's years in the United States. As Héctor is fair-skinned, their features resemble those of their cousins. Nonetheless, Vanessa's brown eyes and hair makes her different from her Tlacopac relatives. In addition, the family's five-year stay in the United States has resonated with her. Upon the family's return from Austin, Vanessa hated the CAAH, and she transferred to finish her education at a Mexican high school. Not surprisingly, she speaks broken German interspersed with English phrases. While she considers herself Mexican, she feels like an outsider. Like her cousin Andy, she loves the United States and longs to return to a city like Austin that, as she believes, accepts multicultural individuals like her. The only U.S. citizen in the Boker family, the native Texan Claudio hardly spoke any German until recently. Since 1999, however, he has spent several summers working on the farm of one of his second cousins in northern Germany and thus has rediscovered his German roots. His German is far better than his sister's, and his blond hair creates the same predicament faced by his Tlacopac cousins.[78]

Not surprisingly, Barbara's two children are the most Mexican of the fifth-generation Bokers. Both her daughter Barbara and her son Roberto consider themselves Mexican, and they speak but minimal German. Both have attempted to come to terms with the limits to assimilation in different ways. A psychologist by training, "Babsi" realizes that her German ancestry and physical appearance will always make a difference in the way other Mexicans see her. She also realizes that these circumstances continue to give her an advantage in Mexican society. Nevertheless, she criticizes her extended family for overemphasizing the German element and for failing to keep Mexican friends not associated with European or U.S. schools and institutions. Born the same day his great-grandmother Luise Böker died, Roberto has attempted to solve this identity problem by embracing his own version of Mexico's indigenous reality. Sporting a tattoo of the Toltec god Quetzalcóatl (but, ironically, also one of Arbolito), he resents his European features and plans to begin a process of reverse whitening by marrying the darkest-skinned Mexican woman that he can find. A Colegio Alemán dropout, he lambastes his relatives from Tlacopac—except Sandra and Jan—not only for socializing in German-Mexican institutions, but also for what he regards as an elitist attitude. By far the most progressive member of his family, Roberto also admires the Zapatista rebellion, likes to speak with a working-class Tepito accent, and strives to convince friends and family alike that he is German in genetic makeup only. This effort to negate his own background demonstrates the painful and contradictory aspect of the Bokers' process of assimilation.[79]

Although rooted in Mexico, all of the fifth-generation Bokers have experienced the limits of assimilation into a society as socially and ethnically diverse as Mexico. Some of them consider their German roots an asset that facilitates their access to elite society; others stress the advantages of bicultural education; yet others express discomfort with being associated with a privileged group. It is no coincidence that the Tlacopac Bokers treasure their German heritage more than the diasporic Bokers, as the Casa Boker and the Casa Amarilla still serve as a reminder of the Bokers' long history. As the following sketch of Liesel's and Gabriele's descendants reveals, however, the Boker legacy influences not only Gunther's progeny.[80]

Based in the small town of Tuxpan, Michoacán, the family of Liesel's only surviving son Dieter Vermehren offers a rural and less assimilated counterpoint to Gunther's clan. Married to one of Luise's nieces, Dieter's father, Alfred, left Germany after the collectivization of his farm in the state of Mecklenburg, then a part of the Soviet-occupied zone. He eventually settled down in Tuxpan, and Dieter helped him build up a small farm, which produced cut flowers along with basic staples. Born and raised in Germany, Dieter never quite gave up his roots. In his own words, he feels "like a foreigner" in Tuxpan, and like his cousin Klaus, he considers himself a mixture of German and Mexican.[81] He married the former Monika Blass, the daughter of a coffee planter in Chiapas and product of the Colegio Alemán, who prefers to speak German and fashions herself German. In the absence of a cosmopolitan bourgeoisie in this small town, the cultural and social gap between the Vermehrens and the Mexicans around them was much wider than what the Bokers experienced in Mexico City. Not surprisingly, Dieter and Monika sent their children to the Swiss school in Mexico City after a two-year experiment with home schooling. Their children's weekend trips to Tuxpan offered a reminder of the difference between their German heritage and their Mexican home.[82] Although their time in Mexico City exposed them to the same elite culture as the Bokers, they developed identities that resembled the ones of their uncles and aunts more so than the ones of their cousins in the capital. Only six years younger than Barbara, Antje married a Swiss-Mexican and followed him to career stops in Orange, New Jersey, and Panama. Her younger brother Jan has helped his father convert their farm into an agribusiness that employs 150 workers and exports flower seedlings to the United States. Married to a fellow German-Mexican, he hedged when asked about his national identity: "Even though I was born here, I can't be completely Mexican since this country is such a mess!"[83] He speaks German both to his wife and to his three blond, blue-eyed children. Claudia, the only Vermehren who lives in Mexico City, became the first family member to marry a Mexican without exposure to German culture, and thus constitutes an exception to this pattern. Predictably, Monika initially disapproved of Claudia's liaison. Finally, the youngest daughter, Katja, followed Antje's lead in marrying a Swiss-Mexican; she lives in the city of Puebla, home to a Volkswagen plant and a German school. All four Vermehrens speak German with their children and Spanish with one another, and they maintain dual citizenship.[84]

Gabriele's descendants, on the other hand, show strong evidence of the migrations in the family's past despite a German upbringing. Her four surviving sons, Helmut, Michel, Ulrich, and Peter, each fulfilled their mother's desire by marrying German spouses and pursuing careers in Germany. For most of the Buchenau clan, the Mexican influence "limits itself to a few Mexican ornaments and tapestries here and there."[85] In fact, Helmut was the only Buchenau to take his own children to see Mexico. Nonetheless, a large part of the next generation—including this author—returned to their international roots, and some have even founded transnational families. Helmut's son Klaus is married to a Russian woman, speaks seven languages, and holds a doctorate in Eastern European history. His daughter Barbara teaches American and Canadian literature at a German university. Michel's eldest daughter Anne lives in rural France with her French husband and children. Ulrich's eldest daughter, Stefanie, a doctoral candidate at Yale, married a French academic of Moroccan Jewish extraction and lives in Paris. In ironic fashion, this generation, dominated by academics in the humanities, may have sought to confront the conservative and nationalist ideology of their grandparents, if not even their past in Nazi Germany. Thus, while Gunther's and Liesel's Mexicans of German origin have not yet become "real" Mexicans, some of Gabriele's German grandchildren are less than "real" Germans.

How can German-Mexicans ever become "real" Mexicans? Roberto Hieber Boker likely provided the best answer to this question: only if immigrants and their descendants breach the social and ethnic gaps separating them from most Mexicans. The social divide will prove the more difficult one to overcome, as well-to-do descendants of immigrants no more understand the poor majority than the Mexican bourgeoisie do. True to the colonial roots of Mexican history, the key to closing the ethnic gap consists in miscegenation as practiced by several of the Bokers. As one student of the German colony in Mexico reminds us, single German men who were cut off from their home culture and married local Mexicans assimilated in isolated areas as early as the nineteenth century.[86] To be sure, as Mexican society becomes increasingly globalized, it will become easier to assimilate into the upper layers of Mexican society. Much of the capitalino elite is as "white" as the Bokers, and the recent election of the son of an Irish father and a Spanish mother to the Mexican presidency signals a change in Mexican attitudes toward immigrants. Yet, if anything, as the multiple attacks on Fox's ethnic background on the campaign trail showed, even a presidential candidate is not free from charges that he is still a foreigner. Hence, the pattern of the nineteenth century still persists in the twenty-first, as many Mexicans cannot conceive of hyphenated identities that bridge the "Mexican" and the "foreign." In fact, three members of the extended Boker family have found the United States—despite its own problems—to be far more accommodating of hyphenated identities than Mexico. Even today, Mexico's supposedly cosmic race is not so cosmic after all.

An era of economic and political turmoil, the years since 1975 have buffeted the Casa Boker as they have other midsized enterprises in Mexico. Bringing hyperinflation and recession, the 1982 debt crisis eroded the Casa Boker's base of customers as well as the real income of its directors and employees. While the crisis destroyed the protectionist barriers that had harmed the Casa Boker during the "Mexican miracle," the Bokers found themselves left out from the new import opportunities that primarily benefited large corporations. More recently, the peso crisis of 1994 and Mexico's plunge into NAFTA have only accentuated these trends.

Nonetheless, the Casa Boker survives, in large measure because the Bokers have converted it into a specialty store that has found its niche in the Mexican economy. Rather than the "Sears of Mexico"—an anachronistic name since the entry of the real Sears corporation into Mexico City—Boker S.A. de C.V. is a midsized enterprise only partially dependent on the import market. While most Mexicans no longer readily recognize the company, and many believe that it never reopened after the fire, it continues to succeed in the wholesale sector.

Just as the monstrous bowels of Mexico City have virtually swallowed up the Casa Boker, so has the process of assimilation continued to chip away at the vestiges of German culture in the Boker family. All of the members of the most recent Boker generation feel most at home in a Spanish-speaking environment, and half of them do not speak much German. Still, the youngest Bokers have found out that their background and physical features still make them different from the people around them. In the words of Jan Boker, "The difference between us and the other German-Mexican families is that no one else maintains the balance between the two cultures as much as we do."[87]

You cannot understand the Mexicans.
The moment you do, you have become one yourself.
—Helmuth Boker

Conclusions

What does the experience of the Bokers tell us about Mexican history? Even though foreigners—and particularly merchants—are only tiny specks on the multichromatic tapestry that is Mexico, they have registered an impact disproportionate to their small numbers. The Bokers and other European families played a crucial role in the Mexican economy by serving as the principal distributors of manufactured imports, whether producer goods or luxury items. Other newcomers from Europe and the United States came to dominate banking, mining, and even landowning in areas engaged in export production. These foreigners assumed the role of a national bourgeoisie when such a group had not yet developed in a country where the principal commercial activity consisted, until recently, in going to the market rather than to the department store or the mall. Far from integrating influential and wealthy foreigners into the fabric of Mexican society, this impact delayed their assimilation. Self-confident and secure in their feeling of superiority over a host society that they considered far beneath their native Germany, the Bokers and other foreign merchants developed ethnic enclaves that sought to isolate them from Mexicans. These enclaves, and the sense of superiority that sustained them, only crumbled after 1945, when import-substitution industrialization created a sizable urban bourgeoisie that competed with the descendants of the trade conquistadors on even terms. This relationship between Mexico and its immigrants shaped the world of the Bokers. The Bokers' position in a small, but wealthy foreign colony in an "underdeveloped" nation joins the diverse strands of the preceding chapters: the life cycle of a department store in Mexico City, the slow journey toward assimilation of a German elite family, and the turbulent local, national, and global contexts in which the family and their business operated.

The first part of this study has examined the ascent of the Casa Boker, and the concomitant adaptation of Robert Böker and his brothers, in the context of Liberal modernization in Mexico and the Industrial Revolution. Merchants like Robert Böker came to postcolonial Mexico in the nineteenth century, filled the void left by the peninsulares who had dominated banking and commerce, and played an important part in the process of modernization that picked up steam just as the Industrial Revolution was at its peak in France, Germany, and the United States. Along with French-owned garment stores such as the Palacio de Hierro and the Puerto de Liverpool, the Casa Boker became one of the most famous commercial establishments in Mexico City, particularly after the construction of the Edificio Boker. Because of the French monopoly on garment sales and the Bokers' reluctance to feed the emergent consumer culture of the era, the Casa Boker never became the equal of U.S. department stores such as Macy's and Sears, Roebuck. Nonetheless, the Edificio Boker building and the company that owned it became one of the icons of the German colony in Mexico City, a relatively small diaspora dominated by merchants and professionals loyal to both Mexican dictator Porfirio Díaz and German Emperor William II. As the colony developed a school as well as a host of athletic and social institutions, and as the era of imperialism increasingly pitted Europe's Great Powers against each other, it progressively isolated itself from both Mexican society and other foreign colonies. This panorama set the stage for the adaptation of the first-generation Bokers and their most significant fellow partners, Rudolf von Lübeck and Carl Friederichs. Although these entrepreneurs never thought of themselves as anything other than temporary residents of Mexico, their business decisions—and particularly their important role in distributing U.S. products and their commitment to building an expensive department store—reflected local conditions. From the beginning, the Casa Boker was an independent company rather than a dependency of "Heinrich Böker."

The second part has analyzed the heyday and stagnation of the Casa Boker, and the reluctant acculturation of Franz and Luise Böker and their family amidst the turmoil of the Mexican Revolution, two world wars, and the Great Depression. The company survived both the revolution and the Allied boycott of the World War I era without any major problems—indeed, the Casa Boker emerged strengthened from the upheaval. After 1920, it weathered both the Depression and postrevolutionary legislation designed to reduce foreign influence in the Mexican economy; even the new UET trade union remained weak throughout the Calles and Cárdenas years. As a result of this success, the leadership of the business missed an important opportunity. As its competitors fell to the wayside, the directors of the Casa Boker privileged dividend payments over the growth of the company, and especially the chance to invest in hardware manufacturing in Mexico, which became the preserve of the Monterrey Group and other Mexican capitalists. Even worse, Mexico declared war on Nazi Germany during World War II, which led to the government takeover of the business and a serious crisis that almost forced the Casa Boker to close its doors forever. Meanwhile, the first Mexican-born Bokers were raised in an exclusively German setting that artificially sought to re-create the world of the lost German Empire: not surprisingly, they clung to a Germany that no longer existed and supported Nazi ideology as a way of unifying all those of German culture worldwide. They also unwittingly accepted many aspects of Mexican culture that made them distinct from the "real Germans" with whom they sought to identify. As a loss of premigratory culture did not yet occur, however, they were acculturated, but not assimilated.

Finally, the third part has delineated the downsizing of the Casa Boker, and the process of assimilation of the fourth and fifth generations, in a megalopolis and an increasingly globalized world in which large-scale family import businesses have lost much of their significance. After 1940, the Mexican government sought to drastically reduce the country's dependence on hardware imports by supporting an ambitious program of industrialization aided by rigid protectionism that kept out many products sold in the Casa Boker. At the same time, commercial activity moved to the suburbs and outskirts of Mexico City, and the Centro declined in importance, especially after the destruction of the 1985 earthquake led to an increase in crime and street vendor activity. Engaged in a difficult process of rebuilding itself from the government takeover and locked in a conflict with its trade union, the Casa Boker belatedly paid the price for not expanding either its market share or its investment in industry. As imports became more difficult to procure, the Bokers switched to Mexican-made products that they otherwise might have produced themselves. By the time of the fire in early 1975, the company stood at the brink of bankruptcy, and only a reorganization that involved a drastic curtailment of the staff ensured its survival through the 1982 and 1994 economic crises. This decline accompanied the crumbling of the German colony, which could no longer reconcile the anachronism of its oldest families with the aspirations and ideas of more recent immigrations. In addition to this fragmentation of the German diaspora, the effective promotion of *mexicanidad* by mass culture encouraged assimilation—a process facilitated by the increasing convergence of the standards of living of German-Mexicans and middle-class Mexicans. With the decline of European influence and the emergence of a sizable entrepreneurial bourgeoisie in Mexico City, the Bokers and other descendants of European immigrants no longer had a reason to feel superior to their host society. As a result, the fourth-generation Bokers adopted a hybrid German-Mexican identity, which has given way to a more pronounced identification with the Mexican bourgeoisie in the fifth generation.

Were the Bokers and most other German merchant families therefore "pioneers of German imperialism," as Brígida von Mentz has suggested?[1] This study has suggested a more nuanced interpretation. For much of its history, the family has served as "cross-cultural Bokers" even as it sought to remain German in a country 6,000 miles away. They not only contributed to the spread of foreign commodities and values in Mexico, but their engagement with Mexico transformed first the business, and then the family itself, reflecting a gradually increasing identification with Mexican society.

Thus, the Casa Boker was never a purely "German" business, and became even less so with the passage of time. In contrast to the large economic interests such as banking and mining that dominated the Mexican economy in the late nineteenth century, foreign merchants bore greater risks as local agents of an increasingly global economy. Whereas the captains of large corporations lived in the comfort of their homes in Berlin, New York, or London and balanced ventures in many different locations, entrepreneurs such as Robert Böker and his descendants lived under local conditions, vulnerable to shifts in the Mexican economy. Therefore, the company initially sold more U.S. than German products, it later followed U.S. precepts of marketing and distribution, and in 1900, the construction of the Edificio Boker highlighted the Bokers' and Carl Friederichs's aspiration to build a department store. Since then, the company has offered a wide array of products from different countries despite German efforts to use merchants like the Bokers as outlets for German merchandise. Since the revolution, the Casa Boker has progressively abandoned its ties to Remscheid and today has become a company of Mexican ownership that primarily distributes Mexican products.

The Mexicanization of the Boker family has proven a much slower process than the Mexicanization of the business. Until the 1950s, the family considered itself German, although evidence of acculturation marked the third-generation Bokers. At that point, however, the assimilation of the Boker family began at the time when both the Casa Boker and the German colony declined in importance. At the beginning of the third millennium, the Bokers continue their lives in between the old German colony and Mexican society at large. However many its newest members might consider themselves Mexicans—the prestige of being European, the lingering vestiges of German culture, and the refusal of the majority of Mexicans to regard the Bokers as Mexicans have thus far combined to limit assimilation.

Throughout their years in Mexico, the Bokers have therefore continually renegotiated their relationship with their host country (Mexico), their home country (Germany), and a hegemonic power that has increasingly affected the histories of both nations (the United States). They have defied the norms imposed by both the German and the Mexican nation-states, and demonstrated that transnational phenomena are not restricted to migrant communities in today's world. While the flags of the imperial powers followed their citizens wherever they invested, entrepreneurs such as the Bokers pursued their business interests and identified their national origin as a cultural rather than a political trait.

Finally, this book has contributed to the discussion about the relationship between economy and culture. As the Bokers' example shows, cultural and economic changes occur in close reciprocity. Cultural change creates new economic realities, and these economic realities in turn produce cultural adjustments. Thus, during the heyday of the Casa Boker, it was easy for its owners to remain German. As the company has assumed its place among the midsized businesses of Mexico City, however, the family that owns it has begun its assimilation into the Mexican bourgeoisie. As the triumph of Vicente Fox has demonstrated, even hyphenless Mexico has recently found a way to claim the descendants of immigrants.

* * *

On a wet June evening in the year 2000, night has already fallen when the American Airlines jet from Dallas touches down at the Benito Juárez Airport in Mexico City. After perfunctory stops at immigration and customs, I hail a taxi to take me across town to my friends' home. Somewhere on a crowded thoroughfare, while chatting animatedly with the taxi driver, I see a billboard that reminds me of the book that I am yet to complete. Against a black background, a fair-skinned woman with European features smiles at me. The caption reads: "Yo soy totalmente Palacio," or "I am totally Palacio [de Hierro]." There will not be another poster showing an engineer and the caption "Yo soy totalmente Boker." While the Palacio de Hierro and the Puerto de Liverpool have become icons of consumption equivalent to Saks Fifth Avenue and Macy's in the United States, the Casa Boker sells a limited assortment of goods to a circle of specialized professionals and retailers. However, the company provokes more admiration for surviving 137 years than pity for not becoming one of the commercial giants in a city littered with the failures of clans far wealthier than the Bokers.

Primary Source Abbreviations in Notes

AB	Archivo Boker, S.A. de C.V.
AdGM	Archiv der deutschen Gesandtschaft in Mexiko
AGN	Archivo General de la Nación
AGNot	Archivo General de Notarías de la Ciudad de México
AHCA	Archivo Histórico, Colegio Alemán Alexander von Humboldt
AHSRE	Archivo Histórico de la Secretaría de Relaciones Exteriores
AMR	Archivo Matías Romero
BAB/AA	Bundesarchiv Berlin, R 901: Auswärtiges Amt
BSI	Bergische Stahlindustrie
BT	Board of Trade
CAAH	Colegio Alemán Alexander von Humboldt
CEPAL	Comisión Económica para la América Latina
CFM	Compañía Ferretera Mexicana
CTM	Confederación de los Trabajadores Mexicanos
DVG	Deutsche Volksgemeinschaft
FA	Fondo Asambleas
FBI/FOIPA	Federal Bureau of Investigation, Files obtained through Freedom of Information and Privacy Act
FCA	Fondo Colegio Alemán
FCP	Fondo Cartas Personales
FE	Fondo Edificios
FFLB	Fondo Franz y Luise Boker
FGMB	Fondo Gunther y Margot Boker
FI	Fondo Intervención
FLC	Fondo Libros de Caja
FM	Fondo Memorias
FO	Foreign Office
FPKB	Fondo Pedro y Klaus Boker
FS	Fondo Sindicato
FOIPA	Freedom of Information and Privacy Act
FRUS	Foreign Relations of the United States
MAC	Fondo Manuel Avila Camacho
MAV	Fondo Miguel Alemán Valdés
MID	Military Intelligence Division
NA	National Archives, Washington D.C. and College Park, Md.
NEL	Nachlass Edda Lucas
NGB	Nachlass Gabriele Buchenau
NMZ	Nachlass Margarete Zantop

NWE	Nachlass Werner Ellerkmann
PAAA	Politisches Archiv, Auswärtiges Amt, Berlin
PARB	Persönliches Archiv Rüdiger Böker
PRO	Public Record Office
RG	Record Group
UET	Unión de Empleados y Trabajadores de la Compañia Ferretera Mexicana
UNAM	Universidad Autónoma de México
USEM	Records of the U.S. Embassy in Mexico City
VDR	Verband Deutscher Reichsangehöriger

Notes

Introduction

1. I will omit the Umlaut in the name Böker when referring to those members of the family born in Mexico, or to the family as a collective.
2. Franz Böker, "Ein Versuch, über den Verlauf meines Lebens etwas aufzuzeichnen," Archivo Boker, Mexico City (hereafter cited as AB), Fondo Memorias (hereafter cited as FM), 37; Helmuth Boker, "Lebenserinnerungen," AB, FM, 1.
3. Oscar Lewis, *Five Families: Mexican Case Studies in the Culture of Poverty* (New York: Basic Books, 1959); Larissa Adler Lomnitz and Marisol Pérez-Lizaur, *A Mexican Elite Family, 1820–1980: Kinship, Class, and Culture* (Princeton, N.J.: Princeton University Press, 1987); and David W. Walker, *Kinship, Business, and Politics: The Martínez del Río Family in Mexico, 1824–1867* (Austin: University of Texas Press, 1986).
4. For the connection between Mexican cultural and economic history generally, see also Eric van Young, "La pareja dispareja: Breves comentarios acerca de la relación entre historia económica y cultural," *Historia Mexicana* 50, no. 3 (2003): 831–70; Eric van Young, "The 'New Cultural History' Comes to Old Mexico," *Hispanic American Historical Review* 79, no. 2 (1999):211–48; and Stephen Haber, "Anything Goes: Mexico's 'New' Cultural History," *Hispanic American Historical Review* 79, no. 2 (1999):309–30. For the importance of "extra-economic" considerations in Mexican business history specifically, consult María Eugenia Romero Ibarra, "La historia empresarial," *Historia Mexicana* 50, no. 3 (2003): 822. For the significance of family history for the study of Latin American economics, politics, and society in the nineteenth century, see also Elizabeth Kuznesof and Robert Oppenheimer, "The Family and Society in Nineteenth-Century Latin America: An Historiographical Introduction," *Journal of Family History* 10, no. 3 (fall 1985): 215–34; and John Kicza, "The Role of the Family in Economic Development in Nineteenth-Century Latin America," *Journal of Family History* 10, no. 3 (fall 1985): 235–57.
5. John M. Hart, *Empire and Revolution: The Americans in Mexico Since the Civil War* (Berkeley and Los Angeles: University of California Press, 2002), passim. For perspectives critical of the world systems and "informal imperialism" approaches that underlie Hart's characterization of merchants, see D. C. M. Platt, "Dependency in Nineteenth-Century Latin America: A Historian Objects," *Latin American Research Review* 15, no. 1 (1980): 113–30; Rory Miller, *Britain and Latin America in the Nineteenth and Twentieth Centuries* (London: Longman,

1993), 16–23; Gilbert M. Joseph, "Close Encounters: Toward a New Cultural History of U.S.-Latin American Relations," in *Close Encounters of Empire: Writing the Cultural History of U.S.-Latin American Relations,* ed. Gilbert M. Joseph, Catherine C. Legrand, and Ricardo D. Salvatore (Durham, N.C.: Duke University Press, 1999), 15–16; and Thomas Fischer, "Ausländische Unternehmen und einheimische Eliten in Lateinamerika: Ansätze zur Interpretation historischer Erfahrungen und aktueller Tendenzen," in *Ausländische Unternehmen und einheimische Eliten in Lateinamerika: Historische Erfahrungen und aktuelle Tendenzen* (Frankfurt: Vervuert, 2001), 13–15.

6. Kelin E. Gersick et al., *Generation to Generation: Life Cycles of the Family Business* (Boston, Mass.: Harvard Business School Press, 1997), 1–3.

7. Interview with Isabel Boker de Willemetz, Mexico City, Jan. 6, 2002.

8. Carlos Morales Díaz, *¿Quién es quien en la nomenclatura de la Ciudad de México?,* 2d exp. ed. (Mexico City: B. Costa-Amic, 1971), 76.

9. "Un comercio moderno con sabor nostálgico. Un siglo de inagotables formas arquitectónicas: Edificio de Casa Boker," *Ferretecnic* 38 (July 2000): 4.

10. Eugene W. Ridings, "Foreign Predominance among Overseas Traders in Nineteenth-Century Latin America," *Latin American Research Review* 20, no. 2 (1985): 3–29. See, however, Carlos Marichal's reply in *Latin American Research Review* 20, no. 3 (1986): 145–50, which points out the important role of Mexican traders and financiers in the city of Monterrey.

11. The term is William Leach's, from *Land of Desire: Merchants, Power, and the Rise of a New American Culture* (New York: Vintage, 1993).

12. The term comes from Arnold J. Bauer, *Goods, Power, History: Latin America's Material Culture* (Cambridge: Cambridge University Press, 2001), 13.

13. José Moya, *Cousins and Strangers: Spanish Immigrants in Buenos Aires, 1850–1930* (Berkeley and Los Angeles: University of California Press, 1998), 6.

14. Jeffrey Lesser, *Negotiating National Identity: Immigrants, Minorities, and the Struggle for Ethnicity in Brazil* (Durham, N.C.: Duke University Press, 1999), 5.

15. Charles Price, "The Study of Assimilation," in *Migration,* ed. J. A. Jackson (Cambridge: Cambridge University Press, 1969), 181–237.

16. This term is Leo Spitzer's, from *Lives in Between: Assimilation and Marginality in Austria, Brazil, and West Africa* (Cambridge: Cambridge University Press, 1989).

17. *Quinto censo de población,* vol. 1: Resumen General (Mexico City: Dirección General de Estadística, 1934), 8.

18. The term is Walther L. Bernecker's, from *Die Handelskonquistadoren:*

Europäische Interessen und mexikanischer Staat im 19. Jahrhundert (Stuttgart: Steiner-Verlag, 1988).

19. Justo Sierra, *Evolución política del pueblo mexicano* [1901] (Mexico City: Fondo de Cultura Económica, 1950); José Vasconcelos, La raza cósmica: Misión de la raza Iberoamericana, Argentina y Brasil [1920] (Mexico City: Espasa-Calpe, 1966).

20. Magnus Mörner, *Adventurers and Proletarians: The Story of Migrants in Latin America* (Pittsburgh, Pa.: University of Pittsburgh Press, 1985). For a recent study of the German enclaves in Latin America, see Jean-Pierre Blancpain, *Migrations et mémoire germaniques en Amérique Latine à l'époque contemporaine: Contribution à l'étude de l'expansion allemande outre-mer* (Strasbourg: Presses Universitaires de Strasbourg, 1994).

21. For this term, see Philip D. Curtin, *Cross-Cultural Trade in Global Perspective* (Cambridge: Cambridge University Press, 1984); and William Schell Jr., *Integral Outsiders: The American Colony in Mexico City, 1876–1911* (Wilmington, Del.: Scholarly Resources, 2001).

22. Robin Cohen, *Global Diasporas: An Introduction* (Seattle: University of Washington Press, 1997), x.

23. Andrew Graham-Yooll, *The Forgotten Colony: A History of the English-Speaking Communities in Argentina* (London: Hutchinson, 1981), especially 188–200.

24. For example, Wilhelm Pferdekamp, *Auf Humboldts Spuren: Deutsche im jungen Mexiko* (Munich: Max Hueber, 1958).

25. Brígida von Mentz et al., *Los pioneros del imperialismo alemán en México* (Mexico City: CIESAS, 1982); Brígida von Mentz et al., *Los empresarios alemanes, el Tercer Reich y la oposición de derecha a Cárdenas,* 2 vols. (Mexico City: CIESAS, 1987); and Luz María Martínez Montiel and Araceli Reynoso Medina, "Inmigración europea y asiática, siglos XIX y XX," in *Simbiosis de culturas: Los inmigrantes y su cultura en México,* ed. Guillermo Bonfil Batalla (Mexico: Fondo de Cultura Económica, 1993), especially 336–65.

26. For example, Linda Basch, Nina Glick Schiller, and Cristina Szanton Blanc, *Nations Unbound: Transnational Projects, Postcolonial Predicaments, and Deterritorialized Nation-States* (Langhorne, Pa.: Gordon and Breach, 1994); Arjun Appadurai, "Global Ethnoscapes: Notes and Queries for a Transnational Anthropology," in *Recapturing Anthropology: Working in the Present,* ed. Richard G. Fox (Santa Fe, N.M.: School of American Research Press, 1991), 191–92.

27. For a perceptive discussion of oral history as a source for Latin American history, see Daniel James, *Doña María's Story: Life History, Memory, and Political Identity* (Durham, N.C.: Duke University Press, 2001), part 3.

Chapter 1

1. Paula von Kollonitz, *Eine Reise nach Mexico im Jahre 1864* (Vienna: C. Gerold's Sohn, 1867), 68–69. All translations mine unless indicated otherwise.
2. Robert Böker, "Lebenserinnerungen," AB, FM, 1–2, 19–20, 24, 26.
3. Carlos Marichal, "Avances recientes en la historia de las grandes empresas y su importancia para la historia económica de México," in *Historia de las grandes empresas en México,* ed. Carlos Marichal and Mario Cerutti (Monterrey: Universidad Autónoma de Nuevo León, 1997), 22; John H. Coatsworth, "Obstacles to Economic Growth in Nineteenth-Century Mexico," *American Historical Review* 83, no. 1 (1978): 92; Jaime Rodríguez O., *Down from Colonialism: Mexico's Nineteenth-Century Crisis* (Los Angeles: Chicano Studies Research Center, University of California, 1983).
4. Moisés González Navarro, *Los extranjeros en México y los mexicanos en el extranjero, 1821–1970* (Mexico City: El Colegio de México, 1993), back cover and passim.
5. George D. Berninger, *La inmigración en México, 1821–1857* (Mexico: Secretaría de Educación Pública, 1974); Bernecker, Handelskonquistadoren, 564–67.
6. For a case study of the struggles of a clan descended from a Panamanian creole, see Walker, *Kinship, Business, and Politics,* particularly 217–19.
7. Ibid., vol. 1; Frederick C. Turner, *The Dynamic of Mexican Nationalism* (Chapel Hill: University of North Carolina Press, 1968), 67–68.
8. Louisa S. Hoberman, *Mexico's Merchant Elite, 1590–1660: Silver, State, and Society* (Durham, N.C.: Duke University Press, 1991), 41; John E. Kicza, *Colonial Entrepreneurs: Families and Business in Bourbon Mexico City* (Albuquerque: University of New Mexico Press, 1983), 25, 45–66.
9. Harold D. Sims, *The Expulsion of Mexico's Spaniards, 1821–1936* (Pittsburgh: University of Pittsburgh Press, 1990); Romeo Flores Caballero, *Counterrevolution: The Role of the Spaniards in the Independence of Mexico, 1804–1838,* trans. Jaime E. Rodríguez O. (Lincoln: University of Nebraska Press, 1974), 14–40; Clara F. Lida, "Los españoles en México: Población, cultura, y sociedad," in *Simbiosis de culturas: Los immigrantes en México y su cultura,* ed. Guillermo Bonfil Batalla (Mexico City: Secretaría de Educación Pública, 1988), 429.
10. Nettie Lee Benson, "Territorial Integrity in Mexican Politics, 1821–1833," in *The Independence of Mexico and the Creation of the New Nation,* ed. Jaime E. Rodríguez O. (Los Angeles: University of California, Los Angeles, Latin American Center, 1989), 275–307.
11. Luis G. Zorrilla, *Relaciones de México con la República de Centro América y con Guatemala* (Mexico: Editorial Porrúa, 1984), 148–67; Jürgen Buchenau, *In the Shadow of the Giant: The Making of Mexico's Central*

America Policy, 1876–1930 (Tuscaloosa: University of Alabama Press, 1996), 3–4 and passim; von Mentz et al., *Los empresarios alemanes*, 1:68–71.

12. Carl C. Sartorius, *Mexico: Landscape and Popular Sketches* (Darmstadt, London, and New York, 1858), 119.

13. David A. Brading, *Miners and Merchants in Bourbon Mexico* (Cambridge: Cambridge University Press, 1971), 97–99; Pferdekamp, Auf Humboldts Spuren, 55–60.

14. Quoted in Ridings, "Foreign Predominance," 6.

15. Bernecker, *Handelskonquistadoren*, 536–67; Jean Meyer, "Les français au Mexique au XIXème siècle," *Cahiers des Amériques Latines* 9–10 (1974): 52–60.

16. Lida, "Los españoles en México," 435–36.

17. Bernecker, *Handelskonquistadoren*, 374–85.

18. Joel R. Poinsett, *Notes on Mexico Made in the Autumn of 1822 Accompanied by an Historical Sketch of the Revolution and Translations of Official Reports on the Present State of That Country* (1823; rpt., New York: Frederick A. Praeger, 1969), 140.

19. Alexander von Humboldt, *Essai politique sur le royaume de la Nouvelle-Espagne*, 5 vols. (Paris: Schoell, 1811); Mary Louise Pratt, *Imperial Eyes: Travel Writing and Transculturation* (New York: Routledge, 1992), 131–32; Susanne Zantop, *Colonial Fantasies: Conquest, Family, and Nation in Precolonial Germany, 1770–1870* (Durham, N.C.: Duke University Press, 1997), 166–67.

20. Zantop, *Colonial Fantasies*, 168.

21. Rodríguez O., *Down from Colonialism*.

22. Interview with Gabriele Buchenau, Warleberg, Germany, June 5, 1992.

23. Charles A. Hale, *Mexican Liberalism in the Age of Mora, 1821–1853* (New Haven, Conn.: Yale University Press, 1968), 35 and 179–80; Juan Bautista Alberdi, "Bases y puntos de partida para la organización política de la República Argentina," in *Obras completas de J. B. Alberdi* (1852; rpt., Buenos Aires, 1886), 3:421.

24. Donathon C. Olliff, *Reforma Mexico and the United States: The Search for Alternatives to Annexation* (Tuscaloosa: University of Alabama Press, 1981), 17–18; González Navarro, *Los extranjeros en México*, 1:230–353; David A. Brading, "Creole Nationalism and Mexican Liberalism," *Journal of Inter-American Studies and World Affairs* 15 (1973): 139–90.

25. See Erika Pani, "Dreaming of a Mexican Empire: The Political Projects of the 'Imperialistas,'" *Hispanic American Historical Review* 82, no. 1 (2002): 1–31.

26. Marianne Oeste de Bopp, "Die Deutschen in Mexico," in *Die Deutschen in Lateinamerika: Schicksal und Leistung*, ed. Hartmut Fröschle (Tübingen: Horst Erdmann Verlag, 1979), 483–84; Hendrik Dane, *Die wirtschaftlichen Beziehungen Deutschlands zu Mexiko und*

Mittelamerika im neunzehnten Jahrhundert (Cologne: Böhlau, 1971), 53–64.

27. Von Mentz et al., *Los pioneros del imperialismo alemán*, 77; Robert Böker, "Lebenserinnerungen," AB, FM, 26.

28. For the early genealogy of the Böker family, see "Stammbaum Familie Böker," Stadtarchiv Remscheid, Remscheid, Germany, R-N-2099.

29. Wilhelm Rees, *Robert Böker und seine Vorfahren als Wirtschaftler und Kommunalpolitiker* (Remscheid: Stadtarchiv Remscheid, 1961), 10–12; Edda Lucas, "Familiengeschichte Böker," Personal Archive Hanneli von Zastrow, Bloomfield, MI, Nachlass Edda Lucas (hereafter cited as NEL), 1. See also Moritz Böker, *Kurze Mittheilungen über die Familie Böker von Mitte des 18. bis Mitte des 19. Jahrhunderts* (Remscheid: Taske und Rittinghaus, 1900); and Moritz Böker, Familie Böker Vieringhausen (Remscheid: n.p., 1924).

30. Rees, *Robert Böker und seine Vorfahren,* 12–17; Lucas, "Familiengeschichte," NEL, 2–5; Böker, *Kurze Mittheilungen,* 6.

31. Lucas, "Familiengeschichte," NEL, 6–8; Edmund Strutz, *Werden und Vergehen Remscheider Familien: Vorträge zur Familienforschung im alten Remscheid* (Remscheid: n.p., 1964), 35–38; von Mentz et al., *Los pioneros del imperialismo alemán,* 35.

32. Rees, *Robert Böker und seine Vorfahren,* 22–23.

33. Helmuth Böker, "Lebenserinnerungen," ed. Joaquín Boker, AB, FM, 17; interview with Helmut Buchenau, Hattiesburg, MS, Nov. 5, 1997, and with Ulrich Buchenau, Jülich, Germany, Aug. 17, 1998.

34. Interview with Gabriele Buchenau, Warleberg, Germany, June 5, 1992.

35. Rees, *Robert Böker und seine Vorfahren,* 26; Lucas, "Familiengeschichte," NEL, 8–10.

36. Friedrich-Wilhelm Henning, *Die Industrialisierung in Deutschland, 1800–1914* (Paderborn, Germany: Schöningh, 1978).

37. Rees, *Robert Böker und seine Vorfahren,* 29–32.

38. Lucas, "Familiengeschichte," NEL, 11.

39. Ibid., 11–12; Rees, *Robert Böker und seine Vorfahren,* 28, 32–33.

40. Lucas, "Familiengeschichte," NEL, 12–15; Rees, *Robert Böker und seine Vorfahren,* 33–38; Robert Böker, "Lebenserinnerungen," AB, FM, 17.

41. Robert Böker, "Lebenserinnerungen," AB, FM, 13–16.

42. Interview with Gabriele Buchenau, June 2, 1992, Warleberg, Germany; Robert Böker, "Lebenserinnerungen," AB, FM, passim.

43. Jürgen Kocka, "The European Pattern and the German Case," in *Bourgeois Society in Nineteenth-Century Europe,* ed. Jürgen Kocka and Allan Mitchell (Providence, R.I.: Berg, 1993), 4–24.

44. Robert Böker, "Lebenserinnerungen," AB, FM, 1, 18–19.

45. Ibid., 19–20.

46. Ibid.

47. Ibid., 20.

48. Ibid., 2.

49. Ibid., 13–15 and 20–23; Rees, *Robert Böker und seine Vorfahren*, 46–48; interview with Pedro Boker, Mexico City, July 27, 1996.
50. Robert Böker, "Lebenserinnerungen," AB, FM, 25.
51. Ibid., 24–25, 28.
52. Kollonitz, *Eine Reise nach Mexico,* 104, 126–27.
53. For the inception of the Paseo de la Reforma, see Barbara A. Tenenbaum, "Streetwise History: The Paseo de la Reforma and the Porfirian State," in *Rituals of Rule, Rituals of Resistance: Public Celebrations and Popular Culture in Mexico,* ed. William H. Beezley, Cheryl English Martin, and William E. French (Wilmington, Del.: Scholarly Resources, 1994), 129.
54. "Geschäftsgeschichte," AB, FM, 1.
55. Robert Böker, "Lebenserinnerungen," AB, FM, 25.
56. Ibid., 25–26.
57. "Co-Partnership Agreement," AB, Fondo Franz y Luise Boker (hereafter cited as FFLB), folder 1324; Jan Bazant, "From Independence to the Liberal Republic, 1821–1867," in *Mexico Since Independence,* ed. Leslie Bethell (Cambridge: Cambridge University Press, 1991), 45.
58. Rees, *Robert Böker und seine Vorfahren*, 66; Robert Böker, "Lebenserinnerungen," AB, FM, 26; AB, Fondo Libros de Cajas (hereafter FLC), vol. 1, 1–4.
59. Robert Böker, "Lebenserinnerungen," AB, FM, 27.
60. Ibid.
61. Ibid., 25; Robert Böker, untitled, AB, FM, 1; Rudolf von Lübeck, "Relación de la fundación y desarrollo de la casa comercial Roberto Boker y Cía," 1, all AB, FM.
62. Robert Böker, "Lebenserinnerungen," AB, FM, 25–26; von Lübeck, "Relación," AB, FM, 1; AB, FLC, vol. 1, 7–17, 242.
63. Robert R. Miller, "Herman Sturm: Hoosier Secret Agent for Mexico," *Indiana Magazine of History* 58 (Mar. 1962): 1–15.
64. Holder, Boker Co. to Matías Romero, Mexico City, Jan. 2, 1869; and Robert Böker to same, Mexico City, Dec. 10, 1869, Banco de México, Mexico City, Archivo Matías Romero (hereafter cited as AMR), doc. 3870 and 8829; Robert Böker, "Lebenserinnerungen," 40.
65. Robert Böker to Romero, Mexico City, Sept. 8, 1871, AMR, 15291.
66. Robert Böker, "Lebenserinnerungen," AB, FM, 30.
67. Pferdekamp, *Auf Humboldts Spuren,* 71.
68. Rees, *Robert Böker und seine Vorfahren*, 71 and 76.
69. Robert Böker to Heinrich Böker, Mar. 10, 1870, AB, FFLB, folder 1324; Robert Böker, "Lebenserinnerungen," AB, FM, 40.
70. Walther L. Bernecker and Thomas Fischer, "Deutsche in Lateinamerika," in *Deutsche im Ausland—Fremde in Deutschland: Migration in Geschichte und Gegenwart,* ed. Klaus J. Bade (Munich: C. H. Beck, 1992), 200–10.
71. Interview with Herbert Bostelmann, Mexico City, June 13, 2000.
72. Von Mentz et al., *Los pioneros del imperialismo alemán,* 333–62; Bernecker, Handelskonquistadoren, 581–93.

73. González Navarro, *Los extranjeros en México,* vol. 1.
74. Katherine Anne Porter, *Ship of Fools* (Boston: Little, Brown, 1962), 79–80.
75. Charles A. Hale, *The Transformation of Mexican Liberalism in the Late Nineteenth Century* (Princeton, N.J.: University of Princeton Press, 1989).
76. David A. Brading, *Los orígenes del nacionalismo mexicano* (Mexico City: El Colegio de México, 1979); and Jacques Lafaye, *Quetzalcóatl and Guadalupe: The Formation of Mexican National Consciousness, 1531–1813,* trans. Benjamin Keen (Chicago: University of Chicago Press, 1976).
77. Alan Knight, "Racism, Revolution, and Indigenismo: Mexico, 1910–1940," in *The Idea of Race in Latin America, 1870–1940,* ed. Richard Graham (Austin: University of Texas Press, 1990), 72–73; Benedict Anderson, *Imagined Communities: Reflections on the Spread of Nationalism* (London: Verso, 1983).
78. For a similar argument comparing the issue of hyphenation in Argentina and the United States, see Donna Gabaccia, "Race, Nation, Hyphen: Italian-Americans in Comparative Perspective," unpublished paper.
79. Von Mentz et al., *Los empresarios alemanes,* 1:328–29.
80. Pedro Boker to Jürgen Buchenau, Nov. 21, 2000.
81. Bernecker, *Handelskonquistadoren,* 567–93; see Chapter 2 for a detailed discussion of the process of transition from expatriate community to "colony."
82. To this day, Mexico City is made up of delegaciones, which in turn consist of colonias.
83. Ethelyn C. Davis, "The American Colony in Mexico City," Ph.D. dissertation, University of Missouri, 1942, ii.
84. Silke Nagel, "Integration oder nationalistische Abgrenzung? Deutsche Einwanderer in Mexiko-Stadt," M.A. thesis, Freie Universität Berlin, 1991, 5.
85. Friedrich Ratzel, *Aus Mexico: Reiseskizzen aus den Jahren 1874 und 1875* (1878; rpt., Stuttgart: Brockhaus, 1969), 379.
86. Bernecker, *Handelskonquistadoren,* 573–76.
87. Oeste de Bopp, "Die Deutschen in Mexico," 518.
88. Robert Böker, "Lebenserinnerungen," AB, FM, 28.
89. Ibid., 29.
90. Robert Böker, "Lebenserinnerungen," AB, FM, 30–35. This episode was printed under the title "Eine Reise mit Hindernissen" in *Deutsche Zeitung von Mexico,* Aug. 14, 1937.
91. Francisco Boker to Miguel Alemán Valdés, Mexico City, Jan. 31, 1947, Archivo General de la Nación (hereafter cited as AGN), Ramo Presidentes, Fondo Miguel Alemán Valdes (hereafter cited as MAV), expediente 562.11/9–8, p. 2–3.

92. *Familiengeschichte Böker,* NEL, 25–26; Auguste Böker diary, AB, FM.

93. Adolfo Schmidtlein, *Cartas de un médico alemán a sus padres* (Mexico City: El Colegio de México, 1978).

94. Auguste Böker diary, AB, FM, 4.

95. Robert Böker, "Lebenserinnerungen," AB, FM, 2; interview with Pedro Boker, July 25, 1996, Mexico City.

96. Auguste Böker diary, AB, FM, 5–7.

97. Lucas, "Familiengeschichte," NEL, 28; Auguste Böker diary, AB, FM, 5–6; Robert Böker to Max Böker, Remscheid, Sept. 1, 1873, AB, FFLB, folder "Hentzen."

98. Böker family tree, Stadtarchiv Remscheid, Germany, N-3000–6.

99. Auguste Böker diary, AB, FM, 22; Robert Böker, "Lebenserinnerungen," AB, FM, 2.

100. Franz Böker, "Vorwort," in Rees, *Robert Böker,* 5.

Chapter 2

1. "Discurso pronunciado por el Presidente Porfirio Díaz," AB, Fondo Edificios (hereafter cited as FE), folder "Einweihung des Hauses."

2. "Paseo por el centro: Casa Boker," *http://www.cultura.df.gob.mx/paseo/r1s10.htm* (May 2, 2001); "El escudo nacional en el suelo: Una infracción que debe corregirse," *El Popular,* July 4, 1900; interview with Pedro Boker, Mexico City, June 17, 1995.

3. Paul Vanderwood, *Disorder and Progress: Bandits, Police, and Mexican Development,* 2d ed. (Wilmington, Del.: Scholarly Resources, 1992); Friedrich Katz, "Liberal Republic and Porfiriato," in *Mexico Since Independence,* ed. Leslie Bethell (Cambridge: Cambridge University Press, 1991), 57; Daniel Cosío Villegas, *Historia moderna de México,* 9 vols. (Mexico City: Editorial Hermes, 1956–73), 2:186–90.

4. Luise Böker, "Lebenserinnerungen," Personal Archive, Rüdiger Böker, Hamburg (hereafter cited as PARB); Helen J. Sanborn, *A Winter in Central America and Mexico* (Boston: Lee and Shepard, 1886), 232–33.

5. John M. Hart, *Revolutionary Mexico: The Coming and Process of the Mexican Revolution,* 2d ed. (Berkeley and Los Angeles: University of California Press, 1997), 103–31; Friedrich Katz, "Liberal Republic and Porfiriato," 57.

6. Alex M. Saragoza, *The Monterrey Elite and the Mexican State* (Austin: University of Texas Press, 1988), 16–71; Aurora Gómez, "El desempeño de la Fundidora de Hierro y Acero de Monterrey durante el porfiriato," in *Historia de las grandes empresas en México, 1850–1930,* ed. Carlos Marichal (Monterrey: Universidad Autónoma de Nuevo León, 1997), 201–39; Memoria, Asamblea Ordinaria, Feb. 11, 1911, AB, Fondo Asambleas (hereafter cited as FA), CFM.

7. Mauricio Tenorio Trillo, *Mexico at the World's Fairs: Crafting a Modern*

Nation (Berkeley and Los Angeles: University of California Press, 1996), 20.

8. Paolo Riguzzi, "México próspero: Las dimensiones de la imagen nacional en el porfiriato," *Historias* 20 (1988): 137–57.

9. John Lear, Workers, *Neighbors, and Citizens: The Revolution in Mexico City* (Lincoln: University of Nebraska Press, 2001), 15–35; Michael Johns, *The City of Mexico in the Age of Díaz* (Austin: University of Texas Press, 1997).

10. Benjamin Orlove and Arnold J. Bauer, "Giving Importance to Imports," in *The Allure of the Foreign: Imported Goods in Postcolonial Latin America,* ed. Benjamin Orlove (Ann Arbor: University of Michigan Press, 1997), 8; and Bauer, *Goods, Power, History,* 150–62.

11. Solomon B. Griffin, *Mexico of To-Day* (New York: Harper and Brothers, 1886), 197–98; Charles M. Flandrau, *Viva Mexico!* (New York: D. Appleton & Co., 1908), 263.

12. Mark Wasserman, *Everyday Life and Politics in Nineteenth-Century Mexico: Men, Women, and War* (Albuquerque: University of New Mexico Press, 2000), 202–3.

13. Pablo Piccato, *City of Suspects: Crime in Mexico City, 1900–1931* (Durham, N.C.: Duke University Press, 2001), 17–23, 35–37.

14. Robert Böker, untitled, AB, FM, 5–6.

15. The term "Porfirian persuasion" comes from William Beezley, *Judas at the Jockey Club and Other Episodes of Porfirian Mexico* (Lincoln: University of Nebraska Press, 1987).

16. John H. Coatsworth, *Growth Against Development: The Economic Impact of Railroads in Porfirian Mexico* (DeKalb: Northern Illinois University Press, 1981), 4–7.

17. Foreign investors who lived outside Mexico were another matter, as the investments of large corporations continued to increase throughout the twentieth century.

18. Schell, *Integral Outsiders,* xiv.

19. Francisco Pimentel, *La economía política aplicada á la propiedad territorial en México* (Mexico City: Ignacio Cumplido, 1866), 183.

20. W. Dirk Raat, *El positivismo durante el porfiriato* (Mexico City: El Colegio de México, 1975); W. Dirk Raat, "Ideas and Society in Don Porfirio's Mexico," *The Americas* 30 (1973): 32–53; Hale, *Transformation of Liberalism,* 215.

21. González Navarro, *Los extranjeros en México,* 101. For the Porfirian exhibits at the World's Fairs, see Tenorio Trillo, *Mexico at the World's Fairs.*

22. Jonathan C. Brown, "Foreign and Native-Born Workers in Porfirian Mexico," *American Historical Review* 98 (1993): 786–818.

23. González Navarro, *Los extranjeros en México,* 2:82–122.

24. Andrés Molina Enríquez, *Los grandes problemas nacionales* (Mexico City: Imprenta de A. Carranza e hijos, 1909), 146.

25. Albert Crosby, *Ecological Imperialism: The Biological Expansion of Europe, 900–1900* (Cambridge: Cambridge University Press, 1986).
26. Delia Salazar Anaya, "Migration: To Mexico," in *Encyclopedia of Mexico: History, Society, and Culture,* ed. Michael S. Werner (Chicago: Fitzroy Dearborn, 1997), 883–84; Katz, "Liberal Republic and Porfiriato," 74–75; Oeste de Bopp, "Die Deutschen in Mexico," 486.
27. Maurice Proal and Pierre Martin Charpenel, *Los Barcelonnettes en México* (Mexico City: Clío, 1998), 15–24.
28. *Tercer censo general de población, 1910* (Mexico City: Dirección General de Estadística, 1921).
29. Eric N. Baklanoff, "From Peddlers to Empresarios: The Lebanese in Latin America," *South Eastern Latin Americanist* 43, no. 1 (1999): 71. For the casta divina, see Gilbert M. Joseph, *Revolution from Without: Yucatán, Mexico, and the United States, 1880–1924* (Cambridge: Cambridge University Press, 1982), 8 and passim.
30. On the growth of the "American colony," see Schell, *Integral Outsiders,* xvii, 51–52.
31. F. C. Rieloff, "Liste der in Mexico D.F. lebenden Deutschen," June 10, 1914, Politisches Archiv, Auswärtiges Amt, Berlin, Germany (hereafter cited as PAAA), Archiv der ehemaligen deutschen Gesandtschaft in Mexico (hereafter cited as AdGM), packet 45, vol. 1.
32. Erich Günther, *Illustriertes Handbuch von Mexico mit besonderer Berücksichtigung der deutschen Interessen* (Mexico City: E. Günther, 1912), 354.
33. Ronald C. Newton, *German Buenos Aires, 1900–1933: Social Change and Cultural Crisis* (Austin: University of Texas Press, 1977), 3–31.
34. *Jahresbericht der Schule der Deutschen Colonie zu Mexico* (hereafter *Jahresbericht*) 1900–1, 1901–2, and 1902–3, Archivo Histórico, Colegio Alemán Alexander von Humboldt (hereafter cited as AHCA), box 1; Matthias Wankel, *Reflejo de la historia de dos pueblos: El Colegio Alemán en México, 1894–1942* (Mexico City: Colegio Alemán, 1994), 183.
35. *Jahresbericht* 1901, AHCA, box 1.
36. Wankel, *Reflejo de la historia,* 186.
37. Grundgesetz der Schule der deutschen Colonie zu Mexico (Mexico City, Hijos de Jens, 1896), 2; AHCA, box 1.
38. Ibid.
39. *Jahresbericht* 1912, 10; AHCA, box 2.
40. Nagel, "Integration oder nationalistische Abgrenzung," 135–37.
41. Robert Böker to Heinrich Böker, Mar. 10, 1870, AB, FFLB, folder 1324; Robert Böker, "Lebenserinnerungen," AB, FM, 40.
42. Hans F. Weise, *Fünfundsiebzig Jahre Deutsches Haus in Mexico (1848–1923)* (Mexico City: Compañía Mexicana de Artes Gráficas, 1923), 23 and 25; American residents to Hayes, May 7, 1877, National Archives, Washington, D.C., and College Park, Md. (hereafter cited

as NA), RG 59: General Records, Department of State, Consular Despatches, Mexico City.

43. More to Rives, Mexico City, June 6, Oct. 10, and Dec. 31, 1888, Apr. 1, 1889; More to Wharton, Mexico City, July 1, 1889, NA, RG 59, Consular Despatches, Mexico City.
44. Luise Böker, "Lebenserinnerungen," Persönliches Archiv Rüdiger Böker, Hamburg, 6–7.
45. Wangenheim to Bülow, Mexico City, Dec. 6, 1905, Bundesarchiv Berlin, R 901: Auswärtiges Amt (hereafter cited as BAB/AA), R 12299, 5–6.
46. Von Mentz et al., *Los pioneros del imperialismo alemán*, 486; Rees, *Robert Böker und seine Vorfahren*, 69–71; von Lübeck, "Relación," AB, FM, 1 and 5.
47. On this distinction, see also Reinhard Liehr and Mariano E. Torres Bautista, "Las *Free-Standing Companies* británicas en el México del porfiriato, 1884–1911," *Historia Mexicana* 187 (1998): 605–7.
48. Rees, *Robert Böker und seine Vorfahren*, 76. The only function of "Heinrich Böker" was the export of hardware from Remscheid and Solingen to the Americas. This company should not be confused with the cutlery producer Heinrich Böker and Co. in Solingen.
49. Franz Böker, "Jahrhundertfeier—und dann: Was?" AB, FFLB, folder 1, 2.
50. Von Lübeck, "Relación," AB, FM, 2–5; Ignacio Mariscal to Stiegler, Mexico City, May 30, 1887, Archivo Histórico de la Secretaría de Relaciones Exteriores, Mexico City (hereafter cited as AHSRE), L-E-1913, 167.
51. "Roberto Boker, Testamento," Dec. 21, 1869, Archivo General de Notarías del Distrito Federal, Fondo Moderno (hereafter cited as AGNot), notaría 100 (Ignacio Burgoa), vol. 618, 789–90.
52. "Sociedad: Robert, Max, Enrique Boker y Carlos Friederichs," July 2, 1885, AGNot, notaría 100 (Ignacio Burgoa), vol. 650, 13–20.
53. *The Massey-Gilbert Blue Book of Mexico* (Mexico City: Massey Gilbert, 1903), 8–397; von Lübeck, "Relación," AB, FM, 2–5.
54. Eduardo Iturbide, *Mi paso por la vida* (Mexico City: Editorial Cultura, 1941), 20–31.
55. Von Lübeck, "Relación," AB, FM, 2.
56. Roberto Boker y Cía to Limantour, Sept. 9, 1901, Archivo Condumex, Mexico City, Fondo CDLIV: Archivo José Y. Limantour, segunda serie, roll 8.
57. Fanny Chambers Gooch, *Face to Face with the Mexicans* (New York: Fords, Howard, & Hulbert, 1887), 170–71.
58. Pferdekamp, *Auf Humboldts Spuren*, 69; Schell, *Integral Outsiders*, 22; von Lübeck, "Relación," AB, FM, 2.
59. Von Lübeck, "Relación," AB, FM, 2.
60. "Vorbilder des unternehmerischen Gemeinsinns," *Remscheider General-Anzeiger*, Mar. 23, 1953, in AB, Fondo Hemerografía; Robert

Böker, untitled ms. [1904], AB, FM; birth certificate, Carlos Friederichs Jr., Jan. 12, 1892, AB, FE, folder "Einweihung des Hauses"; "Geschäftsgeschichte," AB, FM, 4.

61. Cosío Villegas, *Historia moderna de México,* 2:186, 192–97; and 7:710.
62. Von Mentz et al., *Los empresarios alemanes,* 1:29.
63. Friedrich Katz, *Deutschland, Diaz und die mexikanische Revolution: Die deutsche Politik in Mexiko 1870–1920* (Berlin: VEB Deutscher Verlag der Wissenschaften, 1964), 95–98.
64. Jean Meyer, "Les Français au Mexique au XIXème siècle," *Cahiers des Amériques Latines* 9–10 (1974): 62–64; Cosío Villegas, *Historia moderna de México,* 7:710; von Mentz et al., *Los empresarios alemanes,* 1:30.
65. Steven B. Bunker, "'Consumers of Good Taste': Marketing Modernity in Northern Mexico, 1890–1920," *Mexican Studies/Estudios Mexicanos* 13, no. 2 (1997): 234–47.
66. Meyer, "Les Français au Mexique," 64–65; Raymonde Antiq-Auvaro, *L'Émigration des Barcelonnettes au Mexique,* 87–98; Lear, *Workers, Neighbors, and Citizens,* 74–75.
67. *México, ¿quieres tomarte una foto conmigo? Cien años de consumo* (Mexico City: Procuraduría Federal del Consumidor, 1996), 26–31.
68. E. Salazar Silva, *Las colonias extranjeras en México* (Mexico City: n.p., 1937), 40.
69. Pedro Boker, communication to Jürgen Buchenau, Mexico City, Nov. 21, 2000.
70. Michael B. Miller, *The Bon Marché: Bourgeois Culture and the Department Store, 1869–1920* (Princeton, N.J.: Princeton University Press, 1981), 19–35. The first significant department store in London, Harrod's, arrived almost twenty years later, just before the opening of El Palacio de Hierro. Bill Lancaster, *The Department Store: A Social History* (London: Leicester University Press, 1995), 22.
71. William H. Beezley, "The Porfirian Smart Set Anticipates Thorstein Veblen in Guadalajara," in *Rituals of Rule, Rituals of Resistance: Public Celebrations and Popular Culture in Mexico,* ed. William H. Beezley, Cheryl English Martin, and William E. French (Wilmington, Del.: Scholarly Resources, 1994), 178.
72. Tony Morgan, "Proletarians, Politicos, and Patriarchs: The Use and Abuse of Cultural Customs in the Early Industrialization of Mexico City, 1880–1910," in *Rituals of Rule, Rituals of Resistance: Public Celebrations and Popular Culture in Mexico,* ed. William H. Beezley, Cheryl English Martin, and William E. French (Wilmington, Del.: Scholarly Resources, 1994), 152–54.
73. "Geschäftsgeschichte," AB, FM, 5.
74. Bunker, "Marketing Modernity," 227–29; cf. storefronts of the "old" store and the new Edificio Boker.
75. Von Lübeck, "Relación," AB, FM, 3–5; Rees, *Robert Böker und seine*

Vorfahren, 68. For ease of reading, the word "partner" will hereafter refer to propietarios as well as socios.

76. Enrique Cárdenas, "A Macroeconomic Interpretation of Nineteenth-Century Mexico," in *How Latin America Fell Behind: Essays on the Economic Histories of Brazil and Mexico, 1800–1914*, ed. Stephen Haber (Stanford, Calif.: Stanford University Press, 1997), 83.

77. Von Lübeck, "Relación," AB, FM, 3. On the Mexican currency crisis, see William Schell Jr., "Silver Symbiosis: Re-Orienting Mexican Economic History," *Hispanic American Historical Review* 81, no. 1 (2001): 123–27.

78. Von Lübeck, "Relación," AB, FM, 3.

79. Ibid., 3–5; Rees, *Robert Böker und seine Vorfahren*, 68.

80. Von Lübeck, "Relación," AB, FM, 5–6; "Edificio Boker," AB, FE.

81. *Deutsche Zeitung von Mexiko*, July 7, 1900.

82. For information on the architecture, consult *Edificio Boker 100 años, 1900–2000: En memoria al primer centenario de la inauguración del edificio* (Mexico City: n.p., 2000).

83. Rudolf von Lübeck to Franz Böker, Lübeck, Germany, July 6, 1950, AB, FE, folder "Einweihung des Hauses."

84. "Inauguración de la Casa Boker," *El Imparcial*, July 4, 1900.

85. Quoted in Ida Rodríguez Prampolini, *La crítica de arte en México en el siglo XIX* (Mexico City: Imprenta Universitaria, 1964), 1:119.

86. "El escudo nacional en el suelo: Infracción que debe corregirse," *El Popular*, July 4, 1900.

87. "Inauguración de la Casa Boker," *El Tiempo*, July 5, 1900.

88. Rudolf Darius, *Die Entwicklung der deutsch-mexikanischen Handelsbeziehungen von 1870–1914* (Cologne: Welzel, 1927), 60–75.

89. "Discurso en el caso de que venga el Sr. Presidente," AB, FE, folder "Einweihung des Hauses."

90. "Inauguración de la Casa Boker," *El Imparcial*, July 4, 1900.

91. "Pormenor de los gastos . . . ," AB, FE, folder "Einweihung des Hauses."

92. Franz Böker, "Schicksal von Kapital und Arbeit," AB, FM, 2.

93. Von Lübeck, "Relación," AB, FM, 2–4; *Anunciador Boker*, June 1903, AB; *Anunciador Boker*, Oct. 1905, enclosed in Wangenheim to Bülow, Mexico City, Dec. 6, 1905, BAB/AA, R 12299, 5–6.

94. Von Lübeck, "Relación," AB, FM, 4; *Catálogo/Catalog Roberto Boker y Cía*, AB, Fondo Catálogos.

95. For an analysis of the rise of the department store and mail-order house in the United States, consult Alfred D. Chandler Jr., *The Visible Hand: The Managerial Revolution in American Business* (Cambridge, Mass.: Belknap, 1977), 225–33.

96. Franz Böker, "Betrachtung," AB, Fondo Franz and Luise Boker (hereafter cited as FFLB), folder 37, 1–2; Franz Böker, "Schicksal von Kapital und Arbeit im Hause Boker," AB, FM, 1–4.

97. Franz Böker, "Schicksal von Kapital und Arbeit," AB, FM, 4–5;

"Finanzlage und Rentabilitaet des Hauses Roberto Boker & Cia in den Jahren 1895–1909," AB, FFLB, folder 35.

98. Moreno, "Sears, Roebuck Company"; Hart, *Empire and Revolution*.

Chapter 3

1. Franz Böker, "Versuch," AB, FM, 13.

2. Auguste Böker diary, summer 1882, 18–19; Franz Böker, "Versuch," 2–6; Lucas, "Familiengeschichte," NEL, 33–34; interview with Ruth Boker, Mexico City, July 3, 1995.

3. T. B. Holder to Grey, Mexico City, July 14, 1915, Public Record Office, Kew, England (hereafter cited as PRO) Foreign Office (FO) 371/2402, file 113537; Schell, *Integral Outsiders*, 8.

4. Schell, *Integral Outsiders*, 69.

5. Franz Böker, "Versuch," AB, FM, 18.

6. Ibid.

7. Quoted in Wasserman, *Everyday Life and Politics,* 202.

8. Franz Böker, "Versuch," AB, FM, 31.

9. Ibid., 31, 34–36; idem, "Ueber die Lage—1958—in Mexico," AB, FFLB, folder 2, 2.

10. David Blackbourn, "The German Bourgeoisie: An Introduction," in *The German Bourgeoisie: Essays on the Social History of the German Middle Class from the Late Eighteenth to the Early Twentieth Century,* ed. David Blackbourn and Richard J. Evans (London: Routledge, 1991), 7–9.

11. Interviews with Gabriele Buchenau, Warleberg, Germany, June 2 and 5, 1992, and with Helmuth Boker, Warleberg, Germany, July 19, 1994; Franz Böker, "Versuch," 2.

12. Interview with Helmut Buchenau, Hattiesburg, MS, Oct. 27, 1997.

13. Jürgen Osterhammel, *Kolonialismus: Geschichte, Formen, Folgen* (Munich: C. H. Beck, 1995), 95–99; Emily Rosenberg, *Spreading the American Dream: American Economic and Cultural Expansion, 1890–1945* (New York: Hill and Wang, 1982), 38–62.

14. Katz, Deutschland, *Díaz und die mexikanische Revolution,* especially 87–94; von Mentz et al., *Los empresarios alemanes,* 1:34–36.

15. As an example of efforts to encourage German merchants in Mexico to sell German products, see Wangenheim to Bülow, Mexico City, Dec. 6, 1905, BAB/AA, R 12299, 5–6.

16. Nancy Mitchell, *The Danger of Dreams: German and American Imperialism in Latin America* (Chapel Hill: University of North Carolina Press, 1999), chapter 4; Ragnhild Fiebig-von Hase, *Lateinamerika als Konfliktherd der deutsch-amerikanischen Beziehungen, 1890–1903: Vom Beginn der Panamerikapolitik bis zur Venezuelakrise von 1902/03* (Göttingen: Vandenhoeck und Ruprecht, 1986).

17. Friedrich Katz, *The Secret War in Mexico: Europe, the United States, and*

the *Mexican Revolution* (Chicago: University of Chicago Press, 1981), 50–61.

18. Daily Consular Reports (Great Britain), found in BAB/AA, Abt. II: Handelspolitische Abteilung, 4457, p. 59.
19. Franz Böker, "Versuch," AB, FM, 8.
20. Interview with Pedro Boker, Mexico City, Dec. 15, 1998.
21. Franz Böker, "Versuch," AB, FM, passim.
22. See Chapters 4–6.
23. Franz Böker, "Schicksal von Kapital und Arbeit im Hause Boker," AB, FM, 1–2.
24. "Geschäftsgeschichte," AB, FM, 5; Alexander Böker to Heinrich and Luise Böker, various dates, PARB.
25. Interview with Gabriele Buchenau, Warleberg, Germany, June 2 and 5, 1992, and with Margaret Dyckerhoff, Wiesbaden, Germany, May 17, 1996; Franz Böker to Marie Pocorny, Oct. 30, 1919, Nachlass Gabriele Buchenau (hereafter cited as NGB). A history of the Women's Association can be found in *Zum 60 jährigen Jubiläum des deutschmexikanischen Frauenvereins Asociación de Ayuda Social de la Colonia Alemana: Rückblick 1903–1963 mit genauerem Bericht über das letzte Jahrzehnt* (Mexico City: n.p., 1963).
26. Franz Böker, "Versuch," AB, FM, 19.
27. Franz Böker, "Versuch," AB, FM, 29; Franz Böker, "Schicksal von Kapital und Arbeit," AB, FM, 5.
28. Ibid., 4.
29. Sociedad, Compañía Ferretera Mexicana, Nov. 1, 1909, AGNot, notaría 69 (Augusto Burgoa), book 3, vol. 26, 235.
30. Alan Knight, *U.S.-Mexican Relations, 1910–1940: An Interpretation* (La Jolla: Center for U.S.-Mexican Studies, University of California, San Diego, 1987), 55.
31. Franz Böker, "Schicksal von Kapital und Arbeit," AB, FM, 4; Robert Böker, "Lebenserinnerungen," AB, FM, 4.
32. Sociedad, Compañía Ferretera Mexicana, Nov. 1, 1909, AGNot, notaría 69 (Augusto Burgoa), book 3, vol. 26, 236–48.
33. Franz Böker, "Schicksal von Kapital und Arbeit," AB, FM, 2–4.
34. Ibid.; Marichal, "Avances recientes," 28.
35. Hart, *Revolutionary Mexico,* passim. For a critique of Hart's views, see Alan Knight, "The United States and the Mexican Peasantry, c. 1880–1940," in *Rural Revolt in Mexico: U.S. Intervention and the Domain of Subaltern Politics,* ed. Daniel Nugent, exp. edition (Durham, N.C.: Duke University Press, 1998), 25–63.
36. Katz, *Secret War in Mexico,* 75; Franz Böker, "Versuch," AB, FM, 34.
37. The best recent synthetic treatments are Alan Knight, *The Mexican Revolution,* 2 vols. (Cambridge: Cambridge University Press, 1986); Hart, *Revolutionary Mexico;* and François-Xavier Guerra, Le Mexique de l'Ancien Régime à la Révolution, 2 vols. (Paris: Harmattan, 1986);

and Michael Gonzales, *The Mexican Revolution, 1910–1940* (Albuquerque: University of New Mexico Press, 2002).

38. For economic nationalism, see Robert F. Smith, *The United States and Revolutionary Nationalism in Mexico, 1916–32* (Chicago: University of Chicago Press, 1972); Lorenzo Meyer, *Mexico and the United States in the Oil Controversy, 1917–1942* (Austin: University of Texas Press, 1972); and Douglas W. Richmond, *Venustiano Carranza's Nationalist Struggle* (Lincoln: University of Nebraska Press, 1983).

39. Franz Böker, "Versuch," AB, FM, 31, 34–36.

40. Friedrich Bauer-Thoma, *Die Wahrheit über Mexiko und seine deutsche Kolonie* (Berlin: n.p., 1912), 51–52.

41. Franz Böker, "Versuch," AB, FM, 34.

42. Ibid., 37.

43. Ibid.

44. Lear, *Workers, Neighbors, and Citizens,* 273; Hohler to Foreign Office, Mexico City, Feb. 25 and 26, 1915, PRO FO 371/2396, file 15003, and 371/2398, file 40183.

45. Enclosure in Spring Rice to Grey, Apr. 30, 1915, PRO FO 371/2398, file 52164.

46. Franz Böker, "Ueber die Lage," AB, FFLB, folder 2, 2.

47. Interview with Gabriele Buchenau, Warleberg, Germany, June 5, 1992.

48. Interview with Margret Dyckerhoff, Wiesbaden, Germany, May 16, 1996.

49. Interviews with Gabriele Buchenau, Warleberg, Germany, June 5 and 6, 1992.

50. Luise Böker to Marie Pocorny, Mexico City, Feb. 26, 1915, AB, FFLB, folder "Familiengeschichte."

51. Luise Böker to Marie Pocorny, Mexico City, Mar. 11, 1915, AB, FFLB, folder "Familiengeschichte."

52. Franz Böker, "Versuch," AB, FM, 38.

53. Interview with Gabriele Buchenau, Warleberg, Germany, June 5, 1992.

54. Ordinaria—Acta 3, AB, Fondo Asambleas (hereafter cited as FA), May 15, 1912, 2.

55. Arthur G. Magnus to Oficial Mayor, Secretaría de Relaciones Exteriores, Mexico City, Sept. 16, 1914, AHSRE 16–12–165.

56. Franz Böker, "Versuch," AB, FM, 37; Helmuth Boker, "Lebenserinnerungen," 1.

57. Franz Böker, "Versuch," AB, FM, 38; see also Rosa King, *Tempest over Mexico* (New York: Doubleday, 1935), 252–53.

58. It is indicative of the good fortune of the Casa Boker that it did not file a claim with the Mexican-German Claims Commission. See the list of claims contained in Puig Casauranc to Rüdt von Collenberg, Mexico City, May 24, 1934, AHSRE, III-1142–8, and Francisco Boker to Miguel Alemán Valdes, Mexico City, Jan. 31, 1947, AGN, MAV, 562.11/9–8.

216

59. Franz Böker, "Versuch," AB, FM, 38.
60. Ibid., 37; Lear, *Workers, Neighbors, and Citizens,* 228–29.
61. Interviews with Gabriele Buchenau, Warleberg, Germany, June 5 and 6, 1992.
62. Franz Böker, "Schicksal von Kapital und Arbeit," AB, FM, 6; Franz Böker to Heinrich Böker, Mexico City, Nov. 26, 1919, AB, FFLB, folder "Familiengeschichte."
63. Von Mentz et al., *Los empresarios alemanes,* 1:102–5.
64. Message from German consulate in Mexico City intercepted by War Trade Intelligence Committee, May 22, 1916, PRO FO 371/2700, file 48/80209.
65. Katz, *Secret War in Mexico,* 350–67.
66. Note verbale, Spring Rice to U.S. Secretary of State, Washington, D.C., Mar. 1, 1915, Bryan to Page, Washington, D.C., Mar. 5, 1915, *Foreign Relations of the United States* (hereafter cited as *FRUS*) 1915, Supplement: The World War, 127–28 and 132–33; Page to Bryan, London, Jan. 19, 1916, *FRUS* 1916, Supplement: The World War, 337–38.
67. Memorandum, "Home Office and the Blockade," PRO FO 551/11, 4; minutes of Black List Committee, Nov. 2, 1915, PRO TS (Treasury Solicitor), 14.
68. Sinclair to CFM, London, Aug. 9, 1916, AB, Fondo Representaciones.
69. For U.S. counterespionage efforts, see Charles H. Hill III and Louis R. Sadler, *The Archaeologist Was a Spy: Sylvanus G. Morley and the Office of Naval Intelligence* (Albuquerque: University of New Mexico Press, 2003).
70. Lansing to Page, Washington, D.C., Jan. 25, 1916, NA, RG 59, 763.72112/2229.
71. Thurstan to Grey, Mexico City, Dec. 18, 1916, PRO FO 371/2706.
72. Young to Grey, Guatemala City, Jan. 24, 1916, PRO FO 551/10, 17.
73. Franz Böker, "Versuch," AB, FM, 38.
74. Grahame Richards, "Report on the present Mexican situation," Aug. 3, 1917, PRO FO 371/2962, file 48/152598.
75. Message from German consulate in Mexico City intercepted by War Trade Intelligence Committee, May 22, 1916, PRO FO 371/2700, file 48/80209.
76. Memorandum, John Broderick, New York City, Sept. 7, 1915, and Memorandum, Barclay, Mexico City, Sept. 11, 1915, PRO FO 371/2406, file 26624.
77. Durán, *Guerra y revolución,* 258.
78. Thurstan to Grey, Mexico City, Dec. 18, 1916, PRO FO 371/2706.
79. *Jahresbericht* 1915, 11; AHCA, box 2.
80. *Jahresbericht* 1915, 18; AHCA, box 2.
81. *Jahresbericht* 1919, 3; AHCA, box 2.
82. Alan Knight, *U.S.-Mexican Relations,* 15–17.

83. Fletcher to Secretary, Mexico City, Apr. 3, 1918, NA, RG 59, 711.12/77–1/2.
84. Fletcher to Secretary, Mexico City, Mar. 13, 1917, Library of Congress, Manuscript Division, Henry P. Fletcher Papers, box 4, file 9; notes on interview between Carranza and Howard E. Morton for the *Los Angeles Examiner*, Apr. 19, 1917, Archivo CONDUMEX, Mexico City, Archivo Venustiano Carranza, 12837.
85. José Gaxiola to Garza Pérez, Le Havre, France, June 15, 1917, AHSRE 17–8–41.
86. Chamberlain to Secretary of State, Mexico City, Oct. 31, 1917, NA, RG 59, 763.72112/5323.
87. Summerlin to Secretary of State, Mexico City, Jan. 8, 1918, NA, RG 59, 763.72112/6414; Chamberlain to Summerlin, Mexico City, July 31, 1917, NA, RG 84, Mexico City Consulate, 1912–36, vol. 312, file 711.3, 1917; War Trade Board, Confidential List, Apr. 4, 1919, NA, RG 165, Military Intelligence Division, War Department General Staff, box 3802, file 10921–2/26–4; War Trade Board, *Trading with the Enemy. Enemy Trading List revised to Dec. 13, 1918* (Washington, D.C.: Government Printing Office, 1919), 91 and 99.
88. Value in 1913. Asamblea Extraordinaria, Apr. 21, 1914, AB, FA.
89. Asambleas Ordinarias 1913, 1917, 1918, and 1919, AB, FA.
90. Franz Böker, "Der Fondo A und die früheren Aktionäre der C.F.M.," AB, FFLB, folder 1, 2.
91. Frank McIntyre to Lt. F. G. Nichols, Military Censor, Washington, D.C., June 6, 1917, NA, RG 165: Military Intelligence Division, War Department General Staff, box 1932, file 9685–63; H. M. Harrison to District Intelligence Officer, n.p., Apr. 23, 1918, NA, RG 165, box 2156, file 6264–1405/1; M. M. Leeland to Chief, Military Intelligence Section, War College Division, General Staff, Fort Sam Houston, Texas, Sept. 6, 1917, NA, RG 165, box 2164, file 9700–257/1; Henry P. Fletcher to Secretary of State, Mexico City, May 29, 1917, NA, RG 59, 862.20212/348.
92. CFM to Heinrich Böker, Mexico City, Oct. 7 and 19, 1919, AB, FFLB, "Gesandtschaft, 1916–23."
93. Esperanza Durán, *Guerra y revolución: Las grandes potencias y México* (Mexico City: Colegio de México, 1985), 245; Alvaro Matute, *Historia de la revolución mexicana, 1917–1924: Las dificultades del nuevo estado* (Mexico City: Colegio de México, 1995), 20–21.
94. Katz, *Secret War in Mexico,* 446–48.
95. Fletcher to American Consular Service, Mexico City, May 30, 1917, and George T. Summerlin to George A. Chamberlain, Mexico City, Aug. 2, 1917, NA, RG 84, Records of the Foreign Service Posts of the Department of State, Mexico City Consulate, 1912–36, vol. 312, file 711.3, 1917; Duems to von Lübeck, Mexico City, July 1, 1918; NA, RG 84, Mexico City Embassy, 1912–36, vol. 587, file 820.02, 1918,

"Alphabetical List of Subjects of the Teutonic Powers," Sept. 8, 1917, NA, RG 165, box 2031, file 9140–668/3; W. E. Herring to Chief Military Censor, Feb. 17, 1919, NA, RG 165, box 3775, file 10915–201/77; Fletcher to Secretary of State, Mexico City, May 24, 1918, NA, RG 59, 862.20212/1261; Thurstan to Balfour, Mexico City, Apr. 24, 1917, PRO FO 371/2960, file 107189.

96. Von Mentz et al., *Los empresarios alemanes*, 1:55.

97. Luise Böker to Marie Pocorny, Aug. 31, 1919, NGB.

98. Lear, *Workers, Neighbors, and Citizens*, 17.

99. Francisco Boker to Secretaría de Relaciones Exteriores, Mexico City, July 4, 1917, Oct. 16, 1918, Nov. 8, 1918, Oct. 27, 1919; SRE to Boker, Mexico City, July 10, 1917, Oct. 18, 1918, Oct. 29, 1919; AHSRE 14-PB-49; Morgan, "Proletarians, Politicos, and Patriarchs," 153.

100. Franz Böker, "Versuch," AB, FM, 40.

101. Interview with Gabriele Buchenau, Warleberg, Germany, June 5, 1992; photo album, NGB.

102. Pedro Boker to Jürgen Buchenau, Mexico City, Nov. 25, 2000.

103. Franz Böker, "Versuch," AB, FM, 40.

104. Franz Böker to Elisabeth Lucas, Mexico City, Dec. 5, 1919, AB, FFLB, folder 1150.

105. *Deutsche Zeitung von Mexiko*, Dec. 28, 1918, 2.

106. Stefan Rinke, *"Der letzte freie Kontinent": Deutsche Lateinamerikapolitik im Zeichen transnationaler Beziehungen, 1918–1933* (Stuttgart: Verlag Hans Dieter Heinz, 1996), 379–91; Arthur Ruhl, *The Central Americans: Adventures and Impressions Between Mexico and Panama* (New York: Charles Scribner's Sons, 1928), 239.

107. Montgelas to Auswärtiges Amt, Mexico City, Jan. 23, 1922, PAAA, R 79645.

108. Montgelas to Auswärtiges Amt, Mexico City, Sept. 16, 1920, PAAA, R 79645.

109. Franz Böker to Heinrich Böker, Mexico City, Apr. 20, 1920, AB, FFLB, folder 1150.

110. Montgelas to Auswärtiges Amt, Mexico City, Aug. 25, 1921, PAAA, R 79598.

111. Pedro Boker, "Monumento a Beethoven," AB, Fondo Pedro y Klaus Boker (hereafter FPKB); AB, Fondo Theodor von Gosen.

Chapter 4

1. Franz Böker, "Versuch," 40.

2. Frances Calderón de la Barca, *Life in Mexico During a Residence of Two Years in that Country* (London: Chapman and Hall, 1843), 285.

3. Interview with Gabriele Buchenau, Warleberg, Germany, June 6, 1992; personal communication from Pedro Boker, Jan. 2, 2001.

4. Böker family tree, Stadtarchiv Remscheid, Germany, N-3000–6.

5. Diane E. Davis, *Urban Leviathan: Mexico City in the Twentieth Century* (Philadelphia: Temple University Press, 1994), 23–30.

6. Anita Brenner and George R. Leighton, *The Wind that Swept Mexico* (New York: Harper, 1943), 62.

7. Revisionist arguments are analyzed in David C. Bailey, "Revisionism and the Recent Historiography of the Mexican Revolution," *Hispanic American Historical Review* 58, no. 1 (1978): 62–79.

8. Gilbert M. Joseph and Daniel Nugent, "Popular Culture and State Formation in Revolutionary Mexico," in *Everyday Forms of State Formation: Revolution and the Negotiation of Rule in Mexico* (Durham, N.C.: Duke University Press, 1994), 5–15.

9. María del Carmen Collado Herrera, *Empresarios y políticos, entre la Restauración y la Revolución* (Mexico City: Instituto Nacional de Estudios Históricos de la Revolución Mexicana, 1996), 18–26; interview with Gabriele Buchenau, Warleberg, June 5, 1992.

10. Franz Böker to Heinrich Böker, Mexico City, Apr. 20, 1920, AB, FFLB, folder 1150.

11. Interview with Margot Trauwitz, Mexico City, Aug. 9, 1995, and with Carlos Seippel, Mexico City, July 6, 1995. For a detailed discussion of the Nazi period, see Chapter 5.

12. Collado Herrera, *Empresarios y políticos*, 124–25.

13. Böker to G. A. Schmidt, Mexico City, May 31, 1920; and Schmidt to Auswärtiges Amt, Mexico City, July 9, 1920, PAAA, R 91207; von Mentz et al., *Los empresarios alemanes*, 1:147–50.

14. Knight, "Racism, Revolution, and Indigenismo," 71–113.

15. Interview with Gabriele Buchenau, Warleberg, Germany, June 2, 1992.

16. Daniel Cosío Villegas, *Memorias* (Mexico City: Joaquín Mortiz, 1976), 91.

17. Moisés González Navarro, *Población y sociedad en México, 1900–1970* (Mexico City: Universidad Nacional Autónoma de México, 1974), 2:34–56.

18. See also Jürgen Buchenau, "Small Numbers, Great Impact: Mexico and Its Immigrants," *Journal of American Ethnic History* 20, no. 3 (2001): 23–49.

19. Stephen Haber, *Industry and Underdevelopment: The Industrialization of Mexico, 1880–1940* (Stanford, Calif.: Stanford University Press, 1989), 150–70.

20. Ibid., 171; Stephen R. Niblo, *War, Diplomacy, and Development: The United States and Mexico, 1938–1954* (Wilmington, Del.: Scholarly Resources, 1995), 14. See also Table 7 below.

21. Enrique Krauze, Jean Meyer, and Cayetano Reyes, *Historia de la revolución mexicana: Período 1924–28: La reconstrucción económica* (Mexico City: El Colegio de México, 1977), 273–86; Davis, "The American Colony," 100.

22. Helen Delpar, *The Enormous Vogue of Things Mexican* (Tuscaloosa: University of Alabama Press, 1992), 15–53; Drewey W. Gunn, *American and British Writers in Mexico, 1556–1973* (Austin: University of Texas Press, 1974), 76–77; Hart, Empire and Revolution, 367–70.

23. Alex Saragoza, "The Selling of Mexico: Tourism and the State," in *Fragments of a Golden Age: The Politics of Culture in Mexico Since 1940,* ed. Gilbert Joseph, Anne Rubenstein, and Eric Zolov (Durham, N.C.: Duke University Press, 2001), 91. See also Jesús Velasco, "Reading Mexico, Understanding the United States: American Transnational Intellectuals in the 1920s and 1990s," *Journal of American History* 86, no. 2 (Sept. 1999): 643–55. For a view critical of the impact of official nationalism on the average Mexican, see Alan Knight, "Popular Culture and the Revolutionary State in Mexico, 1910–1940," *Hispanic American Historical Review* 74, no. 3 (1994): 395–444.

24. Beezley, *Judas at the Jockey Club*, chapter 1.

25. Delpar, *Enormous Vogue of Things Mexican,* 14 and passim.

26. Henry C. Schmidt, *The Roots of "Lo Mexicano": Self and Society in Mexican Thought, 1900–1934* (College Station: Texas A&M University Press, 1978), 98.

27. Ibid.

28. John Womack, "The Mexican Economy During the Revolution, 1910–1920: Historiography and Analysis," *Marxist Perspectives* 1 (1978): 80–123; George D. Beelen, "The Harding Administration and Mexico: Diplomacy by Economic Persuasion," *The Americas* 41, no. 2 (1984): 151.

29. Thomas F. O'Brien, *The Revolutionary Mission: American Enterprise in Latin America, 1900–1945* (Cambridge: Cambridge University Press, 1996), 267.

30. Haber, *Industry and Underdevelopment,* 143; Jean Meyer, "Mexico in the 1920s," in *Mexico Since Independence,* ed. Leslie Bethell (Cambridge: Cambridge University Press, 1991), 228.

31. O'Brien, *Revolutionary Mission,* 311.

32. Alan Knight, "Revolutionary Process, Recalcitrant People: Mexico, 1910–1940," *The Revolutionary Process in Mexico: Essays on Political and Social Change, 1880–1940,* ed. Jaime Rodríguez O. (Los Angeles: UCLA Latin American Studies Center, 1990), 259.

33. For example, see the costs of advertising in AB, FA, Asambleas Ordinarias, 1920–1941. The advertising budget declined continuously throughout the 1920s and 1930s, demonstrating a lack of commitment to building a larger base of customers.

34. Interview with Carlos Seippel, Mexico City, May 26, 1998. Seippel worked in the Casa Boker as an apprentice from 1935 to 1936 and as the head of the retail department from 1948 to 1996. His father was a client of Don Pancho, a hardware merchant in the city of Tuxtla Gutiérrez.

35. Interview with Margot Trauwitz, Mexico City, Aug. 9, 1995; "Clog Case," [Name blacked out] to FBI, Denver, Aug. 9, 1943, Federal Bureau of Investigation, Washington, D.C., Freedom of Information and Privacy Act file (hereafter cited as FBI/FOIPA, 65–16273–1724.

36. Bunker, "Marketing Modernity," passim.

37. Interview with Helmut Buchenau, Hattiesburg, MS, Oct. 27, 1997.

38. Franz Böker, "Versuch," AB, FM, 11–13.

39. Anselm Doering-Manteuffel, *Wie westlich sind die Deutschen? Amerikanisierung und Westernisierung im 20. Jahrhundert* (Göttingen: Vandenhoeck und Ruprecht, 1999), 20–21. See also Peter Berg, *Deutschland und Amerika, 1918–1929: Über das deutsche Amerikabild der zwanziger Jahre, Historische Studien,* no. 385 (Lübeck: Matthiesen, 1963).

40. Interview with Gabriele Buchenau, Warleberg, Germany, June 6, 1992.

41. Franz Böker, "Versuch einer Rekonstruktion der Hergänge, die unsere heutige Lage herbeigeführt haben," AB, FFLB, 2.

42. Interview with Carlos Seippel, Mexico City, May 26, 1998.

43. Interview with Carlos Seippel, Mexico City, May 26, 1998; AB, Fondo Catálogos; cf. *Catálogo/Catalog,* 1900.

44. List of employees, AB, FE.

45. Earnings after 1935 neither include rent income nor unofficial earnings kept outside the company's books (see discussion below).

46. Franz Böker, "Schicksal von Kapital und Arbeit," AB, FM, 6. From now on, the name Casa Boker will refer to the conglomerate of CFM and La Esperanza.

47. CFM Asamblea Extraordinaria, Aug. 4, 1919, AB, FA.

48. CFM Asamblea Extraordinaria, Nov. 21, 1932, AB, FA.

49. Franz Böker, "Schicksal von Kapital und Arbeit," AB, FM, 6–8.

50. CFM Asamblea Ordinaria, May 25, 1933, AB, FA.

51. Franz Böker, "Über das Problem der heimatdeutschen Teilhaber," AB, FFLB, 2.

52. Ibid.; Gunther Boker, "Unsere Geschaefte waehrend und nach dem Kriege," AB, FM, 2.

53. Contrato Individual de Trabajo (blank), AB, Fondo Sindicato (hereafter cited as FS).

54. Sociedad, Compañía de Inversiones La Esperanza, S.A, June 15, 1931, AB, Fondo Escrituras, leg. Esperanza; Compraventa, June 28, 1935, ibid., leg. CFM.

55. Justus Scharff to Presidente de la Junta de Conciliación y Arbitraje del D.F., Mar. 11, 1932, AB, FS.

56. Gunther Boker, "Unsere Geschaefte waehrend und nach dem Kriege," AB, FM, 5.

57. Nacional Financiera, *Statistics on the Mexican Economy* (Mexico City: Nacional Financiera, 1977), 218.

58. Bilanz 31 Dez. 1940; Bilanz 31 Dez. 1941; Ganancias, pérdidas, y participaciones, 1930–40, AB, FFLB, folders 1, 2, and 37.
59. Contrato Colectivo de Trabajo, 1932, 1933, 1935, 1937, and 1939, AB, FS. For the 1947 strike, see Chapter 5.
60. "El cierre de las casas alemanas," *Excelsior,* Feb. 14, 1936; extracts from Franz Böker's diary, Feb. 11, 12, 13, and 15, AB, FFLB, folder Huelgas y paros; Fernando Amilpa to Lázaro Cárdenas, Feb. 17, 1936, AGN, Ramo Presidentes, Fondo Lázaro Cárdenas, 432.2/187.
61. "Las juventudes socialistas han dado nueva y escandalosa nota," Excelsior, Mar. 11, 1938; Cámara Nacional de Comercio to Jefe del Departamento del Distrito Federal, Mexico City, Mar. 10, 1938, AB, FFLB, folder Huelgas y paros.
62. Interview with Carlos Seippel, Mexico City, May 26, 1998; see also staff lists in AB, FS.
63. Interview with Gabriele Buchenau, Warleberg, Germany, June 5, 1992.
64. Interviews with Gabriele Buchenau, Warleberg, Germany, June 5, 1992; Margret Dyckerhoff, Wiesbaden, Germany, May 16, 1996; von Mentz et al., *Los empresarios alemanes,* 1:326–33.
65. Interview with Carlos Seippel, Mexico City, May 25, 1998.
66. "La Familia Dressel," dir. Fernando de Fuentes, Mexico City, 1935. B/W, 90 mins.; Emilio García Rica, *Fernando de Fuentes, 1894–1958* (Mexico City: Cineteca Nacional, 1984), 129–33; Gustavo García, "Me lo dice el corazón," http://www.unam.mx/univmex/2000/jun-jul/imagenes/ggarcia.html (28 Mar. 2002).
67. Oeste de Bopp, "Die Deutschen in Mexico," 497–500; interview with Gabriele Buchenau, Warleberg, June 6, 1992.
68. See Chapter 3.
69. This pattern was typical of German families in Latin America. Bernecker and Fischer, "Deutsche in Lateinamerika," 213–14.
70. Davis, "American Colony in Mexico City," 18.
71. Franz Böker, "Versuch," AB, FM, 39–41.
72. Interview with Ruth Boker, Mexico City, July 3, 1995.
73. Octavio Paz, *The Labyrinth of Solitude,* trans. Lysander Kemp (New York: Grove Press, 1985), 22.
74. Von Mentz et al., *Los empresarios alemanes,* 1:143–45; Friedrich E. Schuler, *Mexico Between Hitler and Roosevelt: Mexican Foreign Relations in the Age of Lázaro Cárdenas, 1934–1940* (Albuquerque: University of New Mexico Press, 1998), 48–49.
75. Delia Salazar Anaya, La población extranjera en México (1895–1990): Un recuento con base en los censos generales de población (Mexico City: Instituto Nacional de Antropología e Historia, 1996), 240 and 299; Nagel, "Integration oder nationalistische Abgrenzung," 52–65.
76. Traven's origin continues to elicit debate. Karl S. Guthke, in *B. Traven: The Life Behind the Legend* (Chicago: Lawrence Hill Books, 1991),

68–69, accepts the author's claim that he was born in the United States. Heidi Zogbaum, in *B. Traven: A Vision of Mexico* (Wilmington, Del.: Scholarly Resources, 1992), suggests he might have been born in Germany. Both authors concur that Traven was engaged in anarchist activities in postwar Munich.

77. Luise Böker to Marie Pocorny, Aug. 26, 1919, NGB.
78. Oeste von Bopp, "Die Deutschen in Mexico," 487; interview with Carlos Seippel, Mexico City, May 26, 1998. See also Chapter 5.
79. Oeste de Bopp, "Die Deutschen in Mexiko," 491; Rinke, *Der letzte freie Kontinent*, 1:326–27; von Mentz et al., *Los empresarios alemanes*, 2:146; interview with Marianne Frenk-Westheim, Mexico City, June 27, 2000. As a Jewish immigrant who arrived in 1930, Frenk-Westheim was the last living German in Mexico City who remembered the Weimar-era colony.
80. Quoted in Nagel, "Integration oder nationalistische Abgrenzung," 142.
81. Ibid., 139–71.
82. Helmuth Boker, "Lebenserinnerungen," AB, FM.
83. "5 Jahre deutsche evangelische Kirchengemeinde in Mexico," Evangelisches Zentralarchiv, Berlin (hereafter cited as EZA), 5/2827, pp. 66–75; interview with Gabriele Buchenau, Warleberg, Germany, June 2, 1992.
84. Proal and Charpenel, *Los Barcelonnettes*, 73–74.
85. Lida, "Los españoles en México," 434 and 444.
86. Franz Böker, "Versuch," 42; Junta Intersecretarial to Gunther Boker, Mexico City, Feb. 28, 1947, AB, Fondo Gunther and Margot Boker (hereafter cited as FGMB), folder "Correspondencia posguerra."
87. Helmuth Boker, "Lebenserinnerungen," AB, FM, 18.
88. Franz Böker, "Versuch," AB, FM, 43; von Mentz et al., *Los empresarios alemanes*, 1:167; Julius Vermehren, "Lebenserinnerungen," Archivo Personal Dieter Vermehren, Tuxpan, Michoacán (hereafter cited as APDV); interview with Margret Dyckerhoff, Wiesbaden, Germany, May 16, 1996.
89. Interview with Gabriele Buchenau, Warleberg, Germany, June 2, 1992.
90. Interview with Ulrich Buchenau, Warleberg, Germany, Mar. 5, 1995.
91. Interviews with Gabriele Buchenau, Warleberg, Germany, June 5, 1992; Michel Buchenau, Altheim, Germany, May 16, 1996; Ulrich Buchenau, Jülich, Germany, May 16, 1996; and Julieta Hoth, Mexico City, May 15, 1998; Cookbook, NGB.
92. For this concept, see James C. Scott, *Domination and the Art of Resistance: Hidden Transcripts* (New Haven, Conn.: Yale University Press, 1990).
93. Interview with Helmut Buchenau, Charlotte, N.C., Feb. 9, 2001.
94. Gunther Boker to Secretaría de Relaciones Exteriores, Mexico City, Dec. 12, 1935, and Ernesto Hidalgo to Boker, Mexico City, Apr. 20, 1936, AHSRE 2013/36.

95. Interviews with Margot Trauwitz, Mexico City, Aug. 9, 1995; Helmut Buchenau, Hattiesburg, MS, Nov. 5, 1997; and Julieta Hoth, Mexico City, May 20, 1998.
96. "Extragratifikationen auf Grund der Bilanz 1941," AB, FFLB, folder 1; interview with Carlos Seippel, Mexico City, July 6, 1995.
97. Interview with Michel Buchenau, Altheim, Germany, May 16, 1996.
98. Helmuth Boker, "Lebenserinnerungen," AB, FM, 1.
99. Gunther Boker to Gabriele Buchenau, Mexico City, Dec. 18, 1974, NGB. See also Chapter 6.
100. Alfred Vermehren, "Lebenserinnerungen," APDV.
101. Helmuth Boker, "Lebenserinnerungen," AB, FM, 18.
102. Von Mentz et al., *Los empresarios alemanes*, 1:329–33.

Chapter 5

1. Franz Böker to Luise Böker, Sept. 9, 1939, AB, FFLB.
2. Hermann Rauschning, *Gespräche mit Hitler* (Zurich: Europa Verlag, 1940), 66.
3. Klaus Volland, *Das Dritte Reich und Mexiko: Studien zur Entwicklung des deutsch-mexikanischen Verhältnisses 1933–1942 unter besonderer Berücksichtigung der Ölpolitik* (Frankfurt: Peter Lang, 1976), 30–42; and Theodor Schieder, *Hermann Rauschnings 'Gespräche mit Hitler' als Geschichtsquelle* (Opladen, Germany: Rheinisch-Westfälische Akademie der Wissenschaften, 1972).
4. Schuler, *Mexico Between Hitler and Roosevelt,* passim; Alan Knight, "Cardenismo: Juggernaut or Jalopy," *Journal of Latin American Studies* 24 (1994): 73–107; Stephen R. Niblo, *War, Diplomacy, and Development: The United States and Mexico, 1938–1954* (Wilmington, Del.: Scholarly Resources, 1995), 3–62; Thomas G. Powell, *Mexico and the Spanish Civil War* (Albuquerque: University of New Mexico Press, 1980).
5. Friedrich Katz, "Germany and Latin America until 1945," paper presented at the 1995 conference "Rethinking the Post-Colonial Encounter," Yale University, New Haven, Conn., 19. In a widely cited work originally published in 1966, Katz had taken a different stance. "Algunos rasgos esenciales de la política alemana en América Latina," in *Ensayos mexicanos* (Mexico City: Alianza Editorial, 1994), 385–86.
6. Schuler, Mexico *Between Hitler and Roosevelt,* 49–50.
7. Stefan Rinke, "Die Firma Junkers auf dem lateinamerikanischen Markt," in *Grenzenlose Märkte? Die deutsch-lateinamerikanischen Wirtschaftsbeziehungen vom Zeitalter des Imperialismus bis zur Weltwirtschaftskrise,* eds. Boris Barth and Jochen Meissner (Münster, Germany: Lit, 1995), 177–84; Volland, *Das Dritte Reich und Mexiko,* 43, 62–64; Katz, "Algunos rasgos esenciales," 379.
8. Schuler, *Mexico Between Hitler and Roosevelt,* 66–69, 101–3; Schuler, "Germany, Mexico, and the Second World War," *Jahrbuch für*

Geschichte von Staat, Wirtschaft und Gesellschaft Lateinamerikas (1985): 457; Volland, Das Dritte Reich und Mexiko, 83–174; and von Mentz et al., Los empresarios alemanes, 2:71–138. For the financial benefits, see Robert G. McGregor, "Strictly Confidential Report: Nazis, Communists and other Foreign Agents in Mexico," June 28, 1940, NA, RG 165, Records of the War Department: Military Intelligence Division Regional File (hereafter cited as MID), box 2463.

9. Von Mentz et al., Los empresarios alemanes, 2:144.

10. Patrik von zur Mühlen, Fluchtziel Lateinamerika: Die deutsche Emigration, 1933–1945; politische Aktivitäten und soziokulturelle Integration (Berlin: Verlag Neue Gesellschaft, 1988), 160. For the activities of this exile community, see also Renata von Hanffstengel, Cecilia Tercero, and Silke Wehner Franco, ed. Mexiko, das wohltemperierte Exil (Mexico City: Instituto de Investigaciones Interculturales Germano-Mexicanas, 1995).

11. Von Mentz et al., Los empresarios alemanes, 2:144–48; interview with Marianne Frenk-Westheim, Mexico City, June 27, 2000.

12. Von Mentz et al., Los empresarios alemanes, 2:148; Nagel, "Integration oder nationalistische Abgrenzung," 174.

13. Jahresbericht der Deutschen Schule in Mexico: Bericht über das Schuljahr 1939, AHCA, 29 and 41.

14. Heriberto Meili, "El nazismo en México," enclosed in L'Boal to Secretary of State, Mexico City, June (no date) 1940, NA, RG 59, 812.00N/151, 9–11; Gus T. Jones, "The Nazi Failure in Mexico," Stanford University, Hoover Institution Archives, Palo Alto, Calif., 4–13; María Elena Paz, Strategy, Security, and Spies: Mexico and the Allies in World War II (University Park: Pennsylvania State University Press, 1997), 28.

15. Gunther Boker to Peter Brechtel, Tarasp, Germany, July 24, 1967; Bericht des Verwaltungsrats der Deutschen Schule in Mexico 1938, AHCA; Wankel, Reflejo de dos culturas, 228; AB, FFLB, folder 1422; Franz Böker to Rudolf von Lübeck, Mexico City, Feb. 12, 1939, AB, FFLB, folder 1386.

16. Gunther Boker to Miguel Alemán, Mexico City, Mar. 29, 1948, AGN, MAV, 562.11/9–8; Gunther Boker, "Unsere Geschaefte," AB, FM, 3–5.

17. After the war, Kalb wrote a letter in support of the Casa Boker. See Kalb to Secretaría de Relaciones Exteriores, Mexico City, Apr. 1, 1946, AHSRE III-677–1.

18. A. D. Davidson to F. Godber, Mexico City, Mar. 5, 1940, PRO FO 371/24217.

19. Franz Böker officially retired from the CFM in 1937.

20. Franz Böker, "Schicksal von Kapital und Arbeit," AB, FM, 7–10; Franz Böker, memorandum, Apr. 9, 1943, AB, FFLB, folder 34.

21. See list of officers of German Casino, Riding Club, and Rowing Club prepared by the FBI (probably Gus Jones), Feb. 13, 1942, NA, RG 165, MID, box 2460, folder "NSDAP v. 19."

22. "Microscopic Dot Case," NA, RG 59, 862.20212/5–2945; Leslie B. Rout and John F. Bratzel, *The Shadow War: German Espionage and United States Counterespionage during World War II* (Frederick, Md.: University Publications of America, 1985), 53–96; Paz, *Strategy, Security, and Spies,* chapter 9.
23. J. Edgar Hoover to Berle, Washington, D.C., Mar. 16, 1940, NA, RG 59, 812.00N/110; Jones, "Nazi Failure in Mexico," 1–2.
24. Jürgen Müller, *Nationalsozialismus in Lateinamerika: Die Auslandsorganisation der NSDAP in Argentinien, Brasilien, Chile und Mexiko, 1931–1945* (Stuttgart: Verlag Dieter Heinz, 1997), 388–98; see also Volland, *Das Dritte Reich und Mexico,* 200.
25. Interview with Gabriele Buchenau, Warleberg, Germany, June 28, 1992.
26. Ibid.; interview with Margot Trauwitz, Mexico City, Aug. 9, 1995; Helmuth Boker, "Erinnerungen," AB, FM, 19–20, 22–23.
27. Interview with Helmut Buchenau, Chapel Hill, N.C., Jan. 27, 1995.
28. Gunther Boker, diary entries, AB, Fondo Diarios (hereafter cited as FD).
29. Daniels to Secretary, Mexico City, Mar. 21, 1941, NA, RG 84, Mexico City (Mexico) General Records,1937–52 (hereafter cited as USEM), Box 86; Robert McGregor, "Nazis, Communists, and Other Foreign Agents," enclosed in Daniels to Secretary of State, Mexico City, June 28, 1940, NA, RG 165, MID, box 2463; Gunther Boker, diary entry, May 15, 1940, AB, FGMB. Franz and Gunther Boker neither appear on the central, alphabetical list of the NSDAP nor in the records of the AO. NA, RG 242: Berlin Document Center, NSDAP Zentralkartei, Microfilm Publication A3340 (hereafter cited as NSDAP List), roll C0056, and United States Senate, *Nazi Party Membership Records submitted by the War Department to the Subcommittee on War Mobilization of the Committee for Military Affairs* (Washington, D.C.: Government Printing Office, 1946), vol. 2.
30. Franz Böker to Luise Böker, Mexico City, Oct. 4, 1940, enclosed in W. D. Styer to Headquarters Eighth Corps Area, Ft. Sam Houston, Laredo, Texas, Oct. 23, 1940, NA, RG 165: MID, War Department General Staff, box 2920, file 10201–802/3.
31. AB, Fondo Cartas Personales; especially Franz Böker to Luise Böker, Mexico City, Apr. 14 and June 25, 1941.
32. In his memoirs, Franz acknowledged the horrors of the Holocaust and the "criminal" nature of the Hitler regime. He also accepted the German responsibility for the war, although he blamed the Allies for having "poisoned" the atmosphere with the harsh Treaty of Versailles. Franz Böker, "Versuch," AB, FM, 44–45.
33. Gunther Boker to Gabriele Buchenau, Monterrey, July 13, 1939, 4; NGB; Gunther Boker diaries, AB, FD, 4 vols.
34. NA, RG 242, NSDAP List, roll D0037, frame 2530 and 2546; "Microscopic Dot Case," NA, RG 59, 862.20212/5–2945, 70–71; FBI,

"German Espionage in Latin America," June 1946, NA, RG 59, 862.20210/6–1746; Edelmira Aguilar to Avila Camacho, Mexico City, Mar. 11, 1943, AGN, Ramo Presidentes, Fondo Manuel Avila Camacho (hereafter cited as MAC) 550/93; interview with Helmut Buchenau, Hattiesburg, MS, Nov. 17, 1997, and with Sven Diederichsen, Mexico City, July 23, 1996. The FBI report was riddled with factual errors such as the assertions that Gabriele's name was Margarita and that she lived in Buenos Aires, yet was probably correct in delineating Franz's activities in South America.

35. NA, RG 242, NSDAP List, roll C0056, frame 980; Helmuth Boker, "Erinnerungen," AB, FM, 22–45.

36. Interview with Ruth Boker, Mexico City, July 3, 1995.

37. As was custom at the time, Peter's obituary in the German newspaper in Mexico City included the line "Long live the *Fuhrer*" (*Deutsche Zeitung von Mexico,* June 29, 1940, 2).

38. Interviews with Margret Dyckerhoff and Michel Buchenau, May 16, 1996.

39. Ahnenpaß, Gabriele Buchenau, NGB; "Chronik der Familie Carl Mühlinghaus-Sebes aus der Splittergasse zu Remscheid-Lennep," AB, FM, 9–10.

40. Interview with Helmut Buchenau, Hattiesburg, MS, Oct. 28, 1997, and with Pedro Boker, Mexico City, Dec. 12, 1997.

41. Interview with Ulrich Buchenau, Jülich, May 16, 1996.

42. Interview with Pablo Pellat Spitalier, Mexico City, June 13, 2000.

43. Josephus Daniels, Shirt-Sleeve Diplomat (Chapel Hill: University of North Carolina Press, 1947); Niblo, *War, Diplomacy, and Development,* 37–48; Daniels diary, Josephus Daniels Papers, Southern Historical Collection, University of North Carolina at Chapel Hill; Blanca Torres Ramírez, *México en la segunda guerra mundial* (Mexico City: Colegio de México, 1979), 65–66.

44. Daniels, *Shirt-Sleeve Diplomat,* 497.

45. W. Dirk Raat, "Gus Jones and the FBI in Mexico, 1900–1947: A Biographical Essay Writ-Large," unpublished ms., 15 and 19–21.

46. *Excelsior,* May 23 and June 4, 1940; Meili, "El nazismo en México," enclosed in L'Boal to Secretary, Mexico City, June (no date) 1940, NA, RG 59, 812.00N/151; Paz, *Strategy, Security, and Spies,* 30–31.

47. Niblo, *War, Diplomacy, and Development,* 65–66.

48. Ibid.; Torres Ramírez, *México en la segunda guerra mundial,* 9–64.

49. Charles A. Bay, "A Compilation of Information Concerning German Firms in Mexico," enclosed in Daniels to Secretary, Mexico City, Nov. 8, 1940, NA, RG 59, xiii-xiv.

50. J. Edgar Hoover to Adolf Berle, Washington, D.C., Mar. 28, 1941, NA, RG 165, 2657-G-842-99; Franz Buchenau to Auswärtiges Amt, Solingen, Mar. 7, 1940, PAAA, R 114665.

51. Adolf Berle, *The Pattern of Nazi Organizations and Their Activities in*

the *Other American Republics*, Feb. 6, 1941, NA, RG 59, 862.20210/
414A, 36–37.

52. See NA, RG 353: Records of the Division of World Trade Intelligence,
box 9, folders 1–3, and finding aid; Sumner Welles, "Procedures and
Policies on Maintenance of the Proclaimed List of Certain Blocked
Nationals," Aug. 28, 1941, *FRUS* 1941 6:271–83.

53. Summary for Interdepartmental Committee, "Brehme, Hugo," May 1,
1942, NA, RG 353, Division of World Trade Intelligence, box 22,
folder III; Max Paul Friedman, "Nazis and Good Neighbors: The
United States Campaign Against the Germans of Latin America in
World War II," Ph.D. diss., University of California, Berkeley, 2000,
143–44.

54. "Statutory List Cases," PRO BT (Board of Trade) 271/284, no. 3244;
U.S. Department of State, *The Proclaimed List of Certain Blocked
Nationals Promulgated Pursuant to the Proclamation of July 17, 1941*
(Washington, D.C.: Government Printing Office, 1941), 39–40;
Gunther Boker, "Unsere Geschaefte," AB, FM, 1–2.

55. Ibid., 2.

56. "México no se convertirá en campo de maniobra para el ataque sobre
países amigos," Excelsior, July 23, 1941.

57. Interview with Leopold Schubert [Perote inmate], Mexico City, June
6, 1998.

58. Welles to Messersmith, Washington, D.C., May 23, 1942, NA, RG 84,
USEM, box 152; Jones, "The Nazi Failure in Mexico," 1–97.

59. Aide-mémoire, Messersmith, Mexico City, June 1, 1942, AHSRE, III-
2435–2 (I).

60. Daniels to Secretary, Mexico City, Mar. 21, 1941, NA, RG 84, USEM,
Box 86.

61. Robert W. Wagner, "Report on former subversive activities and propaganda of Axis-owned firms in Mexico," in Holland to Secretary, Aug.
12, 1943, NA, RG 84, USEM, Box 316.

62. "Franz Boker," enclosed in [name blacked out] to FBI, July 24, 1945,
FBI/FOIPA, 65–36220–813.

63. See Stephen Niblo, *The Impact of War: Mexico and World War II*
(Melbourne, Australia: La Trobe University Institute of Latin America,
1988).

64. Text of broadcast enclosed in McGurk to Secretary, Mexico City, Dec.
11, 1941, NA, RG 59, 812.00/Avila Camacho, Manuel/171.

65. C. H. Bateman to Anthony Eden, Mexico City, Feb. 27, 1942, PRO FO
371/30574.

66. Bateman to Eden, Mexico City, June 15, 1942, PRO FO 204/639.

67. Torres, *México en la segunda guerra mundial*, 65–153.

68. Interview with Gunther Boker, Dec. 12, 1986, Mexico City.

69. Carlos Marichal, *A Century of Debt Crises in Latin America* (Princeton,
N.J.: Princeton University Press, 1989), 227.

70. Interview with Gunther Boker, Dec. 12, 1986, Mexico City.
71. Junta de Administración y Vigilancia de la Propiedad Extranjera, *Informe sintético de su actuación durante el período comprendido entre el 15 de junio de 1942 y el 15 de junio de 1947* (Mexico City: n.p., 1947); and Junta de Administración y Vigilancia de la Propiedad Extranjera, *Breve Memoria de su Actuación durante el período comprendido entre el 15 de junio de 1942 y el 15 de junio de 1943, redactada por su Vocal Secretario Ing. Luis Topete Bordes* (Mexico: n.p., 1943), 51. Figure does not include coffee fincas.
72. Messersmith to Hull, June 13, 1942, NA, RG 84, USEM, box 152; Marichal, A Century of Debt Crises, 227.
73. "German Community in Mexico," enclosure in Bateman to Eden, Mexico City, Apr. 13, 1944, PRO FO 371/38342.
74. Pedro Boker, personal communication to Jürgen Buchenau, Jan. 2, 2001.
75. *Excelsior*, June 6, 1943.
76. Junta, *Breve Memoria de su Actuación*, 4.
77. Franz Böker, "Versuch einer Rekonstruktion der Hergänge, die unsere heutige Lage herbeigeführt haben—1958," AB, FFLB.
78. Gunther Boker, "Unsere Geschaefte," AB, FM, 2; interview with Margot Trauwitz de Boker, Mexico City, Aug. 9, 1995; Ramón Beteta to Secretaría de Relaciones Exteriores, Mexico City, Jan. 7, 1942, and Ezequiel Padilla to Secretaría de Hacienda, Mexico City, Feb. 7, 1942, AHSRE III-668–1 (2a parte).
79. Gunther Boker to Junta, July 9, 1942, AB, Fondo Intervención (hereafter cited as FI) "CFM Reclamación Intervención."
80. He had used the German passport in a U.S. visa application in November 1935. "Clog Case," [name deleted] to FBI, Mexico City, July 8, 1943, FBI/FOIPA, 65–16273–1802, 4.
81. Jones, "The Nazi Failure in Mexico."
82. "Minutes of Meeting Held at the Foreign Office on April 1, 1943 Between Sr. Tello, Sr. Topete Bordes, Sr. Carvajal, Sr. Sánchez Gavita, Mr. Russell, Mr. Bay and Mr. Holland Concerning Proclaimed List Matters," AHSRE III-668–1 (3a parte); "German Community in Mexico," enclosure in Bateman to Eden, Mexico City, Apr. 13, 1944, PRO FO 371/38342.
83. Franz Böker, "Bewertungs-Grundlage," AB, FFLB, "Accionistas CFM, 1940–60."
84. Gunther Boker, "Unsere Geschaefte," AB, FM, 3–4; von Mentz et al., *Los empresarios alemanes*, 1:212–16; Luis Topete Bordes to Ezequiel Padilla, Mexico City, Dec. 21, 1942, AHSRE III-668–1 (3a parte).
85. Charles A. Bay (Commercial Attaché) to Secretary of State, Apr. 22, 1943; NA, RG 84, USEM, Box 286; interview with Leopold Schubert, Mexico City, June 6, 1998.
86. Junta, *Informe sintético*, 73.

87. "Junta de Administración y Vigilancia de la Propiedad Extranjera—Convocatoria," *Excelsior*, May 12 and June 12, 1945. One of the directors even offered Avila Camacho to help sell the CFM if the Mexican government paid him for his interest in the company. Julio Alcalá Carstens to Avila Camacho, Mexico City, Aug. 29, 1945, AGN, Fondo Presidentes, MAC, 550/35–8.

88. Memorandum, Apr. 2, 1943, NA, RG 84, USEM, item 672, "Records Relating to Lists of Certain Blocked Nationals," folder 1.

89. Gunther Boker, memorandum, Feb. 28, 1950, AB, FI, "CFM Reclamación Intervención."

90. Interview with Carlos Seippel, Mexico City, Dec. 15, 1998; Gunther Boker, "Unsere Geschaefte," AB, FM, 6.

91. For this term, see Stephen R. Niblo, *Mexico in the 1940s: Modernity, Politics, and Corruption* (Wilmington, Del.: Scholarly Resources, 1999), 219–22.

92. CFM to Junta, July 21, 1947; "Contrato de Trabajo," n.d. [1947], AB, FS; Gunther Boker, "Unsere Geschaefte," AB, FM, 5.

93. Ibid., 5 and 7; von Mentz et al., *Los empresarios alemanes*, 1:218–29; Manuel Moreno Sánchez and Luis Cabrera to Alemán, Mexico City, Nov. 11, 1947, AGN, MAV 432/268.

94. Luis Manuel García to Alemán, Mexico City, Nov. 5, 1947; and Rafael Ortiz and Silvestre Ramírez to Alemán, Mexico City, Sept. 22, 1948, AGN, MAV, 432/268; *Excelsior,* Apr. 20, 1948.

95. Gunther Boker, "Unsere Geschaefte," AB, FM, 5–8.

96. Franz Böker, "Schicksal von Kapital und Arbeit," AB, FM, 10.

97. Ibid., 11–12.

98. For these negotiations, see Gunther Boker to Luise Boker, Mexico City, Dec. 1, 1946, Jan. 1, 1947 and Mar. 2, 1948; Gunther Boker to Gabriele Buchenau, Oct. 8, 1947, Oct. 20, 1947, and Feb. 26, 1948; AB, FGMB.

99. Jürgen Buchenau [Sr.] to Werner Ellerkmann, Ixtapaluca, Feb. 8, 1950, AWE.

100. Interviews with Gabriele Buchenau, Warleberg, Germany, June 5 and 6, 1992.

Chapter 6

1. "La 'Casa Boker' Prestigiada Empresa Ferretera Celebra el Centenario de su Fundación," *Excelsior*, Nov. 2, 1965, 5–6B; interview with Claus Schlenker, Mexico City, May 26, 1998.

2. Arthur Schmidt, "Making it Real Compared to What? Reconceptualizing Mexican History Since 1940," in *Fragments of a Golden Age: The Politics of Culture in Mexico Since 1940,* ed. Gilbert Joseph, Anne Rubenstein, and Eric Zolov (Durham, N.C.: Duke University Press, 2001), 25–33.

3. Michael C. Meyer, John L. Sherman, and Susan Deeds, *The Course of Mexican History*, 6th rev. ed. (Oxford: Oxford University Press, 1999), chapters 40–44.

4. For the most recent historiography, see Schmidt, "Making it Real," 37–38, 44.

5. Franz Böker, "Ueber die Lage—1958—in Mexico," AB, FFLB, folder 2, 5.

6. Franz Böker to Walther Hentzen, Mexico City, June 6, 1964, AB, FFLB, folder "Cartas 1962–64."

7. John W. Sherman, "The Mexican Miracle and its Collapse," in *The Oxford History of Mexico*, ed. Michael C. Meyer and William H. Beezley (Oxford: Oxford University Press, 2000), 575–98.

8. Gunther Boker to Alexander Scharff, Mexico City, Oct. 23, 1968, AB, FGMB, folder "Alexander Scharff."

9. Jonathan Kandell, *La Capital: The Biography of Mexico City* (New York: Random House, 1988), 485. This term was also used for the nation as a whole. See Schmidt, "Making it Real," 24.

10. Ibid., 485–86. National growth rates ranged between 6 and 8 percent.

11. Franz Böker, "Ueber die Lage—1958—in Mexico," AB, FFLB, folder 2, 1.

12. Salvador Novo, *Nueva grandeza mexicana: Ensayo sobre la Ciudad de México y sus alrededores; con anotaciones especiales del autor* (Mexico City: Editora de Periódicos, 1956), especially 12–25.

13. Kandell, La Capital, 5.

14. Peter M. Ward, *Mexico City*, 2d rev. ed. (Chichester, England: Wiley & Sons, 1997), 79; Franz Böker, "Gedanken zu dem fuer Gerda und Ellen ausgearbeiteten Exposé," (1958) AB, FFLB, folder 2, 1.

15. David Rock, ed., *Latin America in the 1940s: War and Post-War Transitions* (Berkeley and Los Angeles: University of California Press, 1994); Roger D. Hansen, *The Politics of Mexican Development* (Baltimore, Md.: Johns Hopkins University Press, 1971), 41–70.

16. Alan M. Taylor, "Latin America and Foreign Capital in the Twentieth Century: Economics, Politics, and Institutional Change," in *Political Institutions and Economic Growth in Latin America: Essays in Policy, History, and Political Economy*, ed. Stephen Haber (Stanford, Calif.: Hoover Institution Press, 2000), 124.

17. Olga Pellicer de Brody y Esteban Mancilla, *Historia de la Revolución Mexicana, período 1952–1960: El entendimiento con los Estados Unidos y la gestación del desarrollo estabilizador* (Mexico City: El Colegio de México, 1978), 117–294; Héctor Aguilar Camín and Lorenzo Meyer, *A la sombra de la revolución mexicana: Un ensayo de historia contemporánea de México* (Mexico City: Cal y Arena, 1990), 200.

18. Franz Böker, "Ueber die Lage—1958—in Mexico," AB, FFLB, folder 2, 3; Gunther Boker Pocorny, "Unsere Geschaefte waehrend und nach dem Kriege," AB, FM, 11; and Gunther Boker Pocorny, "Unsere Geschaefte 1964–1975," AB, FM, 2.

19. Ward, *Mexico City*, 187–230.

20. Interview with Helmuth Boker, Warleberg, Germany, July 13, 1994.

21. In the Spanish original, "la región más transparente." Carlos Fuentes, *La región más transparente* (Mexico City: Fondo de Cultura Económica, 1963).

22. Gunther Boker, "Unsere Geschaefte," AB, FM, 7–8; "Devolución CFM intervención," and "Balance General, 30 de nov. de 1948," AB, FI; Gunther Boker, circular, Mexico City, July 26, 1952, AB, FFLB, folder "Familiengeschichte."

23. CFM, Asambleas Extraordinaria, Apr. 19, 1949, AB, FM.

24. Gunther Boker, "Unsere Geschaefte," AB, FM, 7, 10–11. Gunther had desperately tried to obtain more German personnel. Jürgen Buchenau to Anna Buchenau, Ixtapaluca, Dec. 18, 1949, Nachlass Margarete Zantop (hereafter cited as NMZ).

25. Gunther Boker, "Unsere Geschaefte," AB, FM, 9–10; *Contrato colectivo de trabajo de la Unión de Empleados y Trabajadores de la Cía. Ferretera Mexicana, S.A.* (Mexico City: n.p., 1965), in AB, FS.

26. Gunther Boker, "Unsere Geschaefte," 10–12; interviews with Alvaro Gómez, May 25, 1998; Gunther Boker, Dec. 11, 1986, and Carlos Seippel, Dec. 12, 1998 (all Mexico City).

27. Julio E. Moreno, "Sears, Roebuck Company, J. Walter Thompson and the Culture of North American Commerce in Mexico during the 1940's," Ph.D. dissertation, University of California at Irvine, 1998, 230–85.

28. Personal recollection of author [1983].

29. Interview with Carlos Seippel, Mexico City, May 26, 1998, and with Pedro Boker, Mexico City, June 6, 2001.

30. Franz Böker, "Memorandum 15.9.1963," AB, FFLB, folder 2, 2; Gunther Boker, "Unsere Geschaefte," AB, FM, 9.

31. Franz Böker, memorandum, Dec. 31, 1963, AB, FFLB, folder "Fondo A"; Gunther Boker to Carlos Friederichs, Mexico City, Oct. 4, 1965, AB, FGMB, folder "Carlitos."

32. Some years are missing from the archive. After 1971, company balance sheets were not available for consultation. I have not been able to find any sources that explain the erratic numbers after 1959; most likely, changes in Mexican law prompted the CFM to change the way it reported income during this period.

33. Franz Böker, "Der Fondo A und die früheren Aktionäre der C.F.M.," and "Ueber das Problem der heimatdeutschen Teilhaber," AB, FFLB, folder 2.

34. Franz Böker, "Am Scheidewege," AB, FFLB, folder 2.

35. Gunther Boker to Margot Boker, Bad Godesberg, Sept. 25, Sept. 19, and Oct. 13, 1962; Margot Boker to Gunther Boker, Mexico City, Sept. 25, Sept. 28, and Oct. 4, 1962, AB, FGMB, folder "Correspondencia 1962"; Gunther Boker to Franz Buchenau, Bad Godesberg, Sept. 22

and Oct. 10, 1962; Adolf Lucas to Walther Hentzen, Lippstadt, Germany, Jan. 20, 1963; and Franz Böker to Adolf Lucas, Jan. 30, 1963, AB, FFLB, folder "Cartas 1962–64."

36. Franz Böker, "Die Teilhaber in Deutschland, 1964," and "Ueber das Problem der heimatdeutschen Teilhaber," AB, FFLB, folder 2, 3; "Aktennotiz vom 10.12.1984" and Gunther Boker to Gabriele Buchenau, Mexico City, Feb. 6, 1985, AB, FGMB, "Gabriele bis 1983."
37. Lomnitz and Pérez-Lizaur, *A Mexican Elite Family,* 13.
38. Arnold J. Bauer, *Goods, Power, History,* 13.
39. Gunther Boker to Carlos Friederichs, Apr. 5, 1965, AB, FGMB, folder "Carlitos."
40. Asambleas Ordinarias, CFM, 1957–1969, AB, FA; Gunther Boker, "Unsere Geschaefte von 1964 bis 1975," AB, FM, 1–2.
41. Nacional Financiera, *Statistics on the Mexican Economy,* 218–19, 413; Jeffrey Bortz, *Industrial Wages in Mexico City, 1939–1975* (New York: Garland Publishing, 1987).
42. Gunther Boker, "Unsere Geschaefte von 1964 to 1975," AB, FM, 2.
43. This pay scale includes neither agents nor the management level. *Contrato colectivo de trabajo de la Unión de Empleados y Trabajadores de la Cía. Ferretera Mexicana, S.A.* (Mexico City: n.p., 1971), 27–31, AB, FS.
44. Interview with Pedro Boker, Mexico City, June 6, 2001.
45. Mario Ojeda, *Alcances y límites de la política exterior de México* (Mexico: El Colegio de México, 1976), 100–1; Gunther Boker, "Unsere Geschaefte von 1964 bis 1975," AB, FM, 4–5.
46. Gunther Boker to Luise Böker, Mexico City, Sept. 19, 1973, AB, FGMB; Gunther Boker to Gabriele Buchenau, Mexico City, Apr. 29, 1976, AB, FGMB, "Gabriele bis 1983."
47. Gunther Boker, "Unsere Geschaefte von 1964 bis 1975," AB, FM, 5–6; "September 1973," and "10 Oktober 1973," AB, FGMB, folder "CFM-Casa Boker"; Gunther Boker to Gabriele Buchenau, Nov. 13, 1973, and June 19, 1974, AB, FGMB, "Gabriele bis 1983"; interview with Alvaro Gómez, Mexico City, June 25, 1998.
48. Roderic A. Camp, *Entrepreneurs and Politics in Twentieth-Century Mexico* (New York: Oxford University Press, 1989), 36.
49. Adolf Lucas to Walther Hentzen, Lippstadt, Germany, Jan. 20, 1963; and Gunther Boker to Hentzen, Mexico City, Jan. 29, 1963, AB, FFLB, folder "Cartas 1962–64."
50. Pedro Boker to Jürgen Buchenau, Nov. 25, 2000.
51. Interview with Pedro Boker, Mexico City, May 22, 1998.
52. Gunther Boker to Helmuth Boker, Mexico City, Sept. 11, 1961, AB, FGMB, "Correspondenz Eltern."
53. Interview with Gabriele Buchenau, Warleberg, Germany, July 11, 1994.
54. Reinhold Wagnleitner, *The Coca-Colonization of the Cold War: The United States Cultural Mission in Austria after the Second World War*

(Chapel Hill: University of North Carolina Press, 1994). See also Rob Kroes, *If You've Seen One, You've Seen the Mall: Europeans and American Mass Culture* (Urbana: University of Illinois Press, 1996), xii-xiii.

55. Helmuth Boker to Gunther Boker, Bad Godesberg, Aug. 31, 1961, AB, FGMB, folder "Correspondenz Eltern"; interview with Helmuth Boker, Warleberg, July 13, 1994.

56. Interview with Renata von Hanffstengel, Mexico City, June 11, 2000, and with Carlos Seippel, Mexico City, Dec. 12, 1998.

57. Helmuth Boker to Gabriele Buchenau, Mexico City, Dec. 7, 1989, NGB.

58. Laurence McFalls, "Living with Which Past? National Identity in Post-Wall, Postwar Germany," in *A User's Guide to German Cultural Studies,* ed. Scott Denham, Irene Kacandes, and Jonathan Petropoulos (Ann Arbor: University of Michigan Press, 1997), 302.

59. Gunther Boker to Carlos Friederichs, Mexico City, June 22, 1954, Dec. 12, 1962, Dec. 20, 1972, and Oct. 10, 1973, AB, FGMB, folder "Carlitos"; Gunther Boker to Luise Böker, Sept. 14 and 19, 1973, AB, FGMB, folder "Briefe Mutter 1973."

60. Interview with Ruth Boker, Mexico City, July 3, 1995; Gunther Boker to Alexander Scharff, Mexico City, Dec. 15, 1972, AB, FGMB, folder "Alexander Scharff"; Gunther Boker to Carlos Friederichs, Mexico City, Oct. 10, 1973, and June 3, 1974, AB, FGMB, folder "Carlitos"; Gunther Boker to Luise Böker, Mexico City, Aug. 22, 1973, AB, FGMB, folder "Briefe Mutter 1973."

61. Gunther Boker to Carlos Friederichs, Mexico City, Dec. 20, 1972, and Oct. 10, 1973, AB, FGMB, folder "Carlitos."

62. Interview with Carlos Seippel, Mexico City, Dec. 12, 1998; Pedro Boker, personal communication to Jürgen Buchenau, Mexico City, Jan. 9, 2001.

63. Interview with Marianne Frenk-Westheim, Mexico City, June 27, 2000.

64. Interview with Wolfgang Eversbusch, Mexico City, June 8, 1998.

65. M. D. Mónica Palma Mora, "Inmigrantes extranjeros en México, 1950–1980," Ph.D. diss., Universidad Nacional Autónoma de México, 1999, 83–132.

66. Oeste de Bopp, "Die Deutschen in Mexico," 522; AHSRE, Archivo de Concentraciones, Constancias de Nacionalidad.

67. Michael N. Miller, *Red, White, and Green: The Maturing of Mexicanidad* (El Paso: Texas Western Press, 1998), 1.

68. "Club Alemán de México, S.A. de C.V.," http://www.club-aleman.com/hist.htm (Jan. 20, 2001); interview with Pedro Boker, Mexico City, Oct. 2, 1999.

69. Eric Zolov, *Refried Elvis: The Rise of the Mexican Counterculture* (Berkeley and Los Angeles: University of California Press, 1999); Carlos Monsiváis, "Tantos millones de hombres no hablaremos inglés? (La cultura norteamericana y México)," in *Simbiosis de*

culturas: Los inmigrantes en México y su cultura, ed. Guillermo Bonfil Batalla (Mexico City: Secretaría de Educación Pública, 1988), 500–13.

70. Gunther Boker, "Ansprache beim Schulfest 8–10–50," AB, Fondo Colegio Alemán (hereafter cited as FCA), folder "Schule 1950–56."

71. Blanca Huici, "Los años cincuenta," Noticias Humboldt, no. 4–5:5 (1999): 79–82; Arlene Patricia Scanlon, *Un enclave cultural: Poder y etnicidad en el contexto de una escuela norteamericana en México* (Mexico City: CIESAS, 1984); interviews with Dennis Brehme Stappenbeck, Greenville, S.C., May 25, 1999; and Renate Boker, Mexico City, June 1, 1998.

72. A. B. to Richard Eversbusch, Victor Mueller, and Gunther Boker, Mexico City, Oct. 31, 1951, AB, FCA, folder "Schule 1950–56"; interview with Renate Boker, Mexico City, May 28, 1998.

73. Interview with Barbara Boker, Mexico City, June 4, 2001, and with Renate Hernández and Héctor Hernández, Mexico City, May 28, 1998.

74. Gunther Boker, "Aufzeichnung vom 26. Dezember 1960," AB, FCA, folder "Schule—Aufzeichnungen für den Verwaltungsrat."

75. Gunther Boker, "Aufzeichnung fuer den Verwaltungsrat: Streng vertraulich," AB, FCA, folder "Schule—Aufzeichnungen für den Verwaltungsrat."

76. Scanlon, *Enclave cultural.*

77. Interview with Blanca Huici, Mexico City, Oct. 8, 1999.

78. Ibid.; Huici, "Los años cincuenta"; interview with Veronica Kugel, Mexico City, June 9, 1998; *Colegio Alemán Alexander von Humboldt, 1894–1994: Festschrift/Memorias* (Mexico City: Colegio Alemán Alexander von Humboldt, 1994), 21–26.

79. Oeste de Bopp, "Die Deutschen in Mexico," 497; interview with Gabriele Buchenau, Warleberg, Germany, June 5, 1992.

80. Interview with Ulrich Buchenau, Jülich, Germany, May 16, 1996.

81. Jürgen Buchenau, "Small Numbers, Great Impact"; Palma, "Inmigrantes extranjeros," 173–79; interview with Verónica Kugel, Mexico City, June 9, 1998.

82. Gunther Boker to Gabriele Buchenau, Mexico City, Apr. 20, 1978, AB, FGMB, "Gabriele bis 1983."

83. Interviews with Julie Muller, Mexico City, June 13 and Aug. 9, 1995; Ulrich Buchenau, Jülich, May 16, 1995; and Blanca Huici, Mexico City, Oct. 8, 1999.

84. Interview with Barbara Boker, Mexico City, May 27, 1998, and with Renate Boker, Mexico City, Jan. 18, 2002. Pedro disputes this claim. Interview with Pedro Boker, Mexico City, June 6, 2001.

85. Gunther and Margot's second child, Brigitte, died of measles at eighteen months of age.

86. For the same reason, this caveat also applies to the third section of Chapter 7.

87. Interview with Pedro Boker, Mexico City, June 26, 1995.

88. "Club Alemán de México, S.A. de C.V.," http://www.club-aleman.com/ hist.htm [accessed Jan. 20, 2001].

89. Interview with Cecilia Regens, Mexico City, June 1, 1998.

90. Interview with Francisco Regens, Mexico City, June 1, 1998.

91. Interviews with Pedro Boker, Mexico City, June 15 and 26, 1995, and Dec. 11, 1998.

92. Gunther Boker, "Unsere Geschaefte, 1964–1975," AB, FM, 5–9.

93. Interview with Klaus Boker, Mexico City, July 3, 1995, and with Julie Muller de Boker, Mexico City, June 13, 1995.

94. Versión Estenográfica, Sesión pública de la comisión permanente del H. Congreso de la Unión (July 26, 2000), *http://www.senado.gob.mx/ permanente/2000/versiones/v26julio.html* (Jan. 20, 2001).

95. Interview with Klaus Boker, Mexico City, July 3, 1995.

96. Interview with Ruth Boker, Mexico City, June 8, 1998.

97. Interviews with Alvaro Gómez, Mexico City, July 23, 1996, and June 25, 1998.

98. Interview with Víctor Manuel Medina, May 26, 1998; with Pilar Fernández, June 24, 2000; and with Roberto Requejo, June 24, 2000 (all in Mexico City).

99. Interview with Renate Boker, Mexico City, May 28, 1998.

100. Ibid.; Gunther Boker to Gabriele Buchenau, Mexico City, May 14 and 29, 1979, NGB. Helmuth Boker, an M.D., was the first university graduate of his family.

101. Interview with Renate Boker, Mexico City, May 28, 1998.

102. Interview with Héctor Cirilo Hernández, Mexico City, May 28, 1998.

103. Interview with Barbara Boker, Mexico City, May 25, 1998; Gunther Boker to Gabriele Buchenau, Mexico City, Apr. 17, June 23, and Nov. 13, 1973, AB, FGMB, "Gabriele bis 1983."

104. Interview with Barbara Boker, Mexico City, May 25, 1998, and with Barbara Hieber, Mexico City, May 25, 1998.

105. Interview with Maren von Groll, Mexico City, June 12, 2000.

106. Interview with Renate Boker, May 28, 1998.

107. Interview with Ruth Boker, Mexico City, July 3, 1995, and with Isabel Willemetz, Mexico City, Aug. 15, 1995.

108. Interview with Isabel Willemetz, Mexico City, July 27, 1996.

109. Interview with Ruth Boker, Mexico City, July 3, 1995.

110. Renata von Hanffstengel, "La comunidad alemana en México a partir de la Segunda Guerra Mundial hasta la fecha," *BaBel* 1 (1999): 47.

Chapter 7

1. *Excelsior,* "Incendio en Boker," Feb. 9, 1975, 1 and 8.
2. Gunther Boker, "Bericht ueber den Brand in der Casa Boker am 8. Februar 1975," AB, FGMB, "Brand Casa Boker," 2.
3. Ibid.
4. Sydney A. Clark, *All the Best in Mexico* (New York: Dodd, Mead, 1956), 132–33.
5. Interview with Pablo Pellat Spitalier, Mexico City, June 13, 2000.
6. Gabriele Buchenau to Jürgen Buchenau, Warleberg, Germany, Aug. 3, 1983.
7. Kandell, *La Capital,* 574; Gunther Boker to Gabriele Buchenau, Mexico City, Nov. 19, 1982, NGB; interview with Isabel Willemetz, Mexico City, July 27, 1996. For a study of the megacity and its problems, see James B. Pick and Edgar W. Butler, *Mexico's Megacity* (Boulder, Colo.: Westview Press, 1997).
8. Diane E. Davis, *Urban Leviathan: Mexico City in the Twentieth Century* (Philadelphia, Pa.: Temple University Press, 1994), 296.
9. Interviews with Pedro Boker, Mexico City, May 22 and Dec. 15, 1998.
10. Bauer, *Goods, Power, History,* 205.
11. Alexandra Boker Regens, "Diseño de una estrategia de reposicionamiento para una empresa ferretera fundada en 1865 en la Ciudad de México," licenciatura thesis, Universidad Iberoamericana, 1998.
12. Interview with Pedro Boker, Mexico City, June 6, 2001.
13. Néstor García Canclini, *Consumers and Citizens: Globalization and Multicultural Conflicts,* trans. George Yúdice (Minneapolis: University of Minnesota Press, 2001), 52.
14. By 1975, the business in toys had suffered from intense competition for fifteen years. Gunther Boker, "Juguetería," n.d. [1964], AB, FGMB, folder "Juguetes."
15. "Centenario, el edificio Boker muestra que lo antiguo no riñe con la modernidad," *La Jornada,* Aug. 21, 2000.
16. Marina Niforos and Francisco Boker, "Family Firms: Casa Boker— Asking the Right Questions," seminar paper in AB, FPKB, folder "familia," 2–3, 8.
17. Gunther Boker to Gabriele Boker, Mexico City, July 8, 1976, NGB.
18. In the original, "no hay mal que por bien no venga." Gunther Boker to Leuscher, Mexico City, May 19, 1978, AB, FFLB, folder "Hentzen."
19. Interview with Claus Schlenker, Mexico City, May 26, 1998.
20. Gunther Boker, "1. Fortsetzung des Berichts vom Brand in der Casa Boker vom 8. Februar 1975," and "2. Fortsetzung des Berichts ueber den Brand in der Casa Boker und seine [sic] Folgen," AB, FGMB, folder "Brand Casa Boker"; Gunther Boker to Gabriele Buchenau, Mexico City, Oct. 28, 1975, AB, FGMB, "Gabriele bis 1983."
21. "The Boker Group," AB, FPKB, folder "Grupo Boker," 1–2.

22. Francisco Salazar Sotelo, "Balance global de la política económica en el sexenio 1976–1982," in *Estudios cuantitativos sobre la historia de México,* ed. Samuel Schmidt, James W. Wilkie, and Manuel Esparza (Mexico City: UNAM, 1988), 45.
23. Gunther Boker to Gabriele Boker, Mexico City, Dec. 27, 1979, NGB.
24. "Finanzielle Lage im Maerz 1976," AB, FFLB, folder "Familiengeschichte"; "Vermietung an 'Sanborn Hermanos,' S.A.," and "Contrato de arrendamiento," July 1, 1977, AB, FMGB, folder "Sanborns"; Gunther Boker, "Gedanken zur Zukunft von Boker, S.A.— Oktober 1980," AB, FPKB; Gunther Boker to Gabriele Buchenau, Mexico City, Oct. 2, 1974, Mar. 28, 1976, Dec. 28, 1977, Dec. 12, 1980, and Jan. 19, 1981, NGB.
25. Interview with Pedro Boker, Mexico City, June 6, 2001.
26. Gunther Boker to Gabriele Buchenau, Mexico City, Oct. 15, 1976, and Jan. 19, 1981, NGB; Salazar, "Balance global," 54–55.
27. Buchenau, *In the Shadow of the Giant,* 204–5.
28. Gunther Boker to Gabriele Buchenau, Mexico City, Nov. 19, 1982, NGB.
29. Nora Lustig, *Mexico: The Remaking of an Economy,* 2d rev. ed. (Washington, D.C.: Brookings Institution, 1998), chapter 3. See also Alma Guillermoprieto, *The Heart That Bleeds: Latin America Now* (New York: Vintage Books, 1995), especially 47–67 and 237–58.
30. Viviane Brachet-Márquez, *The Dynamics of Domination: State, Class, and Social Reform in Mexico, 1910–1990* (Pittsburgh, Pa.: Pittsburgh University Press, 1994), 130.
31. Lustig, *Mexico,* 69.
32. Pedro Boker, "125-jaehriges Firmenjubilaeum der 'Casa Boker' 1990," AB, FPKB.
33. Gunther Boker to Gabriele Buchenau, Mexico City, Dec. 17, 1982, and Feb. 16, 1983, NGB.
34. Interview with Carlos Seippel, Mexico City, Dec. 12, 1998.
35. Alejandra Boker, "Diseño de una estrategia de reposicionamiento," 41.
36. Kandell, *Capital,* 566–73.
37. Gunther Boker to Gabriele Buchenau, Mexico City, Oct. 11 and 24, 1985, NGB.
38. Interview with Carlos Seippel, Mexico City, Dec. 12, 1998.
39. Ward, *Mexico City,* 79–84; Alexandra Boker, "Diseño de una estrategia de reposicionamiento," 91.
40. "Tradición, Historia y Prestigio: Casa Boker," *La Revista del Centro Comercial de la Ciudad de México 1,* no. 3 (1991): 14.
41. G. Jones and A. Varley, "The Contest for the City Centre: Street Traders Versus Buildings," *Bulletin of Latin American Research* 13 (1994): 27–44; J. L. Lezema, "Ciudad y conflicto: Usos del suelo y comercio ambulante en la Cd. de México," in *Espacio y vivienda en la Ciudad de México,* ed. M. Schteingart (Mexico City: El Colegio de México, 1991), 121–35.

42. Alejandra Boker, "Diseño de una estrategia de reposicionamiento," 88. For Pedro's recent attempts to remove the street vendors, see "Exigen retirar ambulantes del Centro," and "Promete AMLO 'limpiar' el Zócalo," *Reforma,* Aug. 8, 2002.
43. "The Boker Group," AB, FPKB, folder "Grupo Boker," 3; interview with Pedro Boker, Mexico City, Dec. 15, 1998.
44. Guillermoprieto, *Heart That Bleeds,* 250–55.
45. Bauer, *Goods, Power, History,* 202–17.
46. Interview with Helmuth Boker, Mexico City, July 13, 1994.
47. Neil Harvey, *Rebellion in Chiapas: Rural Reforms, Campesino Radicalism, and the Limits to Salinismo* (La Jolla: Center for U.S.-Mexican Studies, University of California, San Diego, 1994).
48. Interview with Cecilia Regens, Mexico City, June 1, 1998; Margot Boker to Gabriele Buchenau, Mexico City, Jan. 31, 1994; Helmuth Boker to Gabriele Buchenau, Mexico City, Jan. 12, 1994, NGB.
49. Lustig, *Mexico,* chapter 6.
50. Ibid.; interview with Víctor Manuel Medina, Mexico City, May 26, 1998.
51. Interview with Claus Schlenker, Mexico City, May 26, 1998; "Breve historia de una familia y ferretería en México," AB, FPKB, folder "historia," 7; "Grupo Boker," AB, FPKB, folder "Grupo Boker," 2; Niforos and Boker, "Family Firms," 8.
52. Interview with Claus Schlenker, Mexico City, May 26, 1998.
53. Interview with Pedro Boker, Mexico City, June 26, 1995.
54. Interview with Klaus Boker, Mexico City, July 3, 1995.
55. Interview with Juan Fernández Vivo, Mexico City, May 26, 1998.
56. Interview with Pedro Boker, Mexico City, May 22, 1998.
57. Avisos, Feb. 7, 2001, "Boker S.A. de C.V., y Compañía Ferretera Mexicana, S.A. de C.V., Acuerdo de fusión; *http://www.ci.shcp.gob.mx/ indice/dof/documentos/2001/febrero/ 07022001/avisos07feb01.html.*
58. Interview with Pedro Boker, Mexico City, May 22, 1998.
59. Jane Bussey, "Salinas de Gortari, Carlos," in Encyclopedia of Mexico: History, Society, and Culture, ed. Michael Werner (Chicago: Fitzroy Dearborn, 1997), 2:1332.
60. Interview with Pedro Boker, Mexico City, June 6, 2001.
61. Niforos and Boker, "Family Firms," 8.
62. Avisos, Feb. 7, 2001, "Boker S.A. de C.V., y Compañía Ferretera Mexicana, S.A. de C.V., Acuerdo de fusión"; *http://www.ci.shcp.gob.mx/ indice/dof/documentos/2001/febrero/07022001/avisos07feb01.html.* Until 1983, the business was known as Boker, S.A.
63. Nicolai Roenne, "Marketingprojekt bei dem Handelsunternehmen Boker in Mexiko-City Januar bis März 1999," AB, FPKB; and Alexandra Boker, "Diseño de una estrategia de reposicionamiento," passim. For the gender breakdown, see also "Clientes tienda BoSA septiembre 1999," AB, FPKB.

64. Interview with Pedro Boker, Mexico City, June 15, 1995.

65. Niforos and Boker, "Family Firms," passim; interview with Francisco Boker, Lippstadt, Germany, Aug. 14, 1998.

66. Heinz Krumpel, *Die deutsche Philosophie in Mexiko: Ein Beitrag zur interkulturellen Verständigung seit Alexander von Humboldt* (Frankfurt: Peter Lang, 1998), 76–77 and 345.

67. See Chapter 6.

68. Niforos and Boker, "Family Firms," 4; interview with Francisco Boker Regens, Lippstadt, Germany, Aug. 14, 1998.

69. Interview with Francisco Boker, Lippstadt, Germany, Aug. 14, 1998.

70. Interviews with Barbara Boker, Mexico City, May 25, 1998; and Renate Boker de Hernández, Mexico City, May 28, 1998.

71. Interview with Francisco Boker, Lippstadt, Germany, Aug. 14, 1998.

72. Interview with Klaus Boker, Mexico City, June 12, 2001.

73. Interview with Francisco Boker, Lippstadt, Germany, Aug. 14, 1998.

74. Interview with Jan Boker, Mexico City, May 25, 1998.

75. Ibid.; interview with Sandra Boker, Mexico City, Dec. 12, 1998.

76. "Up Late: Chismes de los personajes desde la playa de South Beach," http://www.yupi.com/oceandrive/uplate/ 120399/ index.cfm (Jan. 28, 2001).

77. Interview with Susana Boker Muller, Mexico City, Dec. 13, 1998.

78. Interview with Héctor Hérnandez and Renate Boker, Mexico City, May 28, 1998; with Vanessa Hernández, Mexico City, June 6, 2001; and with Claudio Hernández, Warleberg, Germany, Aug. 8, 2001.

79. Gunther Boker to Gabriele Buchenau, Mexico City, Sept. 14, 1977, NGB; interviews with Barbara and Roberto Hieber, Mexico City, May 25, 1998. Roberto Hieber is not mentioned here because Barbara raised the children by herself after their divorce.

80. We have already discussed the case of Helmuth's family in the previous chapter. Roberto and Joaquín are currently single and childless, and Isabel's children are still small, therefore their family will be omitted from the following discussion.

81. Interview with Dieter Vermehren, Tuxpan, June 3, 1998.

82. Ibid.; interview with Monika Blass, Tuxpan, June 4, 1998.

83. Interview with Jan Vermehren, Tuxpan, June 4, 1998.

84. Interview with Monika Blass, Tuxpan, June 26, 1995.

85. Interview with Michel Buchenau, Altheim, Germany, May 16, 1996.

86. Oeste de Bopp, "Die Deutschen in Mexico," 495–96.

87. Interview with Jan Boker, Mexico City, May 25, 1998.

Conclusions

1. Von Mentz et al., *Los pioneros del imperialismo alemán.*

Works Cited

Archives and Private Collections

Germany

Auswärtiges Amt, Berlin. Politisches Archiv.
  Archiv der ehemaligen deutschen Gesandtschaft in Mexico.
Bundesarchiv, Abteilung Berlin.
  R 901, Auswärtiges Amt
    Abt. II: Handelspolitische Abteilung.
Evangelisches Zentralarchiv, Berlin.
Helmut Buchenau, Neuwittenbek. Persönliches Archiv.
  Nachlass Gabriele Buchenau.
  Nachlass Werner Ellerkmann.
  Nachlass Margarete Zantop.
Rüdiger Böker, Hamburg. Persönliches Archiv.
Stadtarchiv Remscheid, Remscheid.

Great Britain

Public Record Office.
BT Board of Trade.
FO Foreign Office.
TS Treasury Solicitor.

Mexico

Archivo General de la Nación, Mexico City.
  Fondo Lázaro Cárdenas.
  Fondo Presidentes.
  Manuel Avila Camacho.
  Miguel Alemán Valdés.
Archivo General de Notarías del Distrito Federal, Mexico City.
  Fondo Antiguo.
  Fondo Moderno.
Banco de México, Mexico City. Archivo Histórico.
  Archivo Matías Romero.
Boker, S. A. de C. V., Mexico City. Archivo Histórico.
Colegio Alemán Alejandro von Humboldt, Mexico City. Archivo
    Histórico.
CONDUMEX, Mexico City. Archivo Histórico.
  Archivo Venustiano Carranza.
  Archivo José Y. Limantour.

Dieter Vermehren, Tuxpan, Michoacán. Archivo Personal.
Secretaría de Relaciones Exteriores, Mexico City. Archivo
    Histórico.
    Serie Gavetas.
    Fondo Reservado.

United States

Federal Bureau of Investigation, Washington, D.C.
    Files obtained through Freedom of Information and Privacy Act
      petition.
Hanneli von Zastrow, Bloomfield, MI. Personal Archive.
    Nachlass Edda Lucas.
Library of Congress, Washington, D.C., Manuscript Division.
    Henry P. Fletcher Papers.
National Archives, Washington, D.C., and College Park, Md.
    RG 59: General Records of the Department of State.
    RG 84: Foreign Post Records of the Department of State.
    RG 165: Records of the Army.
    RG 242: Berlin Document Center.
      NSDAP Zentralkartei.
    RG 335: Division of World Trade Intelligence.
Stanford University, Palo Alto, CA.
    Hoover Institution Archive.
University of North Carolina, Chapel Hill.
    Southern Historical Collection.
    Josephus Daniels Papers.

Interviews (all by author)

Blass de Vermehren, Monica.
Boker de Willemetz, Isabel.
Boker Muller, Marianne ("Susana").
Boker Pocorny, Gunther.
Boker Pocorny, Helmuth.
Boker Regens, Alexandra.
Boker Regens, Francisco.
Boker Regens, Jan.
Boker Schwartzkopff, Joaquín.
Boker Trauwitz, Barbara.
Boker Trauwitz, Klaus.
Boker Trauwitz, Pedro.
Boker Trauwitz, Renate.
Boker, Ruth.
Bostelmann, Herbert.

Brehme Stappenbeck, Dennis.
Buchenau, Gabriele.
Buchenau, Helmut.
Buchenau, Michel.
Buchenau, Ulrich.
Diederichsen, Sven.
Dyckerhoff, Margret.
Eversbusch, Wolfgang.
Fernández Vivo, Juan.
Fernández, Pilar.
Frenk-Westheim, Marianne.
Gómez Vargas, Alvaro.
Hernández Valdés, Héctor Cirilo.
Hernández Boker, Vanessa.
Hieber Boker, Barbara.
Hieber Boker, Roberto.
Hoth, Julieta.
Huici, Blanca.
Kugel, Verónica.
Medina Téllez, Víctor Manuel.
Mueller Hoerig, Julie.
Pellat Spitalier, Pablo.
Regens Galvanduque, Cecilia.
Regens, Francisco.
Requejo Jiménez, Roberto.
Schlenker de Lalande, Claus.
Schubert, Leopold.
Seippel, Carlos.
Trauwitz de Boker, Margot.
Vermehren Blass, Jan.
Vermehren Boker, Dieter.
von Groll, Maren.

Newspapers

Deutsche Zeitung von Mexico, Mexico City.
Excelsior, Mexico City.
El Imparcial, Mexico City.
El Popular, Mexico City.
El Tiempo, Mexico City.
La Jornada, Mexico City.
Reforma, Mexico City.

Published Primary Sources

Alberdi, Juan Bautista. "Bases y puntos de partida para la organización política de la República Argentina." 1852; reprint in *Obras completas de J. B. Alberdi*, 3:421–22. Buenos Aires: n.p., 1886.

Anunciador Boker. Buffalo, N.Y. and Mexico City: n.p., 1901–6.

Bauer-Thoma, Friedrich. *Die Wahrheit über Mexiko und seine deutsche Kolonie*. Berlin: n.p., 1912.

Boker Regens, Alexandra. "Diseño de una estrategia de reposicionamiento para una empresa ferretera fundada en 1865 en la Ciudad de México." Licenciatura thesis, Universidad Iberoamericana, 1998.

Böker, Moritz. *Kurze Mittheilungen über die Familie Böker von Mitte des 18. bis Mitte des 19. Jahrhunderts*. Remscheid: Taske und Rittinghaus, 1900.

———. *Familie Böker Vieringhausen*. Remscheid: n.p., 1924.

Boker, S. A. de C. V. *Edificio Boker 100 años, 1900–2000*. Mexico City: n.p., 2000.

Brenner, Anita, and George R. Leighton. *The Wind that Swept Mexico*. New York: Harper, 1943.

Calderón de la Barca, Fanny. *Life in Mexico During a Residence of Two Years in that Country*. London: Chapman and Hall, 1843.

Chambers Gooch [Iglehart], Fanny. *Face to Face with the Mexicans*. New York: Fords, Howard, & Hulbert, 1887.

Clark, Sydney A. *All the Best in Mexico*. New York: Dodd, Mead, 1956.

Colegio Alemán Alexander von Humboldt, 1894–1994: Festschrift/Memorias. Mexico City: Colegio Alemán Alexander von Humboldt, 1994.

Cosío Villegas, Daniel. *Memorias*. Mexico City: Joaquín Mortiz, 1976.

Cuarto censo general de población, 1921. Mexico City: Dirección General de Estadística, 1928.

Daniels, Josephus. *Shirt-Sleeve Diplomat*. Chapel Hill: University of North Carolina Press, 1947.

Flandrau, Charles M. *Viva Mexico!* New York: D. Appleton & Co., 1908.

Foreign Relations of the United States. Washington, D.C.: Government Printing Office, various dates.

Griffin, Solomon B. *Mexico of To-Day*. New York: Harper and Brothers, 1886.

Günther, Erich. *Illustriertes Handbuch von Mexico mit besonderer Berücksichtigung der deutschen Interessen*. Mexico City: E. Günther, 1912.

Huici, Blanca. "Los años cincuenta." *Noticias Humboldt*, no. 4–5:5 (June 1999): 79–82.

Iturbide, Eduardo. *Mi paso por la vida*. Mexico City: Editorial Cultura, 1941.

Junta de Administración y Vigilancia de la Propiedad Extranjera. *Breve Memoria de su Actuación durante el período comprendido entre el 15 de junio de 1942 y el 15 de junio de 1943, redactada por su Vocal Secretario Ing. Luis Topete Bordes*. Mexico: n.p., 1943.

———. *Informe sintético de su actuación durante el período comprendido entre el 15 de junio de 1942 y el 15 de junio de 1947.* Mexico City: n.p., 1947.

King, Rosa. *Tempest over Mexico.* New York: Doubleday, 1935.

Molina Enríquez, Andrés. *Los grandes problemas nacionales.* Mexico City: Imprenta de A. Carranza e hijos, 1909.

Nacional Financiera. *Statistics on the Mexican Economy.* Mexico City: Nacional Financiera, 1977.

Novo, Salvador. *Nueva grandeza mexicana: Ensayo sobre la Ciudad de México y sus alrededores; con anotaciones especiales del autor.* Mexico City: Editora de Periódicos, 1956.

Pimentel, Francisco. *La economía política aplicada á la propiedad territorial en México.* Mexico City: Ignacio Cumplido, 1866.

Poinsett, Joel R. *Notes on Mexico Made in the Autumn of 1822 Accompanied by an Historical Sketch of the Revolution and Translations of Official Reports on the Present State of That Country.* 1823; rpt., New York: Frederick A. Praeger, 1969.

Porter, Katherine Anne. *Ship of Fools.* Boston: Little, Brown, 1962.

Ratzel, Friedrich. *Aus Mexico: Reiseskizzen aus den Jahren 1874 und 1875.* 1878; rpt., Stuttgart: Brockhaus, 1969.

Rauschning, Hermann. *Gespräche mit Hitler.* Zurich: Europa Verlag, 1940.

Ruhl, Arthur. *The Central Americans: Adventures and Impressions Between Mexico and Panama.* New York: Charles Scribner's Sons, 1928.

Salazar Silva, E. *Las colonias extranjeras en México.* Mexico City: n.p., 1937.

Sanborn, Helen J. *A Winter in Central America and Mexico.* Boston: Lee and Shepard, 1886.

Sartorius, Carl C. *Mexico: Landscape and Popular Sketches.* Darmstadt, London, and New York: n.p., 1858.

Schmidtlein, Adolfo. *Cartas de un médico alemán a sus padres.* Mexico City: El Colegio de México, 1978.

Tercer censo general de población, 1910. Mexico City: Dirección General de Estadística, 1920.

The Massey-Gilbert Blue Book of Mexico. Mexico City: Massey Gilbert, 1903.

"Tradición, Historia y Prestigio: Casa Boker." *La Revista del Centro Comercial de la Ciudad de México* 1, no. 3 (1991): 14.

United States Department of State. *The Proclaimed List of Certain Blocked Nationals Promulgated Pursuant to the Proclamation of July 17, 1941.* Washington, D.C.: Government Printing Office, 1941.

United States Senate. *Nazi Party Membership Records Submitted by the War Department to the Subcommittee on War Mobilization of the Committee for Military Affairs.* Washington, D.C.: Government Printing Office, 1946.

"Un comercio moderno con sabor nostálgico. Un siglo de inagotables formas arquitectónicas: Edificio de Casa Boker." *Ferretecnic* 38 (2000): 3–6.

Vasconcelos, José. *La raza cósmica: Misión de la raza Iberoamericana, Argentina y Brasil.* Mexico City: Espasa-Calpe, 1966.

Von Humboldt, Alexander. *Essai politique sur le royaume de la Nouvelle-Espagne.* 5 vols. Paris: Schoell, 1811.

Von Kollonitz, Paula. *Eine Reise nach Mexico im Jahre 1864.* Vienna: C. Gerold's Sohn, 1867.

War Trade Board. *Trading with the Enemy. Enemy Trading List Revised to Dec. 13, 1918.* Washington, D.C.: Government Printing Office, 1919.

Weise, Hans F. *Fünfundsiebzig Jahre Deutsches Haus in Mexico (1848–1923).* Mexico City: Compañía Mexicana de Artes Gráficas, 1923.

Zum 60 jährigen Jubiläum des deutsch-mexikanischen Frauenvereins (Asociación de Ayuda Social de la Colonia Alemana: Rückblick 1903–1963 mit genauerem Bericht über das letzte Jahrzehnt. Mexico City: n.p., 1963.

Secondary Literature

Aguilar Camín, Héctor, and Lorenzo Meyer. *A la sombra de la revolución mexicana: Un ensayo de historia contemporánea de México.* Mexico City: Cal y Arena, 1990.

Anderson, Benedict. *Imagined Communities: Reflections on the Spread of Nationalism.* London: Verso, 1983.

Appadurai, Arjun. "Global Ethnoscapes: Notes and Queries for a Transnational Anthropology." In *Recapturing Anthropology: Working in the Present,* ed. Richard G. Fox, 191–210. Santa Fe, N.M.: School of American Research Press, 1991.

Bailey, David C. "Revisionism and the Recent Historiography of the Mexican Revolution." *Hispanic American Historical Review* 58, no. 1 (1978): 62–79.

Baklanoff, Eric N. "From Peddlers to Empresarios: The Lebanese in Latin America." *South Eastern Latin Americanist* 43, no. 1 (1999): 65–76.

Basch, Linda, Nina Glick Schiller, and Cristina Szanton Blanc. *Nations Unbound: Transnational Projects, Postcolonial Predicaments, and Deterritorialized Nation-States.* Langhorne, Pa.: Gordon and Breach, 1994.

Bauer, Arnold J. *Goods, Power, History: Latin America's Material Culture* (Cambridge: Cambridge University Press, 2001).

Bazant, Jan. "From Independence to the Liberal Republic, 1821–1867." *Mexico Since Independence,* ed. Leslie Bethell. Cambridge: Cambridge University Press, 1991.

Beelen, George D. "The Harding Administration and Mexico: Diplomacy by Economic Persuasion." *The Americas* 41, no. 2 (Oct. 1984): 177–89.

Beezley, William H. *Judas at the Jockey Club and Other Episodes of Porfirian Mexico.* Lincoln: University of Nebraska Press, 1987.

———. "The Porfirian Smart Set Anticipates Thorstein Veblen in Guadalajara." In *Rituals of Rule, Rituals of Resistance: Public Celebrations and Popular Culture in Mexico,* ed. William H. Beezley, Cheryl English Martin, and William E. French, 173–90. Wilmington, Del.: Scholarly Resources, 1994.

Benson, Nettie Lee. "Territorial Integrity in Mexican Politics, 1821–1833." In *The Independence of Mexico and the Creation of the New Nation,* ed. Jaime E. Rodríguez O., 275–307. Los Angeles: University of California, Los Angeles, Latin American Center, 1989.

Berg, Peter. *Deutschland und Amerika, 1918–1929: Über das deutsche Amerikabild der zwanziger Jahre.* In *Historische Studien,* no. 385. Lübeck: Matthiesen, 1963.

Bernecker, Walther L. *Die Handelskonquistadoren: Europäische Interessen und mexikanischer Staat im 19. Jahrhundert.* Stuttgart: Steiner-Verlag, 1988.

Bernecker, Walther L., and Thomas Fischer. "Deutsche in Lateinamerika." In *Deutsche im Ausland—Fremde in Deutschland: Migration in Geschichte und Gegenwart,* ed. Klaus J. Bade, 194–214. Munich: C. H. Beck, 1992.

Berninger, George D. *La inmigración en México, 1821–1857.* Mexico: Secretaría de Educación Pública, 1974.

Blackbourn, David. "The German Bourgeoisie: An Introduction." In *The German Bourgeoisie: Essays on the Social History of the German Middle Class from the Late Eighteenth to the Early Twentieth Century,* ed. David Blackbourn and Richard J. Evans. London: Routledge, 1991.

Blancpain, Jean-Pierre. *Migrations et mémoire germaniques en Amérique Latine à l'époque contemporaine: Contribution à l'étude de l'expansion allemande outre-mer.* Strasbourg: Presses Universitaires de Strasbourg, 1994.

Bortz, Jeffrey. *Industrial Wages in Mexico City, 1939–1975.* New York: Garland Publishing, 1987.

Brachet-Márquez, Viviane. *The Dynamics of Domination: State, Class, and Social Reform in Mexico, 1910–1990.* Pittsburgh, Pa.: Pittsburgh University Press, 1994.

Brading, David A. *Miners and Merchants in Bourbon Mexico.* Cambridge: Cambridge University Press, 1971.

———. "Creole Nationalism and Mexican Liberalism." *Journal of Inter-American Studies and World Affairs* 15 (1973): 139–90.

———. *Los orígenes del nacionalismo mexicano.* Mexico City: El Colegio de México, 1979.

Brown, Jonathan C. "Foreign and Native-Born Workers in Porfirian Mexico." *American Historical Review* 98 (1993): 786–818.

Buchenau, Jürgen. *In the Shadow of the Giant: The Making of Mexico's Central America Policy, 1876–1930.* Tuscaloosa: University of Alabama Press, 1996.

———. "Small Numbers, Great Impact: Mexico and its Immigrants." *Journal of American Ethnic History* 20, no. 3 (2001): 23–49.

Bunker, Steven B. "'Consumers of Good Taste': Marketing Modernity in Northern Mexico, 1890–1910." *Mexican Studies/Estudios Mexicanos* 13, no. 2 (1997): 227–69.

Bussey, Jane. "Salinas de Gortari, Carlos." In *Encyclopedia of Mexico: History, Society, and Culture,* ed. Michael Werner, 2:1331–32. Chicago: Fitzroy Dearborn Publishers, 1997.

Camp, Roderic A. *Entrepreneurs and Politics in Twentieth-Century Mexico.* New York: Oxford University Press, 1989.

Cárdenas, Enrique. "A Macroeconomic Interpretation of Nineteenth-Century Mexico." In *How Latin America Fell Behind: Essays on the Economic Histories of Brazil and Mexico, 1800–1914,* ed. Stephen Haber, 65–92. Stanford, Calif.: Stanford University Press, 1997.

Chandler, Alfred D. Jr. *The Visible Hand: The Managerial Revolution in American Business.* Cambridge, Mass.: Belknap, 1977.

Coatsworth, John H. "Obstacles to Economic Growth in Nineteenth-Century Mexico." *American Historical Review* 83, no. 1 (1978): 80–100.

———. *Growth Against Development: The Economic Impact of Railroads in Porfirian Mexico.* DeKalb: Northern Illinois University Press, 1981.

Cohen, Robin. *Global Diasporas: An Introduction.* Seattle: University of Washington Press, 1997.

Collado Herrera, María del Carmen. *Empresarios y políticos: Entre la Restauración y la Revolución.* Mexico City: Instituto Nacional de Estudios Históricos de la Revolución Mexicana, 1996.

Cosío Villegas, Daniel, ed. *Historia moderna de México.* 9 vols. Mexico City: Editorial Hermes, 1956–73.

Crosby, Alfred. *Ecological Imperialism: The Biological Expansion of Europe, 900–1900.* Cambridge: Cambridge University Press, 1986.

Curtin, Philip D. *Cross-Cultural Trade in Global Perspective.* Cambridge: Cambridge University Press, 1984.

Dane, Hendrik. *Die wirtschaftlichen Beziehungen Deutschlands zu Mexiko und Mittelamerika im neunzehnten Jahrhundert.* Cologne: Böhlau, 1971.

Darius, Rudolf. *Die Entwicklung der deutsch-mexikanischen Handelsbeziehungen von 1870–1914.* Cologne: Welzel, 1927.

Davis, Diane E. Urban *Leviathan: Mexico City in the Twentieth Century.* Philadelphia, Pa.: Temple University Press, 1994.

Davis, Ethelyn C. "The American Colony in Mexico City." Ph.D. dissertation, University of Missouri, 1942.

Delpar, Helen. *The Enormous Vogue of Things Mexican.* Tuscaloosa: University of Alabama Press, 1992.

Doering-Manteuffel, Anselm. *Wie westlich sind die Deutschen? Amerikanisierung und Westernisierung im 20. Jahrhundert.* Göttingen: Vandenhoeck und Ruprecht, 1999.

Durán, Esperanza. *Guerra y revolución: Las grandes potencias y México.* Mexico City: Colegio de México, 1985.

Fiebig-von Hase, Ragnhild. *Lateinamerika als Konfliktherd der deutsch-amerikanischen Beziehungen, 1890–1903: Vom Beginn der Panamerikapolitik bis zur Venezuelakrise von 1902/03.* Göttingen: Vandenhoeck und Ruprecht, 1986.

Flores Caballero, Romeo. *Counterrevolution: The Role of the Spaniards in the Independence of Mexico, 1804–1838.* Trans. Jaime E. Rodríguez O. Lincoln: University of Nebraska Press, 1974.

Friedman, Max Paul. "Nazis and Good Neighbors: The United States Campaign Against the Germans of Latin America in World War II." Ph.D. dissertation, University of California, Berkeley, 2000.

Fuentes, Carlos. *La región más transparente.* Mexico City: Fondo de Cultura Económica, 1963.

García Canclini, Néstor. *Consumers and Citizens: Globalization and Multicultural Conflicts.* Trans. George Yúdice. Minneapolis: University of Minnesota Press, 2001.

García Rica, Emilio. *Fernando de Fuentes, 1894–1958.* Mexico City: Cineteca Nacional, 1984.

Gersick, Kelin E., et al. *Generation to Generation: Life Cycles of the Family Business.* Boston, Mass.: Harvard Business School Press, 1997.

Gómez, Aurora. "El desempeño de la Fundidora de Hierro y Acero de Monterrey durante el porfiriato." In *Historia de las grandes empresas en México, 1850–1930,* ed. Carlos Marichal, 201–44. Monterrey: Universidad Autónoma de Nuevo León, 1997.

Gonzales, Michael. *The Mexican Revolution, 1910–1940.* Albuquerque: University of New Mexico Press, 2002.

González Navarro, Moisés. *Población y sociedad en México.* Mexico City: El Colegio de México, 1974.

———. *Los extranjeros en México y los mexicanos en el extranjero, 1821–1970.* 3 vols. Mexico City: El Colegio de México, 1993.

Guerra, François-Xavier. *Le Mexique de l'Ancien Régime à la Révolution.* 2 vols. Paris: Harmattan, 1986.

Guillermoprieto, Alma. *The Heart that Bleeds: Latin America Now.* New York: Vintage Books, 1995.

Gunn, Drewey W. *American and British Writers in Mexico, 1556–1973.* Austin: University of Texas Press, 1974.

Guthke, Karl S. *B. Traven: The Life Behind the Legend.* Chicago: Lawrence Hill Books, 1991.

Haber, Stephen. *Industry and Underdevelopment: The Industrialization of Mexico, 1880–1940.* Stanford, Calif.: Stanford University Press, 1989.

———. "Anything Goes: Mexico's 'New' Cultural History." *Hispanic American Historical Review* 79, no. 2 (1999): 309–30.

Hale, Charles A. *Mexican Liberalism in the Age of Mora, 1821–1853.* New Haven, Conn.: Yale University Press, 1968.

———. *The Transformation of Mexican Liberalism in the Late Nineteenth Century.* Princeton, N.J.: Princeton University Press, 1989.

Hansen, Roger D. *The Politics of Mexican Development.* Baltimore, Md.: Johns Hopkins University Press, 1971.

Harris, Charles H., III, and Louis R. Sadler. *The Archaeologist Was a Spy: Sylvanus G. Morley and the Office of Naval Intelligence.* Albuquerque: University of New Mexico, 2003.

Hart, John M. *Revolutionary Mexico: The Coming and Process of the Mexican Revolution*. 2d ed. Berkeley and Los Angeles: University of California Press, 1997.

———. *Empire and Revolution: The Americans in Mexico Since the Civil War*. Berkeley and Los Angeles: University of California Press, 2002.

Harvey, Neil. *Rebellion in Chiapas: Rural Reforms, Campesino Radicalism, and the Limits to Salinismo*. La Jolla: Center for U.S.-Mexican Studies, University of California, San Diego, 1994.

Henning, Friedrich-Wilhelm. *Die Industrialisierung in Deutschland, 1800–1914*. Paderborn, Germany: Schöningh, 1978.

Hoberman, Louisa S. *Mexico's Merchant Elite, 1590–1660: Silver, State, and Society*. Durham, N.C.: Duke University Press, 1991.

James, Daniel. *Doña María's Story: Life History, Memory, and Political Identity*. Durham, N.C.: Duke University Press, 2001.

Johns, Michael. *The City of Mexico in the Age of Díaz*. Austin: University of Texas Press, 1997.

Jones, G., and A. Varley. "The Contest for the City Centre: Street Traders versus Buildings." *Bulletin of Latin American Research* 13 (1994): 27–44.

Joseph, Gilbert M. *Revolution from Without: Yucatán, Mexico, and the United States, 1880–1924*. Cambridge: Cambridge University Press, 1982.

Joseph, Gilbert M., and Daniel Nugent, eds. *Everyday Forms of State Formation: Revolution and the Negotiation of Rule in Mexico*. Durham, N.C.: Duke University Press, 1994.

Joseph, Gilbert M., Catherine C. Legrand, and Ricardo D. Salvatore, eds. *Close Encounters of Empire: Writing the Cultural History of U.S.-Latin American Relations*. Durham, N.C.: Duke University Press, 1999.

Kandell, Jonathan. *La Capital: The Biography of Mexico City*. New York: Random House, 1988.

Katz, Friedrich. *Deutschland, Diaz und die mexikanische Revolution: Die deutsche Politik in Mexiko 1870–1920*. Berlin: VEB Deutscher Verlag der Wissenschaften, 1964.

———. *The Secret War in Mexico: Europe, the United States, and the Mexican Revolution*. Chicago: University of Chicago Press, 1981.

———. "Liberal Republic and Porfiriato." *Mexico Since Independence*, ed. Leslie Bethell, 49–124. Cambridge: Cambridge University Press, 1991.

———. "Algunos rasgos esenciales de la política alemana en América Latina." In *Ensayos mexicanos*, 363–456. Mexico City: Alianza Editorial, 1994.

———. "Germany and Latin America until 1945." Paper presented at the 1995 conference "Rethinking the Post-Colonial Encounter," Yale University, New Haven, Conn.

Kicza, John E. "The Role of the Family in Economic Development in Nineteenth-Century Latin America." *Journal of Family History* 10.3 (fall 1985): 235–57.

————. *Colonial Entrepreneurs: Families and Business in Bourbon Mexico City.* Albuquerque: University of New Mexico Press, 1983.

Knight, Alan. *The Mexican Revolution.* 2 vols. Cambridge: Cambridge University Press, 1986.

————. *U.S.-Mexican Relations, 1910–1940: An Interpretation.* La Jolla: Center for U.S.-Mexican Studies, University of California, San Diego, 1987.

————. "Racism, Revolution, and Indigenismo: Mexico, 1910–1940." In *The Idea of Race in Latin America, 1870–1940,* ed. Richard Graham, 71–113. Austin: University of Texas Press, 1990.

————. "Revolutionary Process, Recalcitrant People: Mexico, 1910–1940." In *The Revolutionary Process in Mexico: Essays on Political and Social Change, 1880–1940,* ed. Jaime Rodríguez O., 227–64. Los Angeles: UCLA Latin American Studies Center, 1990.

————. "Cardenismo: Juggernaut or Jalopy." *Journal of Latin American Studies* 24 (1994): 73–107.

————. "Peasants into Patriots: Thoughts on the Making of the Mexican Nation." *Mexican Studies/Estudios Mexicanos* 10, no. 1 (1994): 135–61.

————. "Popular Culture and the Revolutionary State in Mexico, 1910–1940." *Hispanic American Historical Review* 74, no. 3 (1994): 395–444.

————. "The United States and the Mexican Peasantry, c. 1880–1940." In *Rural Revolt in Mexico: U.S. Intervention and the Domain of Subaltern Politics,* ed. Daniel Nugent, 25–63. 2d exp. ed. Durham, N.C.: Duke University Press, 1998.

Kocka, Jürgen. "The European Pattern and the German Case." In *Bourgeois Society in Nineteenth-Century Europe,* ed. Jürgen Kocka and Allan Mitchell, 3–39. Providence, R.I.: Berg, 1993.

Krauze, Enrique, Jean Meyer, and Cayetano Reyes. *Historia de la revolución mexicana: Período 1924–28: La reconstrucción económica.* Mexico City: El Colegio de México, 1977.

Kroes, Rob. *If You've Seen One, You've Seen the Mall: Europeans and American Mass Culture.* Urbana: University of Illinois Press, 1996.

Krumpel, Heinz. *Die deutsche Philosophie in Mexiko: Ein Beitrag zur interkulturellen Verständigung seit Alexander von Humboldt.* Frankfurt: Peter Lang, 1998.

Kuznesof, Elizabeth, and Robert Oppenheimer. "The Family and Society in Nineteenth-Century Latin America: An Historiographical Introduction." *Journal of Family History* 10, no. 3 (fall 1985): 215–34.

Lafaye, Jacques. *Quetzalcóatl and Guadalupe: The Formation of Mexican National Consciousness, 1531–1813.* Trans. Benjamin Keen. Chicago: University of Chicago Press, 1976.

Lancaster, Bill. *The Department Store: A Social History.* London: Leicester University Press, 1995.

Leach, William. *Land of Desire: Merchants, Power, and the Rise of a New American Culture.* New York: Vintage, 1993.

Lear, John. *Workers, Neighbors, and Citizens: The Revolution in Mexico City.* Lincoln: University of Nebraska Press, 2001.

Lesser, Jeffrey. *Negotiating National Identity: Immigrants, Minorities, and the Struggle for Ethnicity in Brazil.* Durham, N.C.: Duke University Press, 1999.

Lezema, J. L. "Ciudad y conflicto: Usos del suelo y comercio ambulante en la Cd. de México." In *Espacio y vivienda en la Ciudad de México,* ed. Martha Schteingart, 121–35. Mexico City: El Colegio de México, 1991.

Lida, Clara F. "Los españoles en México: población, cultura, y sociedad." In *Simbiosis de culturas: Los inmigrantes en México y su cultura,* ed. Guillermo Bonfil Batalla, 425–54. Mexico City: Secretaría de Educación Pública, 1988.

Liehr, Reinhard, and Mariano E. Torres Bautista. "Las Free-Standing Companies británicas en el México del porfiriato, 1884–1911." *Historia Mexicana* 187 (1998): 605–53.

Lomnitz, Larissa, and Marisol Pérez-Lizaur. *A Mexican Elite Family, 1820–1980: Kinship, Class, and Culture.* Princeton, N.J.: Princeton University Press, 1987.

Lomnitz-Adler, Claudio. *Exits from the Labyrinth: Culture and Ideology in the Mexican National Space.* Berkeley and Los Angeles: University of California Press, 1992.

Lustig, Nora. *Mexico: The Remaking of an Economy.* 2d rev. ed. Washington, D.C.: Brookings Institution, 1998.

Marichal, Carlos. "Foreign Predominance among Overseas Traders in Nineteenth-Century Latin America: A Comment." *Latin American Research Review* 21, no. 3 (1986): 145–50.

———. *A Century of Debt Crises in Latin America.* Princeton, N.J.: Princeton University Press, 1989.

———. "Avances recientes en la historia de las grandes empresas y su importancia para la historia económica de México." In *Historia de las grandes empresas en México,* ed. Carlos Marichal and Mario Cerutti, 9–38. Monterrey: Universidad Autónoma de Nuevo León, 1997.

Martínez Montiel, Luz María, and Araceli Reynoso Medina. "Imigración europea y asiática, siglos XIX y XX." In *Simbiosis de culturas: Los inmigrantes y su cultura en México,* ed. Guillermo Bonfil Batalla, 245–424. Mexico: Fondo de Cultura Económica, 1993.

Matute, Alvaro. *Historia de la revolución mexicana, 1917–1924: Las dificultades del nuevo estado.* Mexico City: Colegio de México, 1995.

McFalls, Laurence. "Living with Which Past? National Identity in Post-Wall, Postwar Germany." In *A User's Guide to German Cultural Studies,* ed. Scott Denham, Irene Kacandes, and Jonathan Petropoulos, 297–308. Ann Arbor: University of Michigan Press, 1997.

Meyer, Jean. "Les Français au Mexique au XIXème siècle." *Cahiers des Amériques Latines* 9–10 (1974): 43–86.

———. "Mexico in the 1920s." In Mexico Since Independence, ed. Leslie

Bethell, 201–40. Cambridge: Cambridge University Press, 1991.

Meyer, Lorenzo. *Mexico and the United States in the Oil Controversy, 1917–1942*. Austin: University of Texas Press, 1972.

Meyer, Michael C., John L. Sherman, and Susan Deeds. *The Course of Mexican History*. 6th rev. ed. Oxford: Oxford University Press, 1999.

Miller, Michael B. *The Bon Marché: Bourgeois Culture and the Department Store, 1869–1920*. Princeton, N.J.: Princeton University Press, 1981.

Miller, Michael N. *Red, White, and Green: The Maturing of Mexicanidad*. El Paso: Texas Western Press, 1998.

Miller, Robert R. "Herman Sturm: Hoosier Secret Agent for Mexico." *Indiana Magazine of History* 58 (1962): 1–15.

Miller, Rory. *Britain and Latin America in the Nineteenth and Twentieth Centuries*. London: Longman, 1993.

Mitchell, Nancy. *The Danger of Dreams: German and American Imperialism in Latin America*. Chapel Hill: University of North Carolina Press, 1999.

Monsiváis, Carlos. "Tantos millones de hombres no hablaremos inglés? (La cultura norteamericana y México)." In *Simbiosis de culturas: Los inmigrantes en México y su cultura*, ed. Guillermo Bonfil Batalla, 455–516. Mexico City: Secretaría de Educación Pública, 1988.

Morales Díaz, Carlos. *¿Quién es quien en la nomenclatura de la Ciudad de México?* 2d expanded ed. Mexico City: B. Costa-Amic, 1971.

Moreno, Julio E. "Sears, Roebuck Company, J. Walter Thompson and the Culture of North American Commerce in Mexico during the 1940's." Ph.D. dissertation, University of California at Irvine, 1998.

Morgan, Tony. "Proletarians, Politicos, and Patriarchs: The Use and Abuse of Cultural Customs in the Early Industrialization of Mexico City, 1880–1910." In *Rituals of Rule, Rituals of Resistance: Public Celebrations and Popular Culture in Mexico*, ed. William H. Beezley, Cheryl English Martin, and William E. French, 151–71. Wilmington, Del.: Scholarly Resources, 1994.

Mörner, Magnus. *Adventurers and Proletarians: The Story of Migrants in Latin America*. Pittsburgh, Pa.: University of Pittsburgh Press, 1985.

Moya, José. *Cousins and Strangers: Spanish Immigrants in Buenos Aires, 1850–1930*. Berkeley and Los Angeles: University of California Press, 1998.

Müller, Jürgen. *Nationalsozialismus in Lateinamerika: Die Auslandsorganisation der NSDAP in Argentinien, Brasilien, Chile und Mexiko, 1931–1945*. Stuttgart: Verlag Dieter Heinz, 1997.

Nagel, Silke. "Integration oder nationalistische Abgrenzung? Deutsche Einwanderer in Mexiko-Stadt." M.A. thesis, Freie Universität Berlin, 1991.

Newton, Ronald C. *German Buenos Aires, 1900–1933: Social Change and Cultural Crisis*. Austin: University of Texas Press, 1977.

Niblo, Stephen R. *The Impact of War: Mexico and World War II*. Melbourne, Australia: La Trobe University Institute of Latin America, 1988.

————. *War, Diplomacy, and Development: The United States and Mexico, 1938–1954*. Wilmington, Del.: Scholarly Resources, 1995.

————. *Mexico in the 1940s: Modernity, Politics, and Corruption*. Wilmington, Del.: Scholarly Resources, 1999.

O'Brien, Thomas F. *The Revolutionary Mission: American Enterprise in Latin America, 1900–1945*. Cambridge: Cambridge University Press, 1996.

Oeste de Bopp, Marianne. "Die Deutschen in Mexico." In *Die Deutschen in Lateinamerika: Schicksal und Leistung*, ed. Hartmut Fröschle, 475–564. Tübingen: Erdmann Verlag, 1979.

Ojeda, Mario. *Alcances y límites de la política exterior de México*. Mexico: El Colegio de México, 1976.

Olliff, Donathon C. *Reforma Mexico and the United States: The Search for Alternatives to Annexation*. Tuscaloosa: University of Alabama Press, 1981.

Orlove, Benjamin, and Arnold J. Bauer. "Giving Importance to Imports." In *The Allure of the Foreign: Imported Goods in Postcolonial Latin America*, ed. Benjamin Orlove, 1–12. Ann Arbor: University of Michigan Press, 1997.

Osterhammel, Jürgen. *Kolonialismus: Geschichte, Formen, Folgen*. Munich: C. H. Beck, 1995.

Palma Mora, M. D. Mónica. "Inmigrantes extranjeros en México, 1950–1980." Ph.D. dissertation, Universidad Nacional Autónoma de México, 1999.

Pani, Erika. "Dreaming of a Mexican Empire: The Political Projects of the 'Imperialistas.'" *Hispanic American Historical Review* 82, no. 1 (2002): 1–31.

Paz, María Elena. *Strategy, Security, and Spies: Mexico and the Allies in World War II*. University Park: Pennsylvania State University Press, 1997.

Paz, Octavio. *The Labyrinth of Solitude*. Trans. Lysander Kemp. New York: Grove Press, 1985.

Pellicer de Brody, Olga, and Esteban Mancilla. *Historia de la Revolución Mexicana, período 1952–1960: El entendimiento con los Estados Unidos y la gestación del desarrollo estabilizador*. Mexico City: El Colegio de México, 1978.

Pferdekamp, Wilhelm. *Auf Humboldts Spuren: Deutsche im jungen Mexiko*. Munich: Max Hueber, 1958.

Piccato, Pablo. *City of Suspects: Crime in Mexico City, 1900–1931*. Durham, N.C.: Duke University Press, 2001.

Pick, James B., and Edgar W. Butler. *Mexico's Megacity*. Boulder, Colo.: Westview Press, 1997.

Platt, D. C. M. "Dependency in Nineteenth-Century Latin America: A Historian Objects." *Latin American Research Review* 15, no. 1 (1980): 113–30.

Powell, Thomas G. *Mexico and the Spanish Civil War*. Albuquerque: University of New Mexico Press, 1980.

Pratt, Mary Louise. *Imperial Eyes: Travel Writing and Transculturation.* London: Routledge, 1992.

Proal, Maurice, and Pierre Martin Charpenel. *Los Barcelonnettes en México.* Mexico City: Clío, 1998.

Price, Charles. "The Study of Assimilation." In *Migration,* ed. J. A. Jackson, 181–237. Cambridge: Cambridge University Press, 1969.

Raat, W. Dirk. "Ideas and Society in Don Porfirio's Mexico." *The Americas* 30 (1973): 32–53.

———. *El positivismo durante el porfiriato.* Mexico City: El Colegio de México, 1975.

———. "Gus Jones and the FBI in Mexico, 1900–1947: A Biographical Essay Writ-Large." Unpublished manuscript.

Rees, Wilhelm. *Robert Böker und seine Vorfahren als Wirtschaftler und Kommunalpolitiker.* Remscheid: Stadtarchiv Remscheid, 1961.

Richmond, Douglas W. *Venustiano Carranza's Nationalist Struggle.* Lincoln: University of Nebraska Press, 1983.

Ridings, Eugene W. "Foreign Predominance among Overseas Traders in Nineteenth-Century Latin America." *Latin American Research Review* 20, no. 2 (1985): 3–29.

Riguzzi, Paolo. "México próspero: Las dimensiones de la imagen nacional en el porfiriato." *Historias* 20 (1988): 137–57.

Rinke, Stefan. "Die Firma Junkers auf dem lateinamerikanischen Markt." In *Grenzenlose Märkte? Die deutsch-lateinamerikanischen Wirtschaftsbeziehungen vom Zeitalter des Imperialismus bis zur Weltwirtschaftskrise,* ed. Boris Barth and Jochen Meissner, 157–84. Münster, Germany: Lit, 1995.

———. *"Der letzte freie Kontinent": Deutsche Lateinamerikapolitik im Zeichen transnationaler Beziehungen, 1918–1933.* Stuttgart: Verlag Hans Dieter Heinz, 1996.

Rock, David, ed. *Latin America in the 1940s: War and Post-War Transitions.* Berkeley and Los Angeles: University of California Press, 1994.

Rodríguez O., Jaime. *Down from Colonialism: Mexico's Nineteenth-Century Crisis.* Los Angeles: Chicano Studies Research Center, University of California, 1983.

Rodríguez Prampolini, Ida. *La crítica de arte en México en el siglo XIX.* Mexico City: Imprenta Universitaria, 1964.

Romero Ibarra, María Eugenia. "La historia empresarial." *Historia Mexicana* 50, no. 3 (2003): 805–29.

Rosenberg, Emily. *Spreading the American Dream: American Economic and Cultural Expansion, 1890–1945.* New York: Hill and Wang, 1982.

Rout, Leslie B., and John F. Bratzel. *The Shadow War: German Espionage and United States Counterespionage During World War II.* Frederick, Md.: University Publications of America, 1985.

Said, Edward. *Orientalism.* New York: Random House, 1979.

Salazar Anaya, Delia. *La población extranjera en México (1895–1990): Un recuento con base en los censos generales de población.* Mexico City: Instituto Nacional de Antropología e Historia, 1996.

Salazar Sotelo, Francisco. "Balance global de la política económica en el sexenio 1976–1982." In *Estudios cuantitativos sobre la historia de México,* ed. Samuel Schmidt, James W. Wilkie, and Manuel Esparza, 41–58. Mexico City: UNAM, 1988.

Saragoza, Alex. *The Monterrey Elite and the Mexican State, 1880–1940.* Austin: University of Texas Press, 1988.

———. "The Selling of Mexico: Tourism and the State." In *Fragments of a Golden Age: The Politics of Culture in Mexico Since 1940,* ed. Gilbert Joseph, Anne Rubenstein, and Eric Zolov, 91–115. Durham, N.C.: Duke University Press, 2001.

Scanlon, Arlene P. *Un enclave cultural: Poder y etnicidad en el contexto de una escuela norteamericana en México.* Mexico City: CIESAS, 1984.

Schell, William, Jr. *Integral Outsiders: The American Colony in Mexico City, 1876–1911.* Wilmington, Del.: Scholarly Resources, 2001.

———. "Silver Symbiosis: Re-Orienting Mexican Economic History." *Hispanic American Historical Review* 81, no. 1 (2001): 89–134.

Schieder, Theodor. *Hermann Rauschnings 'Gespräche mit Hitler' als Geschichtsquelle.* Opladen, Germany: Rheinisch-Westfälische Akademie der Wissenschaften, 1972.

Schmidt, Arthur. "Making it Real Compared to What: Reconceptualizing Mexican History Since 1940." In *Fragments of a Golden Age: The Politics of Culture in Mexico Since 1940,* ed. Gilbert Joseph, Anne Rubenstein, and Eric Zolov, 23–68. Durham, N.C.: Duke University Press, 2001.

Schmidt, Henry C. *The Roots of "Lo Mexicano": Self and Society in Mexican Thought, 1900–1934.* College Station: Texas A&M University Press, 1978.

Schuler, Friedrich E. "Germany, Mexico, and the Second World War." *Jahrbuch für Geschichte von Staat, Wirtschaft und Gesellschaft Lateinamerikas* 25 (1985): 457–76.

———. *Mexico Between Hitler and Roosevelt: Mexican Foreign Relations in the Age of Lázaro Cárdenas, 1934–1940.* Albuquerque: University of New Mexico Press, 1998.

Scott, James. *Domination and the Art of Resistance: Hidden Transcripts.* New Haven, Conn.: Yale University Press, 1990.

Sherman, John W. "The Mexican Miracle and its Collapse." In *The Oxford History of Mexico,* ed. Michael C. Meyer and William H. Beezley, 575–98. Oxford: Oxford University Press, 2000.

Sims, Harold D. *The Expulsion of Mexico's Spaniards, 1821–1936.* Pittsburgh, Pa.: University of Pittsburgh Press, 1990.

Sinkin, Richard N. *The Mexican Reform, 1855–1876: A Study in Liberal Nation-Building.* Austin: University of Texas Press, 1979.

Smith, Robert F. *The United States and Revolutionary Nationalism in Mexico, 1916–32.* Chicago: University of Chicago Press, 1972.

Spitzer, Leo. *Lives in Between: Assimilation and Marginality in Austria, Brazil, and West Africa.* Cambridge: Cambridge University Press, 1989.

Strutz, Edmund. *Werden und Vergehen Remscheider Familien: Vorträge zur Familienforschung im alten Remscheid.* Remscheid: n.p., 1964.

Taylor, Alan M. "Latin America and Foreign Capital in the Twentieth Century: Economics, Politics, and Institutional Change." In *Political Institutions and Economic Growth in Latin America: Essays in Policy, History, and Political Economy,* ed. Stephen Haber, 121–58. Stanford, Calif.: Hoover Institution Press, 2000.

Tenenbaum, Barbara A. "Streetwise History: The Paseo de la Reforma and the Porfirian State." In *Rituals of Rule, Rituals of Resistance: Public Celebrations and Popular Culture in Mexico,* ed. William H. Beezley, Cheryl English Martin, and William E. French, 127–50. Wilmington, Del.: Scholarly Resources, 1994.

Tenorio Trillo, Mauricio. *Mexico at the World's Fairs: Crafting a Modern Nation.* Berkeley and Los Angeles: University of California Press, 1996.

Torres Ramírez, Blanca. *México en la segunda guerra mundial.* Mexico City: Colegio de México, 1979.

Turner, Frederick C. *The Dynamic of Mexican Nationalism.* Chapel Hill: University of North Carolina Press, 1968.

Vanderwood, Paul. *Disorder and Progress: Bandits, Police, and Mexican Development.* 2d ed. Wilmington, Del.: Scholarly Resources, 1992.

Van Young, Eric. "La pareja dispareja: Breves comentarios acerca de la relación entre historia económica y cultural." *Historia Mexicana* 50, no. 3 (2003): 831–70.

———. "The 'New Cultural History' Comes to Old Mexico." *Hispanic American Historical Review* 79, no. 2 (1999): 211–48.

Volland, Klaus. *Das Dritte Reich und Mexiko: Studien zur Entwicklung des deutsch-mexikanischen Verhältnisses 1933–1942 unter besonderer Berücksichtigung der Ölpolitik.* Frankfurt: Peter Lang, 1976.

Von Hanffstengel, Renata. "La comunidad alemana en México a partir de la Segunda Guerra Mundial hasta la fecha." *BaBel* 1 (1999): 41–47.

Von Hanffstengel, Renata, Cecilia Tercero, and Silke Wehner Franco, eds. *Mexiko, das wohltemperierte Exil.* Mexico City: Instituto de Investigaciones Interculturales Germano-Mexicanas, 1995.

Von Mentz, Brígida, et al. *Los pioneros del imperialismo alemán en México.* Mexico City: CIESAS, 1982.

———. *Los empresarios alemanes, el Tercer Reich y la oposición de derecha a Cárdenas.* 2 vols. Mexico City: CIESAS, 1987.

Von zur Mühlen, Patrik. *Fluchtziel Lateinamerika: Die deutsche Emigration, 1933–1945; politische Aktivitäten und soziokulturelle Integration.* Berlin: Verlag Neue Gesellschaft, 1988.

Wagnleitner, Reinhold. *The Coca-Colonization of the Cold War: The United States Cultural Mission in Austria after the Second World War.* Chapel Hill: University of North Carolina Press, 1994.

Walker, David W. Kinship, *Business, and Politics: The Martínez del Río Family in Mexico, 1824–1867.* Austin: University of Texas Press, 1986.

Wankel, Matthias. *Reflejo de la historia de dos pueblos: El Colegio Alemán en México, 1894–1942.* Mexico City: Colegio Alejandro von Humboldt, 1994.

Ward, Peter M. *Mexico City.* 2d rev. ed. Chichester, England: Wiley & Sons, 1997.

Wasserman, Mark. *Everyday Life and Politics in Nineteenth-Century Mexico: Men, Women, and War.* Albuquerque: University of New Mexico Press, 2000.

Womack, John. "The Mexican Economy During the Revolution, 1910–1920: Historiography and Analysis." *Marxist Perspectives* 1 (1978): 80–123.

Zantop, Susanne. *Colonial Fantasies: Conquest, Family, and Nation in Precolonial Germany, 1770–1870.* Durham, N.C.: Duke University Press, 1997.

Zogbaum, Heidi. *B. Traven: A Vision of Mexico.* Wilmington, Del.: Scholarly Resources, 1992.

Zolov, Eric. *Refried Elvis: The Rise of the Mexican Counterculture.* Berkeley and Los Angeles: University of California Press, 1999.

Zorrilla, Luis G. *Relaciones de México con la República de Centro América y con Guatemala.* Mexico: Editorial Porrúa, 1984.

Sources on the World Wide Web

"Versión Estenográfica, Sesión pública de la comisión permanente del H. Congreso de la Unión." *http:/www.senado.gob.mx/permanente/2000/versiones/v26julio.html* (Jan. 22, 2001).

"Me lo dice el corazón." *www.unam.mx/univmex/2000/jun-jul/imagenes/ggarcia.html* (Mar. 28, 2002).

"El Club Alemán." *http://www.club-aleman.com/hist.htm* (Jan. 20, 2001).

"Up late: Chismes de los personajes de South Beach." *http://www.yupi. com/oceandrive/ uplate/120399/index.cfm* (Jan. 28, 2001).

"Paseo por el centro: Casa Boker." *http://www.cultura.df.gob.mx/paseo/r1s10.htm* (May 2, 2001).

"Avisos." *http://www.ci.shcp.gob.mx/indice/dof/documentos/2001/2001/febrero/07022001/avisos07feb01.html* (Apr. 16, 2002).

Film

La Familia Dressel. Dir. Fernando de Fuentes. B/W, 90 mins. Mexico City, 1935.

Index

Camp, Roderic, 154
Campos Hermanos, 176
capitalism: laissez-faire, 180; vs.
Communism, 155
Cárdenas, Lázaro, 93, 102, 118, 128–29
Carranza, Venustiano, 73, 75, 77,
81–82, 92, 94
Carstens Alcalá, Julio, 121
Casa Amarilla, 85–86, 86, 90, 105, 121
Casa Boker: Mexican Revolution and,
72, 76–78; Porfirian era growth,
47–55, 59–60; post-World War II
era, 145–54, 168–69; World War I
era, 78–84
Casa Boker archive, 8
Casa Boker catalogs, 51, 60; national
origin of merchandise, 48, 99, 149,
151–52, 181
Casa del Obrero Mundial, 77
Casino Alemán, 33
censuses of foreign nationals, 14, 108–9
Charlotte (Carlota), 26
Chiapas, 15, 180–81
churches: German Catholic, 46;
Lutheran, 46, 110, 161; Roman
Catholic, 18
Clinton, Bill, 181
cold war, 155–56
Colegio Alemán Alexander von
Humboldt (CAAH), 121, 159–62
Colegio Alemán de México, 45–46, 75,
81, 104, 120 See also Colegio
Alemán Alexander von Humboldt
colonia, 32–33
colonies: American, 46–47, 95; French,
45; German, 7–8, 33, 46–47, 108–9,
194; German, disintegration of, 154,
157, 161, 169; German, Nazi control
of, 118; German, political disagreements within, 109–10, 120; Spanish,
110 See also ethnic enclaves; expatriate communities
colonization, 17, 43–44
Colosio, Luis Donaldo, 181
Comité Internacional, 1, 76, 80
Communism vs. capitalism, 155
Compañía de Inversiones La
Esperanza, S.A., 149, 176; purchase
of Edificio Boker, 102
Compañía Ferretera Mexicana (CFM)

(closely held corporation), 71–72,
175, 183–84; Comité Consultivo, 72,
100; dividend payments, 72; earnings, 77, 99–100, 135–36, 149–51;
Junta supervision of, 117, 132–38;
See also Fondo A
Confederación de Trabajadores
Mexicanos (CTM), 102, 136
Constitution of 1917, 74, 77, 81,
91–93, 180
consulado, 13
consumer culture, 39–40, 51, 53–54, 56,
62, 154; opposition to, 4, 97–98
Cosío Villegas, Daniel, 94, 160
cosmic race, 7
creole elite, 13, 31
Crisol Mexicano S.A. de C.V. (closely
held corporation), 175, 184
CTM (Confederación de Traba-jadores
Mexicanos), 102, 136
Cuauhtémoc brewery, 40
currency, value of the peso, 76–77, 95,
144, 176–77, 179, 181
Curtin, Philip, 43
customer base, 17, 42, 60, 97; female,
53; male, 4, 53, 62, 184
cutlery, 47, 183; Arbolito brand, 30, 56,
57, 149, 172

Daniels, Josephus, 128
Darwinism, social, 31, 42
Davis, William R., 119
de Fuentes, Fernando, La Familia
Dressel, 105
DeLemos and Cordes, 55
department stores, 3, 52–54, 148
dependency analysis, 8
Deutsche Schule von Mexico, 45–46
Deutsche Volksgemeinschaft (DVG),
120
Deutsche Zeitung von Mexico, 46
Díaz, Félix, 76, 82
Díaz, Porfirio, 1, 38–47, 59–60, 154
Díaz Ordaz, Gustavo, 139, 141, 151
Dietrich, Arthur, 122, 129
diplomatic protection of foreign mer-
chants, 73, 92, 101
direct marketing, 147
distribution networks, 4
Dobroschke, Max, 81

Hart, John M., 2, 73
Heinrich Böker, 23
Heinrich Böker and Company
(Solingen), 30, 47, 111, 179
Heinrich Böker (Remscheid), 48
Hella, 176
Hermann Boker and Company (New
York), 21, 80
Hernández Boker, Claudio, 187–88
Hernández Boker, Vanessa, 187–88
Hernández Valdés, Héctor Cirilo (hus-
band of Renate Boker Trauwitz),
165–66, 179, 187
Hieber Boker, Barbara, 187–88
Hieber Boker, Roberto, 167, 187–90
hierarchies: within Böker family, 64, 166;
within CFM, 103–4; within Roberto
Boker y Cía, 49–50
Hitler, Adolf, 2, 118–19; *Mein Kampf,*
120
Holder, Boker y Cía (general partner-
ship), 26–30, 60, 139, 184
Holder, Paul, 26–27, 30
Home Depot, 5
Hoover, J. Edgar, 128–29
Huerta, Victoriano, 73–74
Huici, Blanca, 160
Hull, Cordell, 128

identity: bicultural, 137–38, 162, 167,
191, 195; ethnic, 185; as foreigners,
32; as Mexicans, 31–32; multicultural, 188; national, 5
IMF (International Monetary Fund),
177, 179–80
immigrant communities, New York
City, 12
immigrants: Asian, 44; European,
12–13, 15–19, 44, 161; Guatemalan,
15–16; impact on the receiving society, 7, 16, 191, 193; Lebanese, 44;
Protestant, 15, 18; retention of original citizenship, 43
immigration: of choice, 16, 36; of need,
16, 120; policies, 42–44; regulations,
94, 108, 158
imperialism, German-U.S. rivalry,
66–67, 78
imports: from China and Japan, 182;
dependence on, 145; from Europe,

52; permits for, 144, 151, 179; from
the United States, 52, 67; value of,
99–100
import-substitution industrialization,
96–97, 132, 193
indigenismo movement, 93–94
indigenous population, 31–32, 42, 158
industrialization, 40, 96–97, 132,
142–45, 158–59, 193 *See also* manufacturing
Industrial Revolution, 22
inflation, 136, 144, 152–53, 176–77
insurance business, 47, 51, 79
International Monetary Fund (IMF),
177, 179–80
interviews, oral history, 9, 162, 242–43
investment in Mexico: foreign, 3,
39–40, 43, 180–81; reinvestment of
profits, 84, 86, 96; restrictions on,
78, 91
Iturbide, Agustín, 15
Iturbide, Eduardo, 50

Jones, Gus T., 129, 134
Juárez, Benito, 18, 29, 34, 39
Junta de Administración y Vigilancia de
la Propiedad Extranjera (Junta),
supervision of CFM, 117, 132–38

Kahlo, Guillermo, 69
Kalb, Ysser, 121
Katz, Friedrich, 67, 78, 118

Labor Law of 1931, 93, 102
labor unions, 4, 91–93 *See also* Unión
de Empleados y Trabajadores de la
Compañía Ferretera Mexicana
La Defensa, 83–84
laissez-faire capitalism, 180
la Madrid, Miguel de, 179–80
land ownership, 18, 41, 43, 92–93
Lansing, Robert, 79
Law of Baldíos, 43
Law of Foreignness and Naturalization,
43
lease-purchase agreements, 28
Le Bon Marché, 54
Le Courrier du Mexique, 46
Lemcke, Heinrich, 43
Lenin, Vladimir I., 92

About the Book and Author

Tools of Progress
A German Merchant Family in Mexico City, 1865–Present
Jürgen Buchenau

Founded in 1865, the Casa Boker is one of the oldest and most prestigious stores in Mexico City. At its peak, it was known as "the Sears of Mexico," a department store that sold 40,000 different products across the republic, including sewing machines, typewriters, tools, cutlery, and even insurance. Managed by the great-grandsons of its founder, the Casa Boker continues in business in Mexico City.

Through a revolution, the Great Depression, and two world wars, the Casa Boker thrived as a Mexican business while its owners clung to their German identity. Today, the family still speaks German but considers itself Mexican.

Buchenau's study transcends the categories of local vs. foreign and insider vs. outsider by demonstrating that one family could be commercial insiders and, at the same time, cultural outsiders. Because the Bokers saw themselves as entrepreneurs first and Germans second, Buchenau suggests that transnational theory, a framework previously used to illustrate the fluidity of national identity in poor immigrants, is the best way of understanding this and other elite families of foreign origin.

Jürgen Buchenau is Associate Professor of History at the University of North Carolina, Charlotte. He is the author of *In the Shadow of the Giant: The Making of Mexico's Central America Policy, 1876–1930*.